FIVE FLAGS

THE WARSHIP THAT RESHAPED THE WORLD

STUART BUXTON

STACKPOLE
BOOKS

Essex, Connecticut
Blue Ridge Summit, Pennsylvania

"The best ambassador is a warship."
—*Michelle J. Howard*

STACKPOLE BOOKS

The Globe Pequot Publishing Group, Inc.
64 South Main Street
Essex, CT 06426
www.globepequot.com

Distributed by NATIONAL BOOK NETWORK

British Library Cataloguing in Publication Information Available

Library of Congress Cataloging-in-Publication Data

Names: Buxton, Stuart, 1973– author.
Title: Five flags : the warship that reshaped the world / Stuart Buxton.
Description: Essex, Connecticut : Stackpole Books, 2025. | Includes
   bibliographical references. | Summary: "In a vivid narrative traveling
   from London to Paris, from Copenhagen to Havana, from Washington to
   Tokyo, Five Flags brings to life the incredible true story of the
   Stonewall, one of the first ironclads built during the Civil War"—
   Provided by publisher.
Identifiers: LCCN 2024039249 (print) | LCCN 2024039250 (ebook) | ISBN
   9780811777230 (cloth) | ISBN 9780811777247 (epub)
Subjects: LCSH: Stonewall (Ironclad)—History.
Classification: LCC VA65.S76 B88 2025 (print) | LCC VA65.S76 (ebook) |
   DDC 359.8/35—dc23/eng/20250115
LC record available at https://lccn.loc.gov/2024039249
LC ebook record available at https://lccn.loc.gov/2024039250

∞™ The paper used in this publication meets the minimum requirements of
American National Standard for Information Sciences—Permanence of Paper for
Printed Library Materials, ANSI/NISO Z39.48-1992.

CONTENTS

Preface   v

CHAPTER 1   The Scottish Monster   1

CHAPTER 2   Borrowing an Army   5

CHAPTER 3   The Hopes of a Whole People   9

CHAPTER 4   The Battle of Hampton Roads   16

CHAPTER 5   The Wrong Ships   24

CHAPTER 6   Raiders and Runners   31

CHAPTER 7   The European Solution   37

CHAPTER 8   The Laird Rams   44

CHAPTER 9   An Emperor, a Spy, and a Politician   48

CHAPTER 10 Paper Warships   53

CHAPTER 11 A Second Flag   62

CHAPTER 12 From President to King   66

CHAPTER 13 *Cheops*   76

CHAPTER 14 Of the Amphibian Kind   79

CHAPTER 15 For That Is Music   90

CHAPTER 16 The Hunt Begins   109

CHAPTER 17 If the Thing Is Pressed   121

CHAPTER 18 Aftermath   136

CHAPTER 19 War-Torn Maps   151

CHAPTER 20 Black Ships and Barbarians   159

CHAPTER 21   The Battle of Shimonoseki Strait   174

CHAPTER 22   The Second Battle of Shimonoseki Strait   180

CHAPTER 23   War of the Year of the Dragon   197

CHAPTER 24   The Race to Arms   203

CHAPTER 25   *Kotetsu*'s War   210

CHAPTER 26   Bullets Like Rain   218

CHAPTER 27   Stealing *Kotetsu*   230

CHAPTER 28   My Spirit Guards My Lord in the East   242

CHAPTER 29   The Imperial Pacific   257

CHAPTER 30   Passing the Torch   270

CHAPTER 31   A World of Iron   276

CHAPTER 32   Those Who Served: Officers and Crew of the
              Five-Nation Ship   284

Notes   291

Selected Bibliography   341

PREFACE

May 1869, Miyako Bay, Japan. Everything came down to this. If the Ezo samurai could seize the five-nation ironclad warship *Kotetsu*, their rebellion would have the flagship they needed to divide the country forever. If they were defeated, a reunified Japan could turn to the emperor's imperial ambitions.

Kotetsu was exposed as her Prussian-built opponent steamed toward her, appearing and disappearing in the storm. The sun had just crept above the horizon. Much of her crew was ashore, watching helplessly. Her boilers were under partial pressure. The emperor's fleet around her was still scrambling to their gundecks. She was a heavy ram ship, intended to charge down her targets, lacking the heavy cannon it would take to stop the fast-approaching warship, *Kaiten*, who lowered an American false-flag as she approached.

The attacking Shinsengumi samurai stowed their death poems, carefully placed their grotesque lacquer masks, and readied their katana. *Kaiten* came on, firing a broadside four times heavier than her target, bracketing the *Kotetsu*'s decks, where the first of their own samurai could be seen pushing past bloodied gun crews. The ship that had served as the *Sphinx*, *Stærkodder*, *Olinde*, CSN *Stonewall*, and *Nuetsra Salud del Carmen* offered her first shots from her aftercastle guns in return and braced for impact.

This was the moment. Their gut-wrenching collision was just the start. The Ezo attackers fired a final volley from her 56-pounder cannon, and whistles ordered their assault to begin. *Kotetsu*'s defenders took up their pole-arms and readied a Gatling gun to turn the deck into a killing ground. The next minutes on this extraordinary ship would decide whether Japan would be ruled by shogun or emperor.

Understanding how it came to this starts years before with a rebel American president, a rogue politician, and the French emperor.

Fragments of the five-nation warship's story have been told, here and there, in the context of the American Civil War for more than 150 years. Few record her decisive role in the Japanese Boshin Civil War as anything but a footnote. The more we look at her post-Confederate career, the larger her story grows. In some cases, decisions were made to simplify as a result.

The anglicization of Japanese words uses current translations. Conflicting dates are surprisingly common, due to differences between western Gregorian, lunisolar Chinese, sexagenary, gengo, or Japanese imperial calendars or mistranslation, so while they are not changed in direct quotes, others use the most plausible consensus time line.

It would be more appropriate to cite full names and honorifics for Japanese references, but licenses were taken with the use of surnames throughout. Contemporary names are applied; for example, the Meiji emperor only took on this nomenclature after his death and would more accurately have been referred to in his reign as Emperor Mutsuhito. Times are westernized into the twenty-four-hour day, even though many of the figures cited would have used local Japanese clocks with varying hour lengths that were so complex, many had multiple faces.

Distances have been converted to meters and kilometers when not in quotes. A meter is roughly 1.1 yards. A mile is around 1.6 kilometers (km). A knot is a nautical mile (1.8 km) per hour. A pint is 568 milliliters (ml). An ounce is 28 grams. Guns are referred to by the weight of their shot unless otherwise noted. *Port* is to the left as you look ahead. *Starboard* is to the right. A flagship is strictly the ship a fleet commander has raised his colors on, but the term is used here as it was commonly then, to denote the leading warship in the fleet.

Where a single vessel is referred to by different names in different accounts, they are listed when required for clarity. For example, when the 461-ton British *Lochius* was acquired by Japanese forces, she was variously known as the *Shōō Maru*, *Shōryōmaru*, *Shoho*, or *HoHo*. The prefix *USS* or *CSS* for northern or southern warships is not applied as these conventions were only laid down under President Roosevelt in 1907. Any errors are those of the author.

Thank you to the team at the Virginia Museum of History & Culture for their assistance tracking down and digitizing chief engineer Brooks's steam logs, and to researchers including Courtney Thompson, reference archivist at the Library of Virginia. Thanks, too, go to the teams at the Naval History and Heritage Command, Official Records of the Union and Confederate Navies in the War of the Rebellion, National Parks Service, University of Virginia Library, American Battlefield Trust, Library of Virginia–Charlottesville, Duke University Library, U.S. National Archives in Washington, Cornell University, the Library of Virginia, National Museum of Civil War Medicine, Biographical directory of the United States Congress, the U.S. Naval Institute, Southern Historical Society, Confederate States Navy Research Center, Hampton Roads Naval Museum, U.S. Naval Historical Center, Monitor National Marine Sanctuary, National Diet Library, Japan Centre for Asian Historical Records, National Institute for Defense Studies, National Archives of Japan Shinsengumi-archives, Ministry of Military and Naval Affairs, National Institute of Information and Communications Technology, and a host of digital repositories that have taken huge strides to identify, digitize, and share the past.

As the age of sail gave way to the age of iron, a single warship fought her way through the birth of the United States, Germany, and Japan we recognize today. Built illegally in French shipyards for the Confederacy, she would serve on opposite sides of a European war to her sister-ship, confront Union gunships in the Atlantic, be stormed by samurai, face a shogun's fleet, and serve as the pride of the new Imperial Japanese navy.

Her journey was from rebel to flagship, and spy craft to gunboat diplomacy. This is the incredible life and times of the ironclad warship that served under five flags and seven names, which set entire nations on a new course.

It's time her full story was told.

THE SCOTTISH MONSTER 1

James Dunwoody Bulloch often took a different path from Reverend Tremlett's St. Peter's Church in Belsize Square to the offices of Fraser Trenholm & Company at 10 Rumford Place on Castle Street, Liverpool, England, now the Union had declared him the most dangerous man in Europe.[1] Some days, Tremlett followed in his capacity as secretary of the Society for Promoting a Cessation of Hostilities in America.

Bulloch had served America's rebel Confederacy tirelessly from the moment he landed in England on June 4, 1861. Almost every Confederate dollar spent in Europe went through his hands. Almost every dollar they earned smuggling did, too. He took pride in a list of blockade-runners and raiders acquired, refitted, or commissioned in Europe, which would number more than two hundred vessels.[2] Most were getting through the 5,600-kilometer Union naval blockade at the war's start. Most still did at war's end. The tougher nut to crack was trying to build a navy virtually from scratch with a fraction of the Union's resources. His office was laden with plans for massive broadside ships, ram ships, and more exotic designs, but precious few had been realized, and the war was turning against them. He'd have preferred a command of his own to all this skullduggery—the first time he steamed home to report to the Confederate secretary of the navy, he captained the just-acquired merchant screw steamer *Fingal*, which he'd later rebuild as an ironclad warship.

Bulloch was a man of the sea. He'd left Georgia to sign on as a U.S. Navy midshipman as early he could and served from Brazil to the Mediterranean on warships including the *United States*, *Potomac*, *Decatur*, and *Delatore*, before graduating second in the Philadelphia Naval School class of 1845. While he served in the Mexican War on the *Erie* and was credited with saving the schooner *Shark*'s crew as acting master when she foundered on the Columbia River, few of his generation found career opportunities in a fleet with fewer than ten thousand men in uniform.[3] Coastal surveying followed. He captained the *Black Warrior* when she was seized by the Spanish in Cuba in 1854 in a serious diplomatic incident.[4]

After a fifteen-year naval career, he resigned his commission to serve as a vastly overqualified first officer on the mail steamer *Georgia*, and thought his service was behind him. When the American Civil War broke out in 1861, he dutifully steamed the *Georgia* north, took the U.S. mail steamer *Bienville* to New York to resign, and enlisted in a Confederate navy that had been formed two months before the war by the Provisional Confederate Congress.[5] Simply stealing the *Georgia* was unthinkable. At a time when reputation mattered, the Bulloch name meant enough that few were surprised when his nephew Theodore Roosevelt later rose to the U.S. presidency. Bulloch wasn't a man given to poetic flourishes. He knew ships didn't fight one another. Men did.

The American South had long-standing ties throughout the United Kingdom. By 1860, 125,000 people a year moved from the United Kingdom to the United States. The outbreak of war didn't deter 38,000 following in 1861.[6] No one bought more of her tobacco. Southern trade helped make Liverpool a prosperous shipping hub, and Lancashire the cotton-spinning capital of the world. British consuls stayed on in the rebel South to facilitate trade over the North's protests.[7] Many Scots saw an echo of their own desire for independence or were swayed by southern donations after the Free Church of Scotland split in 1843. Some thought the only color that mattered was the color of money, like the industrialist James Smith, whose ironmaking investments in the South would cost him a brother, killed as a rebel colonel in the Battle of Munfordville.

Western Europe had mixed feelings about the American Civil War. A shortage of Southern cotton led to localized recession in English mill towns, but equally, Northern grain helped address challenges with Ukrainian production. A reduced Union would be less of a threat to English Canada. An independent South would recognize France's newly imposed Hapsburg monarchy in Mexico. The abolitionist author of *Uncle Tom's Cabin*, Harriet Beecher Stowe, had a well-received tour in early 1861 at the invitation of the New Glasgow Anti-Slavery Society, albeit in many of the same venues as black minstrel shows.[8] When escaped slave and emancipationist Frederick Douglass toured Edinburgh, he recorded, "all is smooth—I am treated as a man and as an equal brother." Thirty years after their own abolition of slavery, much of Europe's left, progressives, unionists, and working class were pro-Union, so much so that Glasgow is the only city outside America with a monument to Abraham Lincoln and the Civil War.[9]

At first, Bulloch could work quite openly, just another balding man with overscale moustache and formidable sideburns, even for the day. Foreign ministers initially received the rebel South's representatives, albeit unofficially, even after any notion of them recognizing the Confederacy quickly evaporated. Countless merchants called on him; many of them the biggest names in Liverpool, Glasgow, and London. They made him the biggest provider for the Southern war effort. He made them rich.

Related offices like the Confederate States Aid Association headquarters were openly signposted and so well patronized that when the London Emancipation Society disrupted a meeting there in 1862, no rebels were arrested, but a number of protesters—including a runaway former slave of Jefferson Davis—were arrested for trespass.

Bulloch's network ran through at least a half dozen front firms. Their public face was the Southern Independence Association, whose forty-seven branches boasted members including a future prime minister, a cabinet member, nineteen members of Parliament, thirty-four peers, and others of rank and means. If anyone in Europe's ports was as busy as Bulloch, it was Thomas Haines Dudley, the U.S. consul tasked with dragging his trade and suppliers into the light.

Bulloch's men were rebels. They were spies. They were criminals, and they were there to buy a navy.

For the war's opening six months, the South's first ship agent, Lieutenant James H. North, tried to acquire warships like the French navy's flagship *La Gloire* that were never on sale, complaining, "I can do anything in the way of building if I only had the money," despite more than $2 million having arrived before him.

Most of the records North left were of sightseeing in London and yacht racing in the Channel Islands.[10] The secretary of the navy, Stephen Russell Mallory, was gracious about his lack of progress. "The Department regrets very much to learn that you were unable to purchase or contract for the construction of an ironclad war vessel . . . but it is fully aware of the difficulties with which you had to contend."[11]

If the South couldn't buy what they needed, they'd build. North was directed to construct "one or two war steamers of the most modern and improved description." What he'd contracted in response was a monster with a broadside of twenty 60-pounder rifles and eight 18-pounder smooth-bore cannon that almost brought the whole rebel program crashing down.[12]

Bulloch conceded the challenges North had faced but had a much firmer grasp on what was required. "Inquiries have been and continue to be made. Most of the ironclads already built or now under construction for the European Powers are either too large, and of too heavy draft for our especial purposes, or they are mere floating batteries, too small and heavily armed to cross the Atlantic."[13]

Now that North's single ship—already under construction on the Clyde River—could cost them almost everything they had, Bulloch challenged him directly. North presented a ream of reports in his defense. His ship would be the most powerful in North America. A false paper trail for the fictional *Santa Maria* of Glasgow, or simply for "Hull 61," would keep her a secret.

The press would later describe her as the Scottish sea monster, and rightly so. She was as long as a twenty-seven-story building is high. By the time her 18-inch teak hull was clad in 4.5 inches of rolled iron armor, she displaced more than 4,770 tons without a gun complement, fit-out, or stores. Her draught was more than 19 feet—hardly suited to fight for a Mississippi River as shallow as 9–12 feet. She was so vast that more than 530 men would be required to sail her, more men than the entire Confederate navy had at the beginning of the war. A full complement of guns would need hundreds more at a time when the Union's breakthrough monitor ironclads had just sixty-three men on board. As powerful as her 1,000-horsepower engine appeared on paper, in a vessel of this size, it was marginal. When the Danes built the contemporary ironclad *Peder Skram*, it was 35 percent lighter and featured 40 percent more horsepower. North's sea monster had coal stores so vast—despite a ponderous 8-knot top speed—that she would have exhausted the bunkers of intervening ports like Nassau without dedicated supply. Worse still, with her appetite for iron, reinforced gun decks, and sheer size, she couldn't help but be identified by Union spies no matter what they called her.[14]

If anything, it was a relief for Bulloch when her contracts were exposed by British authorities, and he could extricate himself from the contract with J & G Thompson of Glasgow, Scotland. The South had already invested £182,00 in her unfinished state. They recovered just £40,000 selling her on February 23, 1864, to the Royal Danish Navy then at war with a pre-German Prussia.[15]

The rechristened *Danmark*'s continued fit-out was so slow, she missed the European war altogether. It would be five years before she took her one and only deployment at sea, where she was found to roll alarmingly and consume an astonishing quantity of coal, even with her three-mast rigging set. The *Danmark* sat ignominiously as a floating barracks until her scrapping in 1907.[16] North was quietly reassigned.

Mallory and Bulloch reset their focus on their Laird shipyard rams in England. While smaller, they were such potent designs they became a flashpoint that had some calling for war between England and America. When they were ultimately claimed by the Royal Navy after three years of the American Civil War, the South only had resources for one more roll of the dice. This is the story of the five-nation ship that resulted.

BORROWING AN ARMY

2

Confederate agents commissioned her. Spies tracked her. Men fought and died for her. Millions thrilled at her exploits in newspapers. The war she'd serve would change America forever.

Postindependence America was a rising industrial power, but it was divided, and when the nation elected President Abraham Lincoln in November 1860, they knew it could mean war.

By the time seven Southern states (South Carolina, Mississippi, Florida, Alabama, Georgia, Louisiana, and Texas) seceded from the Union as the Confederate States of America in 1861, their European representatives William Lowndes Yancey, Pierre A. Rost, and Ambrose Dudley Mann had already spent months seeking European diplomatic recognition.[1]

Until the shooting started, there was a Northern view that it wasn't too late to turn back and a Southern view that the North lacked the courage to fight.[2] It's remarkable how lightly militarized their starting points were. Abraham Lincoln was guarded by so few Kansas Frontier Guards that they slept in the same front room of the White House. Jefferson Davis was watched over by just Cassius Clay of Kentucky.[3] The whole U.S. Army amounted to fewer than fifteen thousand men.[4]

Many felt honor-bound by events. The South's General Robert E. Lee wrote, "If Virginia stands by the old Union, so will I. But if she secedes (though I do not believe in secession as a constitutional right, nor that there is sufficient cause for revolution), then I will follow my native State with my sword, and, if need be, with my life."[5] The division between North and South had been widening for generations. They shared a history in agriculture—which was still more than half the North's economy in 1861—but had invested in very different futures. By 1860, 90 percent of the nation's manufacturing was in the North, and 84 percent of the South's workforce was agricultural.[6]

Rivers and coastlines were the lifeblood of the South. When they fought, they fought to control them. On April 12, 1861, the Confederacy fired the first shots of the war at Fort Sumter, which guarded the entrance to Charleston harbor in South Carolina, and forced its surrender. Four further states—Virginia, Arkansas, Tennessee, and North Carolina—joined the rebel Confederacy.

They were confident that victories would see other states follow them. Maryland was an early target for General Lee. Delaware, Maryland, Kentucky, and Missouri—and from 1863, the newly established state of West Virginia—were all slave-owning Union states. None rebelled.

The Crimean War (1853–1856) had ended four years before with an alliance of Ottoman, French, United Kingdom, and pre-Italian states humbling Russia. It had consumed almost 750,000 lives on the battlefield and countless more among civilians, and ushered in terrible new military technologies.[7] Yet, when Fort Sumter fell, there was no loss of life and fewer than 28,000 Americans in uniform. Lincoln's first actions raised 75,000 militiamen and focused on a naval blockade that grew to more than five hundred ships. Within a week, Confederate president Jefferson Davis called on privateers to attack Union merchants, without result, as European powers forbade bringing captured prizes into neutral ports.[8] His treasury appropriated just $2 million for the war effort. Davis's alternative White House on the James River in Richmond, which replaced Montgomery, Alabama, as the Confederate capital, had been built within a year of Washington's white house on the Potomac River by some of the same team. They were scarcely 145 kilometers apart.

The South started by raising one hundred thousand soldiers. They knew there were as many as three men of fighting age in the Union for each of theirs. Before the war was out, more than three-quarters of eligible men had served (against less than half in the North).[9] If the odds of protecting Southern institutions like slavery were against them, well, the odds had been against America in its war for independence, too. Their president, Jefferson Davis, was a U.S. Military Academy (West Point) graduate, a veteran of the Mexican-American War and former secretary of war.

Lincoln hadn't fired a shot in his service with the Black Hawk War; his career was in law and legislation. Union army leadership was quickly handed from the venerable Winfield Scott to the ultracautious George B. "Little Mac" McClellan, who termed Lincoln a "well-meaning baboon" (who quipped in return of his inaction, "If General McClellan isn't going to use his army, I'd like to borrow it for a time").[10] Command would pass again from Henry W. Halleck to Ulysses S. Grant before Lincoln found the drive he needed. What the North had above all was their Anaconda Plan, blockading the South, seizing their rivers and squeezing.

Some of the war's greatest clashes were in the most unlikely places. A local noted that Bull's Run "looks for all the world as though it had done its business, whatever it was, fully eighty years ago, and since then had bolted its doors, put out its fires, and gone to sleep." The first Battle of Bull Run (to the North, who named battles after places and features, and Battle of First Manassas to the South, who favored towns and cities) saw the Union's hesitant advance south checked within 48 kilometers by General Stonewall Jackson's reinforcements. More than five hundred civilian spectators watched, including Judge McCook with one son watching the service of his other son a few hundred yards away.[11]

The nation's navy had become the Union's. The Confederacy's fledgling fleet was entrusted to Secretary Mallory, an admiralty lawyer in his home state of Florida and former U.S. senator and chairman of the Naval Affairs Committee.

Within three weeks, the *Niagara* (5,013 tons; 12 guns), which would one day battle our five-nation ship, was off Charleston, and the *Brooklyn* was at the mouth of the Mississippi to close the South's two largest ports.[12] The Union navy secretary, Gideon Welles, launched a crash program to expand their fleet. Merchants were armed. Paddle wheeler timber-clads hid their wheels. Passenger ships became troop transports. Bulk ships became coalers. By December, their total ships in service spiked from 42 to 264, and work proceeded on purpose-built warships at a rate the South could only dream of.[13]

The Union had almost 21 million citizens in twenty-three states and 88 percent of the nation's immigration. The South's 9.5 million people included more than 3 million slaves in eleven states. The North's industrial capacity was as much as nine times larger and growing faster. While Southern production skyrocketed, it increasingly fell into Union hands, and inflation became a battle of its own. It took $100 in Confederate dollars to purchase $100 in gold in 1862. By April 1865, it took more than $5,500.[14] On Lincoln's election, 97 percent of the country's arms were made in the North, as well as 96 percent of railway locomotives, 93 percent of her pig iron, 90 percent of her boots, and so on. Her land had almost twice the mechanization of the South. Her railway density was double the South's, and quickly became the world's largest network. All the ingredients in gunpowder were imported, for North and South alike, which made control of the nation's ports a deciding factor.

What the South had was land and training, conviction and money, and slaves. The economic value of slaves exceeded all the country's railroads, banks, and factories put together. This "peculiar institution" was a long-standing issue. Missouri's entry to the Union in 1819, when there were eleven free states and eleven slave states, was only accepted with the rule that the western territories above Missouri's lower border would be free. England passed her own Slavery Abolition Laws in 1833, though her efforts to stop African abductions began in 1807 (excluding formerly French acquisitions in the Caribbean). While slavery was always an issue, it only became a defining issue with Lincoln's Emancipation Proclamation in 1863.[15] Much has been made of his assertion, writing to Horace Greeley the year before, "If I could save the Union without freeing any slave I would do it, and if I could save it by freeing all the slaves I would do it; and if I could save it by freeing some and leaving others alone I would also do that," which does him an injustice without adding the qualification, "I have here stated my purpose according to my view of official duty; and I intend no modification of my oft-expressed personal wish that all men everywhere could be free."[16]

The Confederacy started the war with confidence. Seven of the country's eight military colleges were in the South. In the first year of the war, her armies matched the North for troops. The average white citizen was twice as wealthy in the South, and more than 60 percent of the nation's richest men were south of the dividing Mason-Dixon line. While the South had ambitions for a decisive battle in Washington, most of her fighting was on land nearer their homes that they knew better. She had all the food she needed, and all the wealth that king cotton brought. By 1815, it was America's biggest export, and by 1840, it was worth more than all others combined. When the rebel Confederacy gambled it would bring the European powers in on their side, they lost. While European ports remained open for business, they also welcomed rival suppliers in India and Egypt, and rebel cotton trade collapsed 95 percent by the war's end.[17]

The North's initial call-ups were for three months. The South's were for six, not knowing the Civil War would be fought for more than five years in more than ten thousand places. More American lives would be lost to the American Civil War than to World War I, World War II, the Korean War, and the Vietnam War combined.[18]

Even before war on land, tensions had been escalating at sea. In January 1861, when only South Carolina had seceded, the steamship *Star of the West* was fired on in Charleston, South Carolina, and Floridians seized the U.S. Navy Yard at Pensacola.

Despite their great disadvantage, the first shock of the war at sea would be sprung by the Confederacy. The first battle in a new era of ironclad warfare was fast approaching.

THE HOPES OF A WHOLE PEOPLE   3

U nion flag officer Charles Stewart McCauley, a sixty-eight-year-old veteran of the War of 1812, was a desperate man as rebel militia approached. His command, Fort Norfolk and the Gosport shipyards, with their lines of warships "in ordinary," thousands of cannons, and more than 250,000 pounds of powder, was such an intoxicating target, protecting them had been one of naval secretary Gideon Welles's first orders of the war. He knew people whispered he'd "taken to drink," was too old for command, and had put reports of the base's "disorder and confusion" on the record.[1] Though he wanted to show he was the man for the job, he was hopelessly torn between evacuating these Union treasures with the tug *Yankee* or destroying them in place.[2] Now, as dawn broke on April 20, 1861, three days after Virginia had seceded, a decision was being forced on him.

It wasn't the army of Virginia that lined their port fences, it was their neighbors and employees. He couldn't fire on civilians, but nor could he keep them out. Mid-morning, hotheads among them briefly overran the *Yankee* but left as quickly when the *Cumberland* trained her guns on them. It proved to be the final straw. By noon, McCauley resolved to ignore the citizens' council at his gates, dismiss his civilian workforce, and order every man in uniform to begin the base's destruction. Within hours, every heavy ship but the *Cumberland* and *United States* had been scuttled. The *Columbia*, *Pennsylvania*, and *Raritan* had been torched, punctuating the afternoon with explosions as the flames crept through their stores. Rifles were flung as far as into the Elizabeth River as his men could manage. Cannon proved almost impossible to destroy with sledgehammers. By 8:30 p.m., 350 men of the Third Massachusetts Volunteer Infantry Regiment arrived on board the *Pawnee*, found it too late to support the base's defense, and joined in the destruction. By the time Lieutenant Henry A. Wise set the *Merrimack*—a 3,200-ton former

Pacific squadron flagship, and veteran of Cape Horn and South America—alight, flames danced among the yard's buildings. The seventy-four-gun *New York*—hoisted out of the water for works—burned to ash. The dock itself was spared by a petty officer on her explosives detail concerned about the neighboring homes of friends. By 4:20 a.m. the following morning, the last Union men steamed out on the *Pawnee* and *Yankee*, with the *Cumberland* under tow. The conflagration behind them could be seen 48 kilometers away.

McCauley considered it a success, but despite a promotion to commodore, as more details emerged, he was quietly moved to the navy retired list. His war was over. When Virginian militia quenched the last fires on base, by some accounts, they found more than twelve hundred heavy guns, including the latest Dahlgrens, which constituted one-third of their initial field artillery, and half their heavy cannon. The foundry and machine shop were untouched.[3] With them came three thousand surviving barrels of powder, massed pyramids of shot, and eight vessels in whole or part.[4]

A stream of barges, tenders, and wagons distributed their bounty for weeks. And they found the five-year-old *Merrimack*, which the *New York Times*, on March 10, 1862, called the "finest vessel of war of her class that had ever been constructed," whole from the waterline down, ready to be reborn.

Little else could be salvaged. The *Fulton* (2,500 tons), an old 1837 side-wheeler named for the designer of the world's first war steamer, proved too far gone to adapt. The once-mighty three-deck *Pennsylvania* (3,240 tons; 130 guns) was broken up in place. The *Richmond* limped to Richmond, Virginia, for completion. The only ships afloat were three coastal survey vessels, lighthouse tenders, and the revenue cutters *Twilight* and *Petrel*; Petrel's war lasted just two weeks before she was shattered by the larger Union warship *Lawrence*.[5]

The rebel naval secretary Mallory needed a game-changer.

"Inequality of numbers may be compensated by invulnerability. A new and formidable type [of warship] must be created."[6] By July 3, barely three months into the war, he'd tapped Florida-born polymath John Mercer Brooke, an army officer's son, Naval Academy graduate, Pacific explorer, and pioneer in seafloor mapping, for options.[7]

Brooke cycled through possible contractors before settling on the Norfolk Navy Yard's John Luke Porter and chief engineer William P. Williamson, and turned to developing his namesake heavy cannon, founding the Confederate States Naval Academy and serving as chief of the Bureau of Ordnance and Hydrography.[8] Porter worked from an existing ironclad battery ship he'd unsuccessfully offered to France. Williamson worked from a clean sheet of paper. Their joint design proposed a radical submerged bow, hull, and stern with a heavy angled casement to deflect incoming shot.[9]

Merrimack was their chance to make it happen. She was raised and floated to a graving dock for a massive reworking under John L. Porter, whose competing design had been overlooked. Her charred timbers were stripped away to service her machinery and add an armored superstructure with gunport cutouts along two-thirds of her length.[10] Unsure if their newly acquired Gosport guns could penetrate the iron warships already rumored in the North, they reached back to where naval warfare began. Like millennia of ships before her, this new hope, the ironclad *Virginia* was headed by a 1,500-pound iron ram under water.

The ram ship's return was not a lightning bolt, but an evolution. Engineer Charles Ellet Jr., who'd pioneered wire suspension bridges in America and left his mark on railroads, civil works, and canals, wrote as early as 1855, "I have plans to convert a steamer into a battering ram and enable her to fight not with guns, but with her momentum." He went on to develop the Union ram fleet before dying on deck with the side-wheeler *Queen of the West* (406 tons; four guns) at the Battle of Memphis in 1863.[11]

These new iron superweapons were front-page news. In the South, John S. C. Abbot claimed the *Virginia* was not "merely an iron-clad vessel with a turret; but there are, in fact, between thirty and forty patentable inventions upon her."[12] There were not, though her Northern rival would soon file more than 240. The *Chicago Tribune* was closer to the mark, "The [Union's] *Monitor* is no new invention of Mr. Ericsson's, but she is the result of 25 years' study toward an invulnerable siege battery."[13]

At 275 feet, the *Virginia* was as long as a World War II frigate, and at more than 3,200 tons displacement, considerably heavier. Fourteen gunports were laid down with 7-inch Brooke rifles bow and stern, broadsides of 3-inch by 6-inch Brooke rifles and a 9-inch Dahlgren smoothbore, crowned by two 12-pounder Dahlgren howitzers angled 45 degrees to her heading. Eight-inch-wide iron plates from Richmond's Tredegar ironworks were fastened in two 2-inch thick outer layers over 4 inches of oak backing and twenty of pine. With her sides sloped back at 36 degrees, she looked more like a floating barn roof than the ship she'd been.

Timing mattered. Rivers and ports were the South's lifeblood. If they couldn't win on water, they couldn't win at all, and Union forces were advancing steadily. Generals Grant and Charles F. Smith captured Fort Henry to open the Tennessee River in February 1862. The Mississippi's Mosquito fleet was blown away at North Carolina Sounds. In March, Union general Ambrose Burnside captured New Bern, North Carolina, "an immense depot of army fixtures and manufactures, of shot and shell . . . by land and sea," reversing their good fortune at the Gosport Yards.[14] The Battle of Island Number Ten opened the Mississippi River as far as Fort Pillow, Memphis, in April.

Fort Henry's loss a week later opened the Tennessee River, and the Battle of Roanoke Island, North Carolina, cost the South the Pamlico Sound. Taking Fort Donelson in Tennessee opened the Cumberland River. Port Royal fell in South Carolina in November. The North's Anaconda strategy was squeezing, and worse was to come. The South needed results.

On September 17, 1862, the Battle of Antietam in Maryland saw the rebel General Lee's invasion of the North turned back in the bloodiest day in American military history. The North left behind 12,401 dead of 87,000 troops; the South, 10,316 of 45,000 troops. Finally, in December, a failed river crossing saw the Union sharply defeated at the Battle of Fredericksburg, Virginia. The Union's General Burnside had lost 12,653 dead to the South's 5,309. "If there is a worse place than hell," wrote Lincoln, "I am in it." General Lee was somber in victory, "It is well that war is so terrible, or we would grow fond of it." [15]

While the South had lost much of her (smaller) pool of naval crews to the army, officers like Mexican war veteran and torpedo and submarine pioneer Hunter Davidson were still being identified. A new complement of three hundred naval officers was raised and trained under artillerist John Taylor Wood aboard the *Confederate States* for the fleet to come.

Virginia was needed, fast. Expediency was the order of the day. When she rode too high, exposing a vulnerable rim of timber above the waterline, pig-iron ballast lowered her in the water. When her top-heavy design proved unstable, more pig iron followed. Agile, she wasn't. When commissioned on February 17, she was more worksite than warship. Skepticism abounded. To detractors, she was too heavy. Too cumbersome, she could take forty-five minutes and more than 1.6 kilometers to turn a full circle. Too rushed. Too radical. She'd sink. Her chief engineer, Ramsay, was mailed condolences by a peer, as it "would soon be his coffin."[16] Even after appointing Lieutenant John Taylor Wood, the well-connected grandson of President Zachary Taylor and son-in-law of Confederate president Jefferson Davis, it was a scramble to assemble a crew.

She was loud, poorly ventilated, uncomfortable, and unhealthy, conceded her second in command, Lieutenant Catesby ap Roger Jones. "The crew, 320 in number, were obtained with great difficulty, primarily from Norfolk army regiment volunteers, and even then, only four days before she first fought."[17] By the time she steamed out to fight, as many as sixty of them had been hospitalized, and others aboard were on a sick list. Her effective complement was as low as 250, helped by a "sprinkling of old man-of-war's men," recalled Lieutenant John R. Eggleston, "whose value at the time could not be overestimated."[18]

So much was riding on her. One army captain observing this "huge, unwieldy make-shift" craft recorded she was "freighted down to the very guards with the tearful prayers and hopes of a whole people. Every man and officer well understood the desperate hazards of the approaching fight; the utter feebleness of their ship, and the terrible efficiency of the enemy's magnificent fleet."[19]

Virginia's construction practices verged on press-ganging for Norfolk's boilermakers, blacksmiths, and mechanics. It would be a recurring theme, with labor scarcity meaning yard bosses had to divert shipbuilding funds to disgruntled workers and simmering labor tensions. By March 8, *Virginia* moved out under tow, with tradesmen still at work.

With half-empty magazines, Commander Mallory hoped of her ram, "Like a bayonet charge of infantry, this mode of attack, while most distinctive, will commend itself to you in this present scarcity of ammunition."[20]

When reports of a new all-iron rebel ship reached Washington, public reactions ranged from disbelief to near panic, but their navy was sanguine. The previous August, Congress had appropriated $1.5 million to order their own "iron or steel-clad steamships or floating steam batteries."[21]

The South started with the former *Merrimack* and worked their way up. The North started with a clean sheet of paper. A dedicated naval board reviewed a shortlist of sixteen candidate designs. Most were quickly dismissed. Many were slavish copies of the French *La Gloire*. Some had full sail rigs. Some were too heavy to enter the literals they wanted to control. Some were too light to control them when they did. The South went all-in on one option up front. The North had the luxury of progressing with three.

The first, the largest vessel commissioned in the United States to that point, the *New Ironsides* (named for the *Constitution* that was revered as *Old Ironsides* after her battle with HMS *Guerrière* in the War of 1812) was a 4,120-ton, eighteen-gun ocean-going ironclad with 4.5-inch armor from engine builders Merrick & Sons and shipbuilders William Cramp & Sons in the tradition of the French *Gloire*. She was deployed the day she was commissioned to bottle up the *Virginia*, and served in a series of Union fort attacks and Confederate torpedo runs. None of her class followed.

The second, *Galena* (950 tons; six guns), was scaled down to a sloop with 3-inch armor that went on to trade fire with the *Tennessee* at the Battle of Mobile Bay and cycled through fort attacks and repair throughout the war. Damage suffered at the Battle of Drewry's Bluff vindicated fears she was too lightly protected to go toe-to-toe with the heaviest Southern vessels. None of her class followed either.

The third design was controversial. When Cornelius Scranton Bushnell was introduced to the dour and balding Swedish designer, John Ericsson, who'd built a maverick reputation with engines, locomotives, and iron screw ships, to address concerns about *Galena's* stability, he was intrigued by a working model of a radically different design. If anything, selling its designer was harder than selling his work. In 1844, Ericsson had equipped the *Princeton* with a huge gun along French lines he termed the "peacemaker" despite protests from his engineers over its construction. When fired on a full charge in an early trial on the Potomac River, it exploded so violently that six observers—among them the secretaries of state and navy—were killed, and his patron, Captain Robert F. Stockton, was wounded. Ericsson found himself friendless, and it was only with the lone voice of Stephen Russell Mallory (the future secretary of the Confederate navy) that he was repaid his costs. Dahlgren guns were routinely fired with partial charges well into the Civil War as a result.[22] Ericsson took American citizenship regardless and made a respectable living in New York but was determined to rebuild his naval reputation.

Ericsson had unsuccessfully pitched his design for "a new system of naval attack" to the French navy in 1854. Its shallow-drafted, low-freeboard riverine design was not the oceangoing vessel the Union board had called for. Its deck would be less than 2 feet above the water, with only a 6.1-meter by 2.7-meter rotating gun turret housing two monstrous 15-inch smoothbore guns and a small bow house for the helmsman and commanding officer rising above what looked like a low, upside-down armored bathtub. She'd maneuver with a huge 9-foot screw powered by a single-cylinder vibrating-lever steam engine of Ericsson's own design, fed from a 100-ton coal bunker and supplemented by smaller engines for turret rotation and ventilation so she didn't have a vulnerable funnel above deck. Deck armor with 2-inch × .5-inch layers was significantly less than *Virginia*'s, but her turret had 3 to 5 inches of rolled iron over a matching 2 feet of oak and pine.[23]

For Ericsson, there was only one name that would suit. "The impregnable and aggressive character of this structure will admonish the leaders of the Southern Rebellion that the batteries on the banks of their rivers will no longer present barriers to the entrance of the Union forces. The iron-clad intruder will thus prove a severe monitor to those leaders."[24] Critics called it the cheesebox on a raft and bet on its failure, but manufacturing magnate Cornelius S. Bushnell loved it and took Ericsson on a Washington tour so successful that work was already underway when a contract was issued on October 4. When her keel was laid down on October 25, the South had been at work on the *Merrimack* night and day for three and a half months. The plan to catch up started with more than three hundred drawings from Ericsson that machinists called, "marvels of neatness and accuracy to scale."[25]

At every point, Admiral Porter argued for speed of construction, and Ericsson for enhancements that included concealed rudder chains, additional hatches, a reinforced bow, and her turret's sightlines, knowing any flaw would be the end of him. "Ericsson's folly" was considered such a risky venture that his Union contract stipulated that if it was inferior to the *New Ironsides* or *Gelena*, or if the "the impregnable battery" was tested "under the enemy's fire" and found wanting, all payments were to be refunded to the government. He took the project on anyway, declaring, "I love this country, I love its people and its laws, and I would give my life for it."[26]

The 173-foot, 987-ton *Monitor*'s construction was a showcase for Northern industry. Its board of approval included the owners of the Albany Iron Works and Rensselaer Iron Works in Troy, who began rolling iron plates. The Delamater Iron Works, who'd previously built engines for Ericsson, did so again. E. W. Barstow supplied anchor chains. H. R. Worthington supplied bilge pumps. Holdane and Company supplied timber and angle iron. The Novelty Iron Works fabricated her 21-foot gun turret.

When freed slave Mary Louvestre smuggled news of the *Merrimack*'s intended launch date through Confederate lines, a still-formidable pair of 7,300-kilogram, 11-inch guns using 6.8-kilogram powder charges to propel a 61.7-kilogram projectile up to 3,340 meters were stripped from the steam sloop *Dacotah* (996 tons; eight guns, freshly returned from patrol in China) to replace the 15-inch guns intended.[27] Porter and Ericsson aimed to finish her in 100 days. They managed it in 160, and just in time, launching January 30, 1862, with her fit-out still underway. There was a price for such speed. When first trialed, her steam cut-off valves were backwards, reducing her speed from 7 to 3.5 knots. Her complex valve-and-pump submarine toilet launched an untutored user to the ceiling on a water geyser. The rudder was too far back. Hand-cranked friction gears in the turret worked backwards. The gun's initial recoil dented her rear turret wall. Flooding between the turret and deck was persistent. All were addressed.

Her fifty-five-man all-volunteer crew was a cross-section of immigrants: Scandinavian, German, Austrian, English, Scots, Irish, and Welsh. Two were African American. Although their call for recruitment was oversubscribed, it was not for everyone. One veteran seaman, in a "solemn and prophetic tone," proclaimed, "You fellows certainly have got a lot of nerve or want to commit suicide, one or the other."[28] Several sailors deserted on sighting her.

Neither the *Virginia* or *Monitor* was the equal of the European *Warrior* or *La Gloire*. The American ship's laminar armor was weaker than hot-rolled European armor, for example. Testing showed 2-inch by 2.5-inch iron sheets were half as effective as a single 5-inch-thick sheet, and 5-inch by 1-inch sheets were only a quarter as effective. The gap would later close, but for the South, it was yet another reason to look to Europe for her navy. Ultimately, neither European ship could fight their way down a river, and neither American ship could fight their way out to sea.

When *Virginia* launched March 7, 1862, under Lieutenant John L. Worden, the stage was set for a clash that would change naval warfare forever.[29] The five-nation ship was only twenty-seven months away.

THE BATTLE OF HAMPTON ROADS   4

T he *Virginia*'s officers might have had every confidence in their fighting men, but their ship was an unknown. Prior to steaming out March 8, 1862, Lieutenant Wood noted of the *Virginia*, "not a gun had been fired, hardly a revolution of her engines had been made." Her internal compartments were incomplete, leaving fumes and noise to run her length. Lieutenant Jones noted that her forward gun shields had dropped several inches, leaving a narrow band of wood exposed as she turned. She inspired as much disbelief as awe, with her surgeon, Dinwiddie Phillips noting, "many predicted a total failure."[1]

It took the gunboat *Beaufort* to nudge her underway. Within her first 3 kilometers on the Elizabeth River, her steering was so erratic that twin tugs were attached to guide her. With a draft of 19 feet, and depth soundings in places of less than 14 feet, Southern pilots vetoed any night fighting and worried about her reaching Union forces at all. The *Raleigh* joined her before a rendezvous with the James River squadron gunboats *Patrick Henry*, *Jamestown*, and *Teaser* (64 tons; two guns, with the five-nation ship's future first officer aboard). The skies were blue. Temperatures, warm. Making just 5 knots gave the people of Norfolk more than an hour to cheer her on. Lunch was called onboard, though the sight of the assistant surgeon laying out his instruments just a curtain away limited their appetites. Afterward, Captain Franklin Buchanan declared his intention to ram the *Cumberland*. His final speech centered on the South's desire to strike back, and simply closed, "Those ships must be taken. . . . Go to your guns."[2] At her tallest, her casement was under 7 feet high. Under her sloping casement facings, her gunners kneeled and waited.

Five warships from the Union North Atlantic Blocking Squadron awaited them. The sloop *Cumberland* (1,726 tons; twenty-two guns), which had a whole gundeck "razed" away from her original build, and the frigate *Congress* (1,867 tons; fifty-two guns), which had served as far afield as the Uruguayan civil war (1839–1851), were anchored across a shoal channel near the Newport News. The marginal sail frigate *St. Lawrence* (1,726 tons; fifty guns), which had already been decommissioned and resurrected four times, the twice-decommissioned steam frigate *Roanoke* (4,544 tons; six guns), which might as well have been a sail ship with her engines undergoing a rebuild, and the *Minnesota*★ (3,360 tons; forty-four guns) were moored under the guns of Fort Monroe.

There could be little excuse for surprise—newspapers had speculated on the clash for weeks, and thousands of spectators already jostled with observers like Gustavus Fox, assistant secretary of the Union navy, for vantage points onshore. This would be a recurring theme. Picknickers watched the First Battle of Bull Run. Numerous references are made to spectators on hilltops, rooftops, and balconies throughout the war. Major General "Fighting Jo" Hooker records of Antietam, "The progress of the battle on this part of the field was watched with anxious interest for kilometres around, and while it elicited the applause of the spectators, they could not fail to admire the steadiness, resolution, and courage of the brave officers and men engaged."[4]

When the Union fort commander saw the small French paddle wheel gunboat *Gassendi* readying to move without notifying the port, he was right to be suspicious. Observers aboard the French ship had kept the *Virginia*'s secrets for months. Additional lookouts were posted. At 11:00 a.m., Brigadier General Joseph K. Mansfield noted heavy smoke, without reporting it ahead. At 12:45 p.m., *Virginia* was spotted. Union general quarters were sounded. Signal flags alerted the fleet. Military drums replaced idle harmonicas. Guns were manned. The *Virginia*'s chief engineer, Ramsey, recorded, "long lines of tugs and boats scurried to the far shore like chickens on the approach of a hovering hawk."[5] The *Cumberland* had her crew's washing strung across her rigging, looking oddly festive. She was a good eighty men short of her full complement, even with eighty marines aboard. The 5,000-ton paddle wheel liner *Vanderbilt* was unarmed, unready, and unable to respond. *St. Lawrence* and *Minnesota* attempted to get under steam. *Roanoke* sat becalmed, with her engine disassembled.

The diminutive Union steam tug *Zouave* (127 tons; two guns) fired first. The gunship *Beaufort* replied. *Virginia* held her fire. *Congress* opened up on her with 4-inch by 8-inch smoothbore and forty-eight 32-pounders as *Virginia* passed, recording hit after hit to no effect.

★One notable crewman of the *Minnesota* was Welsh explorer and writer Henry M. Stanley, of "Dr. Livingstone, I presume?" fame, who managed to serve the Confederate army, the Union army, and the Union navy throughout the Civil War.[3]

The wood-and-sail *Cumberland* chimed in with a state-of-the-art broadside of 9-inch Dahlgren guns. *Virginia* finally replied with three 9-inch Dahlgren guns and a Brooke rifle on each flank, and Brooke rifles fore and aft, deafeningly loud in the closed iron casemate as she charged. *Virginia* pierced *Cumberland* with an explosive shell below decks and followed it with a ram strike so violent that her iron ram was split from her keel and disappeared. When the rebel ironclad's engines could separate them, the hole rent in *Cumberland*'s side was so large she went down with her colors flying and took 111 Union sailors with her, some "gallantly fighting her guns as long as they were above water," testified Buchanan.[6] Ten more would die of their wounds in the days ahead. Rebel captain Franklin Buchanan ordered *Virginia* to turn on the *Congress*, despite knowing his brother McKean Buchanan served aboard the Union ship.

Without steam power, by the time the *Congress* set topsails and jibs and slipped her anchor, she faced the concentrated fire of Tucker's James River Squadron and chose to ground herself. *Virginia* closed on her stern, and together they poured fire into her for more than an hour, inflicting such heavy damage that when her captain, William Smith, was decapitated, her executive officer, Austin Pendergrast, struck her colors and ordered abandon ship at 4:00 p.m. When the *Virginia*'s Confederate captain Franklin Buchanan exited her superstructure to observe, he was struck in the thigh by infantry fire from the riverside that had peppered her throughout. In revenge, *Congress* was raked with incendiary hot shot that set her ablaze. Union fire parties later finished what she had started.[7]

Meantime, the James River Squadron had concentrated on the *Minnesota*, which had slipped her moorings under Fort Monroe and run aground. *Virginia* attempted to close on her but couldn't against the channel's shallow run and ebbing tide. With daylight fading, she retreated to wait out the night in the relative safety of the Elizabeth River, steaming off at little more than a walking pace. Behind her, two Union ships had been sunk. Three others were grounded. Two further tugs were destroyed, and a transport was captured. *Virginia* had had two guns disabled in return. Her ram was gone. Her smokestack was riddled with holes and leaking fumes below deck, but above all, her armor plate, while heavily marked, held. Command passed to executive officer Lieutenant Catesby ap Roger Jones, who'd overseen the ship's fit-out.

It was a shocking outcome for the North. Stephen Russell Mallory described it as "the most remarkable victory which naval annals record." When briefed on the day's battle, Lincoln was speechless. The Union secretary of war, Edwin Stanton, declared the "whole character of the war" had changed. "The Merrimack [*Virginia*] would sink every vessel in the navy, capture Fort

Monroe, cut off Burnside in the Carolina sounds, retake Port Royal, and lay New York and Boston under 'contribution.'" Gideon Welles, the Union secretary of the navy, called it "the worst day of the war." They would have more to fear from the ironclad warships being negotiated with European shipyards. The Union was already reeling from defeats in Tennessee and the Carolina Sounds. Secretary Mallory speculated *Virginia* could "make a dashing cruise on the Potomac as far as Washington, [as] its effect upon the public mind would be important to our cause."[8]

The fight was far from over, though. Union forces, lit by the burning *Congress*, repositioned the *Minnesota* and *St. Lawrence* behind a strange, low-slung shape overnight, black as coal, and so low in the water that *Virginia* initially ignored her when she returned. This new Union warship only narrowly made it. Her tug, the *Seth Low*, had twice pulled her inshore for fear of her being swamped, and the whole time she fought the next day, crewmen with hand pumps fought the river.[9] The *Monitor*'s captain, John L. Worden, reminded his men they were all volunteers at first light. When he asked if any man wanted to walk away, he received three cheers, and none left. "I will stand by you to the last if I can help you," Lieutenant Worden, *Monitor*'s commander, told *Minnesota*'s Captain Van Brunt.[10] At 7:20 a.m., they piped all hands to stations and waited.

Morale was high among the Confederates on their return. "There isn't enough danger to give us glory," recorded acting paymaster Frederick Keeler.[11] Confident of the kill, Lieutenant Jones and the *Virginia* made straight for the stationary *Minnesota* after 8:00 a.m. *Virginia* opened fire first. When the *Minnesota* replied, further blasts could be seen from a strange vessel beside her. The *Monitor* had opened fire, and ironclad warships were engaged for the first time. Her Union captain later wrote, "The Negroes {who formed an aft gun crew} fought energetically and bravely—none more so. They evidently felt that they were thus working out the deliverance of their race." More than 17,600 African Americans would follow them in the Union navy, making up as much as 16 percent of their complement, twice the rate of the army.[12]

As *Virginia* punched through the *Minnesota*'s gun smoke, the *Monitor*'s large twin-gun turret became clear, and the ironclads traded fire. The *Monitor*'s guns took five to seven minutes to load. Her cast-iron balls shattered against *Virginia*'s armor with the conservative 6.8-kilogram powder charges being employed (later tests showed twice as much could have been sustained[13]). Buchanan, with a rebel magazine primarily of explosive shells better suited to wooden hulls, saw shot after shot burst on the *Monitor*'s turret in reply.

The *Monitor*'s turret was rotated closed during reloading for protection. In action, it was so difficult to see from and operate, her gun crew kept it spinning rather than try and track back and forth, leaving them almost completely disoriented. With her speaking tubes failing, orders could only travel from captain to engineer as fast as a man could run. Inward opening port stoppers (which kept water out in bad weather) meant she could only fire one gun at a time. Conditions on both ships were hellishly hot, loud, and concussive. As her ammunition ran low, *Virginia* tried to reorient to the wooden *Minnesota*. When *Monitor* moved with her, a ramming duel developed that neither ironclad was maneuverable enough to win. *Virginia* had the same engines that saw *Merrimack* laid up in the first place, and even if she could make full steam, her ram was gone. *Virginia* readied her boarding crew. At one point, *Monitor* fired her primary battery almost touching the *Virginia*. Her plates buckled but held. Sporadic fire continued.

Finally, after four hours of exchanges, a final shot struck the *Monitor*'s pilothouse, temporarily blinding Captain Worden. Executive officer Samuel Dana Green took command and ordered her to shallower water to assess damage to her captain and turret alike. The deeper-drafted *Virginia* couldn't follow. With a growing struggle against the tide, wounded men of its own and little ammunition remaining, the *Virginia* reluctantly broke off and made for the shelter of Portsmouth. When the *Monitor* returned to the channel beyond Fortress Monroe, her opponent was gone. The *Monitor* had been struck twenty times. *Virginia*, more than a hundred.

The South had proved an ad hoc crew could match some of the most experienced officers in the Union navy. Flag officer Buchanan reported, "The bearing of [*Virginia*'s] men was all that could be desired. Their enthusiasm could scarcely be restrained. During the action, they cheered again and again. Their coolness and skill were the more remarkable from the fact that the great majority of them were under fire for the first time. They were strangers to each other and to the officers and had but a few days' instruction in the management of the great guns."[14]

Minnesota's volume of fire was astonishing. She'd fired 141 (10-inch) solid or explosive rounds, and 225 more 8-inch shells and expended more than 2,260 kilograms of powder. Three crewmen had died. Not a single shot of it had holed anything but *Virginia*'s smokestack.[15] The Union rushed in the converted civilian steamships SS *Arago*, SS *Illinois*, and SS *Ericsson* to join the SS *Vanderbilt* as reinforcements until the new ironclads *E. A. Stevens* and *Gelena* could join them.[16]

Both sides claimed victory.

The popular press clearly afforded it to the South. It's hard to overstate the shock a single rebel ship had inflicted. The *Philadelphia Daily News* spoke of "disaster and . . . unheard-of treason" from her navy. The *Bangor Daily Whig and Courier* (Maine) shouted, "Fiasco . . . or something worse."

The *Philadelphia Inquirer* observed Union ships were deployed "as to invite their sad fate." Congress demanded an investigation of the "deplorable calamity." The *Boston Daily Evening Traveler* claimed (falsely) that Secretary Welles had dismissed ironclads as "humbugs." The *New York Times* spoke to the North's lack of confidence against a scratch-built opponent: "What the next naval disaster may be, we shall all know after it occurs." The *Times* placed Hampton Roads in a "long series of national disgraces."[17] The fear in the North was very real, and important to remember as rumors of new European-built rebel ships followed.

Southern engineers worked forty-eight hours straight on repairs. A new smokestack needed fabrication. There wasn't a flagpole, rail, or stanchion left to fly the flag. Her bow leaked. The port anchor, two cannons, both anti-boarding mortars, and cutter boats were replaced. Further armor was grafted below the waterline. On came barrel after barrel of gunpowder, as her boarding parties practiced driving wedges between the *Monitor's* deck and turret. She steamed out on April 10 without battle being offered.[18] She did again on April 11, but the *Monitor* remained under the protection of Fort Monroe and their distant exchange of fire amounted to nothing before the *Virginia* withdrew.

While the *Monitor* remained on station throughout the spring and summer of 1862, they never faced one another again. The North didn't have to defeat the *Virginia* to negate her. On May 3, their army's advance on Sewell's Point bottled her in. By May 10, 1862, Northern troops occupied both sides of the Elizabeth River. Captain Josiah Tattnall ruled out a solo fight for the *Virginia* against a reinforced Union fleet, "playing around us as rabbits around a sloth" as no way to spend the lives of his crew.[19] Her only option was to chance the James River's shallows to make for Richmond and the rebel fleet.

Stripped of her ballast, water, and nonessentials but fully armed, she grounded herself in the attempt and stuck fast. When removing armor plating wasn't enough to free her, it was clear she couldn't escape in fighting shape. To avoid her capture, they stripped her of her guns, evacuated her crew, and lit a fire that blasted her clear out of the water, could be heard for kilometers, and sent her to the bottom when it reached the 36,000 pounds of powder still in her magazine. It was May 11. Tattnall sadly telegraphed Mallory, "the *Virginia* no longer exists."[20] Her career spanned just 83 days.

The Union's flag officer, Louis M. Goldsborough, declared the James River closed to him, and he was accused of having "ram fever" or "Merrimac on the brain." Southern historian Virginius Newton, in a postwar reading attended by General Robert E. Lee, summarized, "The brief career of the Merrimac in Hampton Roads, delayed the advance of McClellan on the Peninsula—gave you the much-needed time to put the defences of Richmond in order."[21]

The Union navy was convinced of John Ericsson's design. The *Monitor*'s payments were duly made, but she wouldn't see the year out either. If there was an Achilles' heel to her design, it was her seaworthiness. From the moment sharks tailed her out of New York harbor under tow from the *Rhode Island* (1,517 tons; eleven guns) on December 30, stormwater began shipping across her deck, leaking through her deck-plates, ebbing through the seals of her turret and down her funnel and ventilator fairings. As the swell worsened into the evening, her crew were ordered below deck with the cry, "Hurrah for the first iron-clad that ever rounded Cape Hatteras! Hurrah for the little boat that is first in everything!" When one of her tow's hawser ropes snapped shortly afterward, violent rolling began filling her bilges. Wet coal struggled to make a quarter of her normal 80 pounds of pressure. The slower she moved, the more she rolled, and the more frequently her pilothouse was submerged. By 8:45 p.m., her tow ship stopped. At 10:00 p.m., a red distress lantern went up. At 11:00 p.m., she signaled for rescue. *Monitor* was sinking. Her crew began a desperate scramble through the hatch in her turret. When she went down, sixteen men went down with her.[22] One-fifth of the ship, including the turret, still bearing impacts from *Virginia*, was raised in 2002 and restored by the Mariner's Museum in Newport News for display at the Batten Conservation Complex.[23]

The Confederacy lost 7 killed and 17 wounded at Hampton Roads.[24] The age of high-masted, wooden-hulled warships was closing. Two hundred and sixty-one Union sailors had died; 108 were wounded—more than in any sea battle in the fledgling nation's history, and more than would again until the Japanese attack on Pearl Harbor in 1941. They were shots heard around the world. The *London Times* called it the end of an era. "Before the duel off Hampton Roads, the Royal Navy had 149 first-class warships. After the battle, it has just two."[25]

The *Virginia*'s loss meant the upper Mississippi, Cumberland, and Tennessee Rivers now served the North. The race for new ironclads was on. The rebel *Arkansas* launched in April, but her war ended when her engines died in August in waters said to be haunted by the fearsome White River Monster.[26] Her larger sister, the first *Tennessee*, was overrun by the North and burned in her shipyard.[27] Ultimately, the Confederacy started construction on thirty-four ironclads within its borders, of which twenty-five entered service and most were sunk at their own hands to avoid capture. Only the small *Manassas* in 1862 and *Albemarle* in 1864 were ever sunk by enemy action.[28]

Ericsson argued that his monitors would always prevail in candid public talks, declaring, "The next time they go out, I predict the third round will sink the Merrimac [Virginia]."[29] Monitor fever gripped the North. Of the eighty-four ironclads they built, sixty-four were evolved monitor types with raised freeboards, improved seals, and 15-inch Dahlgren guns.[30] By war's end, they boasted twin turrets that retracted into the hull for reloading (which Ericsson felt was so redundant, he compared them to having "two suns in the sky"[31]). The others were legacy paddle wheelers, a four-ship run of James Ead's Milwaukee-class shallow-draft ironclads, one of which limped on in service as a side-wheeler ferry as late as 1945, the heavy ships-of-the-line *New Ironsides* and *Dunderberg*, which only launched after the war's end, and two much larger ocean-going monitors, the *Dictator* (4,438 tons; two guns) and *Puritan* (3,265 tons; two guns).

The South launched a crash course in industrialization to close the gap. A 3.2-kilometer run of Confederate Ordnance Bureau factories sprouting along the Augusta canal produced up to 6,000 pounds of gunpowder daily, requiring imported saltpeter. The Columbus arsenal factory produced ten thousand small arms rounds a day. Dalton made swords. Rome made cannon. Griswoldville, pistols and bayonets. Athens made rifles, and so it went. Between 1860 and 1870, Georgia's factories alone spiked from 1,890 to 3,836.[32]

It wasn't enough. Of the nation's ten shipyards, eight were in the North. Only two Southern mills could produce rolling stock. The Tredegar Iron Works at Richmond was their only factory casting heavy guns. None made ship engines or percussion caps. There were no Southern rope walk factories of note. The North produced twenty times more pig iron and thirty times more firearms. The price of iron quickly spiked from $25 a ton to more than $1,300 and was scarce at any price. Even when material made it through the blockade—and more did than didn't—the South needed 50,000 tons of rail annually for her transport connections alone.[33]

The solution for Southern naval supremacy wasn't in the Confederacy. It was in Europe's shipyards.

THE WRONG SHIPS 5

For Secretary Mallory, the answer to the North's overwhelming wooden naval blockade was iron. The age of sail was ending. Steam engines and screw propellers had freed captains from the wind and unleashed new designs and tactics. The challenge was innovating fast enough to impact the war.

By December 1861, his agents were scouring the world for warship acquisitions, and five ironclad warships were under construction to "enable us with a small number of vessels comparatively to keep our waters free from the enemy and ultimately to contest with them the possession of his own."[1] Mallory had been raised on stories of the sea. When his family lost his father and brother to accidents in his youth, it was letting rooms out to seamen that funded his education. He'd worked as a customs inspector, served in the Second Seminole Indian War (1835–1837), and been elected senator in 1850. As the son of an engineer, he'd always been a practical man. When consulting on grand schemes to develop Florida marshland, for example, he cited their low elevation and said, "he might as well have surveyed the moon." His loyalty to the South was absolute. "It is not for me to indicate the path she [the South] may, in her wisdom, pursue; but, sir, . . . my whole heart is with her, and she will find me treading it with undivided affections."[2]

He'd imagined the new Porter-designed *Virginia* setting New York to such panic that the North would surrender. For years, he was convinced he was one ship away from success. The next ironclad launched, for example, the *Louisiana* (1,400 tons; sixteen guns), improvised in New Orleans with machinery from the river steamer *Ingomar*, "if completed, would raise the blockade of every Gulf port in 10 days."[3]

It was not a fanciful idea. While the North was developing ironclads of their own, blockading more than 5,600 kilometers of coastlines meant much of the work fell to light wooden craft, including fifty-seven revenue cutters with a single gun like the rebel-captured *Hercules*.[4]

For all his ambition, his ironclads were evolutionary, not revolutionary.

British commercial interests had used the flat-hulled iron paddle wheel steamboat *Nemesis* to shatter the Chinese middle-kingdom's navy and turn Lord Nelson's famous adage "a ship's a fool to fight a fort" on its head in the Opium Wars (1839–1841).*

France launched the *Napoleon* in 1849 as the first steamship of the line. England fitted her HMS *Agamemnon* with auxiliary engines in reply the following year.

The Crimean War (1853–1856) between Russia and an alliance of the Ottoman Empire, France, England, and pre-independence Italians—to which Confederate president Jefferson Davis dispatched observers as secretary of war—showcased further disruption.[6] Russian admiral Pavel Nakhimov's 700-gun Russian squadron didn't just defeat the opposing Vice Admiral Osman Pasha's 510-gun Turkish fleet in the Battle of Sinope, they shattered it, showcasing the power of new explosive shells against wooden warships. Only one Turkish ship escaped with the news. Turkey lost more than 3,000 lives. Russia lost 37.[7]

England and France used early armored battery ships like the *Devastation*, *Lave*, and *Tonnante* to open the Dnieper and Rostov-on-Don Rivers Russia thought her forts had closed, though despite being only 50 meters long, they were already displacing more than 1,700 tons without machinery and had to be towed into place. Cowper Phipps Coles and the great British engineer Isambard Kingdom Brunel pioneered rotating turrets on the test ship HMS *Trusty*, which meant they could aim their guns for the first time, not their whole ships.[8] Russia's humiliating defeat sent her into a wave of modernization—and the emancipation of her serfs.

No one had more to lose from the sudden vulnerability of wooden warships than the great rivals, England and France. Emperor Napoleon III had his namesake warship *Napoleon* rebuilt as the first ocean-going ironclad, *La Gloire*, in 1859 with a 5-inch armored belt (6,000 tons; thirty-six 30-pounder guns).[9] Queen Victoria's navy replied with the HMS *Warrior* the following year (6,109 tons; forty guns).[10] *Warrior*'s 4,000-horsepower engine was the largest ever put to sea. Her speed (14 knots) was faster than any warship afloat. In a four-month tour of England in mid-1863, more than three hundred thousand people toured her, including American observers. Her cost equated to the kind of money it took to build a twentieth-century escort aircraft carrier.

---

*Having declared "a ship's a fool to fight a fort," Lord Nelson promptly did in Copenhagen against Danish forts and won.[5]

As many as twenty iron warships of some description had launched world-wide before *Virginia*.[10] Russia ordered a 3,300-ton ironclad with a ram bow in 1861 from the *Warrior*'s shipyards. Ottoman Turkey ordered 6,400-ton ironclads from England. Spain ordered ships in France even as she began her first ironclads at home. Austria contracted for new iron corvettes and a trio of French *La Gloire*–class warships. A pre-Italy Sardinia ordered the ironclads *Formidabile* and *Terribile* (2,807 tons; twenty guns) from France and the sea-going turret ram *Affondatore* ("Sinker"; 4,307 tons; four guns) from Armstrong's yard at Elswick, England.[11] A new age had arrived.

The U.S. Navy had monitored these developments. Though it was never completed, the floating battery ship *Robert Livingston Stevens* started development with shells replacing round shot in 1842.[12] For Mallory, Confederate ironclads would not be auxiliaries that supported ships of the line, they would displace them entirely. "Such a vessel at this time could traverse the entire coast of the United States to prevent all blockades, and encounter, with a fair prospect of success, their entire navy."[13]

The South's navy needed their army to buy her time.

In May 1861, the North crossed the Potomac River, occupied Alexandria, and suffered her first large-scale casualties. In June, fighting started in the east near Philippi, West Virginia, and escalated with the Battle of Big Bethel in Virginia, which resulted in West Virginia becoming the twenty-fifth state of the Union. In July, the Battle of Bull Run saw Union forces retreat toward Washington. By August, a rebel victory at the Battle of Wilson's Creek, Missouri, and the death of General Nathaniel Lyon, shattered any notion of a quick end to fighting. The North's focus on ports began with the seizure of Fort Hatteras at Cape Hatteras, North Carolina. It was progress, but it was a strategy that would take years.

When it became clear England and France would not officially recognize the Confederacy, further outreach to Belgium and Russia was cancelled, and the Confederacy's European operatives were refocused on supply and acquisition.[14] A battle for hearts and minds started with both sides printing propaganda newspapers two doors apart on London's Fleet Street.[15]

At the outset of war, 321 of 1,563 officers in the U.S. Navy pledged to serve the South despite the odds against them. The rebel navy triaged their resources into five streams for them that culminated in the five-nation ship.

The first was gathering everything afloat in fighting shape. Captain C. W. "Sea Wolf" Read, who would capture twenty-two Union vessels with the *Clarence*, *Tacony*, and *Archer*, records, "As the different States seceded from the Union, each sovereignty made efforts to provide for a navy. . . . A few revenue cutters and merchant steamers were seized and converted into men-of-war. . . . The secretary of the navy, Mr. Mallory, immediately turned his attention to the building of a navy."[16] Long odds were little deterrent to men like him, who moved directly from the American Civil War to rebellion in Spanish Cuba.[17] By war's end, the Confederate navy had grown from a scratch fleet of fourteen vessels to more than a hundred, with a further fifty contracted or linked to the rebels.[18] Vessels like the *McCrae* (680 tons; eight guns), a former Mexican navy gunboat (*Marquis de la Habana*) captured by the *Saratoga* during the March 1860 Battle of Anton Lizardo, were quickly readied.[19] The age of paddle-steamers with their high drag, high center of gravity, and frailty was ending, but where there were no alternatives, they made do, like *Jamestown* (1,300 tons; two guns) or the former mail ship *Nashville* (1,100 tons; four guns), which fired the first rebel shots at sea, and was sunk, hopelessly outmatched, by the monitor *Page*. The side-wheeler *Star of the West* (1,172 tons), which was fired on approaching Fort Sumter in the war's opening clash, served as a transport and ended her war scuttled as part of the defense of Vicksburg. The ironclad sloop *Whitehall* used machinery grafted from a sawmill. The *Seabird* (202 tons; two guns) was rammed and sunk by Commodore Perry. The *Pontchartrain*, originally the side-wheeler *Lizzie Simmons*, burned in the docks while undergoing conversion to an ironclad ram.[20] The side-wheelers *Bigbee* (1,716 tons) and *Montgomery* were never commissioned.[21] The initiative behind them was remarkable. Their results were not.

Private owners donated or sold a handful of other vessels to the fledgling Confederate navy, which added the *Patrick Henry* (formerly the *Yorktown*, 1,300 tons; ten guns) and "mosquito fleets" of lighter craft including the *Beaufort* (85 tons; one gun), the screw-tugs *Winslow* and *Ellis* (100 tons; two guns) and the *Everglade* (406 tons; one gun), which served as the *Savannah*, *Old Savannah*, and *Oconee* before foundering at sea as a blockade-runner.[22] None made a lasting contribution to what sceptics called Stephen Mallory's "soapbox navy."

A second stream of ships were gathered to raid Union shipping like the *Sumter* (437 tons; five guns), a Philadelphia-built barque-rigged wooden steamer that took eighteen prize-ships before reassignment to blockade running. Commerce raiders like the *Florida* (nine guns), the English-crewed *Alabama* (1,050 tons; eight guns), *Georgia* (600 tons; five guns), *Shenandoah* (1,160 tons; eight guns), and *Tallahassee* (700 tons; three guns) thrilled the South with their successes.

An often overlooked third stream were the wooden warships advocated by Matthew Fontaine Maury, along the lines of the 141-foot, twin-screw *Chattahoochee* (six guns), a section of which survived its spectacular boiler explosion and was raised for display at the National Civil War Naval Museum at Port Columbus. Their simplified requirements raised the number of potential rebel shipyards to more than 150, but they proved as much a dead end as paddle wheelers. Even when we consider others from Europe, like the *Florida* (obscured during construction as the *Oreto* [700 tons; nine guns], which was later ravaged by yellow fever), none were material to the war.[23]

Secretary Mallory concluded, "I regard the possession of an iron-armoured ship as a matter of the first necessity."[24] Despite a multimillion-dollar authorization for European-sourced vessels within the first months of the war, urgency dictated that he had to start his warship building at home.

An ingenious fourth stream of ships saw wooden vessels radically rebuilt as ironclads, like the *Virginia* or the merchantman *Fingal*, which relaunched as the ironclad *Atlanta* and served both sides of the war. Five were under construction by February 1862.[25] While a series of launches followed at Norfolk, Richmond, Wilmington, Charleston, Savannah, Mobile, New Orleans, and elsewhere, only the *Louisiana* and *Mississippi* (each 1,400 tons; sixteen guns) captured in the fall of New Orleans on April 24, 1862, were ever seen as a profound threat by the Union's Admiral Porter.[26] The first of them to fight was the *Manassas* (387 tons; one gun) in the bloodless Battle of the Head of Passes.

On October 12, 1861, the low-slung turtle-backed ironclad adapted from the heavy tug *Enoch Train* with a fixed 64-pounder gun and disturbing system for pumping boiling water to repel boarders, steamed on Union forces on the Mississippi River. This beast, looking like a half-submerged iron egg, led a mosquito fleet with the *Calhoun* (509 tons; five guns), *Ivy* (447 tons; two guns), side-wheeler *Tuscarora* (357 tons; two guns), flagship *Jackson* (297 tons; two guns), and *Pickens* (155 tons; three guns). Opposing them were the Union's wooden screw sloop *Richmond* (2,700 tons; twenty-two guns), which boasted a greater broadside than the South's entire squadron, and the sloops *Vincennes* (eighteen guns), *Preble* (sixteen guns), and *Water Witch* (255 tons; three guns), which the five-nation's ship's first captain had made famous in South America years before.

The *Preble* fired first, futilely, over the rebel *Manassas*, which rose barely six feet above the waterline. In return, the unwieldy Southern ironclad wedged herself between the *Richmond* and coal schooner *Joseph H. Toone*, tearing off an engine. Her struggle to free herself wasn't helped by her signal rockets accidentally ricocheting inside her. By the time she was clear, her smokestack had been shot clean away, forcing a very, very slow retreat. *Richmond* was hit twice, without damage, and the greatest risk the Union fleet faced was when the *Vincennes*'s misnamed Captain Handy tried unsuccessfully to torch his own ship when he misunderstood a signal.[27]

It was an inauspicious omen. *Manassas* was a nightmare to handle. While she later withstood a murderous weight of fire in the Battle of Forts Jackson and St. Philip, she only managed to miss a ram run on *Pensacola* (3,000 tons;

seventeen guns), scrape along the *Mississippi* (3,272 tons; ten guns) without effect, and lightly damage the wooden sloop *Brooklyn* (2,532 tons; 21 guns) before being grounded and abandoned, which lightened her enough to float empty downriver until she exploded spectacularly.[28]

The Mississippi River was fickle. From the middle of the nineteenth century, engineering works had set about creating a narrower, faster flow to accelerate trade. It could flood 4.8 kilometers wide or more and run fast or slow, shallow or deep. Her course could change so radically that she didn't just wreck ships, she hid them. In 1988, the steamboat *Great White Arabia*, sunk in 1856, revealed 200 tons of preserved cargo when found in the middle of a Kansas cornfield. The champagne tasted as good as ever. The ship-wrecked steamboat *Malta* was later found nearby.[29]

It took time to rebuild donor hulls into angular ironclads like the Gatling gun–equipped *Atlanta* (700 tons; four guns), which was crowd-funded with donated jewelry.[30] A series of new warships launched in the second year of the war, including the *Charleston* (600 tons; six guns), *Fredericksburg* (700 tons; three guns), and the *Arkansas* (1,200 tons; six guns), which ran the blockade at Vicksburg before engine failures saw her scuttled in August 1862.

On it went, with the *Richmond* (four guns), *Raleigh* (65 tons; four guns), *North Carolina* (600 tons; seven guns), *Chicora* (six guns), and the evolved *Virginia* design, *Palmetto State* (four guns), which was torched by her crew when Charlestown was overrun in 1865. Others included the Kinston-built *Neuse* (two guns), *Savannah* (406 tons; four guns), *Tuscaloosa* (five guns), *Albemarle* (376 tons; two guns), *Huntsville* (four guns), and the *Nashville* from the Confederate States Naval Iron Works at Columbus, Georgia (1,221 tons; four guns), which became the first Confederate ship to reach European waters. The *Tennessee* (1,273 tons; six guns) used engines stripped from the *Alonzo*, which author Mark Twain had piloted.[31] Once again, none changed the war.

Louisiana's rush to service was illustrative. With her heavy rail iron armor, even at maximum steam pressure, she could barely make headway against the Mississippi's current. Her gun carriages were mounted irregularly, making sighting problematic. She was short handed, and the crew she had were more soldiers than sailors. When she fought, she fought at anchor. When her guardian shore forts mutinied and surrendered, she was untenable alone and was destroyed by her crew.[32] As each rebel warship was lost, Union control of her rivers tightened, and the pressure on their railways grew.

The South tried different tactics with these disparate forces. In May 1862, a mixed fleet of wooden, cotton-clad, and ironclad gunboats concentrated to relieve Fort Pillow in Tennessee. Though the Union's casemate gunboats *Cincinnati* and *Mound City* (both 512 tons; fourteen guns) were rammed and sunk, the Confederate squadron was shattered in a pyrrhic victory, and their code books were found, copied, and distributed across the Union fleet. With the river lost, Memphis fell within a day. Within weeks, both Union losses were raised and refitting. The South didn't just need more ships, it needed different ships.

In October 1862, shipbuilders J. L. Porter Builder, T. Weldon, and J. McFarland of the Yazoo City Navy Yard, Mississippi, laid down the biggest warship ever produced inland. With a 3,410-ton displacement, 4.5 inches of sloped armor from the Shelby Iron Company, a dozen 7-inch RML cannon, and a speed of up to 6 knots, the *Yazoo Monster,* which was far too big to be any kind of secret, was a new source of hope. Agonizingly for Mallory, she too was destroyed in place on May 21, 1863, to prevent her capture by advancing Union forces. In all, thirty-four domestic ironclad ships advanced to naming ceremonies, although only twenty-five were commissioned.

None could prevent the relentless Northern Anaconda Plan. The loss of ports in Memphis, Norfolk, Jacksonville, New Bern, and Pensacola made on-shore production a diminishing effort. The loss of New Orleans in 1862, the South's largest city, through which more than $500 million in trade passed in the last ninety days before the war, was lamented by Secretary Mallory as "a sad, sad blow" that "has affected me bitterly, bitterly, bitterly."[33]

Local deterrence wasn't enough. Local parity wasn't enough. The South needed local supremacy, and for that, they needed Europe's shipyards.

This fifth stream of warships would take years and millions of dollars, but even if European governments wouldn't recognize the South, their merchants certainly would. While the Scottish sea monster had proved a dead end, the South's agents in Europe were already developing ships unlike anything that had gone before them.

RAIDERS AND RUNNERS   6

F inding European shipyards willing to take Southern gold without too many questions wasn't the hard part. Concealing their production, quite illegally, was. Any weak link between President Jefferson Davis's white house in Richmond, Virginia, his agent's Little White House in Liverpool, England, and their shipyards could do more damage than any Northern cannonball. Indeed, it wasn't a battle that cost them their two greatest ships, but a humble clerk for the Savannah, Albany and Gulf Railroad Company.

The war had started brightly for Clarence Randolph Yonge, with enlistment, an early role with the converted tugboat *Lady Davis* (250 tons; two guns), and a chance encounter with James Dunwoody Bulloch, who found him "a quiet, modest young man . . . whose conduct was most exemplary," that would change both their lives.[1]

As a freshly promoted acting assistant paymaster—entrusted with enough cash, gold, and bonds for a warship to cross the world—Yonge returned to Europe with Bulloch and worked closely with him on the mysterious "hull 290." By the time 290 was rechristened the raider *Alabama*, though, the mentorship had soured, and Bulloch deemed him "an unsteady and unreliable young man, whose judgement and discretion were not to be trusted," though he still had "no reason to suspect his honesty."[2] It would have been better if he had.

Yonge was deployed to their new raider as acting paymaster and went some way to restoring his name in five months at sea until he went missing with more than £400 while settling the *Alabama*'s accounts in Port Royal, Jamaica, in January 1863. A frantic search found him AWOL, drunk and fraternizing with a Union consul and paroled Union seamen. It was unforgivable. A shipboard hearing took less than thirty minutes to find him guilty of "behaving in a most disreputable manner by talking to the enemy," strip him of his rank and uniform, and order him left behind. It was not the last they'd hear of him.

The Union's European network by this point documented almost "any persons who may have given aid to the rebellion by furnishing blockade-runners or munitions of war."[3] Northern agents watched every coaling station from Wales to Spain, the Bahamas, Brazil, and West Indies, who, while they could not seize ships, could bribe, cajole, or threaten Southern suppliers. Reports on thousands of shipping departures were compiled into intelligence summaries by the Department of State for the Navy, which briefed the North Atlantic Blockading Squadron.

Despite having left a wife behind in the United States, within weeks Yonge fell in with a widowed owner of a Jamaican boardinghouse and her mother, proposed marriage, and convinced them to sell everything to fund a voyage to Liverpool on the steamer *Askalon*. On arrival in England, Yonge abandoned them, broke and destitute in an alien land, and marched into the office of the Union minister, Charles Francis Adams, to lay out every trick, supplier, and payment it took to get the raider *Alabama* made.[4] U.S. secretary of state William H. Seward ordered Adams to expose the vessel's construction to the British press, and the clear violation of neutrality was greeted with all the outrage they'd hoped for.

The Crown hoped the focus would fade. The Union made sure it didn't. On June 22, 1863, Yonge testified before the Lord Chief Baron, Sir Frederick Pollock. The government rebuttal of his testimony was quite accurate but, equally, quite irrelevant. Here was "a man who commenced his career by abandoning his wife and child in his native country, who betrayed every one of his friends and fellow officers in the cause of the country to which he had promised allegiance, and who tricked a young widow into marriage in order that he could ruin and plunder her property. And then brought her to Liverpool, where he turned her adrift penniless in the streets before hurrying up to London to pour into the ear of Mr Adams, the American minister, his tale of treachery."[5] The British played for time. Paperwork was requested and rejected and changed. Anonymous informants needed to be named. Thomas Haines Dudley retained local lawyers and recruited Crown agents including Liverpool port authorities and customs agents the South had swindled en route. By July 29, the weight of evidence Dudley presented was undeniable, and law officers of the Crown conceded, "the vessel, cargo, and stores, may be properly condemned."[6]

Too late. The fictional HMS *Enrica* was soon rechristened the *Alabama* with a largely British crew under Captain Raphael Semmes and escaped through Scottish waters. Without ever reaching a Confederate port, the *Alabama* became the South's most successful commerce raider, boarding more than 450 ships and capturing 65 Union vessels across the Atlantic, Pacific, and Indian Oceans. At least four were carteled to transport his prisoners to safety. Others—including one with 140 soldiers aboard—were allowed to go if he could not safely accommodate them.[7] Semmes epitomized the courage and chivalry that was hard to find in the bloody, industrialized, and relentless campaigns waged on land, and the Southern press lionized him for it. In all, she claimed more than two thousand Northern prisoners without taking a single life.[8] No ship sank more American merchants. Even when we review World War I, with the German U-boat *Lothar von Arnauld de la Perière*'s 195 kills, and every hunter in World War II, she was the most successful such raider of all time.[9]

In 657 days of service, 534 were spent at sea while a dozen Union warships pursued her. She was finally tracked down undergoing repairs in Cherborg, France, in June 1864 by the sloop *Kearsarge* (1550 tons; seven guns), under Captain John Ancrum Winslow, who'd previously overcome the *Sumter*. The future captain of the five-nation ship was en route to assume command, but it was Captain Semmes, who'd had a previous command seized by Union forces in Gibraltar, who steamed out to fight. And why not—his only previous clash with the Union navy had been sinking the side-wheeler *Hatteras* off Galveston, Texas.

A Confederate observer recorded "a naval combat fought so near the shore as to be witnessed by thousands of excited spectators. . . . When the Alabama steamed out to meet her adversary the port and the sea seemed as if they had found voices of thunder to bid her God speed."[10] Semmes's memoir omitted the fact he was seriously ill (and the hand wound suffered in battle). Captain John A. Winslow had had the *Kearsarge* refitted with "chainclad" armor improvised from iron chain links hidden with a facing of wood planking in readiness. His magazine was full. His powder was fresh. *Alabama* fired first at 1,000 yards before they began a circling exchange of broadsides.

Cannon fire was hugely labor intensive. By far the largest complement of nineteenth-century warships were their gun crews. In both ships, gunports were opened, their tampion plugs were stowed, and a tightly choreographed dance began. Each gun was muscled back on its tracks. A worm was thrust in and out to ensure the bore was clear. A wet swab cleared residue from the prior shot to ensure embers didn't set off the next shot prematurely. Gunpowder was run from the magazine by powder boys, either loose or, preferably, in a measured cloth or parchment cartridge. A reamer checked the vent (the ignition touch hole) was clear. Next came a wad, often improvised from old sail or cordage. The rammer packed it in. Another wad followed to hold the shot. Brute strength was required to run out the gun carriage to the ship's bulwark with its barrel protruding. It was deafening, quite literally, and dangerous, with even secondary guns weighing over four tons moving in a rolling platform with only the gun crew and rope between each man and disaster. The touch hole in the rear breech was then lit with fine priming powder, sometimes premeasured with a natural carrier like a quill, and the gunlock was set. Finally, the gun captain sighted their enemy down their barrels, and the firing cord was pulled to fire.[11] On a moving platform, against moving targets, and at average ranges, it's estimated as few as 4 percent of shots of the era hit.[12]

Several Confederate shells failed to explode, including one found lodged in the Union ship's vulnerable stern after the battle. Being exposed on deck was a terrifying proposition. Semmes's officers recorded, "Smoke stung their eyes until, red and watered, they could hardly see. Each roar of a gun assaulted the ears until they were temporarily deaf. It was nearly impossible to breathe as particles of gunpowder, smoke, dust, and fumes from the ship's stack choked their lungs nearly shut. Snaking lines wrenched arms and legs; deadly splinters flew with each shot the enemy landed; shrapnel was always flying about, and the noise and the pounding literally rattled their brains inside their skulls."[13]

Alabama had pierced her opponent's chain cladding with at least two 32-pounder strikes. Either could have been final, if they'd come from her 100-pounders. In all, she fired more than 370 rounds, at better than a round a minute. Her steering was shot away. An 11-inch round penetrated her at the waterline and began drowning her boilers. After thirty minutes, Winslow noted *Alabama* was readying a boarding party, even as she began to list, with holes "large enough to admit a wheelbarrow."[14]

After an hour, it was clear she was "in a sinking condition." She struck her colors—taking at least five further hits until *Kearsarge* held off. The dying rebel raider launched her twin boats, one for her crew, the other to appeal *for Kearsarge*'s help. The array of spectator pleasure craft and pilot boats that gathered around her survivors was captured by painter Édouard Manet. Semmes wasn't one to go down with the ship. He threw his sword into the ocean and swam for an observer's yacht. The Union lost three crew. The Confederacy lost 30 of the 150 men aboard. Their ship-buying agent, George Terry Sinclair, later claimed her gunpowder had deteriorated throughout her twenty-two-month voyage, though Captain Semmes did not.[15]

The *Kearsarge* was still on station months later when the five-nation ship followed. Captain Winslow was promoted to commodore.[16] A Southern spectator recorded, "When the *Kearsarge*, after her victory, entered the same harbor there was an angry silence like that which accompanies the progress of some hated malefactor."[17] Semmes recuperated for a time in Father Tremlett's house across the street from the Confederate haven of St. Peter's Church,

Belsize Square, somewhat mollified by the grand warship plans Bulloch and others were developing, before returning to a hero's reception in the South and promotion to rear admiral.[18]

One ship could make a world of difference.

Dudley took hull 290's success as a personal afront. He'd almost choked her from funding, until French loans bridged the gap. He'd caught her in the yards, and escalated so forcefully that the British foreign office secretary had been forced to respond, albeit too damn slowly.[19] Adams was there to see that this could never happen again, making Yonge an absolute gift. After informing on the *Alabama*, Yonge was dispatched to Liverpool to flush out greater warships, the formidable hulls 294 and 295, which he'd seen plans for in his work for Bulloch. He delivered a second round of affidavits that ensured the Union were far better placed to force Britain to intervene. Even then, his revenge was incomplete, and he testified against the *Alexandria* being built in Liverpool by the Confederate front Fraser, Trenholm & Company as a raider, which spent her war in legal limbo.[20] Despite recognizing his motivation as greed and revenge, and declaring Yonge "quite likely a bad man," assistant secretary Benjamin Moran arranged for a weekly stipend and return passage to the United States for him "and the (second) wife he'd deserted."[21]

Yonge had had more impact on the Civil War at sea than almost any man short of Secretary Welles. If he had wished for recognition and glory in the North, what he got was enlistment in the Union army's Twenty-Fifth Regiment of New York Cavalry under the name "James Edwards Davies," before he was quietly discharged and his war ended, as it started, with him an anonymous clerk.

The *Alabama* was one piece in a much larger puzzle. Confederate president Jefferson Davis divided his forces thinly across the Arkansas-Missouri and Tennessee-Kentucky borders, to the Gulf and Atlantic coasts and across the Shenandoah Valley, western Virginia, and Manassas. No matter the tactics they employed, they needed supplies, fast. The distances involved were huge—the Confederacy was as big as Russia west of Moscow, and twice as large as the founding thirteen colonies. His rhetoric shifted from the legal to the militant. "A question settled by violence, or in disregard of law, must remain unsettled forever" had become "the South is determined to maintain her position, and make all who oppose her smell Southern powder and feel Southern steel."[22] It was time for the navy to respond. Moving huge sums of money around the globe was slow and costly. Every transit meant provisioning, crewing, repairs, coaling, and more. John Slidell had to build a network of suppliers from Bermuda to Gibraltar and Cadiz and on to their UK ports to get his ships to battle. As early as January 1862, the *Sumter* was delayed by outstanding Spanish tradesmen's bills. for example.[23] Congress worked through it with him in voluminous correspondence, ship by ship, port by port, captain by captain, bill by bill.

The blockade-runners came first.

Their first weeks at sea were chaotic. What U.S. naval ships would defect? Where did each captain's loyalties lie? Each owner's or investor? Each nation? Who around the world would trade for gold, contraband, or Confederate dollars? Organization took time. Early rebel blockade-runners were filled with confounding cargo. Luxury goods were substituted for war materials. Armaments were procured without munitions and vice versa. Cargos were spoiled or missing. Spot markets rose and drove up prices.

The Confederacy formed a one-hundred-strong merchant fleet, supplemented by private for-profit blockade-runners. By 1864, five Southern conglomerates were contracted to build a further eight ships each, leveraging cotton futures. Their success was notable. Throughout the Civil War, only one in six ships were stopped by the Northern blockade. Even among their heaviest (and slowest) merchantmen, four in five got through.[24] Cotton remained the South's lifeblood. Between a half million and a million bales of cotton still reached European mills annually, down from more than three million prewar. These ships returned with more than four hundred thousand rifles, 3 million pounds of lead, more than 2 million pounds of saltpeter for gunpowder, a million pairs of boots, and more.[25]

As 1861 turned to 1862, it was clear the Union blockade may help win the war, but that it wouldn't do so alone. Maintaining it was a huge investment. The North's coal consumption quickly exceeded 3,000 tons a week, and more than one in five ships was steaming to or from a coaling station at any point.[26] They were still dependent on a wood-and-sail fleet as a result.

The stage was set for a new generation of European-sourced ironclads that threatened to change everything.

THE EUROPEAN SOLUTION 7

The South had gone as far as they could to build the raiders, runners, and warships they needed domestically. Localized defense hadn't stopped the Union's advance. To reclaim her rivers and ports and force a peace, they needed warships like none the world had never seen.

Shipbuilding was an industry of state. It was prestige, writ large. Warships were the face of a nation to the world.

This was gunboat diplomacy at its height. In 1858 alone, Britain had deployed her gunboats to New Zealand, Jamaica, Panama, Honduras, Siam (Thailand), Brazil, Sarawak (Malaysia), Egypt, Jeddah (Saudi Arabia), Canada, Mexico, Morocco, and Newfoundland's fishing banks. They investigated murder in the New Hebrides, aided Dr. Livingstone in Zambezi (Namibia), freed prisoners in Taiwan and Sierra Leone, and protected guano traders in Oman, archaeology in Crete, and missionaries in Borneo.[1] The Confederate navy didn't just need to win at sea, it needed to convince the world they were a nation.

A formal plan for the Confederate States of America navy reached James Dunwoody Bulloch, September 26, 1861. By December 19, speed had surpassed all else in ship buying, and the secretary of the navy was authorized to act without Congress or the president. One hundred gunboats were preapproved in December.[2]

It was a seller's market. The South faced an overheated market of existing vessels, new proposals, speculators, and ghost ships that simply didn't exist. Japan, after the humiliation of the "unequal treaties" imposed by Commander Matthew C. Perry and the American black ships, was particularly active, with the Satsuma, Chōshū, Hizen, Tosa, and Kaga clans all dispatching buyers to Europe, claiming the Dutch-built frigate *Kaiyō* (2,632 tons; thirty-one guns), corvette *Kanrin* (295 tons; twelve guns), and *Chōyō* (600 tons; twelve guns).[3]

Their competition was so intense, it extended to ships laid up, paid off, and condemned. The first steam-powered side-wheeler of the Prussian navy, SMS *Danzig*, a veteran of the Battle of Tres Forcas in 1856 against Riffian pirates from present-day Morocco, had been retired due to dry rot. The English firm Dorset and Blythe purchased her for 56,000 taler, repaired and refitted her with thirteen cannon, and flipped her to the Japanese shogun as the *Kaiten* (356 tons; five guns), which would one day lead an assault on the five-nation ship to come. A speculative consortium in Aberdeen started a 1,500-ton, six-gun broadside armored corvette for what was rumored to be a Confederate buyer, which only surfaced after the Civil War as the Bizen clan's warship, *Ryūjō*, that served alongside the five-nation ship under her final flag. When Russia declared a disputed French-built warship "not sufficiently advanced for their purposes" on June 26, 1863, the Confederate States Congress immediately, but unsuccessfully, pursued it.[4]

Everything had a price—cruising ships, gunboats, blockade-runners, tugs, coalers, troop transports, supply ships, and later, torpedo boats. Waves of agents, starting with Lieutenant North's fanciful approaches to try and acquire the *Gloire* or the Scottish sea monster, were appointed to pay it. If anything, the odds against the South were increasing. Union shipbuilding ramped up so fast, they were being contracted by fleets as far afield as a newly unified Italy's, and in a strange twist, Russian czar Alexander II, still licking his wounds from the Crimean War, even dispatched little-known six-ship merchant-escort squadrons to New York on the East Coast and San Francisco on the West Coast.[5] While the czar talked of brotherhood, it's likely this owed more to the North's acceptance of his brutal suppression of the 1863 Polish rebellion, to preposition them for any armed response from England, and his desire to sell Alaska (which followed in 1867).

Chief among the rebel buying agents was John Slidell, who, despite studying in New York and being bankrupted by the 1812 War of Independence, was from one of the South's most esteemed naval families. His brother was a naval captain and veteran of the antislavery blockade of Africa in 1842. His brother-in-law, Commodore Matthew C. Perry, had led the black ships that forced Japanese ports open, and led to a civil war that his rebel flagship would help decide.[6]

When Slidell and James Mason were identified boarding the mail steamer *Trent* in Cuba, the American consul general Robert W. Shufeldt advised San Jacinto's Captain Wilkes (incorrectly) their seizure would be legal. Wilkes put two shots across the British steam packet ship's bow and arrested them in international waters, triggering a diplomatic crisis between the Union and the Crown on November 8, 1861.[7] The ship was neutral and released. The Confederates were not and were held until January 1, 1862, amid popular outrage in Britain and saber rattling in Washington. Westminster's threats were very real. The number of troops mustered in Canada was expanded to thirty thousand. Their North American fleet was reinforced, and their salt-peter trade—a crucial requirement for gunpowder—was briefly suspended. Plans were drawn up to challenge the Union blockade. Within a month, Abraham Lincoln had eased tensions with diplomacy but without apology.[8] The monitor's designer later acknowledged that a potential confrontation with a European power became a design requirement. "A foreign war must be waged almost exclusively upon the ocean . . . in view of the settled hostil-ity of England and France . . . we ought to prepare ourselves to cope with their navies, through which alone they can strike us."[9]

An unrepentant Shufeldt was dispatched to Mexico where, wildly over-reaching his orders, he tried to arrange a new home for freed slaves and was quickly recalled. His ability to brush off failure was Churchillian. When try-ing to open Asian port access in 1881, his rant—that the Chinese empress was "an ignorant capricious, & immoral woman," that "deceit & untruthfulness pervade all intercourse with foreigners," and that anything less than force was a waste of time—was the diplomatic setback you'd expect. He finally redeemed himself by opening Korea to trade with a treaty in 1884.[10]

Within months, walking into Liverpool's "Little White House" at 9 Ab-ercromby Square was like walking into chaos. Southern agents feuded and bid against one another. What they were doing was illegal, so by necessity, con-tracts were loose, misleading, or absent. Astonishing amounts of money were moving in cash, gold, and bonds without oversight. Agents appeared without orders. Not all had a working knowledge of riverboats, much less transatlantic warships. Their bureaucracy for shipping, ports, and registration was far from perfect. Key requirements were missed, misunderstood, or misquoted. Slidell started, quite rightly, spending more time with bankers than sailors.

By January 10, 1862, policies were in place to identify sailors among the rebel army to man their fleet. Money was not a barrier. The Confederate States Congress had recognized a state of war on May 6, 1861. Within three days, $1 million was appropriated for six iron steamers that the blockade-run-ner George Trenholm carried to Liverpool in gold.[11] Confederate president Jefferson Davis dictated two further ships be sought ten days later.

On May 10, 1861, Congress appropriated a further $2 million. On May 13, Mallory appointed Lieutenant James H. North and arranged for money trans-fers with the secretary of the treasury. Speed was everything. The new vessels ordered from Europe couldn't arrive soon enough; in some cases, requests for updates in July and August overtook their agents even arriving in Europe.

On April 11, 1862, a new series of ironclads were authorized, with a fur-ther $1 million allocated. Millions followed.[12]

Slidell was an ambitious man who had surrounded himself with Grecian-style busts and finery, married up, and campaigned relentlessly to secure a congressional term (1843–1845). A subsequent appointment to the U.S. Senate in 1853 was a backroom deal for someone else's unexpired term; he repaid the debt as a kingmaker for James Buchanan's election for president in 1856. When Louisiana seceded, he had little doubt how the war would go. Foreign powers would prevent blockade. The Confederacy would never fire the first shot but, if fired upon, would prevail "with efficient weapons." When proved wrong, he refocused on arming the rebellion.[13] Numerous agents followed.

The renowned Southern oceanographer Matthew Fontaine Maury, all five feet six and sixty years of him, having launched a program to deliver a hundred wooden gunboats at home, sought warships in the courts of Europe with an appetite for the good life and an unquenchable thirst for awards. Never a small man, he was positively rotund by the time his European tour ended. Class mattered. He was aided by a series of worthies, such as the Netherlands navy's Captain Marin Jansen. Like Bulloch, Maury started with a win, securing the Scottish-built 233-foot iron brig-rigged propeller ship *Japan*, commissioned near Brest, France, as the *Georgia*. She claimed nine prizes before limping into Cherbourg on October 28, 1863, in need of repairs so serious she was withdrawn from service and stripped down; she never fought again.[14] He also secured the former HMS *Victor*, a screw sloop built in 1857, which had been paid off the fleet as being "defective and worn out beyond economic repair." She was refitted as *Rappahannock*, named after a beloved river in Richmond, but frozen in France when she was publicly called out. Though never seized, like the growing number of others, she remained in limbo until the war's end.[15]

Less successful among the South's agents was Louis Merton, who'd been dispatched in 1862 for wooden gunboats. By 1863, he was rebriefed to pursue ironclads with Archduke Ferdinand Max, younger brother of Emperor Franz Joseph, head of the Austrian navy and the future emperor of Mexico. While he sought the thirty-one-gun frigate *Radetzky* (a veteran of the Battle of Heligoland), two twenty-two-gun corvettes, and lesser gunboats, Austria was expanding her navy with an eye on a newly unified Italy's growing fleet. No deals resulted.

George Terry Sinclair, who later watched *Alabama*'s last battle from the heights above Cherbourg, contracted with the Thompson yards in Britain for an auxiliary cruiser scaled up from the raider *Alabama*.[16] Named *Canton* as a cover while under construction, she was notionally ordered by London shipowner Edward Pembroke through the Scottish brokers Patrick Henderson and Company. Once again, their project was uncovered by the Union consular network. After the *Alexandra* case, it was simply too public to be allowed to proceed, and she was "exchequered" to prevent her leaving

Glasgow.[17] Even then, the cat-and-mouse game continued. Her contractors Messrs. Fawcett, Preston & Company rechristened her the *Mary* and transferred ownership to another Confederate agent, Henry Lafone, to slip her away. Union consul Thomas Haines Dudley knew better than to rely on British assurances. She made it as far as mounting four guns before she was libeled in Nassau December 13, 1864, and sat out the remainder of the war, in another tantalizing what-if for the rebel navy.[18] Captain Caleb Hughes was yet another agent in Europe, who established that, while the channel nations would take their gold, the continental peers would not; his only achievement was a brief arrest in Stuttgart, Germany.[19]

None of their acquisitions turned the tables on the North. The Scottish-built *Ajax* made it no further than Nassau. The *Louisa Ann Fanny* from John and William Dudgeon of Millwall, London, was never armed and served instead as a tender to the five-nation ship and others. The *Mary Augusta* only fought postwar in South America. By 1863, secured loans and all-gold offers from Liverpool's "Little White House" had devolved into a murky web of futures, middlemen, and contraband. Union victories at Gettysburg and Vicksburg, which Ulysses S. Grant said he could not have accomplished without the navy, had been covered around the world, and by 1863 President Lincoln could write of the Mississippi, "The Father of Waters again goes unvexed to the sea."[20] Bulloch lamented, "It will now, I think, be admitted that the fall of Vicksburg, by which the Mississippi was opened through-out its whole course to the United States gunboats, and the Confederate States severed in twain, and the nearly simultaneous repulse of General Lee at Gettysburg, were the turning-points of the war."[21] Rebel casualties were mounting, and her stores were depleting, with seventy thousand rifles lost in the first nine days of the year alone.[22]

The South's rivers now served the North.

Despite all their protestations of innocence, shipyards producing vessels with ram bows, reinforced decks, gunports, and magazines knew why. These secret ships were front-page news. By the time Union treasury secretary Salmon P. Chase dispatched private agents John Murray Forbes and William H. Aspinwall with $6 million in bonds (which went unspent and were returned unopened) in April 1863, the *London Times* openly reported, "two well-known merchants, one from Boston and one from New York have been commissioned by the Washington government . . . to employ part of the 2 million pounds" they brought with them to buying up "the gunboats now building in England for the rebels."[23]

Twenty-seven shipyards on the river Clyde had built, modified, or contracted for more than two hundred ships with labor laid off from cotton mills.[24] A third of all blockade-runners were Scottish built. Rebel investment was transformative. By 1876, when the five-nation ship was twelve years old and a veteran of the civil war in Japan, there were more iron ships produced along the Clyde River than there were in the rest of the world put together.[25]

It was a high-tide mark for European funding. Lieutenant North's reports were already protesting he was personally paying for cannon, and that warship production was stopping between each blockade-runner's arrival as fewer and fewer yards were prepared to accept payment in cotton certificates.

Many ships were constructed as warships, but not initially armed. Fraser, Trenholm & Company contracted William Denny of Dumbarton to launch four twin-screw ships that ran to America as merchants, and were fitted out domestically as warships, including the 170-foot gunboats *Ajax* and *Hercules* (1865, 500 tons). Others included the larger 250-foot vessels *Adventure* and *Enterprise* from the same yards, which were simply too late to matter.

Some didn't make it that far. The would-be rebel gunboat *Iona 1* sank on the Clyde River after a collision in 1862. The *Lellia* sank in a storm off Liverpool in 1862. The ill-named *Iona 2* went down in the Bristol channel in 1864 with the loss of forty-seven lives, long before the South could commission her. The *Matilda* likewise sank in dense fog in the Bristol Channel in 1864.

The *Alabama* wasn't a lone hope at sea. The *Albemarle* under Commander J. W. Cooke sank the *Southfield* on April 19, 1864, forcing the whole Union squadron at Plymouth, North Carolina, to withdraw, and ensuring the city fell to the Confederates the next day, neatly showcasing everything the South's millions could achieve.

Union officials maintained that the Confederates were rebels, not nationals. Some Southern suppliers got the carrot, and Northern grains deals to offset Southern cotton. Others got the stick and were pursued for every dollar Dudley could take through the courts, some long after the shooting stopped.[26] At different points suspicions were raised about rebel ties to warships including the *Lima Barros* (Brazil; 1,705 tons; two guns), *Huascar* (Peru; 1,870 tons; six guns), *Rolf Krake* (Denmark; 1,360 tons; two guns), and *Arminius* (Prussia; 1,829 tons; 4 guns).[27] The Royal Navy's own HMS *Hector* (7,000 tons; forty-two guns) was watched until the day she launched.[28] If any started as rebel projects, none finished that way.

William H. Seward's eyes were the consuls of the U.S. Department of State, appointed to assist international shipping, collect fees and taxes, and report corporate, diplomatic, shipping, and military news, many of independent means.[29] His ears were spies from the highest men at Lloyd's Registry to the lowest dock workers, bribing, cajoling, and stealing as required. He didn't question the character of the men he paid. "To watch the movements of Southern agents who are here purchasing arms and munitions of war and engaged in fitting out vessels for the so-called Southern Confederacy" required "not very estimable men . . . who are the only persons we can get to engage in this business."[30] It was war. Only results mattered.

As a neutral party, British subjects were forbidden from "equipping, furnishing, fitting out, or arming, of any ship or vessel, with intent or in order that such ship or vessel shall be employed in the service" of a belligerent nation on the penalty of forfeiture and gaol. He knew England was violating her neutrality flagrantly. England knew they knew and traded on. Seward took the pursuit of rebel ships very personally. The raider *Florida* had steamed out of Liverpool on his watch, and reports of mysterious new ships were still reaching him with so little detail, he could only refer to them by hull numbers.[31] By war's end, dozens of his agents solicited, gathered, and reported intelligence for a cost measured in just the tens of thousands, which was surely their best investment of the war.

The South fought on with what they had.

The First Battle of Charleston Harbor in April 1863 saw a Union fleet with seven improved monitors, *New Ironsides*, and the experimental twin-turret *Keokuk* (677 tons; two guns) under Rear Admiral Samuel Francis Du Pont test rebel coastal defenses. After picking their way through rebel mines, the low-slung Union warships fought a turning tide as much as they did Fort Moultrie and Fort Sumter. In two hours of fire, they inflicted immaterial damage, had the *Nahant* (1,905 tons; two guns) briefly out of control after the death of her pilot, and left the *Keokuk* grounded under Fort Sumter's guns, where her thin armor was riddled with more than ninety hits, most of them penetrating, some below the waterline. Twenty-one crew were wounded before the ex-slave pilot Robert Smalls freed her and coaxed her through a long night as her wounded died, only for her to founder in the morning after barely a month's service. The South lost five killed and eight wounded in return but had managed to see off the greatest monitor concentration ever assembled.[32] The rebel navy longed for a day when they could swing onto the offensive.

Blockade, drought, slave desertions, labor shortages, rampant inflation, and faltering logistics were worsening as the Union anaconda squeezed. Just twenty-one of the eight hundred papers the South started the war with survived. By 1863, food riots in the South were so severe that President Davis authorized the (never enacted) use of fire by militias on women to break them up. There could be no victory without supply, and no supply without naval victories.[33]

While innovation continued—with incendiary rockets, torpedo explosives, and, later, submersibles—the fundamental ascendancy of full armor over shot had been well established.

The South now had years of learnings on what their flagships required. The result was twin Laird rams so powerful that they didn't just threaten any Union ship afloat, they almost drove the United States and England back to war.

THE LAIRD RAMS   8

The year 1863 started brightly for the Confederates. The side-wheel cotton-clad *Bayou City*, fighting with the converted tugboat *Neptune*, destroyed the Union side-wheeler *Westfield* (822 tons; six guns) and seized the cutter *Harriet Lane* (730 tons; six guns) off Galveston, Texas, January 1. Ten days later, *Alabama* sank the North's *Hatteras* (1,126 tons; five guns). With her crew netting £400 to £500 a month from prizes, the *Alabama* was becoming a beacon for English recruitment.[1]

On land, Union efforts were stalling in the west. Lee's army of Northern Virginia was threatening in the east. Lincoln considered growing "copperhead" and "peace democrat" protests a "fire in the rear."[2] It was clear by now there would be no single day, and no single battle that could end things, steering both protagonists to mass recruitment. Abraham Lincoln approved black regiments. The North's Enrolment Act launched the first conscription America had ever seen. Some in the South thought the ability of the wealthy to buy their way out said a lot. Some in the North did, too.

Northern pressure continued. After the ironclad Battle of Hampton Roads in March, the Union's General Ulysses S. Grant prevailed at the Battle of Shiloh in Tennessee, and the North fell into a rhythm of ying-and-yang land and sea actions.

President Davis assured the South their position was better than it had been a year before. It was not. The red river was under Union control. Men, orders, and supplies on one side of the Mississippi were cut off from the other. Exacerbated by drought, agricultural production was in decline. The prospect of hunger and shortage was very real. Labor shortages were biting. Alabama's governor John Gill Shorter raged, "Failing to accomplish our subjugation by the force of arms and the power of numbers, the enemy has called to his aid the terrible appliances of want and starvation."[3]

They fought on, regardless. In August, the Battle of Second Bull Run had been fought on the same ground as the year before, with another Confederate victory. Stephen Russell Mallory regaled James Dunwoody Bulloch with his conviction, "our people are united, thoroughly aroused, and determined to listen to neither truce nor peace until every hostile foot shall be driven from our soil." Then it was down to business. "If you can purchase 10,000 good Enfield rifles, or rifled muskets with bayonets, do so at once, without regard to price."[4] They needed surer supply. Time was running out for European-sourced warships to deliver it.

In December, Union forces had been heavily defeated in a river crossing below the Marye heights at the Battle of Fredericksburg, Virginia, and again at the Battle of Ball's Bluff, Virginia. The chivalry of Captain Raphael Semmes and the *Alabama* was hard to see on land. "Old Jack" Stonewall Jackson was so appalled at the Union's occupation that when a staff officer asked what should be done about it, he was unequivocal. "Kill 'em. Kill 'em all."[5] His namesake five-nation warship was still sixteen months away.

In Europe, the Confederacy walked away from her least promising deals, slashed the number of buying agents, and doubled down on her best, the mysterious hulls 294 and 295, who were obscured with contracts with the Russian-owned, Paris-based Bravay & Company. Any inquiries were met with the cover story they would serve Egypt as the patrol ships *El Tousson* and *El Monassir* for the Khedive and *Ismail Pasha* on behalf of the Ottoman sultan.[6]

The Union never found their initial £93,760 contract, but at 230 feet in length and 40 feet wide, there was no disguising the sheer volume of rolled iron shipping to Birkenhead, and only so many times Bulloch could explain his constant travel to Liverpool. "The ribs of one is up," consul Thomas Haines Dudley reported, "and they have commenced to put on the plates."[7] There were no guns, but the deck reinforcement for them was unmistakable. The wildly successful raider *Alabama* had a merchantman's bones. These Laird ironclads would be purpose-built twin-turreted warships, developed in consultation with the Royal Navy's Captain Cowper Coles. With 2,795 tons displacement and a bow ram, they represented a new class of vessel. A battery of four 220-pounder Armstrong guns in elevated turrets angled down to pierce enemy decks meant she could track and fire on two targets while ramming a third. A three-masted barque's sailing rig would free them from predictable re-coaling.

Four and a half inches of armor would be intricately latticed to provide up to 10 inches of protection at her gunports, and so complete it would plunge 3.5 feet below the waterline. Double hulls beneath the engine and boiler rooms, and twelve watertight bulkhead doors would protect her. Remarkably, for their size, their full complement would be just 153 men.

They were everything Johnny Reb needed and became an obsession for William H. Seward's consuls and Dudley's turncoats, dockworkers, and clerks as a result. "I shall send for my special detective at London endeavour at the proper time to get up some evidence and have it laid before the government," Dudley advised Seward.[8] His source delivered. "I enclose you a correct Photograph of Laird Rams. The first sketch made was not accurate. The artist made it from memory after seeing the vessel. This one shows her (like one in the Great Float at Birkenhead) just as she lays."[9] Days passed. Weeks, then months as their construction progressed. Dudley's London consul, the wonderfully named Freeman H. Morse, successfully slipped a young mechanic past the rebel's vetting to work on them until his mother tumbled onto his scheme and threatened to talk unless he was slipped right back out again.[10]

Bulloch sweated on them from France, and briefly, it looked like his audacious gamble would pay off. The day after General Robert E. Lee's second attempted invasion of the North was defeated at Gettysburg, Dudley reported to Washington that the ships were launching shakedown cruises from Liverpool harbor. On April 5, 1863, the turncoat Confederate paymaster Clarence Randolph Yonge was dispatched to Southern suppliers to learn more about hulls "294" and "295."[11] His reports were alarming. If correct, there was scarcely a ship in the Union fleet that could withstand the would-be *Mississippi* and *North Carolina*, named for lost Richmond class rams built in Wilmington in 1862.

Bulloch was in no doubt of their potential. If the "Liverpool rams, with those built at Bordeaux, had been permitted to go to sea, the Confederate Government would have been able to open some of the Southern ports to private enterprise, and could have made far more formidable and effective attacks. . . . The weak and accessible points along the Northern coast were well known to the Confederate naval authorities, and the Liverpool rams would have been sent to them."[12]

The Union felt so, too. News of their advanced construction raced through the Union American Foreign Office like fire. In Washington, British ambassador Lord Richard Lyons was summoned by Secretary of State William Seward and told in no uncertain terms that Lincoln was prepared to interdict British trade if these mysterious British-built hulls reached the Atlantic. He knew the stakes if the Royal Navy stared him down, but equally, they knew he was prepared for confrontation after the Trent Affair.

It was not to be. On April 6, just weeks from their intended delivery, Yonge's affidavit dragged the Laird rams into the light, and cost Lieutenant Thomas Jefferson Page, who would later helm the five-nation ship, their captaincy. Bulloch tried desperately to pivot, later writing, "Emperor Napoleon was appealed to by Messrs Bravay, to intervene and request the release of the rams as the property of subjects of France, but he refused to take any steps."[13] It was not the last time Napoleon III would disappoint them. In September 1863, the American minister to England, Charles Francis Adams, warned Lord Russell of the British Foreign Office unequivocally: "it would be superfluous in me to point out to your Lordship that this [releasing the twin Laird rams to the South] means war."[14]

There was no defense for this repeated violation of neutrality. On October 10, 1863, armed elements from the HMS *Majestic* seized the "Birkenhead" rams. The Laird shipyards sued for their return and failed. Now in English hands, they were a dilemma. Ninety percent of the Royal Navy was wooden hulled, and only a handful of their leading ironclads could oppose them. What if they were sold on to France? The Crown ultimately agreed to purchase the vessels for the Admiralty as HMS *Scorpion* and HMS *Wyvern* for £220,000, netting their illegal builders a tidy profit of £30,000 each.

The South's share of the sale went toward the raider *Shenandoah* and a final series of runners under General Colin McRae, which, yet again, proved too little, too late. Six completed a single run. Three were stranded in transit at war's end, and six more were orphaned at different stages of production.[15] The balance went to one final warship project across the channel. This was it. With the Scottish sea monster and Laird rams lost, there wasn't a shipyard of scale in the British Isles they hadn't sounded out. Dutch yards were closed to them. Russia was in the North's camp. Prussia, Austria, and Italy were beating their own war drums. France represented their last throw of the dice.

The HMS *Warrior* had been laid down more than three years before, but no U.S. ship—*Old Ironsides* and monitors included—had equaled it. No further ships had followed *Galena*'s design. The Union fleet was even more wooden hulled than the Royal Navy, and what ironclads she had were riverine classes that an oceanic ironclad ram could avoid offshore at will. A window of opportunity remained. As desperate as the rebel army was for manpower, Secretary Mallory oversaw legislation that any "webfeet" who volunteered for the navy were to be transferred.[16]

Three years of warfare had delivered a series of bloody lessons. Coal was a steamship's Achilles heel, and a sail rig would help her cross the Atlantic and strike with surprise. Twin screws would ensure the speed and maneuverability required to pin her opponents. Armor was ascendant over even exploding shells. Ram ships could—and had—sunk even the strongest ironclad opponent. Fewer, heavier guns, mounted high and angled down, would reduce crew requirements and raise the chance of catastrophic penetrations.

While the outline of the new five-nation ship started with Bulloch's sketches, and an early consensus was found, countless questions remained on how she would be hidden, how she would be built, and how she would fight.

In a private audience, off books and well attended, the French emperor, Napoleon III, quietly began the five-nation ship's journey.

AN EMPEROR, A SPY, AND A POLITICIAN

9

The Confederacy's move in 1862 to the "Little White House" built by Charles Prioleau, a partner at the Confederacy's leading cotton traders and bankers at 9 Abercromby Square, wasn't spy craft. It was a function of the growing bureaucracy it took to manage a global supply chain. No effort had been made to conceal the original offices they used throughout the war, and little effort followed now. Prioleau's senior partner lived in South Carolina and later served as Confederate secretary of the treasury. The Bonnie Blue star flag of the Republic of Texas flew over a first-floor window. The portico columns were decorated with the cabbage palmetto, the state tree of South Carolina.[1] When the socialite Rose O'Neal Greenhow—convicted as a spy by the Pinkerton agency and jailed after the Battle of Bull Run—made a fund-raising tour of the United Kingdom, they promoted a society dinner in her honor (too successful a trip as it happens, as she drowned on her return to the United States, slipping away from the blockade-runner on the Cape Fear River with $2,000 in gold sewn into her dress).[2]

Congressional correspondence with the Navy Department approved a shift to French production. A May 26 briefing to James Dunwoody Bulloch "announces additional assurances have been received that iron-plated ships of war can be constructed in France by French shipbuilders and delivered ready for service on the high seas, and wishes enquiries made so as to reach the Emperor of France."[3] By the time the Confederate turncoat Clarence Randolph Yonge was testifying to the Laird rams' true buyer in England in June 1863, John Slidell, an entertaining, diplomatic, and ruthless French speaker, was proving himself the right man to make it happen.[4]

Union steamships took about three weeks to reach western Europe. The journey from New York to Washington added another. Rebel communications took longer through Halifax, Havana, Nassau, or Bermuda. While telegraph networks were expanding, they were costly and insecure, forcing each side into coding and code breaking. The net effect was that Bulloch and Slidell were more like captains than mere agents, and talks progressed rapidly.[5] Napolean III summoned Lucien Arman to get down to business.

Arman, a heavy-set man with great tumbles of dark hair that turned sharply white as it met his sideburns, proved the perfect bridge between the buyer and seller. Not only was he a respected shipbuilder, politician, and businessman with seats in the French legislator, French Academy of Sciences, National Order of the Legion of Honour, and Bordeaux Chamber of Commerce, but he was of a class that gravitated together. The French emperor and Empress Eugénie were guests of honor at his son's wedding. His support opened doors to a similarly elite group of builders, including M. Voruz and his peers of the Jollett & Babin and Dubigeon Brothers shipyards in Nantes.[6]

Napoleon III declined any contracts on the record, but he continued discussions in private. Bulloch engaged with good faith and gold, up front. If anything, the next year would show he was too loyal to Napoleon III and received too little loyalty in return. Napoleon Bonaparte's nephew, Napoleon III, was a worldly man, raised in exile in Switzerland, schooled in Germany, and influenced by travel throughout pre-independence Italy. His youth suggested rashness and entitlement—he narrowly survived his role in a plot against papal Rome in 1830 that claimed his brother. Years spent publishing treatises on a polyglot of subjects did nothing to dull his ambitions. He was exiled to America in 1836 after a premature coup attempt in France, only to slip back via Britain in 1840 to launch another failed attempt. Far from harming his brand, he was increasingly seen as a last chance for change, and he was elected to France's post-revolution parliament, and popularly to the office of president in 1848. He finally launched a successful coup in 1851 that restored universal suffrage but dissolved the Legislative Assembly and found that victory in the Crimean War did more to legitimize him than a series of plebiscites.

Napoleon III's foreign policy was mixed. He supported Italian independence and sponsored the Suez Canal but exploited French Indochina and West Africa shamelessly and installed a proxy monarchy in Mexico that ended in disaster. His larger Latin American ambitions overlapped with the Confederacy's. By the 1850s, illegal American or American-backed private armies operated in Mexico, Cuba, and South America, and one, led by William Walker, briefly ruled Nicaragua in 1856–1857. The Kentucky-born U.S. vice president, John Breckinridge, warned prewar that "the Southern states cannot afford to be shut off from all possibility of expansion toward the tropics by the hostile action of the federal government." Rebels like John T. Picket openly fomented Mexican rebellion to support "the permanent possession of that beautiful country." While never a defining Southern goal, their future president, Jefferson Davis, hinted at "new acquisitions to be made south of the Rio Grande" postwar for the slave trade.[7]

Few shipyards on earth were better suited than Arman's in Bordeaux, whose first awards for composite wood and iron construction dated back to the Exposition Universelle of 1855.[8] Less than a year had passed since the Battle of Hampton Roads between the ironclads *Monitor* and *Virginia*, but naval design had changed forever. A decision had to be made between Stephen Mallory's vision of a larger fleet of shallow-drafted rams to open river mouths and Bulloch's for a smaller blue-water fleet that could prevail in New York, Boston, or Baltimore. "I designed these ships for something more than harbor or even coastal defense," he wrote in 1863. "I confidently believe, if ready for sea now, they could sweep away the entire blockading fleet of enemy vessels."[9] Bulloch prevailed, and a first payment of 720,000 francs changed hands June 10 "for two steamers now building for the confederate states."[10]

After Gettysburg in 1863, Emperor Napoleon III began to hedge his bets. Arman was instructed to obfuscate their rebel engagement with complicated cutout arrangements with Swedish third parties.

Bulloch drew heavily on the solicitors of Liverpool's Fraser, Trenholm & Company, who "piloted me safely through the mazes of the Foreign Enlistment Act."[11] Loopholes for European construction remained when a legitimate third party served as a cut out, when a vessel couldn't be proved to have military purpose, or when there was no overwhelming proof of its end user. It was one thing for Union agents to suspect warships attributed to second- and third-tier nations who could not conceivably have paid for them, but it was quite another to prove it. In Britain, Union envoys Charles Francis Adams Sr. and Thomas Haines Dudley were Bulloch's antagonists. In France, U.S. envoy John Bigelow matched Slidell move for move. Bulloch knew the game. Vessels were contracted without weaponry, for dummy corporations, ostensibly serving other governments. They exited port under factory crews. External vessels were arranged to furnish weaponry and crews in international waters, away from prying eyes.

This pair of final ironclad rams would be supported by four screw corvettes that, Bulloch noted, "have been designed as tow boats, to deceive the Federal spies, but [which] will require insignificant alterations to convert them" with 8- and 9-inch gun batteries.[12] Split, they'd form two squadrons that would force the Union to consolidate her ironclads, recall much of her wooden fleet, and trade off protection for her cities, merchants, ports, and armies.

Arman reserved the lead ship—our five-nation ship—for his yards in final contracts signed with Bulloch and his agent, French captain Eugene L. Tessier. The corvettes were contracted to the yards of Jollett & Babin and Dubigeon Brothers in Nantes through a member of Arman's business network, fellow legislator and engine maker M. Voruz. The French emperor wasn't just aware—he participated in their cover story and placated a French navy with nothing comparable.

The corvettes quickly abandoned any pretense of being tugboats and were said, instead, to be for the launch of a new steam packet line between San Francisco, Japan, and China. If a provision for armament was clear in the heavy reinforcement of her gundecks, it was to allow a potential sale to either China or Japan. By July 20, 1863, Bulloch was regularly reporting on their progress. On June 1, 1863, as required by law, Lucien Arman identified the four initial ships under construction to his government and requested permission to arm them, citing their intended service for merchants fearing pirates in the China Sea. It wasn't consistent with stories told before or after, but hardly needed to be. Permission from minister of marine Prosper Chasseloup-Laubat took just five days. Arman was no Confederate. He was a businessman, deeply networked with his peers. Banker Emile Erlanger, who engineered the release of cotton bonds across Europe's exchanges to smooth Southern cash flows, took a 5 percent commission for underwriting Bulloch's payment. Henri Arnous de Rivière pocketed 3 percent. The Blakely Company of England took a 10 percent fee to act as cutout for her armaments.[13]

A false paper trail for the rams *Sphinx* and *Cheops* recycled the Egyptian navy cover story that failed the would-be Laird rams. No armaments were commissioned with French foundries; guns would be procured separately in England. Bulloch, writing to Secretary Mallory on June 10, 1864, revealed, "As Denmark was then at war it had been arranged that the nominal ownership of the rams should vest in Sweden [which had] consented to do this piece of good service for Denmark . . . a Swedish naval officer was then at Bordeaux superintending the completion of the rams as if for his own Government."[14]

Arman would complete delivery in Gothenburg. "When the first ram is ready to sail, the American minister will no doubt ask the Swedish minister if the vessel belongs to his Government; the reply will be 'yes'; she will-arrive at her destination according to contract. This will distract all suspicion from the second ram and when she sails under like circumstances with the first, my people will deliver her to you." Arrangements were made for "the best mode of shipping the guns, the engagement of reliable captains, and the possibility of getting seamen from the ports of Brittany.[15]

The fear that even this new layer of Swedish actors may not be enough was very real. The Confederacy's agents in London, Liverpool, and Glasgow were hunted men by 1864. It was only in late 1864 that they tried to conceal their operations with a secret headquarters 51 kilometers from Clyde by rail in the sedate Stirlingshire village of Bridge of Allan, capped at under ten agents.

Even then, to follow the money, you just had to follow the accents—"big hats and smoking large cigars"—openly commented upon in local press. By early 1864, the amateur detectives of the antislavery Dundee Ladies' Emancipation Society marched themselves into the U.S. consul's office to call the rebels agents out, a good year before the English-built Laird ram's flashpoint was resolved.[16] No action followed.

It was proving a good war for men like Prioleau. By the time their rebel operations moved, he was making more than $500 million a year from cotton alone, not all of which made its way back to the cause.[17] A series of business leaders followed, with some trading at arm's length like Charles Kuhn Prioleau. Others like J. H. Ashbridge were all-in on securing armaments.[18] The sums involved were huge—a half dozen small arms manufacturers including Bond, James, Scott & Son, Kerr, and Freed & Company had already supplied more than 350,000 rifles, more guns than the British had soldiers in the War of 1812, Opium War, Crimean War, NZ Māori Wars, and Sepoy Mutinies combined.[19]

Diplomatic outreach continued to flounder. When Alabama's William Yancey, the Confederate commissioner to London, marched from Half Moon Street to propose Britain and the Confederacy restart the transatlantic slave trade, he was rejected with a speed rarely seen in the Foreign Office.

There would be no more moves for the rebel agents, and no further flagship designs. This was it.

A ship could have anything on paper. The scale of the Scottish sea monster. Powered turrets. Impervious armor. Unprecedented broadsides. A ram. Speed. More men, less men. River access. Oceanic range. But many aspirations were contradictory. More armor needed more power, larger engines, larger coal stores, and more armor to protect them and so on.

Time was not on the Confederacy's side. While the Union simply needed not to lose, America's rebels needed a radical reversal with her rivers and ports to win.

While the killing went on, the Confederacy was about to launch one last, best hope.

PAPER WARSHIPS   10

In a world of iron, decisions lasted.

France's pioneering *La Gloire* had evolved into Provence-class iron-clads of more than 5,700 tons. With a naval complement of 579 men, they were as poor a fit for the rebel navy as the Scottish sea monster had been. Across the channel, England's designers were responding with Ocean-class ironclads displacing more than 7,600 tons, crewed by more than 750 souls.[1] *Sphinx* and *Cheops* took a very different path.

Each was 56.9 meters long, 15 meters shorter than the Laird rams, but still larger than the Paris Arc de Triomphe or Nelson's column in London. With a beam of 9.9 meters, they were as wide as a three-story house is high. While the Mississippi could be as deep as 18 meters at New Orleans, its run past Saint Louis, Missouri, and Cairo, Illinois, averaged just 9 meters. A draft depth between 4.3 meters and 4.8 meters was the sweet spot, shallow enough for key ports but substantial enough to cross an ocean.

The future CSS *Stonewall*'s construction began with a backbone of pre-aged, scarph-joined keel timbers. Giant ribs followed, and upon them, decks on longitudinal frames supported by transverse bands of wood and iron. In places, her hull planking and forecastles and aftercastles were as much as 2 feet thick. Oak predominated, despite its cost. Cultivating it for ships was a long game. Between 1830 and 1840, after the Napoleonic Wars, Sweden laid down a grove of more than three hundred thousand oaks on the slender island of Visingsö for her navy. By the time they were ship ready, World War II was finished.[2]

Leaks were a part of life for sea-going ships of the era. Her hull beams were sealed with a combination of oakum rope fiber and pitch that required constant maintenance. Copper sheathing was added to mitigate the risk of marine life like the Teredo Nanalis, which grew up to a half meter long, lived their whole life in the holes they've bored, and left larvae to do likewise. To manage the Mississippi's notorious current, and outmaneuver opponents, twin sternposts, twin screws, and twin rudders were specified with a goal for her to turn in her own length.

The devil was in the detail. Too little protection, and a ram may not survive a broadside from her targets. Too much protection and she may not ram them at all. Her contract specified a speed of 12 knots, up to 4.5 inches of armor, and a 280-ton coal bunker for a range spanning London to Boston.[3]

Armor wasn't the only force behind the rams' return. Innovators like French Crimean War veteran Rear Admiral Labrousse quickly grasped the implication of steam power for ramming. English conflicts with France and Spain had led a transition from medieval ship designs with raised forecastles and aftercastles like landed battlements toward long, level decks with clear sightlines, massed cannon, and lowered centers of gravity. Gradually a culture of shooting down rigging and boarding targets as prizes gave way to standing off to destroy targets outright with cannon fire. These new rebel ironclads turned back the clock, with a dominant 10-inch single-gun forecastle and twin 6.4-inch-gun aftercastle. Forgoing massed deck cannon meant faster construction, smaller machinery requirements, smaller crews, and the kind of agility a ram would need. Raised castles angled her fire to potentially pierce a deck seeking a catastrophic boiler or magazine penetration, clearing their armored hulls. The trade-off was controversial. Despite their comparable sizes, *Louisiana* had a sixteen-gun battery, to the three guns of *Sphinx* and *Cheops*.

Form followed function, so instead of a bow jutting toward the sky, she led with a 7-meter ram below the waterline, longer than a soccer goal is wide. She flared out within paces and held her width her whole length.

Given that the *Virginia*'s ram had sheared off on its first collision, her ram was tightly integrated with the hull and reinforced with iron place, socket, and bow pieces. It was her raison d'être, after all. The Battle of Hampton Roads had descended into failed ram runs. The rebel flagship *Queen of the West* had been rammed by the *Monarch*, mortally wounding the commander, Colonel Charles Ellet Jr., and later rammed and captured the *Indianola* when she was raised. In 1864, their smallest-ever ironclad casemate, *Albemarle* (376 tons; two guns), roughly fashioned in a cornfield on the Roanoke River by an eighteen-year-old foreman, sent the *Southfield* (750 tons; four guns) to the bottom by ramming, before her war was ended by a spar torpedo attack from a Union lieutenant named Cushing in a steam launch too small to be named, which left a hole "big enough to drive a wagon in."[4]

Twin masts, anchored into the ship's keel, were sealed at each level with wedges and reinforced at the deckline with hardwood. Each supported twin mast cross beams wider than the ship, as well as a small observation platform that offered access to the upper rigging and sails. A smokestack almost as wide as a man is tall neatly split the distance between them. A second smokestack half its height provided ventilation for her machinery. Below deck, her carpenter's station included timbers to fish the masts together in the event of battle damage, inset timbers with mortice and tenon joints, and, for dire straits, rope and chain for emergency woolding. Two large air scoops just forward of the smokestack gave her a curious look and did what they could for the crew below. Nothing but the thick armored gunwales came between her crew and the ocean to either side.

Scarcely a decade from the first crude Crimean gun platforms, ocean-going rams represented a new, if brief, pinnacle in naval design. English demonstrations in 1859 with an Armstrong 40-pounder and in 1869 with a rifled 100-pounder failed to penetrate 10 centimeters of armur at ranges within 100 yards.[5] Even a decade after the American Civil War, ironclad warfare between Peru and Chile showed as few as one shot in four hundred penetrated.[6]

Thicker, hot-rolled European armor made for greater protection than matching her specs to U.S.-built ships suggests, as their higher-temperature Bessemer process burned off more impurities and left armor plate that was significantly stronger.[7] The twin rams were reinforced with hardwood backing as much as three times thicker than *Virginia*'s. Extending her armor belt up to 1.5 meters below the waterline propelled her displacement to more than 1,590 tons in transit and as much as 1,720 tons in a combat-ready configuration with full stores, powder, and coal.[8] Given her need to enter the Mississippi River mouth, this was an impressive engineering feat. The first 50-meter gun platforms of the Crimean war were little more than unpowered barges and weighed more. With 11 centimeters of flank armor over 38 centimeters of aged teak, and 14 centimeters of armor over 60 centimeters of oak to her castles, she was designed to withstand 15-inch (38.1-centimeter) shells, and did, albeit for another nation.

American ships followed European conventions from the age of sail. A sloop had a single mast and head sail. A schooner, two or three masts, rigged fore and aft. A barque sported as many as three to five, and so on. Categories overlapped. At some point a single deck sloop became a corvette or frigate as it scaled. Warship ratings were largely driven by crew numbers, as they were the most labor-intensive part of any ship. First-rate ships caried one hundred guns or 1,000 men; second raters carried more than eighty guns, or 800 men; third raters carried sixty guns and 600 men; fourth raters carried 410 men, and fifth raters had 300 men until a sixth rate was deemed any ship with an appointed captain, but these classifications were already unraveling. The *Monitor* had as few as 49 crew but fought *Virginia*'s 320 to a standstill. *Sphinx* and *Cheops* defied them completely. With fewer than 140 men, given the right circumstances, they had greater punch than any Union ship afloat.

Tough design choices continued, some with little more than dead reckoning. The British engineer Cowper Phipps Coles—a world leader in turret design, sponsored by Prince Albert—showcased this when his HMS *Captain* (1869; 7,070 tons) launched with such profound design flaws that she capsized within months with the loss of more than 480 lives, including his own.[9]

When chief engineer Alban C. Stimers up-armored Ericsson's initial monitor design with the Union's Casco-class ironclads, miscalculated weights resulted in the *Chino* sinking in the East River as soon as she launched. Even with Ericsson consulting for urgent redesigns, just eight of the class followed, stripped back to a single turret and gun and an experimental spar torpedo, none of which saw action.[10] The South had their failures, too. The would-be *Phoenix* from the engineers behind the *Nashville* (which has no surviving photos and a bewildering array of contradictory descriptions), had her keel fail on launch, sending her straight to the bottom, where she can still be seen today. Another side-wheeler built at Anderson was so damaged in her attempted launch, she was scrapped for parts.[11]

Their anchors were of the modern British Rogers type introduced the decade before, weighing 4,000 pounds or more. Even with the mechanical advantage of a ratcheted windlass, it was a bastard of a job to raise them. Her capstan to do so was amidships, with a turning slot bar for her chains that could be removed to free space. On a merchant ship, the men who worked it may sing a "forebitter" song. On a warship, they shut up so the captain could be heard giving orders. As the anchor rose, its length ahead of the ship shortened, and the rigging officer informed the captain she was at "long stay," "short stay," then "up and down" before the anchor left the water and was "catted" in place with rope.

Steam was still a relatively new marine technology. While demonstrators had launched in the eighteenth century, the first working steamboat, the *Charlotte Dundas*, had only been built by Scottish engineer William Symington sixty-two years before. In the South, machinery had become a new shipbuilding bottleneck, with sloops like the *Whitehall* using sawmill machinery so marginal it could barely make headway against the tide. In France, *Sphinx* enjoyed the absolute latest.

France's pioneering *La Gloire* could steam for fourteen days at up to 11 knots with a full sail rig. Working from the same requirement tables, the *Sphinx* and *Cheops* designers estimated a 280-ton coal bunker was required to see her across the Atlantic in fighting shape. Her contract stipulated her twin boilers would be set below the waterline. To accelerate production, neither were, and their placement together in a single boiler room between coal storage bunkers shrank her potential range.[12] Twin horizontal direct-acting two-cylinder single expansion powerplants from Mazeline in Le Havre were a generation ahead of earlier box-type designs with more complicated gearing. Surface condensers enabled higher pressures. They provided steam to the engines at 1.5 standard atmospheres (150 kilopascals), mated to two tubular coal-burning boilers that developed 1,200 PferdStarke (1,184 indicated horsepower). Together, they enabled speeds more than 12 knots, 2 knots per hour faster than the monitor's design goal, and 4 knots faster than the Union ironclad ever actually moved. Twin four-bladed, 12-foot screws were mounted in large protruding fairings.

Sails had made row-powered rams obsolete millennia before. While a person can deliver more than 1 horsepower in bursts, they sustain under 0.1, so the five-nation ship alone had the equivalent of almost five thousand men before her sails were deployed.[13] Provision was made to steam her with one engine at a time at 5.8 knots as required. Her steaming range was as much as 5,600 kilometers, depending on prevailing weather, her brace of sail, her hull maintenance, and the quality of coal.[14] At full steam, her bunkers would empty in five days, with broad-backed first-class firemen like James Stewitt shifting more than a ton of coal an hour in temperatures that routinely climbed above 50 degrees Celsius.

Alongside her magazine, her boilers were the greatest point of risk aboard. Boiler explosions had been recorded throwing iron plates more than 400 meters. Ironclads like the Japanese *Koshin* and Italian *Re d'Italia* sank in less than two minutes after boiler explosions. In 1865, with the American Civil War winding down and the mass repatriation of servicemen underway, a boiler explosion on the steamboat *Sultana* in Memphis cost more than seventeen hundred lives—more than were lost on the *Titanic*—in what's still America's greatest maritime disaster.[15]

Her sailing rig was a careful balance of speed and simplicity. Large fore-and-aft rigs maximized area, speed, and control sailing into the wind. Smaller square-rigged sails, being lighter, were easier to manage with fewer hands, and better suited to jibing downwind and tacking upwind. The rebel rams mixed both. *Sphinx* featured two square-rigged masts (the foremast being taller) with mainsails and gaff-rigged spankers (also known as the boom mainsail and trysail). Further studding sails like wings could increase her total sail area. Jibs ran from the foremast and horizontal bowspar. Conflicting accounts agree on at least 740 square meters of sail to supplement her engines, with the largest estimates exceeding 1,400 meters. Each used local three-strand (hawser-laid) or four-strand (shroud-laid) hemp cordage, with comparable rigs consuming more than 43 kilometers of rope or more.

Her control helm was on the aftercastle deck, with a view obscured by the masts, funnel, and forecastle, at just the wrong height for her secondary smokestack in an unkind wind. Although her huge twin rudders could turn her in her own length, making it happen was a battle for two to four men on the helm and twice as many on the rudder station, and heavily dependent on the sea state. In a following sea, the risk of yawing or ploughing under the waves was very real.

She featured five service boats on small davit cranes, two each to the port and starboard and one on an elevated rear poop deck. Their purpose was the transfer of crewmen and supplies and not as lifeboats. If she started sinking, there were too many men aboard for them, and the expectation was that they'd go down fighting.

Locks were everywhere: on the Confederate marine's armory, on the cutlery and utensils, and on stores lockers and liquor cabinets, though alcohol wasn't the touchstone it had once been. British navy rations had halved in 1824 and again in 1850. Men like General Stonewall Jackson, for whom this warship would one day be named, disavowed drink, not because they hated it, but because they loved it too much. The Union navy banned grog from 1862, but the Confederates provided a gill of spirits (four shot glasses) or 280 milliliters of wine per day until the very end. A man could choose to trade this in for an allowance of 20 cents a day, but few did. The *Sphinx* was hard on her crews, and pleasures were few and far between.[16]

Sphinx and *Cheops* were being built in France, but their armaments were carefully secured from English suppliers. Armor may have been in the ascendancy, but the firepower of the modern gun or rifle had ramped as much as five times over since the Battle of Trafalgar sixty years earlier. New casting and machining techniques allowed for larger guns that extended the fighting range of ships from hundreds of yards to thousands. A gun's firepower scaled up sharply as the calibers rose—one 68-pound shot had the destructive power of five 32-pound shots.[17] Arming the five-nation ship required choosing from overlapping generations of technology.

Older Carronade were squat, wide short-range designs launched by the Carron Company of Scotland in 1776 to reduce older gun weights by as much as two-thirds. Suddenly, guns no heavier than a 12-pounder could throw a 68-pounder's shot. Their shorter ranges suited the English in an age when privateers wanted to de-rig and board an opponent to gain her as a prize. With a limited battery available, *Sphinx* made heavier selections instead.

French Paixhans guns developed by General Henri-Joseph Paixhans from 1822 to 1823 were designed to use the first explosive shells. They used a flatter trajectory that made sighting down a gun barrel accurate enough to move from de-rigging to targeting vulnerable spaces. No wooden vessel was safe against such firepower, no matter what guns they mounted. Admiral Sir

John Hay of the Royal Navy put it succinctly in 1861, "The man who goes into action in a wooden vessel is a fool, and the man who sends him there is a villain."[18] *Sphinx* and *Cheops* passed them over for heavier options, too.

American Dahlgren guns were the result of Rear Admiral John A. Dahlgren applying scientific rigor to the danger of cannons exploding. While he was inspired by a deadly explosion of a 32-pound gun test in 1832, it was a familiar risk for the monitor's designer, Ericsson, whose own demonstration in 1864 had killed six. Weight was the enemy of the naval designer. Too little and the gun would fail. Too much and a ship's stability could be compromised. Dahlgren's solution was an ingenious "soda bottle" shape that thickened toward its rear where explosive forces were greatest. Dahlgren was emphatic, "The difference between the system of Paixhans and my own was simply that Paixhans guns were strictly shell guns, and were not designed for shot, nor for great penetration or accuracy at long ranges."[19] This strength allowed new breech-loading designs, where crews could rapidly reload at the gun's rear and not her muzzle, and more aerodynamic bullet-shaped shells that flew further and hit harder. While breech-loaders fired faster, they were slower and more costly to build. In 1863, their rollout across the Royal Navy was suspended. By 1864, they concluded, "Muzzle-loading guns are far superior to breech-loaders in simplicity of construction and efficiency."[20] *Sphinx* and *Cheops* used muzzle-loaders as a result.

Guns had smooth barrels. Rifles had spiraling grooves in their barrels that spun a projectile for greater range and accuracy. Howitzers were longer ranged weapons that could elevate to 45 degrees for higher ballistic arcs and indirect fire. Mortars threw even higher arcs up to 70 degrees. The *Sphinx* and *Cheops* would do their fighting in close. If their battery needed fewer, more-powerful guns sourced in England, they had to be Armstrong's.

Sir William Armstrong, the son of Newcastle-on-Tyne's corn-merchant mayor, became the lawyer his father wanted and hated it. He was twenty-seven before rambling across a hopelessly outdated watermill inspired a pursuit of engineering. Within fifteen years, he owned patents on everything from hydroelectric machines to hydraulic cranes and was a fellow of the Royal Society. By 1854, his military inventions included a submarine mine, lighter artillery, and a night scope called a "nyctoscope" designed so he could experiment on guns around the clock.

After successful demonstrations in 1854 for the secretary of state for war, he was challenged to progressively scale his novel cannon designs up to 6-, 9-, and 12-pounder light field guns by 1858. Armstrong didn't believe they could be scaled further. The ministry did: 20-, 40-, and 110-pounder heavy guns followed for immediate service in the New Zealand Māori wars and Second Opium War in China. The term *pounds* here refers to the weight of their shot. Guns were otherwise described by their muzzle, for example, a 40-pounder Armstrong was a 121 millimeter (4.75-inch) gun. They supported explosive shells like Paixhans. They retained the Dahlgren curves that put their strength where the stress was. His innovation was in layering their construction.[21]

By 1863, he was delivering rifled barrels in toughened mild steel, reinforced by wrought-iron coils that kept them under compression with remarkable precision. Like the new Minié infantry rifle, Armstrong guns used shells fractionally larger than the bore, with the outermost layer finished in softer lead so they could deform into the barrel rifling and take on its spin when fired. Each barrel had a squeeze bore fractionally smaller again, which center the round and sheared off the last outer lead for the cleanest possible flight.

The Royal Navy went all-in rolling them out, making Armstrong director of rifled ordnance, a knight, and member of the order of the Companion of the Bath (though his designs were shamelessly cloned by the Elswick Ordnance Company founded by the secretary of state for war and partners). The five-nation ship would not only mount Armstrong guns, but she'd be hit by them in her Japanese service.

Revolving turrets had been a part of the Laird ram design, but they added weight and complexity at a point when the South's future might be measured in months, not years. The resulting compromise saw a fixed 10-inch (25-centimeter) 300-pounder Armstrong gun mounted in a forecastle that ran 20 feet back from the bow, so it could fire on her ramming targets. Test firings were supervised in England. It used more than 50 pounds of powder though it was tested with as much as 80 pounds, and it claimed to penetrate 5.5 inches of armor with a first shot at less than 200 yards and penetrate it wholly with a second and third.[22] Armor might have had the upper hand, but this was still enough to potentially pierce the *New Ironsides*, then the largest ship in the Union. At longer ranges, a shot of this weight could "ring the bell" of its target with concussive force and splintering even if it didn't penetrate. Reloading it was laborious. Today's twenty-one-gun salutes can be traced back to ships firing their cannon before entering a neutral port as a goodwill gesture, rendering themselves impotent while they reloaded.

The largest guns that the aftercastle could mount were twin 4-ton, 16-centimeter (6.4-inch), 70-pounder rifled muzzle-loading designs thought to be a late substitution from a Royal Navy vessel in another indication the British Admiralty knew more than they admitted.[23] One faced each side. Both were cast iron. The alternative was bronze, which was easier to cast and longer serving due to its greater elasticity, but more than four times as expensive. These were claimed (without proof and very optimistically) to penetrate 4 inches of armor over a backing of 9 inches of oak from 200 yards with less than 10 pounds of powder.

While the rear castle was fixed (something Prussia later addressed in a major refit of her sister ship with a turret), her designers installed multiple cutouts so the guns could be manually shifted between them to aim.[24] The precise transfer of dimensions from plans to molds was challenging. When the two guns for the aft turrets arrived, they found the turrets more than a foot narrower than drawn, and their gun carriages were cut down to fit. Her rear plate armor was methodically stripped back, reforged and reset, in another setback for her battle with weight distribution. The resulting spacing was so tight, both guns couldn't face out perpendicular to the hull at the same time, and each gun's crew was endangered by the recoil of the other. Hydraulic controls were still decades away. All three guns were mounted on four-wheel truck carriages, with only breeching ropes attached to the hull protecting their crews from their recoil.

Though improved, their gunpowder looked much like it had since its discovery in second-century China by alchemists seeking an elixir of life. Key advances like the nitrates German chemist Christian Friedrich uncovered blowing up his lab or the nitroglycerin Ascanio Sobrero identified and Alfred Nobel stabilized, were too powerful for metallurgy to harness for cannon fire. While the United States tested compressed air guns in the Spanish-American War a generation later with the *Vesuvius*, black powder was there to stay.[25]

Their ammunition varied. Solid shot was best for piercing iron hulls. Explosive shot could hole a wooden vessel like never before, especially with contact fuses displacing hand-cut fuses. Chain shot joining two balls with a length of chain to reduce rigging was fast disappearing. Shotgun-like grape-shot was selected to target men, not ships. Using a reduced powder charge could allow for double-shotting with reduced range but greater impact.★ Rates of fire varied wildly, but a well-drilled crew would take four minutes or more to fire each round. Battles of the era could take hours.

London-based recruiters and Captain William H. Parker's Confederate naval academy were already assembling new rebel crews. Many, like her first captain, served with coastal artillery, pending reassignment.[26]

In this pre-radio era, her communications were confined to the nine colors, compass points and letters of their signal flags, based on code books kept under lock and key in the captain's cabin. When they passed from sight warships of the day were like islands, and their leaders like presidents.

Against the odds, Bulloch's team were delivering a disruptor no Union monitor could follow and no wooden ship could match. But she had a court-room and an ocean to overcome before she could fight.

★Mortars firing such rounds were the "bombs bursting in air" over Fort McHenry in the American national anthem.

A SECOND FLAG

11

On September 10, 1863, a disgruntled Arman shipyard employee named Trémont walked into the Union's stately three-story Parisian embassy with an offer that seemed too good to be true.

He knew the Confederates had lost their Laird rams to the turncoat Clarence Yonge's testimony. Would they pay for information on new rebel warships in France? His price was 20,000 francs. There was hardly a figure he could have quoted that Consul General John Bigelow wouldn't have happily paid. Sample documents were requested and supplied. This was no mere tip-off—it was a paper trail all the way to the Little White House. Twenty-one documents followed, laying out French complicity in black and white. Bigelow raced the documents to the US minister to France, William L. Dayton, who very publicly called the French out, and to William H. Seward, who added a threat to embarrass Napolean III with their lucrative rebel tobacco trade and designs on a proxy Mexican monarchy.

This was the final straw for senior French officials who'd indulged the emperor to this point. Foreign affairs minister Edouard Drouyn de Lhuys took both threats at face value and was so exasperated he later said of Napoleon III when he'd led them to ruin against Prussia, "The emperor has immense desires and limited abilities."[1]

French officials presented Lucien Arman with papers alleging the twin rams under construction were not for Sweden and could represent a violation of neutrality. It was enough to force Arman, who was, after all, a national legislator himself, to distance himself from them, too. Arman was summoned to the king, "who rated him severely, threatened imprisonment, ordered him to sell the ships at once. . . . The two corvettes at Nantes [*Texas* and *Georgia*] were also ordered to be sold. The order is of the most peremptory kind, not only directing the sale but requiring the builders to furnish proof to the minister of foreign affairs that the sale is a real one . . . in a style of virtuous indignation."[2]

Bigelow called it out for the theater it was, "when you call to mind the fact that this same Minister of Marine on the 6th day of June, 1863, wrote over his own official signature a formal authorization to arm those very ships with 14 heavy guns each 'canons raye de trentes,' the affectation of having just discovered them to be suitable for purpose of war is really astonishing."[3]

A chastened French government declared that the twin rams and four corvettes under construction would be sold to governments then at peace. Perhaps they even meant it, though they certainly didn't honor it. Confederate efforts to use new cutouts were rebuffed. James Dunwoody Bulloch advised the rebel Congress that the French administration was becoming "more unfriendly than Earl Russell," the two-time prime minister of England.[4]

With the question of who they wouldn't serve settled, Arman turned to who they would. Denmark was at war with Prussia and Austria. Two corvettes and the second flagship ram, *Cheops*, were sold to Prussia. The other ram was sold to a Swedish banker acting for Denmark after initial approaches to the Italian and Mexican navies amounted to nothing.[5] Two corvettes were sold to Peru. Bulloch stayed in touch at every step, looking for a loophole, and later affirming, "I believe that M. Arman has acted in a perfectly loyal manner thus far in these transactions, and he sincerely regrets the present turn of events. He has proposed that a nominal sale of the vessels should be made to a Danish banker, and that there should be a private agreement providing for a redelivery to us at some point beyond the jurisdiction of France."[6]

Bulloch's belief in Napoleon III never wavered, convinced he "favours us so far as to tell us frankly to sell out and save our money," though "there was still a large balance in question at the end of the war, which has never been settled." Despite the hope of a later resale, Bulloch despaired at their loss. "The two Bordeaux ironclads and the four corvettes would have been a formidable attacking squadron and would have enabled its commander to strike severe and telling blows upon the Northern seaboard. The loss of the ironclads changes the whole character of the force, and deprives it of its real power of offence. . . . There really seems but little for our ships to do now upon the open sea."[7]

Bulloch ordered down-scaled steamships as a last-gasp option with smaller European yards prepared to face penalties for a customer paying overs. Six modest iron-hulled twin-screw torpedo boats were contracted in London. Six variants were contracted in Liverpool. More detail survives on the London designs, which featured a semi-submerged hull for a low silhouette on the water and light armor. None are recorded as having served, though at least one completed trials on the Thames, and at least three were shipped to

North America as deck cargo on the Confederacy's largest blockade-runners. Though these were ultimately reported by the Union's consular network to Charles Francis Adams, no formal protests were made, and the Navy focused on intercepting their carriers.[8] None fought.

As late as October 1864, new agents like chief engineer Quinn were still being dispatched to Europe with plans for a torpedo boat fleet that amounted to nothing. The South's last gasp was the 230-foot steamship *Hawk*, which was funded by the speculative Scottish firm Henderson and Colborne and fitted out by the blockade-runner Thomas Sterling Begbie, but stranded in Bermuda by their bankruptcy.[9]

Numerous other projects were rumored. The five-nation ship's future captain noted, "Every ship then being built in Europe acquired this reputation."[10] The British Crown's representative in America, Sir Frederick W. A. Bruce, recorded, "There is no doubt that agents of the confederates were on the look-out to purchase the more powerful vessels of the squadron from the Chinese," when the Qing emperor rejected them. Four were returned to Britain, while the remainder transferred to new owners in Bombay (followed partway by the raider *Alabama* trying to persuade a former Fraser, Trenholm & Company employee to hijack them, who declined, but later helmed the blockade-runner *Lady Stirling*).[11]

Commander M. F. Maury still dreamed of a twin-turret oceanic ironclad with a full spread of sail and a 16-knot top speed and progressed to securing loans against future crops and having drawings made, before cooler heads prevailed. Confederate diplomat John Slidell directed no further ships could be commissioned unless the Confederacy was granted diplomatic recognition, or they could be openly contracted for.[12] Their window had closed.

Bulloch was indefatigable. If guns and rams couldn't get the job done, perhaps new technologies could.

When the North declined the Winans steam gun, which looked like a five-ton steampunk tank with a steam-powered centrifugal gun capable of flinging two hundred rounds per minute, it was smuggled to Harper's Ferry, though it ended the war with a whimper stored in Lowell, Massachusetts.[13] In 1862, architectural engineer William C. Powers built a full-size mock-up of a steam-powered Archimedean screw helicopter in Mobile, which could never have worked.[14] Experimental double-barreled cannon failed trials in Georgia when they only managed to damage a chimney in one direction and a cow in another.[15] Henry Clay Pate's Confederate revolving cannon, which scaled up a revolver action to field artillery, failed. Desperation closed in. When Georgia governor Joe Brown ordered ten thousand pikes to arm local troops, he knew what chance medieval weapons would stand on a modern battlefield.[16]

Not all innovations floundered. The Union's *Cairo* was sunk by an electrically detonated naval mine on the Yazoo River in Mississippi in December 1862.[17] Armored railcars defended against raiders. Both sides developed a balloon corps for observation. The North's Thaddeus S. C. Lowe had been about to attempt a lighter-than-air crossing of the Atlantic when war broke out, and he oversaw new designs with generators and telegraph sets. The Confederates matched them, barely, with silken petticoat donations, wood, fabric, and the heat of oil-soaked pinecones. Because neither side commissioned these aeronauts into the army, the legal situation for these pioneers was murky so they risked being hung as spies.[18]

Finned grenades were first thrown. New rifled barrels transformed infantry range and firepower. Terrible new 0.58 Minié bullets almost as big as a dime flattened as they pulled skin, bacteria, and clothing into their wounds and often failed to exit, driving a wave of brutal battlefield amputations. Triage surgeons quickly learned who to treat first. Seventy-one percent of those hit in their extremities survived, but gut shots were almost always fatal.[19] Changes quickly rippled out from their battlefields. The anesthesia inhaler was a new mercy. Income tax was introduced for the first time, though at just 7.5 percent at war's end. Clothing and shoe sizes were standardized. Lime lights made new night action possible. Jellybeans were conceived to reach beloved soldiers.

The Confederate Torpedo Bureau under Lieutenant H. Davidson continued the pioneering work of Commander M. F. Maury. Though America's Robert Fulton had demonstrated the destruction of the brig *Dorethea* with floating mines in 1805, neither England nor France was moved to buy a weapon "that would give great advantage to weaker maritime nations." Improvised versions in the War of 1812 were seen more as terrorism than warfare. British captain Thomas Hardy of the HMS *Ramillies* declared if America used any "torpedo boat" in this "cruel and unheard-of warfare," he would "order every house near the shore to be destroyed." Russia has no such qualms employing mines in the Crimea, and the Confederacy didn't either. While they were a defensive deterrent for the South—and certainly sunk Union vessels—they couldn't address the Union blockade.[20]

In all, just five ships built in western European ports provided active service in the Confederate navy. At least five ironclads, fourteen cruisers of varying sizes, and numerous smaller gunboats had been thwarted by the Union's policing.

Everything the South had to fight with was already at sea. Their would-be flagships, now in service to Prussia and Denmark, then found themselves not fighting for Southern secession, but on opposite sides of a sharp continental war that would be instrumental in shaping the future German state.

FROM PRESIDENT TO KING   12

T he duchies of Schleswig and Holstein were a complicated question in a complicated time.

Schleswig was predominantly Danish in its north, German to the south, and mixed in-between. It had variously been a Danish dependency to the fourteenth century, united with Holstein from 1386 to 1460, a separate duchy under the king of Denmark, a fief of the Holy Roman Empire, and a member of the German confederation.[1] Denmark considered it theirs. Holstein was largely German, and a target for nationalists wanting it incorporated into a new Germany.

Denmark's constitutional reforms under the new King Frederick VII in 1848 made no claims to either territory. The situation was complicated by the usual tangle of conflicting interests. England preferred that Prussia not be strengthened by access to the Baltics. Russia supported Denmark's claim to avoid her joining a Scandinavian union.

While the German states were slowly coalescing, their path to statehood was unclear. By the late eighteenth century, a bewildering array of alliances, marriages, and conflicts had reduced the Holy Roman Empire in the west to a Hapsburg dynasty centered in Austria. The Office of the Holy Roman Emperor was dissolved in 1806. A loose federation emerged in 1815. France's 1848 revolution motivated Prussia's King Friedrich Wilhelm IV to accede to an elected representative body to avoid bloodier alternatives.

When the city of Kiel in Schleswig-Holstein proclaimed a provisional government without the consent of either nation, Prince Frederik of Noer led volunteers into the open fortress of Rendsburg, seized its armories, and expelled those loyal to Denmark. An equal-sized force of Danes forced their retreat in return. The result was the First Schleswig War (1848–1851), which made their admirals buyers on the world's ship markets.

Though Denmark's navy was clearly superior, its early surge from Co-penhagen to Jutland underwhelmed. In April 1849 a Danish fleet trapped by unfavorable winds before the Eckernförde fjord forts lost the frigate *Gefion* spectacularly after a magazine explosion, as well as the flagship *Christian VIII.* They were cheered entering Sonderborg but ignored as Flensberg, Aabenraa, and Fehmarn fell to Prussian advances on land. On April 18, the wider Ger-man confederation declared war. Victory at Schleswig on April 23 forced a series of Danish withdrawals. Denmark resorted to a blockade of Prussian ports and appeals to Europe's great powers. Within a week, every Baltic Sea port was closed. This Danish blockade was a lesson to all. Union leaders cited it while developing their Anaconda Plan. Two generations hence, World War I repeated it on a continental scale.

After their defeat by a twenty-eight-thousand-man Prussian-led army, eleven thousand Danes retreated to Als island. Prussia invaded Jutland, which escalated it to a wider European concern. Sweden landed seven thousand troops in support of Denmark. Russia threatened Prussia with counterinva-sion and partially mobilized. England threatened naval action. The net result was that the German confederation grudgingly accepted the truce of Malmo, which Frederick VII broke seven months later with an eighty-thousand-man invasion of the disputed territories. At sea, while lighter Prussian forces like the Von Der Tann skirmished with heavier opponents like Denmark's *Hekla,* the Danes' ability to move troops by sea delivered a major land victory July 6, forcing Prussia to sue for peace a second time.

With Schleswig and Holstein still contested, a third round of fighting in 1851 saw a thirty-thousand-man pro-German force raised in the disputed territories so overwhelmingly defeated, Prussia felt bound to invade Holstein again with forty thousand soldiers that suffered their own defeat at Isted, which forced their return of Jutland to Denmark.[2] Schleswig and Holstein were reunited with Denmark in the resulting Treaty of London. The Prussian statesman, Otto Von Bismarck, was outraged. The German Diet refused to recognize it, and tensions simmered.[3] Prussia, Austria, and Denmark's diverg-ing positions within the German federation complicated any political resolu-tion. All three eyed the world's military shipyards hungrily.

In 1863, with fighting in the American Civil War in its third year, the victorious Danish king Frederick VII died, and King Christian IX assumed the throne. He immediately launched his predecessor's new "November" constitution, which annexed Schleswig. Denmark was confident that Eu-rope's powers would back her. Prussia was confident that only force would prevail. By November 21, a German alliance threatened to tear up the Treaty of London and invade. On December 7, Denmark marched in troops to dis-puted territory in defiance.

Denmark's naval superiority was built upon the generation of wooden-hulled warships, and it was ripe for disruption. The French Arman shipyards, despite pledging that the *Sphinx* and *Cheops* wouldn't be sold to combatants, dispatched Baron Henri Arnous de Rivière to pitch both ships for a tidy profit at 2.4 million francs each in December. On January 16, Austro-Prussian representatives demanded Denmark withdraw her troops and roll back her constitution. Denmark refused, and Prussia took it as a casus belli gleefully. On February 1, Austria and Prussia invaded Schleswig a final time.

The Second Schleswig War of 1864 was very different to the first. Prussia was on the rise. Denmark entered the war outnumbered, fought it at great disadvantage, and was defeated decisively. Her fortifications at the Danewirk—the Maginot line of their day—surrendered inside a week. France and Russia favored the Prussian position. Britain and Sweden stood back. Denmark looked to her fleet to offset her disadvantages on land.

The Danes deployed an east Baltic fleet under Rear Admiral C. E. van Dockum and a west Baltic fleet under Commander F. Muxoll to restart their blockade. Individual ships like *Niel Juel* patrolled the English Channel.[4]

On February 18, the Danish turret ironclad *Rolf Krake* was ordered to destroy a bridge the Prussians had built across Nybøl Nor. Doing so meant the two-turret, four-gun ship running the gauntlet of Flensburg Fjord's artillery. By the time the Danish warship was driven off, she had taken more than a hundred hits with just three wounded aboard, in yet another showcase of armor's ascendency.[5] Within days of Germanic invasion, Denmark acquired the 5,000-ton-plus Scottish sea monster from the Confederacy and began her slow (and unsuccessful) completion. The rebel *Sphinx* and *Cheops* offered more immediate service. The director of the Royal Holmen Dockyards, Otto Frederik Suenson, traveled to Bordeaux for inspections in early March. The Danish emissary in Paris, Count Molkte, endorsed them, vowing, "Prussia will not bring these vessels out of Bordeaux, but perhaps we can."[6] Suenson endorsed their purchase, March 13.

Otto von Bismarck signed a Prussian alliance with Austria, on March 6, 1864, to invade Denmark and contest the Danish naval blockade. Prussia's navy was a coastal gunboat flotilla with little naval tradition and a checkered recent history. In 1860–1862, the fledgling Prussian Brandenburg navy had clashed with Spain over debts incurred as allies against France, swarming an isolated frigate with seven ships under Claes van Beveren, before fleeing from the Spanish escorts of a silver fleet from South America.[7] Austria's larger fleet, operating from bases in the Adriatic, was divided by tensions with Italy, who'd declared their independence June 6, 1861, after their victory with Napoleon III's Second French Empire over Austria.

After the seizure of numerous merchants in Baltic waters, Admiral Prince Adalbert of Prussia ordered Captain Eduard von Jachmann to test the blockade. On March 16, a Prussian squadron was spotted but lost in snow flurries in the Baltic by Danish pickets.

Jachmann steamed out from the Oder the following day with the corvettes SMS *Arcona* (2,353 tons; twenty-six guns) and SMS *Nymphe* (1,183 tons; sixteen guns). With no immediate Danish response, they were joined by the side-wheeler SMS *Loreley* (420 tons; two guns) and six light twin-cannon gunboats headed by the *Comet*. After finding nothing steaming east, they turned west toward Greifswalder Oie island. At 1:15 p.m., their lookouts spotted smoke on the horizon. Their three heavies formed a firing line ahead of their gunboats in heavy rain. The Battle of Jasmund, depicted in a painting by Danish artist Carl Frederik Sørensen, was about to begin.

The smoke soon resolved itself as a Danish squadron with the ship-of-the-line *Skjold*, corvettes *Sjælland* (2,132 tons; forty-two guns), *Thor* (790 tons; twelve guns), and *Hejmdal* (878 tons; sixteen guns) under Rear Admiral C. E. van Dockum. By 2:30 p.m., they formed opposing lines off Rügen island, and *Arcona* was first to fire on *Sjælland*. Initial exchanges were inconclusive, but as the larger *Skjold* closed on her, the Prussian *Arcona* turned to starboard without a clear signal. The divided Prussian forces enabled the Danes to concentrate their fire on the remaining *Nymphe*, which was quickly hindered by damage to her funnel. At 3:00 p.m., the additional Danish propeller frigate *Tordenskold* (1,453 tons; thirty guns) was sighted steaming in from the north. By 3:40 p.m., she fired briefly on Prussian gunboats that wanted nothing to do with her and were last seen steaming off with the gunboat *Hay* under tow. Within minutes, the dated Prussian side-wheeler *Loreley* broke off to the west. By 4:45 p.m., the remaining Prussian corvettes had put enough distance between the two fleets for firing to taper off. By 6:00 p.m., the Danish chase was called off.

It was a mixed result for both. The blockade held, but the Prussian navy retreated in good order. It was yet another testament to the ascendency of armor—*Nymphe* alone had been hit more than seventy times, but casualties were light, with six dead and sixteen wounded for Denmark and three dead and three wounded for Prussia. Though Jachmann was promoted to rear admiral, the Danes reinforced their fleet, and the Prussian navy remained pinned in port until hostilities ended.[8]

On March 28, the Danish turreted ironclad *Rolf Krake* absorbed Prussian land fire while trying and failing to prevent the Prussian seizure of Dybbøl. Arman sought to exploit a seller's market, asking 937.500 rigsdalers for the *Sphinx* or *Cheops*, but the Danes were his equal across the bargaining table. When Denmark settled on a single hull by March 31, it wasn't just for 800,000 rigsdaler, it was with several terms in their favor, including a maximum displacement (her effective depth) and a handover in the sound between Denmark and Sweden by June 10, 1864.

The contract reads, in part:

- Displacement: 1400 tons, 1535 deep load
- Dimensions: 171 feet, 10" (between perpindiculars), 187 feet overall × 32 feet, 8 inches beam (52.38, 56.99 × 4.37 meters)
- Machinery: 2 tubular boilers, 2-shaft RCR (return connecting rod), 1200 ihp (indicated horsepower)—10 knots—coal: 200/280 tons
- Armour: Iron. Side: 4 inches–3½ inches; turret—4½ inches, after guns: 4 inches
- Armament: 1–10 inch, 300-pounder wrought iron Armstrong rifled muzzle-loader and twin 6.4 inch, 70-pounder Armstrong rifled muzzle-loading gun
- Complement: 130
- Builder: Arman, Bordeaux
- Contracted—July 16, 1863
- Launched: June 21, 1864
- Completed: January 1865[9]

When the deputy director of the Copenhagen Royal Dockyard, G. P. Schönheyder, was ordered to Bordeaux to inspect her, we see her new name, *Stærkodder*, for the first time, calling back to an epic hero in old Norse mythology descended from giants, capable of both heroism and ignominy.[10]★ She would never be referred to as the *Sphinx* again.

G. P. Schönheyder's supervision of the new Danish warship's completion was meticulous and dispassionate. His first report, dated April 18, was riddled with concerns. "The woodwork is not as beautiful as the work done at home." "Coal trimmings on board will be difficult." "[The constructors] have not made any calculations regarding the displacement. The Coal stores can only hold 200 tons instead of the promised 280 tons. I dare not insist on a larger increase than to 220 tons—which Arman has promised to make."[11]

Urgent missives reached Schönheyder every week. Denmark's position on land was becoming untenable. While her blockade of German ports continued, rumors of Prussian efforts to reinforce her fleet were everywhere. The war's most decisive clash at sea was fought off Heligoland Island, then under British control, but later swapped with Germany for Zanzibar in search of spices.

On May 9, 1864, the Danish frigates *Niels Juel* (1,934 tons; forty-four guns) and *Jylland* (2,450 tons; forty-four guns), and corvette *Hejmdal* under Admiral Edouard Suenson, spotted the neutral British frigate *Aurora*. Beyond

---

★Which makes the alternative translation as "strong otter" somewhat underwhelming.

her sailed the Austrian frigates *Schwarzenberg* (2,614 tons; thirty-eight guns) and *Radetzky* (2,334 tons; thirty-one guns) leading three marginal Prussian gunboats (three guns). They closed aggressively.

Opposite Denmark's Suenson was the esteemed admiral, Wilhelm von Tegetthoff, widely considered the father of the subsequent Austro-Hungarian navy. They drew line abreast and closed in. By 1:45 p.m., Tegetthoff's flagship, the *Schwarzenberg*, opened fire on Danish forces who maintained disciplined silence until the gap between them fell under 1.6 kilometers. Tegetthoff turned to try and execute a classic T intersection where his ships could release a full broadside and only Danish bow gunners could fire in return. Suenson's countermaneuvers positioned them in two parallel lines, crossing 1,800 meters apart at such speed that the Prussian gunboats began to fall behind their Austrian escorts. Tegetthoff broke contact to regather them in a line southwestward, which the Danes quickly matched, so both could bring all their firepower to bear. *Niels Juel* concentrated her guns on the *Schwarzenberg*. *Jylland* and *Hejmdal* trained theirs on the smaller *Radetzky*.

While both fleets observed impacts, they were indecisive until, after some two hours, *Schwarzenberg* was seen to be burning fiercely and so stricken that Tegetthoff attempted a run for neutral British waters. While the Danes initially closed, firing, the HMS British *Aurora*, which had observed throughout, faced them to enforce their island's neutrality. Suenson veered off at the 4.8 kilometer territorial limit, watching Tegetthoff's burning flagship edge away as darkness fell. Austro-Prussian forces escaped to Cuxhaven overnight with their rigging compromised and the *Schwarzenberg* heavily damaged.[12] Each ship survived. Danish forces lost seventeen killed and thirty-seven wounded, including the whole of *Jylland*'s gun crew of nine; the Austrians lost thirty-seven dead and ninety-three wounded. The Prussians lost none among gunboats so diminutive that they made no material contribution.

None of it mattered on land. By June 14, Denmark sued for peace, and control of Schleswig-Holstein passed to Germany (only to return, in part, after Germany's defeat in World War I). Denmark continued supervision of the *Stærkodder*'s construction in France. With Prussia closing in on the *Cheops*, there's every chance their agents crossed paths in Arman's docks. Their navies wouldn't clash again after what would prove to be the last all-wood battle at sea between major powers. The London Conference of European Powers was convened April 25, 1864, over Prussia's protests, with a French motion to survey the disputed duchies on their preferred future.

Schönheyder, the Danish deputy director, stayed on station in Bordeaux, day in, day out, battling delays. Ten days after *Stærkodder*'s contracted delivery date—June 20—he reported, "The engines and the boilers have arrived. I will travel to Rochefort in order to compare the ship with French naval units, in particular in regard to the putting on of the armoured plates." On June 21, the five-nation ship launched for the first time, and her shakedown trials began. On June 27 he reports, "It will most likely draw four inches too deep. My studies of the French naval vessels regarding the armour indicates that the accurate adaptation of the armoured plates are not as good as planned. We can do nothing about this, but it is important in regard to the decision whether or not to accept the ship."[13]

By June 19, Prussia and Austria had resolved how they'd carve up the contested duchies.[14] Without the European intervention of the First Schleswig War, Denmark's defeat on land was absolute. Her refusal to offer immediate terms meant Germany continued advancing. Jutland was invaded again on June 25. On June 26, Prussian storm-boats ferrying troops between Jutland and the island of Als were scattered by the arrival of the turret-ironclad *Rolf Krake*. While they'd landed enough troops to prevail in the war's last major action, it was another reminder how badly a new flagship that could oppose the Danes was needed.

Construction proceeded on the Arman rams, night and day. James Dunwoody Bulloch's man, Captain Eugene L. Tessier, remained onsite, working on a cover story for "the China trade" if they could somehow be reacquired for the Confederacy.[15] Bismarck was dissatisfied enough with his dependence on Austria at sea that he met Arman's price for the *Cheops*. The announcement of its acquisition on June 28 sent a jolt through Danish circles. There wasn't a more powerful ship for sale on earth. Here was a vessel that could face them directly, force them to compress their fleet, and break their blockade—everything it was designed to do for the Confederacy.

Arman now had two nations pushing for delivery. Managing the weight distribution of new ship classes had always been challenging. On July 11, Schönheyder reported further concerns about her steerage way—the headway required for the ship to be responsive to the helm.

Denmark's return to negotiations was now on German terms. Schleswig and Holstein were gone. The most she could hope for was her own borders. The final Treaty of Vienna, signed on October 30, 1864, was a capitulation costing Denmark more than 30 percent of her land and almost as much of her prewar population.[16] Less than a year later, the Convention of Gastein ceded Holstein to Austria and Schleswig to Prussia.

On July 22, Schönheyder reported concerns that rushed construction had compromised *Stærkodder*. "The draught aft is 1½ feet to [*sic*] great, the steerage way is too big and the armouring inadequate. The armoured plates have been fashioned very carelessly. Have requested that these faults be corrected before we can accept the ship." Arman protested but agreed to remediation.

Although *Sphinx* and *Cheops* were indeed sister ships, variations between them were multiplying with a more heavily armored *Sphinx* sitting lower in the water. The Danish Ministry of Naval Affairs replied, "whether or not we accept the *Stærkodder* depends more on . . . that the draught and speed of the ship are as stipulated in the contract, than whether the work has been done with more or less accuracy and care," and counseled the work was not to be judged unduly before she was finished.[17]

The former *Sphinx* left the water for dry docks and extensive modifications. Selected armored plates were remounted, and others were replaced outright, four layers thick in places, on the understanding it would cancel any subsequent claims for compensation. Her sister ship *Cheops*, without these modifications, would later suffer for it.

Arman was hardly alone. Mounting ever-heavier armor was throwing shipyards around the world back to the drawing board. In Alabama, for example, the shipbuilders J. T. Shirley and David Dehaven were horrified when the new *Memphis* (2,046 tons; six guns, fashioned from the former *Alonzo Child*) broke her back under the weight of 4-inch armor and could only serve as an unarmored transport until being sunk as a harbor obstruction.[18]

By September 30, she was back in the water, and Bulloch's efforts to build a fleet around her continued. The *Sea King* was his latest win, a fully rigged steamer built on the Clyde River in Scotland, whose first charter had been carrying troops more than 18,000 kilometers to the Māori Wars in New Zealand. When her government service ended, Bulloch diverted her from transporting tea between England, Japan, and China to a notable run through the Atlantic, across the Indian Ocean, in Japanese waters and as far as the Australian colonies as the raider *Shenandoah* (1,018 tons; eight guns). She took six prize ships rounding the Cape of Good Hope before settling in the Bering Strait, where she ran riot, destroying thirty-two fishing vessels and capturing more than one thousand prisoners.[19]

By October 14, already four months overdue, Danish reports suggested the new ram's depth issues had worsened, and her variances from the contract were as much as 30 centimeters aft and 17 centimeters down her centerline. Schönheyder summarizes her progress:

Advantages

- The ship is strong build [*sic*]
- Has a powerful armament
- Good engines
- Handles well
- Good stock

Faults

- Constructed in wood and iron
- The armoured plates are below minimum thickness and are very badly fitted
- Not enough room in the aft. gun tower
- Aft. gun tower does not have a free field of fire abeam
- The boilers are exposed
- Bad sea boat
- Limited room on the deck and in the crew's quarters
- Poor coal trimming conditions[20]

A week later, his telegrams added, "Speed during trials [is] 10.8 knots. Handled well. Speed with only one engine [is] 5.8 knots. The engines worked well. Easy movements, but takes a lot of water in [over the stern]." On October 23, the head of the third department in the Ministry of Naval Affairs was ordered to the Arman shipyards to determine if she'd be accepted. It was one thing for Denmark to spend heavily when at war. It was quite another at peace, after withering losses. "The Naval Ministry is ready to accept the ship, if Arman will accept a 80,000 frcs. reduction of the price. However, the penalty for a late delivery (1000 francs. a day) is still to be paid by Arman."[21]

Two days later, Deputy Director Schönheyder reported that "the Stærkodder has left for the Sound. Arman entrusts it to the Ministry of Naval Affairs to decide whether or not they will accept the ship on other conditions than the one stipulated in the contract."[22] It is not clear which nation's colors she flew.

On October 29, Danish short payment demands rose to 300,000 francs over variations in her handling, depth, and delivery delays. Arman countered with 200,000 francs, and when not initially accepted, ordered her to return to port at Cherbourg. A flurry of conflicting cables followed among Danish officials. On November 2, the Naval Ministry was advised the deal was off and immediately wrote back to their emissary with, "Why? The offer from Arman was reasonable."[23]

The Second Schleswig War had been fought and lost. Denmark had a third fewer citizens within her borders. The Scottish sea monster was proving to be a money pit. *Stærkodder*, for all her potential, now had little to offer a Denmark who'd learned supremacy at sea could not offset weakness on land.

By November 11, the newspaper *Berlingske Tidende* took up the story. "The new armoured vessel *Stærkodder*, which has been built in France and is rigged as a brig, arrived at the Copenhagen Roads yesterday evening." The first allocation of supplies for her crew and medical staff are recorded November 10, 1864. By December, *Stærkodder* had been delivered by a French captain and crew and was front-page news again. On December 1, we see "the new armoured brig *Stærkodder* carried out a trial run in the Sound." On December 5, "The armoured brig *Stærkodder* yesterday moved from the Royal Dockyard [Holmen], to the Copenhagen Roads."[24] It was only then that Denmark declined delivery in a written submission that compared her build quality unfavorably to the armored battery ship *Lindormen* (2,048 tons; six guns), then taking shape in the Royal Danish dockyards. Negotiations restarted with a widening array of diplomatic and military officials on both sides. Did she meet her contract specifications? Did Arman still hold her title? Who could arbitrate? With a fixed price contract signed, Arman was concerned about the cost overruns they'd sustained, and he was keen to see the impasse resolved.

The deeply unpopular Danish king Christian IX served on through a series of parliamentary disputes over who held what authority. Time helped rehabilitate his reputation. By his death in 1906, he was a respected figure, whose children's royal marriages saw him dubbed "the father-in-law of Europe." Denmark was left so averse to war, she declared herself neutral in World War I.[25]

Prussia's Otto von Bismarck, who felt passionately that "the main thing is to make history, not to write it," was only getting started. He wanted Europe back at the center of the world with a unified Germany at its heart. He had little regard for the upstart new world, later opining of America's relentless post–Civil War ascent, "God has a special providence for fools, drunkards, and the United States of America."[26] In 1866, he defeated his former ally Austria in the seven-week war and expelled her from the Germanic league. In 1870, France was defeated by the North German federation, Prussian troops staged a victory march in Paris, Alsace and Lorraine were taken as Schleswig-Holstein had been taken before them, and the seeds for World War I were sown.

The question of Schleswig and Holstein had been answered. Now it was time to ask if the five-nation ship would be the one to break the Union's blockade and reframe the American Civil War forever.

CHEOPS

13

With the Second Schleswig War raging, it was Denmark—despite her clear superiority at sea—that was the first to move on the fugitive French Arman rams. While she held contracts for both at one point, money talks, and Prussia secured the *Sphinx*'s sister ship, *Cheops*, on May 25, 1864.

Without a dedicated inspector in her yards like Denmark's G. P. Schön-heyder for the *Sphinx*, almost every account of her acquisition is clouded by concerns and disputes. The armor that was replaced and refitted on *Sphinx* went largely untouched on her. Her displacement and steering way exceeded their contractual limits and stayed that way. There is no record of the shortfall in her coal bunkers being addressed. Even when compared to her sister ship, the quantity of water she shipped over her prow in heavy seas was shocking. In June 1865, she ran aground while conducting trials off the Danish coast. Crewmen talked about ill luck. Engineers spoke of unseasoned wood and hurried construction.

A series of construction delays saw her commissioned on October 29, 1865, months after hostilities ended. As the new Prussian flagship, she was honored with the name SMS *Prinz Adalbert*, after the brother of Wilhelm I and proponent of German naval power. With Denmark humbled, Prussia turned her sights on an Austrian Hapsburg monarchy weakened by the failed Hungarian Revolution and second Italian War of Independence. As soon as the Cowper-design, London-built turret ship *Arminius* joined her navy (which some suspected also had been commissioned first by the Confederacy), *Prinz Adalbert* was hauled out of the water for refit and repair. Out went her initial three-rifled 36-pounder muzzle-loading guns, positioned at the bow and in fixed turrets amidship, and in came a single 21-centimeter gun in the bow and two 17-centimeter guns from the Krupps works. Revisions to the gun turrets saw her two midship guns traverse for the first time; revisions to her 11-centimeter armor plate and an expanded magazine accommodated seventy-six rounds (forward) and seventy-one rounds (aft). With a transatlantic crossing no longer required, her rigging was slashed some 740 square meters to 677 square meters.[1]

In 1866, in what the victors celebrated as the seven-week war, and their opponents lamented as the Civil War (or Brothers War), a Germanic alliance of Prussia, Oldenburg, Mecklenburg-Schwerin, Mecklenburg-Strelitz, Brunswick, and the Kingdom of Italy, then on the verge of their third independence war of unification, sharply defeated the combined forces of Austria, Bavaria, Saxony, and Hanover. The contrast to the start of the American Civil War is notable. When hostilities between the North and South erupted, the U.S. army had fewer than 16,000 men, and no draft, reserve, or mobilization plan against a population of 34.8 million. Prussia mustered more than 342,000 men at arms, with 260,000 actively deployed, from a population nearer 18 million.

Prussia entered the war at a considerable advantage with Austria pinned between her and Italy. Her soldiers reloaded prone with breech-loading rifles, while her opponents stood upright with their muzzle-loaders (although Austria reversed this advantage in artillery). Prussian conscripts had been drilling for three years while Austria released most men back to their civilian lives. Prussian forces were raised close to their home. Austrian forces were distributed far and wide for fear of insurrection. Prussia's railways concentrated her forces faster. Her telegraphs reached more widely.

In June 1866, after an initial refit and eight months of service, SMS *Prinz Adalbert* joined *Arminius* in Kiel to head an expanded Prussian fleet under Vice Admiral Eduard von Jachmann.[2]

While the war opened with a sharp Austrian defeat of Italy on June 24, it quickly turned with Prussia's crushing victories throughout June and July. Wilhelm von Tegetthoff, who'd been checked in the Battle of Heligoland two years before, shattered the Italian fleet at Lissa on July 20, in a rare highlight for the Austrian alliance, which saw him become immortalized much like Nelson was for the British after Trafalgar. It did little for their cause on land.

When Prussia shattered the Austrian alliance at Tauberbischofsheim (July 24), she'd already occupied Bohemia and northern Württemberg, and only her opponent's capitulation stopped her marching on. Business was concluded with a peace treaty and compensation (8 million gulden to Prussia) within weeks. The German federation was dissolved. Four territories were consumed by Prussia. Austria was expelled from German determination. Lichtenstein became an independent microstate. Presciently, Prussia didn't take a single inch of land from Austria, who, with her fear of Italian and Slavic claims to her east, she felt would be a natural ally in future.[3]

The Prussian navy became the Norddeutche Bundesmarine in 1867 with five ironclads in service. While the five-nation ship served on with distinction, her sister, *Prinz Adalbert* (1560 tons; two guns) was already in her last years of service.[4] While Denmark's navy was saddled with the disastrous Scottish sea monster, Prussia strengthened theirs with the formidable *Friedrich* (6,900 tons, from the French yard Cie des Forges et Chantiers of Toulon, which soon fought against her builders), the *Kronprinz* (6,300 tons; sixteen guns), and *Konig Wilhelm* (ordered by the Turks from the Thames Iron Works, but purchased while still under construction, which served beyond World War I).[5] In January 1871, as the last independent states joined a unified Germany, her navy reorganized as the Kaiserliche Marine under the king of Prussia and first German emperor, King William.

Despite SMS *Prinz Adalbert*'s refit, issues with her armor and sail rig persisted. Under-seasoned framing timbers saw her copper-sheathed hull leaking so badly that she spent the war with Austria confined to port-guard duties. Her challenges were so debilitating that she was hauled from the water and laid up again in the Geestemünde naval depot in 1868–1869 for heavy work. Armor plating was removed and remounted. Her main mast was relocated as part of a major rerigging of her sails to a schooner's set. A breakwater was installed at her stern. None of it redeemed her reputation as a poor steamer, and none of it stopped the leaks.[6] In May 1870, she toured Britain as far as Plymouth with three armored frigates, before running aground and limping back to Kiel for repairs. On July 13, amid rising tension with France over the German Hohenzollern dynasties' claim to the then-vacant Spanish throne, she was ordered to Dartmouth. When all German vessels were recalled on the eve of war, *Prinz Adalbert* made such poor headway that she was taken under tow by the *Kronprinz*. They arrived three days before France declared war over the Ems dispatch. France imposed a naval blockade.

Prinz Adalbert saw out the war (1870–1871) as a static guardship in Hamburg, by which point she was no longer considered worthy of her name. Rotting timbers forced her decommissioning later that year. By October 23, she was removed from service. In 1875, she was disarmed and stricken from the register. When broken up in Wilhelmshaven, she was in such a poor state that only her engine was reused.[7] It was an ignoble record and highlights the debt the former *Sphinx* owed the interventions of Schönheyder, deputy director of the Copenhagen Royal Dockyard, in the Arman yards.

The United States, Italy, Netherlands, and Germany we know today were now largely in place, though the Austro-Hungarian Empire limped on, wounded and vulnerable until defeat and dissolution in World War I. Few who saw *Prinz Adalbert*'s last days would credit that her sister ship not only had faced down two greater Union warships and survived the American Civil War but also would decide the civil war of the other great power coalescing across the Pacific.

The five-nation ship's story had only just begun.

OF THE AMPHIBIAN KIND   14

While Lucien Arman worked to reclaim the *Stærkodder* from Denmark, the United States was bleeding. The American Civil War was three and a half years old. Conscription was ruthlessly enforced, North and South. In the eighteen months since the emancipation proclamation, the Bureau of Colored Troops had swollen Union ranks by 10 percent, and the South had resorted to enslaving (or reenslaving) them as "contrabands" when captured and, in some cases, executing their white officers.[1] If anything, their positions had hardened.

The Confederate Congress was adamant, "No . . . law denying or impairing the right of property in negro slaves shall be passed." Vice President Alexander Stephens explained that the American Union "rested upon the assumption of the equality of the races," but "our new government is founded upon exactly the opposite ideas: its foundations are laid, its cornerstone rests, upon the great truth that the negro is not equal to the white man; that slavery is his natural . . . condition."[2] His statue still stands in Washington alongside Jefferson Davis's and General Lee's.

Stephens's peers still thought the North's will would give out before theirs. There had been victories for the South at Chancellorsville, Virginia, where a larger opportunity to shatter divided Union forces is a frequent what-if scenario (April–May 1863). In June, though, the largest cavalry clash of the war, the Battle of Brandy Station, Virginia, opened the Gettysburg campaign, which became the bloodiest of the war—and the largest ever waged in the Western Hemisphere. The Union lost 23,049 dead. The South, 28,063.[3] It's likely that a turning point had been reached. A victory at Winchester in June was General Lee's last window for an invasion of the North. Vicksburg fell the following day, leaving the Mississippi firmly in Union control. Raiders and runners had prolonged the war, but they couldn't end it.

Arman never closed the door to the South. Confederate agents had inspected the *Sphinx* before her departure from Bordeaux for Copenhagen on June 21, 1864, when an impressed Danish crew noted she "certainly did then show no sign of weakness."[4] Her sale price was still being negotiated when their Prussian truce broke on June 24. Within a week, *Cheops* was publicly Prussian. With defeat at the Battle of Lundby on July 3, and the occupation of Jutland after July 14, *Stærkodder* arrived in a Denmark awash with recrimination and debt, too late to do anything about it.

The Danish negotiators who then declined her delivery weren't remotely interested in where she may end up. No questions were asked. While their navy was wary of her seakeeping, they never doubted the ram's ability, with one official summarizing she "was a terrible vessel, and was going to make terrible havoc among the blockading squadrons of the Federals" once her new owners were revealed.[5]

James Dunwoody Bulloch offered Arman 373,000 francs for his shipyards and a further 80,000 francs for their agents and financiers to reacquire the *Stærkodder*. It was a fraction of what the Danes had contracted, but it was the only option left for Arman. When he agreed, it was just as illegal as their original deal.

Her first rebel captain recorded slipping abroad in a strange third-person perspective in his biography.★

"Before leaving [her Danish] port a Confederate navy officer, who was curiously interested in all such naval architecture, had been often on board and inspected the vessel throughout—her armament, gun gear, projectiles, naval stores, &c.—for in her construction, equipment, &c., she was quite unique. Pleased with the appearance of the vessel and all on board, he accepted the invitation of the builder's agent and took passage in her for France." When she was driven back to port by storms, the captain noted, this "Mr. Brown, whose status on board was known only to the captain, urged him to 'put to sea' on the least abatement of the gale."[7]

His urgency was understandable. By 1863, the South was planting food instead of cotton, impairing their ability to fund European arms. With the loss of her rivers, new railways were consuming her iron. By 1864, as younger boys and older men were being called up and more resources were diverted to recapturing slaves and deserters, the Gulf states expanded enlistment among plantation workers in a classic butter or guns dilemma.[8]

★The blurb for *The Career of the Confederate Cruiser "Stonewall"* by Captain Thomas J. Page, CSN, modestly disclaims, "In presenting this blurred picture of the "Stonewall," its imperfections should be attributed more to the shortcoming of the artist than to the intrinsic worth in the subject presented." It's a curious work that strays in and out of a third-person perspective and makes incorrect references, such as it being a "cruiser" in its title, which suggests a ghostwriter on the other side of the world with limited engagement by Page. Nevertheless, well said.[6]

Plantations were asked to release their labor, produce more, and support the growing number of wounded returning. Inflation was rampant. Food shortages were spreading, often due to distribution rather than supply. Southern liberties were declining. The Confederate constitution did not allow for states to secede. Speech was not free. Opposition parties were banned. Only 1.5 million men among their 9 million people could vote. The few remaining papers were indignant, "Seizures of persons and property have become as common as they are in France and Russia. Personal liberty has been made dependent on the mere will of army officers appointed by the President. Hundreds have been arrested for opinion's sake." Habeas corpus and freedom of protest were likewise suspended in the North. No amount of censorship could conceal the scale of the South's losses—every plantation and most families had been impacted. Tithing was imposed. Food riots diverted more men to policing. Texan protestors railed against "[t]he tyrannical conduct of the rebel authorities in impressing men and seizing provisions produced great dissatisfaction."[9]

Morale wavered. A favorable cease-fire needed victories. Victory needed supply. Supply needed ports and rivers. No scenario for the war's end could start without disrupting the Union navy, and now only the five-nation ship could make it happen. On the continent, rebel agents had assembled a crew of their best and brightest, boasting no fewer than four former ironclad captains, under a leader who'd fought on the international stage long before the American Civil War began, and not a moment too soon.

The five-nation ship's time had come.

Naval warfare is often romanticized. Ships are anthropomorphized, characterized as feminine, heralded for their beauty and said to engage one another. But it was men who built them, men who sailed them, and men who fought and died on them. By November 1864, while the five-nation ship was still in Danish hands, work was already underway in the South to crew her.[10]

While similarly rigged merchant schooners could be sailed with as few as a dozen men, the ram's battery and machinery, the risk of injury and illness on long voyages, and the need to board or repel other warships meant she'd need a complement of 10 officers and 120 men. This was the scale the Confederates needed. Both the renamed *Stærkodder* and *Prinz Adalbert* could fight with less than the gun crews alone of the Scottish sea monster still fitting out in Denmark.

At no point were all rebel sailors American. As many as three thousand Scots served on Southern ships, a few for ideology, but more for the money. Some blockade-running captains were paid as much as $3,000 to reach the Confederate states with European food, arms, and supplies. Filling their holds with rebel cotton for the return journey could provide a 30 to 1 return on investment that captains had a leading stake in, but all crew shared.[11]

Enlistees under twenty-one needed their parents' consent, in theory if not in practice. No man over thirty-five could be accepted, though it's said some were asked their birthdates as many times as it took to get it right. While it was their policy that no one under fourteen was to serve, this is hard to reconcile with the thousands of child-musicians employed on both sides or the navy's use of young "powder monkeys" running up leather satchels of powder barefoot from warship magazines. Some looked older. Some lied about their age. Some, like Heck Thomas, whose law enforcement days are immortalized in 1908's silent film *The Bank Robbery*, served from the age of twelve. A cartoon of the time shows a boy writing the number "18" on the soles of his shoes, and pronouncing he was "over 18."[12]

The Royal Navy built her officer classes by apprenticing junior midshipmen of social standing or merit to captains and promoting them through ranks by examination. A decade's service aboard an armed merchantman might be required before rising above sixth-rate vessels.[13] The Confederate navy had no such luxury. Most of her officers attended their naval college and graduated with a 32-inch cutlass from the Ames Manufacturing Company of Massachusetts, but far from all.[14]

The South clung to an image of themselves as gentlemen-warriors. The previous July, ads ran in the *Liverpool Courier* newspaper directing claims of pay for the deceased crewmen of the *Alabama* to Mr. R. W. Curtis, for example, who W. S. Wilding, U.S. vice consul in Great Britain, immediately flagged as a Confederate agent. A photo of Curtis captured in Cherbourg, France, shows him to be a tall figure with a long bulldog face, a beard trimmed oddly below his chin, and a shock of wavy hair. He'd been in place at least since April 27, 1863, when his signature approved fourteen crew members recruited from the prize ship *Dictator* for the *Georgia*. Union agents confirmed, "the orders given to the men for 10 pounds each were drawn by Richard W. Curtis, understood to be a person in the rebel naval service."[15]

Curtis had chosen the sea well before the war, with the brewer's son leaving clerking in London to join Isambard Brunel's monumental *Great Eastern* on its maiden voyage with four hundred crew and four thousand passengers, and relocating to New York. He enlisted in the Confederate navy in March 1863, and first served on the steamer *Georgia* (600 tons; five guns).[16] The Confederacy was a rebellion, not a nation. What paymaster Curtis was doing to assemble a new rebel crew for the five-nation ship was illegal. With his identity exposed, on January 6, 1865, Curtis was assigned to the rebel navy's last great hope, freshly back from Danish hands, so his life would be in the hands of men he recruited. Regular briefings with James Dunwoody Bulloch began in Liverpool, reviewing expenses drawn from a reported 600-pound pool of gold coins he administered with astonishingly little oversight.[17]

Signing up had a low bar to clear—the minimum height required was 4 feet 8 inches. African Americans could enlist in theory or be enlisted more likely as vassals to a master onboard. The money on offer was more than many had ever seen. Starting salaries were $12 a month for landsmen, $14 a month for ordinary seamen, and $18 a month for seamen while men earned $4 and $9 a week in the mills. Boys, officially fourteen or older, were rated as third, second, or first class according to their skills and strength, earning $7, $8, or $9 a month.[18]

Ideally, recruits would start their service on a receiving ship, typically wooden sail ships, some little more than floating dormitories, for a few weeks of basic instruction. Without these resources in Europe, Curtis prioritized men with experience. Fishermen. Postmen. Lighthouse men. Whaling men. When assigned to the new ram, they reported to the officer of the deck to be captured in the ship's log. For the former *Stærkodder*, this would be one of Curtis's first appointments, Marine Sergeant John M. Prior. With the basics of rank and order established, practical instruction continued below decks for machinery, larders, magazines, caulking, and coal and above deck for everything from steering to heaving the lead to determine depth, handling tenders and rowboats, knotting and splicing ropes, sewing, reefing sails, or drilling to board or be boarded. Inspections were typically by the master-at-arms, the ship's senior rating or chief petty officer, at least initially Maryland's William H. Savage, who was responsible for discipline together with a petty officer appointed ship's corporal. Woe be to any who crossed them.

Securing executive officer Robert Randolph Carter was an early success, after his work with Bulloch on the *Shenandoah* affair, overcoming Union efforts to have her seized in Australia. As acting first mate, he was responsible for day-to-day operations, supervision in port, her log, watches, and supporting her captain at sea. It would prove a fine pairing. Carter was a former ironclad officer on the *Mississippi*, who'd arranged the surreptitious coaling of the *Stærkodder* in Niewe Diep, Netherlands, long before her ownership had been resolved, and who Bulloch trusted even above the taciturn and close-mouthed captain who followed.

In the small community of rebels on the continent, she was such a prize that posting men turned down lucrative blockade-runners, jostled for position, and, in some cases, accepted demotion to sign on. Flag officer Samuel Barron, for example, arranged for his son to sign on as lesser watch officer after his earlier command of a gunboat in Virginia. A former captain himself, Barron was appointed a bureau chief in the navy department on the outbreak of war, had overseen the defenses of North Carolina and Virginia as a flag officer, was captured as Fort Hatteras fell, and was freed in a prisoner exchange, before his posting to outfit blockade-runners in Europe.[19]

Next to be assigned was the Kentucky-born Lieutenant George M. Shyrock, who'd enlisted in the first three months of the war as an officer and was himself the former commander of the *Segar* and *Mobile*. In all, she'd have four former captains aboard at her commissioning. Shyrock had escaped the surrender of forts Jackson and St. Philip and served in the attack on the federal blockading squadron off Charleston, South Carolina, before reassignment to Europe in 1863. With him came Virginian lieutenant Edmund G. Read, who, like so many Southern naval officers, started with shore batteries and worked his way from midshipman, serving on a string of warships, including the *Patrick Henry*, *Mississippi*, and *Baltic*, before being posted to Europe in 1863.[20]

The acting second mates, twenty-six-year-old George A. Borchert and Edmund Gaines Read, each ran half the crew, and shared the sailing rig, in a senior role typically attained by talent who had worked their way up from the lowest ranks. Borchert was a Georgia-born U.S. Naval Academy graduate who'd joined the Union navy in 1855 but resigned to join the rebels after a final voyage captaining the captured slave ship *Triton* back to the United States. He'd cut his teeth as an officer on the runner *Sirius*, the warships *Morgan* and *Baltic* (together with Lieutenant Read), and the English acquisition, *Rappahannock*.[21]

The boatswain, John M. Dukehart, was responsible for the maintenance and repair of her plant, hull, and fittings. No ship of this size would be complete without their carpenter, Joseph Mather, his sail-making peer, and their respective crews, who were integral to waterproofing, repairs, caulking, and, in battle, applying wood and canvas shot plugs to seal penetrating cannon fire. Both roles were sometimes called idlers, though rarely to their face, for their being exempt from watch duties measured one 30-minute sand glass cycle at a time.[22]

Virginia's Bennett W. Green was the first officer posted to her medical staff. After joining the U.S. Navy a month before the war's outbreak, he'd served at the Naval Hospital, Richmond (1862–1863) before his repeated requests to take to sea were granted and he transferred to the Provisional Navy on June 2, 1864, as passed assistant surgeon.

Chief engineer William P. Brooks was a veteran of the raiders *Sumter* and *Alabama*, who selected C. J. Kolsh as his right-hand man for his engineering group.[23] No ship could ram under sail. Her engines meant everything. His steam logs are the most detailed surviving record of her service, tracking his team, time, steam, vacuum, temperature, water density, revolutions, and coal from his first day of service aboard to his last.[24] His attention to detail is impressive, and in all the warship's record keeping, there is just a single error, crossed out and neatly corrected.

Sergeant John M. Prior of the Confederate States Marine Corps was a veteran of the would-be raider *Rappahannock*, assigned as their leader in boarding, repelling assaults, weapons drill, and the enforcement of Page's will on board. The keys to the armory stayed with him. While the HMS *Warrior* had had 122 marines on board, he had as few as two. If they had to fight for their ship, it was every man's job.

Gunnery officer J. B. King was responsible for their cannon's maintenance and operations, including powder, cartridges, and safety, which was paramount on a wooden-decked ship. Every man's life was in his hands. Guy Fawkes had attempted to bring down the British Houses of Parliament with thirty-six barrels of powder. The new rebel flagship could store more than 150. Every precaution was taken with them. Striking matches were strictly banned. Lamps were lit behind glass screens. No metal could enter the magazine, where slippers were worn, or their powder monkey's feet went bare. Gun crew records have not survived, but up to eighteen men were assigned to comparable aftercastle guns on HMS *Warrior*, and at least eight to twelve men are likely to have manned her foregun.[25]

If something went wrong, Surgeon Bennett W. Green and the aptly named assistant surgeon James W. Herty were all that stood between a man and his maker. All the medicine he had came aboard in a single chest, along with a torturer's-dungeon assortment of saws, clamps, and other tools. Their remit included the ship's utensils, coppers, and provisions. Any injury came with the dual threat of infection. Surgery could be immediate, but with germ theory still years away, it wasn't sterile. Warship surgeries were periodically cleaned down with lye and lime, but they were often painted blood-red for a reason.

Doctors dispensed their own medicine, mostly botanicals, and mostly unproven. Even the contemporary Oliver Wendell Holmes stated at the Massachusetts Medical Society annual meeting, "I firmly believe that if the whole materia medica, as now used, could be sunk to the bottom of the sea, it would be all the better for mankind,—and all the worse for the fishes." It was a brutal era. A majority of battlefield surgeries were amputations with more than 26 percent mortality rate within the first twenty-four hours. It was so invasive that speed was everything. As few as one in fifteen Civil War doctors could perform the procedure, the best in as little as two minutes. Chloroform was available for some limited pain relief in this period, but there is no record of it aboard, where a shot of grog may have been all men could hope for.[26]

Every man's first physical included his sight, hearing, and speech, as well as a naked inspection. What the doctor couldn't see, he couldn't know. A sick man's nurse was any man the surgeon assigned to do it. If a man could push on though ill health—even consumption—he did. Communicable diseases saw men separated, as far as their cramped confines could allow.

Where crew slots could be filled with Confederates, they were. First rollcalls would sound out Jermiah Sheehan and fireman James Stewitt who'd never served on a warship before her and never would again, and others including Isaac J. Redmond, John Christian, Manuel A. DeBaron, Robert Smith, Iveson Robinson, John Baptiste, Joseph N. Mayne, and Joseph Dean with varied experiences from the lowliest gunboats to the fastest raiders. Scores of others joined them, unrecorded.[27]

Above them all was Captain Thomas Jefferson Page. A ship was not a democracy. On board, he was general, priest, navigator, disciplinarian, and, as he had learned in Paraguay, diplomat. His word was law. *Heart of Darkness* author Joseph Conrad put it succinctly. "In each ship is one man who, in the hour of emergency of peril at sea, can turn to no other man. There is one who, alone, is ultimately responsible for the safe navigation, engineering performance, accurate gunfire and morale of his ship. He is the commanding officer. He is the ship."[28]

Officers shared rooms. Captain Page was afforded his own. On a full-deck warship, most crewmen slept on the gun decks, in hammocks slung 18 inches apart; they could at least ventilate and light with open gunports if the weather allowed. With only a raised fore and aftercastle, on the five-nation ship they slept in packets here and there, most without open light or air, and their tight quarters were noted by G. P. Schönheyder and others, time and again. They ate where they slept. When the ship faced Spanish heat, they sweated. When they faced the Atlantic cold, they shivered with no heating but their machinery. The only fire permitted outside the engine room was with coal in the galley. If charcoal burners were brought below decks, it was to dry her out, and never their comfort. Fire was every sailor's nightmare—even these burners were half buried in sand. Regulations said no man should sleep in wet clothes or a wet bed, but their authors had never steamed on a ship like this. On the five-nation ship, with the water she plumed over her bow, and the modest number of uniforms assigned, this was aspirational. With barely half a gallon of water a man a day allocated, once you started smelling you stayed that way. Fresh water was stored in barrels, and without boiling as a common practice, you only knew it was a problem when the first men came down sick.[29]

Weevils were an everyday fact for oceangoing crews. Most learned to snap the hardtack bread they dismissively called ship's biscuits and scrape them out with a knife before soaking them. Pork and beef were prized stores but were roughly butchered and stored in barrels that kept them edible long after worms appeared. Their preservation depended on salt so heavy, it was often all the men could taste, though they at least benefited from fast-improving canning and preservatives. Sailors of the era often carried this through their lives—without enough salt, nothing tasted quite right. While scurvy was largely understood—the Royal Navy had issued citrus as part of a daily diet since 1795—it was not unheard of. For the Japanese crews who would one day serve on board, scurvy wouldn't be their bugbear, but beriberi, due to a lack of vitamin B1 in a rice-based diet, was to come. There is no record of the live chickens or goats typically carried on transatlantic voyages for fresh eggs, milk, and meat. This was a warship. Her decks must be clear to fight.

Personal hygiene was an issue on land. It was a greater issue at sea. Their toilets, or heads, were as simple as wooden boards on deck with a hole with sluices that used gravity, water, or both to clear them. The result was a constant smell. Some could not be used at all in heavy weather, leaving their bilges rank with waste.

Washing was in salt water, infrequent and usually limited to just hands, feet, and faces, so fleas and lice were constant companions. Clothes reached a point where they became so salt stained and encrusted that they could almost serve by themselves. As unpleasant as this was, it also provided a vector for shipborne diseases such as typhus and yellow fever, which were then claiming ten thousand lives a year in the North, leading to rumors of Confederate biowarfare. Dr. Luke Pryor Blackburn, a known gunrunner, was accused of the crime and, while charged, was not convicted. The case for his planning to do so is strong, with the intention to include Southern states then in Northern occupation like North Carolina and Virginia, and was almost certainly discussed with President Jefferson Davis.[30] Rats and mice were constant companions. Food stores spread from their holds into any available space under the supervision of master's mates J. B. King and William H. Savage.

The differences between merchant and navy service were drilled and drilled. Cleaning was constant. Heavy work on a freighter might be accompanied by shanties and working songs, but the work was done in silence on a warship, so any order could be heard. Talking on watch—especially at night when sound carried—was done in a habitual whisper. Few crewmen had a long-standing apprenticeship or formal training unless they were sourced from merchant service. Naval academies were for officers. Their crews learned at sea. Live gunfire was rare—given their limited powder and shot—but drilling was free, particularly for the aftercastle gun crews, who had to manage their guns recoiling back toward each other and wrestle them between the cutouts in the bulwarks to target a moving enemy.

Discipline was rigid. Cross a line, and you'd be punished at the captain's discretion, or held for court-martial in port, as a Union commander would soon be for shirking a fight with the rebel flagship. The era of flogging and keelhauling was over. Most infractions were simple drunkenness, sleeping on duty, damaging gear, disobedience, or theft. Sergeant John M. Prior could put a man in irons, on bread and water, or expel a man from a crew altogether, as the Confederates had with informer Clarence Yonge who'd cost the South their Laird rams. More common was punishment with the worst assignments—like the never-ending battle of their bilge pumps. A crew member who'd crossed another was less likely to come to blows than be stonewalled, have his hammock cut, draw the worst watches in the worst weather, and the like.

Any ship of the era had its dangers. Warships especially so. Any compromise to steam systems under pressure meant appalling burns, and worse. Damaged funnels could make breathing in the machinery spaces a struggle. You only discovered a gun was compromised when it detonated, as John Ericsson's had, killing the secretaries of navy and state prewar. Shirkers in the face of the enemy could be imprisoned, or, though extremely rare, summarily executed at the captain's discretion—seamen by hanging; officers by pistol.[31]

With Southern labor now at such a premium, the Confederate navy made choices others would not. Estimates put the number of black rebel sailors at more than 1,150 by February 1865, both slaves and free men. It's an extraordinary figure when we consider their total wartime fleet ran to twenty-three primary warships and some five thousand men. Confederate navy regulations not only allowed for up to 20 percent of crews to be black but had an established exemption process that suggested it was far from a cap. Black representation in the Union navy peaked at 23 percent.[32] This is not to say they were equal aboard. Their inferiority was assumed, and their segregation maintained as far as cramped quarters allowed. Their pay was lower. Their ranks were capped. Their work was the hardest and longest. Even after the Civil War, it would be 1948 before the U.S. Army was desegregated.

The North had as many as 180,000 black Americans in their land forces. More than 20,000 served in their navy—almost four times as many as the South had total servicemen, though it would be June 1864 before they received the same pay as white Americans, and they faced the additional threat of enslavement on capture.[33] None are thought to have served on the five-nation ship, though records are incomplete. The records of their Marine Corps were deliberately destroyed at war's end, erasing the service history of men like Sargeant John M. Prior.[34]

Pilots who guided the South's warships, gunboats, troopships, and merchant marine could be surprisingly independent, whatever their background. Moses Dallas, for example, serving with the Savannah Squadron from 1862 to 1864, was recorded in correspondence from the squadron commander to the secretary of the navy, "I have also been compelled to increase the pay of Moses Dallas from $80 to $100 per month in order to retain him. He is a colored pilot and is considered the best inland pilot on the coast." The sum was academic. Moses was one of six sailors killed boarding the *Water Witch*; he was so respected, however, that the Confederacy paid for his casket and service. As for so many others, it was ultimately in vain. The whole Savannah Squadron in which he'd served was destroyed on December 21, 1864, to keep them from falling into Union hands.[35]

No civilian clothing was allowed in Union naval vessels. In the South, it varied from crew to crew and time to time. They started their war in Union kit captured at Norfolk and Pensacola. On the home front, they turned from Union blue to rebel grey for want of dyes. Abroad, as they outgrew their Union caches, they turned to Bulloch's European network for a sharper look.[36] For a navy with scarcely four hundred men at war's start, the scale of her orders in 1861 is instructive: Two thousand pairs of pants, cloth or cassinette; two thousand sweaters and duck pants; two thousand flannel overshirts and drawers; two thousand pairs of shoes with a not-very-generous total of three thousand pairs of socks; and blankets, cloth caps, frocks, and silk handkerchiefs, as well as one thousand round jackets (often referred to as shell jackets after the term *shellback* for British sailors) and one thousand pea jackets. Rakish French-derived 4-inch-high caps were issued, though in the Spanish heat, straw hats were permitted. One glance told each man's story. Lieutenant Robert R. Carter's blue-wreathed cap marked him as executive officer. Lieutenants like Edmund Gaines Read and George S. Shyrock sported a single star. Paymasters sported green caps. Engineering, dark blue. Medical, black. The devil was in the details—chaplains' uniforms varied from officers only in the number of buttons of their frock coat.[37] Officers were issued a muzzle-loaded 36-caliber navy revolver, which spent most of its time in their cabin under lock and key. A proud nation needed a proud navy. These were for the men who would make it happen.

Now *Stærkodder* was out of Danish hands and being transferred by the French; a series of coded transmissions about tea and teak wood from Bulloch (ostensibly between a Mrs. Puggard of Copenhagen and Mrs. Mabbs of London) instructed her new Captain Page to assume command of the *Stærkodder* as soon as she made international waters.[38] It had been a long time coming. He had been the intended captain for the Laird rams now in English service and was about to relieve Captain Raphael Semmes on the triumphant raider *Alabama* before her showdown with the *Kearsarge*.

Captain Thomas Jefferson Page stepped aboard the last warship command he would ever hold. The South's last great hope at sea had arrived.

FOR THAT IS MUSIC   15

U nder the alias "Mr Brown," her new captain had been onboard in Danish waters before any of them. Captain Thomas J. Page was born January 4, 1808, on the Rosewell Estate's Shelley Plantation in Glouchester County, Virginia, as the eighth of fourteen sons in a distinguished Southern line. His mother, Elizabeth Nelson, was a noted belle whose father, Major General Thomas Nelson, was a former state governor, and whose grandfather had signed the Declaration of Independence. Page's father, the respected lawyer Mann Page, secured entry to West Point for two of his sons with endorsements from President John Quincy Adams.[1] This pedigree was typical of the South's small band of career naval officers. The captain of the *Tallahassee*, John Taylor Wood, for example, was a grandson of President Zachary Taylor and nephew of Jefferson Davis. His ship evaded eleven of the fifty ships blockading North Carolina in her first twenty-four hours, sunk or seized thirty-three Union ships, fought on as the *Olustee*, and ultimately surrendered to James Dunwoody Bulloch in London as the degunned blockade-runner *Chameleon*.[2] West Point had been Page's father's dream. Instead, he resigned to pursue a naval career.

Captain Page was every bit the Southern gentleman, and his posting to the West Indies as the youngest midshipman on the sloop *Erie* (509 tons; twenty-two guns) was as much for excelling in mathematics and the classics as any naval prowess. It was the making of him. After a grueling three-year tour, a yellow fever outbreak wracked the ship. The captain summoned Page from bed. "I am a sick man and all of our officers are down with fever; here is an appointment for you as acting Lieutenant. Take us home; steer for Norfolk." He braved treacherous weather turning Cape Hatteras with a single midshipman officer to support him and got every crewman home alive. He cultivated a love of science surveying the hydrography of New York's coastline and at the Naval Observatory in Washington with Lieutenant Matthew Fontaine Maury.[3] His wife, Benjamina Price, was a navy wife. His five children, four sons and a daughter, were navy children. It was all he'd ever wanted. It was everything that made him.

He commanded the *Plymouth* on assignment to the South China Sea and Sea of Japan in 1849, where he battled Malay pirates in the headwaters of the Yangtze River at the request of the Qing government but was so disturbed by Western conduct in the first Opium War (1839–1842) that he declined to serve in the Perry expedition that forced Japan's ports open.

At the outbreak of war, he was one of four hundred naval officers who resigned their federal commission to join the rebel cause and was immediately promoted to commander. His peer, Captain C. W. Read, would later record, "I met several naval officers in Montgomery who, like myself, had resigned from the United States service, among them the gallant Lieutenant Hartstine, of Arctic exploration fame. There were a great many strangers from the different sections of the country, at that time in the capital of the Confederacy . . . the people of the South were almost unanimously in favor of the secession of the States, for the reason that they could see no other way of protecting their rights; but they hoped for peace and the friendship of the people of the North."[4]

With only a scattering of inherited or adapted ships available, he was first deployed as a battery commander at Glouchester Point, Virginia, and promoted to a colonel of artillery in the Provisional Army of the Confederate States in 1862 before transferring to command Magruder's Light Artillery at Drewry's Bluff, Virginia. The sea remained his passion—even as battery commander, he was instrumental in securing an official marque legitimizing the privateer schooner *Onward*. He kept his hand in developing small gunboats on the York River that, like so many others, were destroyed by rebels in retreat. He was an early and ardent supporter of pursuing European-built warships.[5]

It would be 1863 before he secured reassignment to Europe only to see the Laird rams slip through his fingers. By 1864, he was in Copenhagen, preparing for his first rebel command at sea.

Page was bold, resolute, and steeped in a Southern code of honor that held that, while no gentlemen should offend another, no gentleman should stand for it should it occur. Honor was so integral to the South's notion of gentleman-captain that her naval code's first three articles were about duty, respect, and "if an inferior feels himself aggrieved."[6] He was quite aware of his command's cover story, later noting, "She was built with the knowledge and sanction of the late Emperor of France" and that, when rumors of the ship's Confederate agenda surfaced, "he was officially informed, from high authority, that if this or any other such vessel should be permitted to leave

France and fall into the possession of the Confederate Government, Mexico would be made untenable ground for French troops."[7]

He was also aware that *Stærkodder* was the rump of a greater fleet of iron-clad rams the South had envisaged, recording, "A similar diplomatic game had already been successfully played in England, in the case of the 'Birkenhead rams'—as two vessels built on the Mersey were called; for a like issue had been made on the charge that they were designed for the Confederate Government." Page was convinced, "Had all the vessels charged to the Confederate account so actually belonged, that Government would have been the most formidable of all naval powers."[8]

His appointment was a triumph for a man whose prewar career had stalled over a deadly diplomatic incident in South America. In 1851, the secretary of the navy, John P. Kennedy, ordered ports in Argentina, Brazil, Uruguay, Paraguay, and Bolivia to accept American trade as part the Monroe Doctrine opposing European interests in the Western Hemisphere. The warship they selected to enforce their demands was the *Water Witch* (464 tons; six guns), which had pioneered the "Hunter wheel" that hid her paddle wheel horizontally under the waterline in an evolutionary step that competed unsuccessfully with John Ericsson's patent screw propulsion under trial on the *Princeton*.[9]

Page's misfortune was his appointment coinciding with the hot-headed twenty-two-year-old American consul to Paraguay, Edward A. Hopkins, whose family's influence over his appointment was so absolute he was the only recorded applicant. Though the role was almost entirely ceremonial, he thought it put him on a path to greatness. Hopkins was no diplomat. Hopkins was no businessman. His first posting to Paraguay resulted in a recall after an unauthorized and inept attempt to mediate a dispute between Paraguay and Argentinian dictator Juan Manuel de Rosas. When Rosas simply ignored him, Hopkins sent him a letter so insulting that his government issued an apology.

Undeterred, Hopkins raised $100,000 for the United States and Paraguay Navigation Company he claimed would make a fortune civilizing the country, and he later returned. Before departing the United States, he signed on as general agent for the competing Rhode Island Company in a shameless conflict of interest. His second Paraguayan effort started with the loss of his investor's machinery when his chartered steamboat was shipwrecked. On reaching Paraguay, he borrowed heavily from dictator-president Carlos Antonio López to establish a series of sawmill and cigar ventures he managed to run into the ground, despite their conscript labor. And he feuded.

Hopkins feuded over matters of ceremony. He demanded apologies in the national press. He fought over rights of way on the road (after one such dispute with military officers, he burst into the presidential audience chambers still brandishing the whip he'd threatened them with). He feuded over his brother's illegal land purchases and how uncivilized he found Paraguay, which was exiting a traumatic period in its history and had already signed treaties of friendship with Great Britain, France, and Sardinia. His proposed follow-on treaty with America was so poorly drafted that neither party was prepared to sign it.[10] Within months, he'd turned $100,000 of his investors' money into millions of dollars in debt to López.

President Carlos Antonio López was a corpulent and irascible dictator with such a need for control that his foreign service was forbidden to open any correspondence without him.[11] López was wary of foreign actors on a border with Brazil defined by rivers that bore little relationship to any map. It had led to skirmishing in the past, centered on Itapiru, which was one of the few firm border crossings in otherwise swampy ground that Paraguay bolstered with a semicircular ten-gun brick fortress. Captain Page was given permission to steam the *Water Witch* that far on the La Planta River, but no further.

When Page first arrived in September, "The reception of the expedition in his waters, and his entire course towards us, until his outbreak with [consul Edward Hopkins], was characterized throughout by generous hospitality."[12] Within days, however, López advised Page that Hopkins was no longer accepted as U.S. consul, and that he would not be allowed to leave the country until his debts were paid and certain papers were returned. When Page was advised no further correspondence would be conducted in English, he transported Hopkins to Argentina for his own safety. Whatever he thought of Hopkins, he was American and Page understood gunboat diplomacy. When he steamed past the presidential palace, he did so with all guns trained on it.[13]

López forbade foreign ships from entering Paraguayan waters in response. With Paraguayan trade now favoring new treaty partners in Europe, the U.S. secretary of state, James Buchanan, complained at being denied a treaty over "frivolous and even insulting pretexts."[14] By January 1855, while Page led a scientific expedition in Argentine rivers in a lesser vessel, he ordered his executive officer, Lieutenant William Nicholson Jeffers, to explore the upper Paraná River in the *Water Witch*. In places it was kilometers wide. Where it narrowed around the island of Carayá, one side was Paraguayan and the other Brazilian.

The *Water Witch*'s exact orders were unclear. What was clear, however, was a decision by acting captain Jeffers to approach the Paraguayan channel on February 1, 1855, in a classic show of strength. While he would later claim he'd been forced into this channel by Argentine pilots, his moving his cannon to one side showed premeditation. Forty shrapnel loads, twelve regular shells, and thirty stands of grapeshot were prepared.[15]

The fort sent a copy of López's directive against foreign vessels out to the *Water Witch* at 1:20 p.m., which Jeffers disregarded as it wasn't drafted in English. He steamed within 300 yards of the fort, ignoring all directives that he stop. Two blank shots were fired by the fort. Jeffers continued. A third cannon report from the fort was live, and it struck the helmsman, Samuel Chaney, killing him outright. *Water Witch* opened fire with her three howitzers. With the Argentine pilots leaving her helm, Jeffers reversed course and made a second pass. The fort's fire pierced her hull in ten places, shattered two boats, and damaged machinery portside before Jeffers could break away. When word of the incident reached Page, he demanded permission from Commodore William D. Salter, commander of the U.S. squadron in South America, to attack the fort. Salter refused, and the matter was escalated to Washington.

Page claimed it had occurred in international waters, without provocation. President Buchanan claimed that President López's prohibition did not apply because the *Water Witch* was a vessel of science, not war. The secretary of state, William L. Marcy, was not convinced by either argument and restarted efforts to sign a treaty the following year (without success). What little press there was turned out to be unflattering to Hopkins and Page, even after his scientific reports and surveys were published over two volumes.

Inexplicably, President Buchanan launched a punitive fleet against Paraguay three years later. Some saw it as enforcing the Monroe Doctrine. Others dismissed it as a distraction from domestic criticism. In either case, it ended in fiasco. The opposing Congressional Committee held that "Mr Buchanan's war on Paraguay was not for glory, but to furnish means of corruption."[16]

On its departure in 1858, it was the largest expeditionary naval force America had ever deployed. Its nineteen ships were led by the sail frigates *Sabine* (1,726 tons; forty-four guns) and *St. Lawrence* (1726 tons; fifty guns, which had the ugly distinction of being decommissioned six times before being struck), commanded by flag officer William B. Shubrick. In all, it boasted two hundred guns and twenty-five hundred men and included seven steamers purchased for a lengthy deployment. Former Missouri congressman and judge James Butler Bowlin joined as its commissioner with a list of demands for apology and reparations. It cost more than $3 million, consumed more than one-quarter of the navy's resources, and revealed deep-rooted problems in a navy three years from civil war.

Only one ship went further than Argentina. When the *Fulton* reached Asuncion, Commissioner Bowlin realized the Rhode Island Company claims against López were baseless and America's conduct leading to the incident was deeply flawed. He had been ordered to accept nothing less than $500,000 compensation. Instead, the fleet waived its demands for apology or reparations other than 10,000 pesos for the family of deceased helmsman Chaney and, ultimately, signed the treaty of friendship they had fought over. López would be remembered as a modernizer and nation builder. Hopkins, not at all.

Though Captain Page and the *Water Witch* returned with this fleet, he was conspicuously absent from the senior command group. Instead, he watched and learned. The fleet had launched with such slight provisions that a single seven-hour engagement would have exhausted every magazine. No thought was given to how their deeper-drafted vessel could navigate the La Plata River system. Allegations of corruption and price-fixing were rife. Crewmen had limited small arms to defend their ships. Missing gun carriages meant their largest 11-inch Dahlgren guns could not fire at all. Coal supplies were sporadic and at the whims of private contractors who gouged shamelessly. The seven steamers acquired were deemed unfit for further service and abandoned.

Page had learned the risk of abdicating command. So much rode on the South's new flagship, he would never do so again. As the handover of the newly rebel-owned ship neared, his spycraft was impeccable. Others were not. When Bulloch ran into a cluster of young rebel officers in France with their paramours, they immediately appealed to join the supposedly secret new flagship. "It forced me to make a partial confession in order that I might warn them to secrecy and caution."[17]

As few as forty sailors had been recruited to this point: it was little more than a skeleton crew.[18] Recruiting en masse was too public to be kept from the Union, but more bodies were urgently required. As it happened, gaining a crew required them to lose a ship.

When the rebel *Florida* docked at Bahia harbor on October 4, 1864, it was protected by Brazil's neutrality. When the Union *Wachusett* followed her in the day after, Brazil stressed their willingness to act, and redocked *Florida* beside a Brazilian warship. Forts Santa Maria and Barr were on high alert. Regardless, the Union's grandly named Captain Napoleon Collins took it upon himself to attack her at 3:00 a.m. on October 7 while half the rebel crew were asleep onshore. It was so dark, and the weather was so bad, his 6-inch guns hit nothing on approach. He was so close to the rebel ship by the time they made him out, it became an exchange of small arms fire until Collins fired a full broadside, raking the rebel deck and dropping their mizzenmast. Boarding parties stormed the *Florida*, seizing the deck, and firing shamelessly at rebel sailors swimming for it. By the time they took their prize under tow, they had to race responding Brazilian gunboats out to sea. Five rebels were killed and nine wounded. Twelve officers and fifty-eight crew were captured. Brazil demanded the ship's return. The law on the matter was clear. The U.S. Navy agreed, before claiming the *Florida* had sunk accidentally in a collision near where *Virginia* and *Monitor* had fought. Collins was court-martialed, though with so little sincerity, he faced no punishment and was promoted.[19]

It was a national embarrassment. Even the Union secretary of state conceded it was an "unauthorized, unlawful and indefensible exercise of naval force of the United States within a foreign country." Lincoln considered it a war crime.[20] Gideon Welles was so keen to put the embarrassment behind them that he ordered their crew released from Fort Warren without a prisoner exchange. After almost two months of detention, their arrival in Liverpool lined up perfectly with manning the *Stærkodder*.

By 1864, only Mobile Bay, Charlestown, and Wilmington ports remained open to host her in the United States. On the home front, the Southern navy's other great hope was the casemate ironclad ram *Tennessee* (1,273 tons; six guns) built in the first of these ports, for Captain Buchanan, who'd faced the *Monitor* inconclusively with the *Virginia* and recovered from his wounds. With 6-inch armor and heavy rifled guns, she was arguably the South's most capable broadside warship.

At home, the Union captain D. G. Farragut sought to close Mobile Bay with four of the latest twin-turret monitor designs. The Canonicus-class *Tecumseh* and *Manhattan* had 15-inch guns and up to 11 inches of armor, while the Milwaukee-class *Winnebago* and *Chickasaw* sported 11-inch guns and 8 inches of armor. Farragut was an old-fashioned blood and thunder leader, keen to reduce the rebs to just two deepwater ports. "Give me plenty of iron in the men," he declared, "and I don't mind so much about iron in the ships."[21]

He attacked Mobile on April 5, 1864, with the four iron monitors to port and fourteen wooden ships lashed in pairs to starboard to make them harder to sink. The assault started disastrously with the ironclad monitor *Tecumseh* veering to port past the last red marker buoy, striking a rebel mine and sinking with such speed she went down with 113 of 121 crew. A sailor later testified that "her stern lifted high in the air with the propeller still revolving, and the ship pitched out of sight like an arrow twanged from a bow."[22] The wooden *Brooklyn* began tacking violently in response, leaving Farragut fearful the whole column would slow and scatter in front of the defending Confederate forts. The *Brooklyn* despaired, "Our best monitor is sunk!" Farragut, however, would have nothing of it, ordering them on with the cry, "Damn the torpedoes! Full speed ahead!" (torpedo then being any waterborne explosive).

Damn them, it was. Several ships reported the sounds of mines scraping along their hulls and, in some cases, their firing mechanisms closing shut without detonating.[23] The Confederate forts Morgan and Gaines, together with the ironclad *Tennessee* and gunships *Selma*, *Morgan*, and *Gaines*, concentrated on the North's wooden warships. Farragut's flagship, the *Hartford* under Captain Drayton, led the monitors through the minefield, and outran them charging the *Tennessee*, whose screen of light gunboats quickly fled for the shallows. Each side regrouped—Buchanan so calmly that he ordered breakfast for his crew. The Union monitors advanced slowly against the current.

The wooden *Brooklyn* narrowly missed a ram run from the *Tennessee*, which was limited by her surplus riverboat engines. As the wooden Union warships cleared the minefield in pairs, the sloop *Monongahela* and gunboat *Kennebec* rammed the *Tennessee* in turn, without effect.

The monitor *Manhattan* then appeared through the thickening smoke and penetrated the Southern ironclad with a 15-inch shot weighing 350 pounds. *Lackawanna* missed another wild ram run, but her fire severed *Tennessee*'s exposed steering chains. *Hartford* then attempted to ram the rebel ironclad, missed, and was struck by the *Lackawanna* in the growing confusion. *Chickasaw*, without any clear approach, held off and fired steadily at the Confederate defenders. Without steerage, and with mounting casualties, the *Tennessee* was in an untenable position. Commander James Johnston conferred with Buchanan, who was bloodied and broken legged, before striking her colors to end the clash. The Union had lost 325 casualties to the Confederates, but owning the bay forced the rebel city to surrender within days.[24] The Gulf of Mexico was now closed to the South. Their last domestically built warship of note was gone.

Domestically built warships in the North were growing. In the South, they were shrinking. Next to launch was engineer John L. Porter's *Savannah*, with 2-inch armor, 6-knot speed, and a four-gun battery.

Union gains continued throughout 1864 in Louisiana, Tennessee, Florida, Georgia, and Virginia. Eighty-five thousand men clashed in the Union's victory at Nashville. The Confederate navy's Savannah Squadron was destroyed by their crews to keep them out of Union hands. On October 19, 1864, the raider *Shenandoah* became the second-last Confederate ironclad launched in European waters.[25] While she took a string of Union prize ships and was the last rebel warship to fire a shot, her teak hull was never intended to break the Union's blockade. On December 14, 1864, the deal for the *Stærkodder* was finally completed.[26]

Page was formally assigned January 5, but he was hemmed in by heavy snowfalls that left him fretting that his secret ship was "very generally talked about in Paris."[27] When she left Copenhagen on January 7, under the Danish captain G. L. Moeller and crew, heading for Bordeaux, she used the name *Olinde*, her third, in a flimsy attempt at concealment. The Danish flag stayed onboard. The photographic record doesn't indicate when she lost the elaborate Danish naval coat of arms on her stern.[28]

Bulloch was appalled at the indiscretion of *Rappahannock*'s officers, including Lieutenant Arthur Sinclair: "The result of all this has been to bring the Niagara to Dover and spies have been sent from here to Calais to tamper with men." Those responsible, he raged, "should forthwith be sent out of Europe." When Page boarded his new command, it was with a letter from Bulloch noting, "Niagara is now at Dover, waiting, I fear, to intercept your ship. I offer no suggestion on this point, because you will know how to give her the slip when you get to sea, far better than I."[29]

The plan was for the runner *City of Richmond*, chartered from London with railway equipment, to ferry out her new rebel crew and return her delivery crew to shore.[30] While Denmark was now off the hook, a rendezvous in French waters with a British ship could have resulted in a complicated international incident.

By afternoon, snowfalls were behind them. Captain Page, a thin, bald figure with a cold stare, given to looking off-camera, gathered his men on deck in the bracing cold. In a short commissioning ceremony, he raised the Confederate "blood-stained banner," their third and final national flag, and rechristened her in honor of the venerated Southern general killed at Chancellorsville.

Thomas Jonathan "Stonewall" Jackson was born in 1824 and raised by his extended family after the early death of his father in Virginia. He graduated seventeenth in his class at West Point Military Academy in 1846 and took his epithet for a cool nerve under fire. He was famous for it, and the lengths he'd go to preserve it—avoiding pepper, which he felt weakened his legs; standing ramrod straight at all times to "align his organs"; and holding one arm above his head under duress to "re-establish equilibrium."[31]

However it looked, it worked for him. Stonewall was a Mexican war veteran and former slave owner with an aversion to alcohol, a remarkable ability to sleep anywhere, and an uncomplicated approach to war. "War means fighting. The business of the soldier is to fight," he offered. "Never take counsel of your fears," he chided, and, more practically, "Shoot the brave officers, and the cowards will run away and take the men with them." His victories in a series of engagements including the Second Battle of Bull Run enabled the Confederate invasion of Maryland and saw him promoted to command one of two corps for General Lee. On May 2, 1863, fresh from his victory rolling the Union flank at Chancellorsville, he was shot by a jumpy Confederate picket while returning from scouting. While his arm was amputated, he rallied and gave some hope of recovery before succumbing to infection a week later. Few what-if reviews of the war overlook his loss.[32]

Religion was Stonewall's bedrock. "My religious beliefs teach me to feel as safe in battle as in bed. God has fixed the time of my death. I do not concern myself with that." In his last delirious moments, he started an order to prepare for action, paused, and settled instead for, "Let us go over and sit in the shade of the trees," as his last words. General Lee, on hearing of his death said, "I'm bleeding at the heart. . . . I have lost my right arm."[33]

There was little place left for honor at this point. Prisoner exchanges had largely ended. Lincoln's General Order 252 held that if rebels wouldn't regard blacks as soldiers or prisoners of war, then a Confederate prisoner would be killed in turn for every execution, though it was rarely applied. The Confederate cavalry massacred more than 300 predominantly black surrendered Union troops at Fort Pillow on the Mississippi River. The rebel sacking of Lawrence, Kansas, ended in the murder of more than 150 men and boys (August 1863). Union general "Uncle Billy" Sherman vowed to "make Georgia howl" and began systemically destroying rail, warehouses, and telegraph lines, which he later conceded was "simple waste and destruction."[34] The rebel prison master at Andersonville would swing for the number of men who died as prisoners of war, which all puts Captain Raphael Semmes's chivalry at sea with the *Alabama* into perspective.

Captain Page was effusive. "The "spar deck" of the vessel presented, on that bright, sunny morn, a busy scene. The Confederate flag was "run up" at the peak, and the pennant at the main masthead, when the commander, surrounded by the little band of officers and men, with caps in hand, pointed to the pure emblem at her peak, the token of the nationality of the vessel, and announced her 'The Stonewall'—[an] ever to be remembered name."[35]

Page was moved. "Certain preliminaries, the 'shipping' of men, assignment to specific duties, &c., having been gone through with, the deck was soon cleared of the various articles, so generously presented and as gratefully received from the steamer in company. . . . The anchor was 'hove up' under the inspiration of that joyous music, familiar to every sailor man, when the 'boatswain calls all hands up anchor for home'; for that is music, though it comes from nature's roughest cut, whose melody touches the soul and causes a responsive vibration of the tenderest chords of the heart."[36]

Page continued: "The Bay of Biscay, whose normal condition is that of a boisterous sea, lay like a mirror, reflecting the bright rays of the sun; while balmy air, fanned into the gentlest of breezes by the 'headway' of the vessel, promised a happy entrance into the broad Atlantic. 'Man proposes but God disposes.'"[37] America beckoned.

She was not the first ship to be named for General Stonewall. She wasn't even the first ram of that name. The first *Stonewall* was a Southern pilot boat (1863; 30 tons; one gun), captured by the Union screw gunboat *Tahoma* on February 24, 1863.[38]

As General Stonewall's profile rose, so did the stature of his namesakes. The next *Stonewall Jackson* was selected by Captain J. E. Montgomery for conversion to a one-gun side-wheel cotton-clad ram in the Confederate River Defense Fleet. By March 1862, work sheathing her bow with compressed cotton, double-pine beams, 4 inches of oak, and 1 inch of iron was complete, and she was deployed under Captain G. M. Phillips in a five-ship squadron protecting New Orleans. On April 24, 1862, a Union fleet under flag officer D. G. Farragut, USN, ran the gauntlet of forts Jackson and St. Philip to support the capture of New Orleans. In the ensuing confrontation, the *Stonewall Jackson* made a successful ram-run on the USS *Varuna*, which was locked in a duel with the *Governor Moore*. *Varuna* maintained her fire, point blank, as the ram disentangled itself and completed a second ram run. The force of this second impact not only opened the Union ship but also spun the *Stonewall Jackson* around, exposing her weaker stern to four penetrating 8-inch shells. *Varuna* grounded herself to avoid sinking. The *Oneida*, too late to save her sister ship, drove the heavily damaged *Stonewall Jackson* ashore, where she was abandoned and burned.[39] It was an agonizing defeat for the South—with a pair of heavy ironclads including New Orleans's namesake sitting idle nearby and later burned for want of prop shafts to complete their construction.[40] On October 15, 1864, a further schooner named *Stonewall* suffered the ignominy of being burned, alongside the schooner *Lone Star* and Confederate barracks, by raiding boat crews from the *Rachel Seaman* and *Kensington*.[41] The five-nation ship would be the last of her name.

A Confederate jack flag was raised at the bow. Her commission pennant was run up the aft mast. Her ensign—the Confederate flag to the top left of a white flag—flew from her stern. This was the "stainless banner" adopted in 1863, one of the first examples of which was laid to rest in Lieutenant General Thomas J. "Stonewall" Jackson's burial place in Richmond. This is not to say it was a wholly Confederate crew. In February 1864, the *Rappahannock*'s Commanding Lieutenant Campbell conceded his goal of having a third of his crew as sons of the Confederacy would not be reached. Semmes had fewer Confederates than foreigners on the *Alabama*. Page exceeded this only because of the *Florida*'s newly freed donor crew. Numerous Southern ships sailed with multinational crews. Adventure called some. Money called others. The cause, still others. This held for captains and officers as much as their men. The blockade-runner Joannes Wyllie, for example, was Scottish.

Newspapers leaned into the noble and dramatic. Readers on the Battle of Shiloh—the deadliest of the war to that point, where General Johnston failed to prevent two Union armies joining in Tennessee with the loss of 13,047 Union and 10,669 rebel casualties—were treated to accounts of a glowing greenish-blue light in wounds that could only be the work of angels.★ It was five times as bloody as the Battle of Bull Run the year before. Senior commanders had hardened themselves for losses on this scale. Union general Will Tecumseh sought out his commanding officer, General Ulysses S. Grant, that night. "Well Grant, we've had the devil's own day, haven't we?" Yes, he conceded around his cigar, but "we'll lick 'em tomorrow."[43]

It was a common refrain. It will be over soon. I'll survive. Victory is coming. Believe. General Grant, of Shiloh, concluded, "I saw an open field, in our possession on the second day, over which the Confederates had made repeated charges the day before, so covered with dead that it would have been possible to walk across the clearing, in any direction, stepping on dead bodies, without a foot touching the ground." Others might still believe some single battle could end the war, but he no longer could.[44]

It was down to business for *Stonewall*. There was no question of French complicity—her first task was meeting the French-flagged supply ship *Expeditif* off Belle Isle to fill her coal bunkers. With the pomp and ceremony complete, Page recorded a more candid position for the rebel flag officer, Samuel Barron, in a letter written that night, "You must not expect too much [of] me; I fear that the power and effect of this vessel have been too much exaggerated."[45]

Her civilian enlistees quickly learned the rudiments of military life. Drilling. Managing her sail and rigging. Manning her boats and guns. Rifle and bayonet work. The work was physical, repetitive, and demanding. Coal bunkers were trimmed for balance, meticulously tracked by chief engineer William P. Brooks, and fed by leading firemen like James Stewitt. Stores were managed. Food was prepared. Decks, guns, and living spaces were cleaned, salt stained, and cleaned again.

Without another flag officer aboard, the stateroom was Page's. The Wardroom officers shared cramped compartment spaces. Further astern, steerage officers shared berth rooms with lockers and fold-out mess tables. For seamen in their hammocks, a blanket was the navy's responsibility, but if you wanted a mattress, you brought it. The crew were first assigned to their officer and stations on the guns under J. B. King, the deck under Robert Carter, engineering under William P. Brooks, in the tops, and so on. Each had a mess and hammock allocated. A crewman might be assigned to the third division of the master's mate J. B. King's battery in the aftercastle, gun two as first loader, lower aft mess, and hammock 70. They were then divided into watches around the clock. That sailor might then work the port yard-

---

★One hundred forty years passed before it was found the bioluminescent bacteria P. luminescens had entered wounds from the soil and killed other microbes in the wounds.[42]

arm of the mizzen topgallant yard or form a party to launch or repel boarding actions as required. When the anchor was raised, he might be assigned to the winding capstan gear and more according to the station bills posted by officers.[46] Sickness and injury were part of life at sea. If you had to cover for another man, you did.

After so many disappointments, Bulloch was all for a first strike at Port Royal, South Carolina, where his last reports placed the heart of Sherman's Union army.[47] If anything, Commodore Barron was even more enamored of their new flagship. His correspondence was rife with targets for her on both coasts: breaking the blockade of Wilmington; capturing Californian gold steamers running from Aspinwall to New York; and even "a dash at the New England ports and commerce might be made very destructive. A few days of cruising the banks may inflict severe injury on the fisheries of the United States," which was at least borne out by the *Shenandoah*.[48]

She'd have to cross the Atlantic first.

Her seakeeping was immediately tested in the Baltic between Elsinore in Denmark and Sweden. As soon as they left the lee of Belle Isle, she became a storm's plaything; her ventilation was shuttered closed, fires were extinguished down to the last candle, and those men without their sea legs began a brutal period of seasickness. Trips on deck to the head were replaced by an ordeal in the dark with a chamber pot, and the bilges were soon fetid. Few letters survive because few could be written in the dank and gloom. The heavyweight ironclad did not ride across the swells but, instead, plunged through them, shipping huge quantities of water that could knock a man clean off his feet and left everything water slicked. Her cyclopean foregun port was capped off and, in all but calm seas, would stay that way. Her anchor hawseholes were covered with a buckler. Her carpenter, Joseph Mather, pressed more and more men to caulking and pitching. She leaked all the same.

Within twenty-four hours, seepage where the sweep of the outer hull met her vertical armor threatened to flood the bilge, and Page sought shelter at Kristiansand in southern Norway. Already, whole watches could pass without a man being able to get on deck outside his duties, much less light a cigar or pipe from the foredeck's whale oil lamp. The thought of crossing the Atlantic was a daunting one.

Courage was not an abstract for leaders of the day. Leading from the front meant a general was more likely to be killed than a private. The notion that a captain must go down with the ship was not expressed anywhere in law, but it was understood in battle that the captain would stand amidships or the rear castle as prominently as he could to see and be seen. *Stonewall* would be a test for them all. While his peers likened their vessels to great beauties, Captain Page was more direct. "Her performance in the North Sea somewhat dampened the ardor of these hardy seamen of the North, for they looked upon her as being more of the amphibian kind than of that class of vessels in which they had been accustomed to navigate the ocean."[49]

The *Stonewall* soon won him over. "It is true she had no very great respect for the heavy waves of the sea—she defied them—and if they did not permit her to gracefully ride over, she would go through them—protruding her long elephantine proboscis as the seas receded; and, rising from her almost submerged condition, would shake the torrent from her deck and again walk the water like a thing of life."[50]

When she pushed offshore a third time, her leaks were immediate and serious. She would sport them all her life, notably in the captain's stateroom and principal supply storeroom. Page learned to live with them. "The only danger lay in stopping the engines; that, in a word, the safety of the vessel and all on board depended entirely on the continuous movement of the engine, and the watchful care of it by the engineers." Chief engineer Brooks's meticulous log records as much.

On January 14, she made for a strange arrival to an anchor point in Quiberon Bay on France's Breton Island to take on further supplies and crew, though her efforts to hide under a Danish flag were undermined by the close attention of the *City of Richmond*, one of whose officers recorded, "She '(the Stonewall)' was in a filthy condition, and required more labour to clean her than to get the stores on board and stowed afterwards."[51] The French chargé d'affaires, who didn't know her backstory, lodged a protest on her arrival, which French minister Edouard Drouyn de Lhuys, who did, completely ignored.

If anything, anchoring meant more work, with stores taken onboard one box, barrel, or sack at a time, and drills continuing. Page wanted cross-skilling to the least ship's boy and landsmen in ropework, steering, gauging water depth, rowing, sewing, and managing sail, although her machinery made for more specialized work. Everything had a hierarchy—even a coal loader or landsman would have to progress to be a fireman, like the first-class crewman, James Stewitt.

The flags of at least three nations were already aboard. Much of her signage was still in French or Danish. New signal flags were added, including, it was rumored, Union examples. Page's journals are silent on the subject, but his peers weren't always above using deception, and he'd cloak himself in French colors at least once. Honor was honor, but war was war. Submersibles had been unthinkable for Europe's navies. In America, the *H. L. Hunley* sinking the *Housatonic* in February 1864 showed that the new world played by new rules.

Back in Denmark, agent James H. North's Scottish sea monster was finally launched as the warship *Danmark*. She proved as poorly suited to their navy as she would have the Confederacy's. Too late for the war against Prussia, she struggled through a fraught five-month deployment that showed such poor seakeeping she was confined to serving as a fixed barracks ship for thirty-eight years.

At home, the North had set a policy of relentless contact with the South. General Grant accepted casualties in May's Battle of the Wilderness, in Virginia, that would have checked Winfield Scott, George B. McClellan, or Henry W. Halleck before him, and marched on, declaring, "I'm prepared to fight it out on this line if it takes all summer." Scott's Anaconda Plan had squeezed, but Grant "had no quit in him." It was more industrial than any war before it, but just as personal. At one point in Saunders Field, during the Wilderness Campaign, two opponents dived into the same gully for shelter and started a fistfight so intense combat actually stopped as other soldiers cheered them on. The Confederate prevailed and took his Northern opponent prisoner, as agreed, before the killing resumed.[52]

General Grant was a nuanced leader, and remarkably candid, writing of the Mexican War, for example, "I do not think there was ever a more wicked war than that waged by the United States on Mexico. I thought so at the time when I was a youngster, only I had not the moral courage enough to resign."[53] On it went: the Battle of Resaca, Georgia (May); the Battle of Cold Harbor, Virginia (June); the Battle of Brice's Crossroads, Mississippi; the Battle of Petersburg; and the Battle of Kennesaw Mountain, Georgia (June) just days before the *Kearsarge* sank the raider *Alabama*. Not all were Northern victories, but each left the South with fewer men, less supply, less space, and less time.

The North was ascendant, but that had been true for three years without a final victory. Only six months earlier, fighting had been so close to the Union capital that Lincoln saw it for himself (though public tours of the White House had continued).[54] The South still had hope, and the *Stonewall* was coming.

Confederate agents were actively promoting her as a wonder weapon, prescribed by Commander Bulloch to both "animate the spirits of the Southern people in the struggle" and "cause some delay or confusion in the proposed operations against Wilmington and other ports on the coast of Georgia and the Carolinas," which paid off spectacularly for them off the Spanish coast.[55] Word reached around the world. The *Dallas Herald* newspaper declared that *Stonewall* and her sister ship were the "two most formidable ironclads ever designed at sea" and destined to break the Northern blockade.[56] By February

1, the Confederate Congress cheered "reports that Captain T. Jefferson Page has taken command of C.C.S. *Stonewall*, and commends Captain Bulloch for his tact, energy and management in getting possession of the Stonewall, which is a difficult matter."[57]

As each new observer noted the new rebel flagship's brutal seakeeping, Captain Page began to take perverse pride in it, recording, "Battened down, she was 'water tight', and, although she was no 'Mother Cary's chicken' to gracefully dance on the crest of waves, and would, in her lazy way, receive them over her bows, in cataract form, and give them free exit through the quarter ports to their mother ocean." When he next met a Confederate vessel, Page conceded that it "anxiously watched her performance in this terrific gale, in order to render other assistance if needed—telegraphed or signalled to know 'how she was getting on'; for at times when the *Stonewall* would be in the trough of the sea, partly submerged, there could be nothing seen of her."[58]

When she steamed out again, her gunnery officers noted that great plumes of water over her bow made using the forward 300-pounder next to impossible. The flow of water from her deck and out through her scupper holes was almost constant. Once again, Page recorded, "that water was flowing into the captain's cabin from 'abaft' in a very unusual manner; and, although men were set to bailing with buckets, the water gained on them. The storeroom for the men's clothing and other purser's effects was 'abaft' the cabin, whence came the water. On opening this apartment, a very discomforting spectacle met the eye. The caps over the two 'rudder heads' were, by the force of the sea, as the *Stonewall* would occasionally dive beneath, being gradually lifted, the bolts yielding to the pressure, and the water gushing in every direction with great force. Had these blocks been suddenly lifted from their places there would have been opened two holes of ten inches diameter each below the water line, apertures well calculated to endanger the safety of the vessel. A temporary repair was soon made by malling the blocks into their places, and the rush of water partially arrested." He'd later concede, "With exhausted bunkers and paralysed engine" the *Stonewall* would have been a prey to the raging storm; she was not capable of contending under sail alone against a severe gale.[59] Everything depended on engineer Brooks's command of the twin Mazeline engines. Three times she'd pushed out to sea. Three times, she'd been driven back.

No observation of her position had been made in two days. Proceeding on dead reckoning, they made for the nearest Spanish port: "The pulsations of every heart beat quickly, and every eye was anxiously strained to descry, midst the obscurity of the atmosphere, the crescent shaped contour of the coast, in which lay the port hoped for. Not more joyously did the cry of 'land ho!' find an echo in the hearts of Columbus' crew, than it did in the hearts of the *Stonewall's* on this occasion."[60]

With her bilge almost filled with water and her coal stores depleted, the *Stonewall* docked in A Coruña, on Spain's northwest coast in Galicia on February 3, 1865. While Spanish yards were happy enough to take the work, they wanted *Stonewall* out before the Union navy came in. While numerous Northern ships operated off the continent, it was the formidable *Niagara*, Page noted, that "had given them apprehension."[61]

Barron was less comfortable with Page's third run to shore than Bulloch, and he was growing concerned his captain was too careful and methodical to show the urgency needed. While Page sang *Stonewall's* praises in public, in private he feared when she reached American shores the ship "would not be in condition to accomplish anything nearly adequate to the slight chance of success attending the efforts of making the passage." His diary captures his underlying anger, railing, "everyone connected with her outfit and delivery" was "guilty of neglect, deception and cheating."[62] Page, Eugene L. Tessier, Barron, and Bulloch hastily converged onshore to discuss the *Stonewall's* preparedness. Bulloch spared no expense for her repairs. Barron rebuked Page for sharing the concerns his junior officers were expressing. Tessier fretted at how soon she could steam out.

Stonewall was not fully crewed, even then. The Union's efforts to check their every move continued. Parisian consul John Bigelow reported that "the Confederates were using the *Rappahannock*, still tied up at Calais, as a collecting point for a crew for the *Stonewall*. This is absolutely contrary to French neutrality laws." Seward ordered Bigelow to escalate. His protests to the French court "in as strong a language as diplomacy permitted" were acknowledged at the highest level, satisfying him for the moment that "this effort was successful in obtaining French government action to stop the recruitment."[63]

Even after their big wins against the Laird rams and others, European intransigence was maddening. When the North presented evidence of English ports re-masting a known runner, one British naval officer was reprimanded, and the Sheerness dockyard dismissed a single man. As consequences go, they could hardly have been smaller.[64] Though Page was confident in their Spanish repairs, not all officers shared the view, with one recording, "what a devil of a scrape we have gone ourselves into with this *Stonewall*, but you can not laugh at us, for I knew what was coming of her and felt the sacrificial knife."[65]

Page was ordered to cross the Atlantic via Nassau to strike at key Union supplies in Savannah, Georgia. Behind him, Bulloch never gave up. With European yards now shut to them—at least publicly—he proposed a new hybrid construction model for more warships. "Vessels [should] be laid down at once at the various ports in the Confederacy where timber is abundant, then by sending over scale drawings or working plans of their decks and sides, the iron plates, rivets, bolts, etc., could be made here [in Europe], marked, and shipped to arrive as soon as the vessels would be ready to receive them." President Davis declined the recommendation. He'd allocated $14,605,777 to the navy of $347,272,958 spent in the war's first eighteen months, with few results. Officials in the Treasury Department and elsewhere were actively hostile to further naval funding.[66] Their inability to spend more, faster had undoubtedly cost them opportunities. The private East India Company, for example, had reportedly offered a ten-ship fleet that an embittered General Pierre Beauregard, who'd started the war with the attack on Fort Sumter, felt had been bungled.[67] For "Johnny Reb," it was now *Stonewall* or nothing.

Page was very much the gentleman officer. Even while tradesmen crawled over her, day and night, so did dignitaries and visitors, men and women. It wasn't just the Union consular network that watched it all. There were plenty of Union navy uniforms on the docks and A Caruña was only so big. Nearby at sea aboard the Union warship *Niagara* was twenty-six-year-old William B. Gould, who'd escaped slavery by rowing out to the blockading federal gunboat *Cambridge* in 1861, that, for want of crew, enlisted him as a first-class boy on the spot. His diary of prior trips to A Caruña were rife with encounters with rebel sailors that escalated bloodlessly as "some of our men meet some of her crew on shore and they Braught of[f] a Rebs cap as a trophy."[68]

While fighting was illegal in a neutral port, it's easy to picture Union sailors mocking their counterparts on the war's progress, and their rebel opponents exaggerating the warship now coming for them in return. The latter was telling. Union dispatches breathlessly repeated claims her 6-meter ram was longer than 12 meters, and her 12.5-centimeters of armor was closer to 25 centimeters.

Page was keen to show the urgency Barron demanded. While his superiors returned to Liverpool and Bordeaux, he finalized payments for the work completed with paymaster Curtis, took on a last run of fresh food, and resumed command from Lieutenant Carter. The weather, which had held off enough for the heavier yard works, promptly turned for the worse. By the time he was in the Bay of Biscay, fierce storms provided an immediate test of her repairs. He didn't need emergency reports to know the leaks continued—his own cabin had resumed its commitment to leaking as soon as they left the breakwaters behind. Even more serious was a report of further damage to her rudder assembly. Recognizing she was in no shape for a transatlantic voyage, he limped *Stonewall* the 14 kilometers to the Spanish naval base, El Ferrol. His fourth run offshore had failed before Bulloch even reached Bordeaux.

Curtis opened his purse strings again or, rather, unlocked a quantity of gold bullion, this time for a larger berth with heavier equipment. Lieutenant Carter assumed portside responsibilities again. Spain provided a "good dry hulk" to transfer heavy stores to, to float her higher in the water while they hunted down new leaks in her rudder housing and all the usual suspects. Special permission was granted for an extended stay, as international law held that "no vessel or privateer of either belligerent is permitted to remain in port for a longer time than 24 hours." Works were completed without incident by March 21. "Ship carpenters were immediately at work repairing damages, and at the same time a supply of coals was being taken on board. . . . The intelligence of her arrival was not to be confined to Ferrol. There were here, as in every other part of Europe, curious gentlemen, whose avocation was to find out other people's business. The wires soon flashed the news of this arrival, under a novel flag, to the American Minister at Madrid."[69]

The Union's European blockading fleet dispatched its two leading warships to intercept her. *Stonewall* was not alone. The next time she took to sea, it would not be the elements she was fighting.

THE HUNT BEGINS   16

The Union squadron patrolling European waters continued to grow. First came the *Kearsarge*—which destroyed the celebrated raider *Alabama*—then her sister ship the *Sacramento* and the frigate *Niagara*. More would follow, as reports filtered back from *Stonewall*'s coast hopping.[1] John Bigelow's network had recorded the *Stærkodder*'s departure from Copenhagen. By January 28, he knew she traveled under the non de plume *Olinde*. He tracked her to Ferrol and lodged an immediate protest, where he "insisted that a crime against the laws of France had been committed."[2] Bigelow's counterpart, Horatio J. Perry, contacted the Spanish government, writing to the U.S. secretary of state, William H. Seward, "after a good deal of difficulty, I procured a counter order . . . to suspend the work" on *Stonewall*.[3] Perry was wrong. Work continued.

Spies and informants were contacted. U.S. agents spoke to the crew of the French *Expeditif* on her return from supplying *Stonewall*, gleaning details on her coal bunkers that helped estimate the stops she'd make in transit. On February 4, the chargé d'affaires in the U.S. embassy in Madrid, Horatio Perry, was briefed on the *Stonewall*'s repairs at A Caruña. John Bigelow, chargé d'affaires in Paris, conceded that moving against her in port would be "sufficiently uncertain to make it a bad policy risk."[4] No one wanted a repeat of the Brazilian fiasco of *Florida*'s seizure, especially with many of the same men aboard.

The wooden steam frigate *Niagara* had patrolled for weeks further north in a futile search for the English-built raiders *Sea King* (later the *Shenandoah*) and *Laurel* operating out of Liverpool. Her frustration was tempered by news of a victory at Appomattox so complete that it would be the last battle General Robert E. Lee and the Army of Northern Virginia would ever fight. *Niagara* left Antwerp on new reports of the *Stonewall*, so close to her target that the crew were ordered to sharpen their cutlasses.[5] The wooden steam sloop *Sacramento* (2,100 tons) launched from Cherbourg to join her. She was *Stonewall*'s length, but a generation older, with a hardwood hull and heavier mixed battery with a 150-pound rifled gun, two 11-inch smoothbore guns, one 30-pounder rifled gun, two 24-pounder howitzers, two 12-pounder rifled guns, and two further smoothbores.

Niagara was 100 feet longer. When she launched in 1857, she was the largest vessel ever built in the United States; she had so much deck space that she was selected to lay telegraph cable across the Atlantic prewar.[6] She mounted a formidable battery of twelve 11-inch Dahlgren smoothbore guns that threw 135-pound shells. Like the *Sacramento*, her hull was hardwood. While this left *Niagara* vulnerable to explosive shells, much of *Stonewall*'s loadout was solid shot more suited for armored targets.

On land, James Longstreet's Confederate chief of artillery, Edward Porter Alexander, had developed the art of ricocheting 12-pounder fire off the ground with so much energy there are reports of single shots carrying away ten men or more. At sea, a generation before, gunners aimed to de-rig and de-mast opponents. Now, the usual goal was to get stern-on to a target, so a penetrating shot could run the length of their decks wreaking destruction, as the *Virginia* did to the *Congress*, and the *Varuna* did to the *Stonewall Jackson*. *Stonewall*'s goal was different again. Strike hard enough amidship, and she'd send anything to the bottom.

The United States petitioned Spain that *Stonewall* was not a sovereign belligerent afforded rights under international maritime law but simply a pirate. Despite nineteen meetings with Perry insisting works stop, they continued.[7] From the moment *Niagara* and *Sacramento* took up stations offshore to bottle *Stonewall* in, the rebel ironclad could only come out fighting. Many saw echoes of the English HMS *Shannon* lying off Boston harbor in 1813, taunting the refitted American *Chesapeake* out to meet her, which resulted in the U.S. ship's capture in less than fifteen minutes with seventy-one lives lost.[8] Captain Thomas J. Page noted Spain's precautions against any Union incursion. "Two guard-boats were also stationed near us, and remained there every night while the *Niagara* was in port. However, we kept steam all night, and the chain unshackled, so as to get the ram pointed fair, in case the Niagara moved our way."[9] Lessons had been learned from the *Florida*'s seizure in Brazil, so the crew spent night after uncomfortable night on board, in sight of warmer, drier accommodation dockside, with gun crew and rifle picket duties on top of everything else.

Page received legal updates daily. "The wires soon flashed the news of this arrival, under a novel flag, to the American Minister at Madrid, who forthwith protested to that Government that the admission of such a vessel—a pirate, an enemy to all mankind, a reckless rover of the sea—was an infringement of international law, a violation of the rights of nations, and that the Government should eject her from that port and prohibit her entering another, though she might go to the bottom—the only port the hospitalities of which she was entitled to."[10] Their legal defense fell to him.

Spanish officials began to equivocate. The withdrawal of their dry hulk forced executive officer Carter to lead a second exhausting transfer of stores. Page responded with his Confederate commission and a summary of the Union case against them. "It is eminently proper here to state the ground on which rested the nationality, not only of the *Stonewall*, but of every other Confederate man of war, because it was not an uncommon assertion in high places, and eagerly embraced in some quarters, that inasmuch as these vessels under the Confederate flag had been neither built, nor fitted out, nor commissioned in some Confederate port, they were not, in view of international requirements, men of war; and consequently not entitled to the hospitality usually accorded to belligerents in neutral port."[11]

His case in return was that "[p]ublic ships of war in the service of a belligerent, entering the ports or waters of a neutral, are, by the practice of nations, exempt from the jurisdiction of a neutral power. To withdraw or refuse to recognize this exemption without previous notice, or without such notice to exert or attempt to exert jurisdiction over any such vessel, would be a violation of a common understanding which all nations are bound by good faith to respect. A vessel becomes a public ship of war by being armed and commissioned. There are no General rules which prescribe how, when or in what form the commissioning must be effected, so as to impress on the vessel the character of a public ship of war."[12]

Page's approach was "trust but prepare." First mate Carter's correspondence confirms, "We of course got ready for accidents, and in lighting fires sparks flew from the funnel." With her crew confined to the *Stonewall*, he drilled them into a high state of readiness and maintained sentries around the clock. Union observers reported the smoke rising from her stack at all hours. Page had no doubt he was only buying time for repairs. Sooner or later, what awaited him was an "unequal engagement" with Union forces.[13]

Spain was already entangled in what became the Spanish–South American War, pitting her fleet against those of her former colonies Peru, Chile, Ecuador, and Bolivia from 1865 to 1879. Coupled with colonial commitments spanning Morocco, the Philippines, Mexico, and the Dominican Republic, if Spanish courts ordered *Stonewall* seized, they had no ship capable of doing so to hand.

Perry advised Secretary of State Seward that the Spanish representative, Mr. Banuelos, "could not undertake to arrest her definitively in their port, first, because they had not the material power to do it, and, second, because they did not think they had a right to do it. If they let her go away in precisely the same condition in which she was when she entered the Spanish jurisdiction, they were not responsible for anything this ship might do afterwards." Of his agent in Ferrol, he "authorized him to employ what people he might need to watch the ram and see that she made no repairs; that she took no coals, nor provisions and water, except what might be necessary to keep her crew from day to day, etc."[14]

It was the second time Spanish assurances had amounted to nothing. El Ferrol's captain general, an admiral in the Spanish navy, simply directed that no military staff could participate in repairs, to the bemusement of the private contractors who'd been working without them all along. Directives that works be limited to her seaworthiness and not her fighting ability were loose enough to encompass anything short of her guns. Captain Page maintained courteous daily calls on port officials and ensured no action from her crew jeopardized local relations.

If the *Stonewall*'s smokestack didn't confirm her willingness to fight, intercepted mail did. On March 14, Vice Consul Henry Wilding in Liverpool reported to Perry in Madrid that they'd "received a letter from a man on board the *Stonewall*" who "says the *Niagara* and *Sacramento* are outside, but give us little concern, as we shall run right into one of them and send her to the bottom. The man to whom this is addressed . . . expects to go to the *Stonewall* as a gunner, and that men are still being engaged for her, and that a Dutch vessel is to take them to her."[15]

Repairs continued. Newspapers maintained daily coverage. Those that were Southern leaning speculated on her power. Those that were Northern leaning focused on whether *Stonewall* would be seized or face the waiting Union warships. Both featured Northern victories on land.

By September, Atlanta had fallen, and redoubts like Fort Harrison near Richmond, Virginia, were lost. In October, the Battle of Cedar Creek, Virginia, saw the control of the Shenandoah valley resolved in the Union's favor. The momentum was unmistakable. In November, Abraham Lincoln was reelected to see the war out in a comprehensive defeat of the failed general, George B. McClellan, in another key what-if moment for the war's end. Rebel counterattacks continued, as in the Battle of Franklin, Tennessee, but in December, another great Southern city, Savannah, was lost, and the Battle of Nashville saw the North consolidate control in the secessionist states.

Captain Page already had a pair of larger ships offshore. More were on their way. Whatever the state of *Stonewall*'s repairs, it was time for him to act.

Preparing for battle meant choices. First officer Carter supervised the stowage of her upper sails and paring back her running rigging, so if shot away, they couldn't become a sea anchor or entangle her propellers. Chief engineer William P. Brooks kept her Mazaline boilers under pressure and kept watching briefs with assistant engineers J. C. Closh and William Hutcheson Jackson twenty-four hours a day. Dr. Green readied a ghoulish array of medical devices, and he discussed how and where they'd triage her wounded with Dr. Herty. Officer J. B. King moved between his trio of guns, drilling his gun crews on sighting, loading, and manually tracking their aft guns. Lead Carpenter Mather readied the chocks, braces, and caulking that would fill a piercing shot, or brace her if she was stove-in by collision. Sargeant John Prior reviewed what he'd run up from the armory, and who he'd put behind it. Too many small arms would be a shrapnel risk, and leave other tasks undone. Too few, and King's crews could be picked off.

There is no record of rousing speeches. Page was a man who expected a lot of his men and led by example. When the shooting started, his place would be amidships or on the rear castle, more visible a target than any other man aboard. Forty tons of coal were removed to lighten her handling, some of it only just taken aboard. She wouldn't be transiting out of port. She'd be fighting.

Every ambition they had was 7,500 kilometers away. Failing at this remove was unthinkable. Captain Page recorded, "The gallant spirits on board of the *Stonewall* were not dismayed in the face of this superior force; but trusting in the Omnipotent Ruler, and in the justice of the cause represented by that emblem at the 'peak,' they were of one mind to do their duty. The small sum of Government money on hand was sent on shore, and the officers sent, each one, his watch—a memento of his last gallant deeds—to some dear relative."[16] James Dunwoody Bulloch had expressed a concern that Page may be too careful a captain.[17] He would not do so again.

Page made ready. Decks were cleared. Hammock rolls were fixed along the bulwarks. The magazine was opened. Shot was readied. Powder was run in hessian and leather. Messages were chalked on guns and shells. Prayers were offered. Last smokes were capped from the foredeck lamp. On March 24, 1865, *Stonewall* raised her colors and steamed into the Ferrol estuary at 10:00 a.m., followed "by a very imposing Spanish frigate, whose object—doubtless coupled with a little curiosity to witness a fight—was to see that in the impending conflict between the belligerents there should be no violation of Spanish territory."[18]

For days now, it had been a steady 16 degrees by day and 8 degrees overnight, but once again, *Stonewall* timed her run with a turn in the weather that dumped much of the region's 4-inch monthly average rainfall within days. Her forecastle gunport remained closed fast.

The heavier Union pair was ready. Aboard the *Niagara*, William B. Gould recorded, "At Ferrol. As soon as day dawns the Crew was all eagerness to fight [the] monster that have vow'd vengeance for us. She looks like an ugly customer for anything she can hit with her prow but we do not think she can come it over this ship."[19] As soon as *Stonewall* cleared the breakwaters, she began ploughing into the surf, looking like a ghost to the waiting Union warships, appearing and disappearing. Her twin rear castle guns, while strong, and capable of some manual traverse, had a limited firing arc due to her sailing rig. She had no guns facing behind her. It was imperative that Page outmaneuver his opponents. If they could keep her at arm's length or, worse, offer a combined broadside, his firepower was wildly overmatched.

Union warships struggled almost as much with the brutal conditions. While they fired first, it was quickly apparent in the surging white-capped waves, that spotting where their shots landed and adjusting was almost impossible. Neither could turn a tighter circle than the rebel warship to close in. With neither party able to land a blow, *Stonewall* retreated to port to await calmer seas, and the Union boats waited out a tough night at anchor. Though they stood-to at dawn, there was no sign of Page, and regular timetables resumed. Gould noted, "Inspection at 10. Divine serve 10.30. Visitors. Locals vending fruits and articles from tender boats. 'fight certain. All talk is of the ram,' with an, ugly customer to handle, but we will not be dismayed."[20]

On Tuesday, March 24, Gould noted her fighting trim, "The upper spars, to the lower masts, were struck and stowed on deck, and the boats were detached from the davits." It took on a cadence. "We are expecting to fight . . . but who will be the victor remains to be seen." Nothing happened. Again, outside Ferrol, "we expect a fight tomorrow."[21] With his crew buttoned down, some still adjusting to her rolling, and with her ventilation openings shuttered tight, it was a long night outside the breakwaters, with more than a few men unable to keep down what they ate, and every surface wet and slick.

Page carefully balanced his coal stores. Too little, and he couldn't make the crossing ahead. Too much, and *Stonewall* would be too sluggish to ram. A bruise-dark sky offered no respite. Loading 40 tons took him to 100 in total and left his bunkers more than half empty. He steamed out again on March 22, but after ploughing 3.2 kilometers out, he found just making headway was challenging with his ram biting so deeply into the storm-tossed waves that her rudders were lifting from the water. Smoke from the three combatants' stacks bled into gray skies. With the *Niagara* and the *Sacramento* closing toward a firing range, he returned to the harbor yet again. It was a risk, with further Union reinforcements being just as likely as a break in the weather. Chief engineer Brooks continued his nightly routine, fighting off exhaustion, banking her fires, pumping and blowing to freshen his water, raising the Havaline engine's safety valves, and attending to detailed tasks like tightening their stuffing ropes.[22]

Page was undaunted. He ventured out again on March 23, only to find the sea state was, if anything, even worse. Back he went. On deck, the Union navy's crews were resolute, but below decks on the *Niagara*, Captain Thomas Tingey Craven, a forty-three-year navy veteran and father of eight who'd served from the Antarctic to the Mediterranean (and whose brother had gone down with the monitor *Tecumseh* in Mobile Bay), was wavering. "The *Stonewall* is a very formidable vessel. If as fast as reputed to be in smooth waters she ought to be more than a match for three such ships as the *Niagara*. Should we be so fortunate, however, as to catch her out in rough water, we might possibly be able to put an end to her career. Our main change now depends upon the possibility of detaining her where she is until the Government sees fit to send out reinforcements."[23]

Less than 3,000 meters away, overnight, Page's diary recorded reservations about the "Yankee nightmare," *Niagara*, in turn. The sea taught a man patience. It had taken four hops for *Stonewall* to reach this far. Finally, on March 24, the call of divers, herons, and cormorants could be heard in the yards of the national naval arsenal again, and he had the calmer waters he needed. Out they steamed for a fourth sally. This was it.

Once again, the Spanish navy trailed him out, but now, after days of breathless newspaper coverage and the sun breaking through the clouds, civilian crowds gathered. Page noted, "The day was very fine, earth, sky and sea were alike beautiful, and nothing could be more lovely and picturesque than the mountains behind Ferrol and Corona [*sic*], alive with human beings; the whole population of Ferrol, Corona [*sic*] and the neighboring villages and hamlets seemed to have gathered there to witness the battle of the little 'Stonewall' and the two goliaths."[24] It's unclear how many men *Stonewall* was lacking for a full complement. It's certain many were still learning the ropes, quite literally. They were about to be tested.

Black smoke marked their intent as chief engineer Brooks gave Page everything their twin two-cylinder single expansion engines had. Page threw caution to the wind, with no deeper stratagem than heading straight for his opponents and counterpunching with a ram-run once they'd fired everything they had at him. The *Sacramento* was nearer. Page made for her, with his aft gun crews firing on *Niagara*. On she came as Union gun captains looked to their commanders for the order to fire, and they sheared off to avoid *Stonewall*'s ram. Page came about for another pass in a tighter arc than Commodore Craven could have expected. Union gun crews held her in their sights, waiting, waiting.

The order to fire never came.

For Captain Craven on the *Niagara*, despite seeing *Stonewall* repeatedly return to port, the decision on whether to confront her was already made. "A dead calm prevailing, with a smooth glassy sea, she again made her appearance. At this time the odds in her favor were too great and too certain, in my humble judgement, to admit of the slightest hope of being able to inflict upon her even the most trifling injury, whereas, if we had gone out, the Niagara would most undoubtedly have been easily and promptly destroyed. So thoroughly a one-sided combat I did not consider myself called upon to engage in."[25] If he was thinking of his brother's recent loss, it went unrecorded.

The *Sacramento*'s captain, Henry A. Walke, also in firing range, was of the same opinion. "Her turrets are of the heaviest plating and, as reported by Mr Palmer (an American and now a chief engineer in the Spanish navy) she is shot proof from any quarter."[26]

Both Union vessels had an edge in speed over *Stonewall*'s ponderous bow ram. Both multiplied *Stonewall*'s weight of shot—many times over. Both had larger crews of greater experience.[27] What both lacked was the formidable press the rebel ram received while under construction. *Stonewall* circled, but commanders Craven and Walke refused to be drawn into battle. "With feelings no one can imagine, I was obliged to undergo the deep humiliation of knowing that it (the 'Stonewall') was there, steaming back and forth, flaunting its flags, and waiting for me to go out to the attack. I dared not to do it!"[28]

Page defied his enemy, steaming to and fro until 8:30 p.m. "Thus passed the day, in hopeless anticipation. The spectators on the mountain side had disappeared, and the Spanish frigate, seeing there would be no violation to Her Majesty's territory, had returned to Ferrol while the *Stonewall*, at the close of the day, abandoning all hopes of meeting her fellow travellers of the sea, for they evidently desired none of her company, stood on her course for Lisbon."[29]

Morale on both Union ships plummeted. Aboard the *Niagara*, Michael Murphy waged a months-long legal battle against charges of everything from brawling to drunkenness, before he established his deafness was from the navy's guns and won a small pension. First-class boy Gould was dismayed. "She passed close to us and it was very mortefying to see her go out so close to us flaunting the Rebel Rag in our very face and we dare not follow."[30]

Captain Page was stunned. "This will doubtless seem as inexplicable to you as it is to myself. To suppose that these two heavily armed men-of-war were afraid of the *Stonewall* is to me incredible."[31] *Niagara* had seen off the worst storms the Atlantic could offer laying telegraph cables. She'd carried Japan's delegation to the states. She captured the former warship *Georgia*. She'd been ship enough to fight the forts at Mobile Bay, Fort Pickens, Florida, and Fort McRee, Pensacola, which no sane captain would have asked of a wooden ship before the war.

Page was gracious in his subsequent book. "Perhaps the weather was too good, the sea too smooth—conditions most favorable to the *Stonewall*, for in a heavy sea she could not have fought her guns at all, while the *Niagara* could have not only fought her but, towering above, could have run over her, provided she had not run 'afoul' of her most salient point, the spur at the bow." Suddenly, *Stonewall*'s near-sinking weeks before was dismissed. "She was not so dangerous. She was dangerous only when coming in conflict with one of her own kind; and even in this respect her reputation subsequently grew to vast proportions—far exceeding her capacity to do damage."[32]

It was reported as the greatest naval embarrassment of the American Civil War. Without firing a shot, *Stonewall* was free to make her way along the coast toward Lisbon, shadowed at a wary distance by the *Niagara* and *Sacramento*.

With all engineering hands at work in a single shift on March 24, the supervision of her machinery became an exercise in fatigue management, and command of her engineering spaces was handed over up to seven times each twenty-four hours. Further fresh water had to be taken on, with chief engineer Brooks's meticulous steam logs recording an ongoing battle with cracking in the fresh water "donkey" condensers.

When *Stonewall* arrived in Lisbon under the guns of the imposing sixteenth-century Belem Tower on the northern bank of the Tagus River three days later to take on additional supplies, Commodore Craven made an inexplicable mistake. Under international maritime law, once he followed Page into a neutral port, a belligerent must be allowed twenty-four hours of grace when leaving. Not only could he and *Sacramento* not wait in ambush at the port for *Stonewall*'s departure, they'd now also have to give her a twenty-four-hour head start when she left.

Page explains, "It became necessary to 'put into' this port, though so near, because the *Stonewall* had taken on board in Ferrol only a limited quantity of coals. This was done in order to enable her to carry the '4 bow gun' as high as possible above the sea, and thereby be more efficient. She conceived the chances of victory greatly against her, and that she would not require coals if captured or sent to the bottom."[33] Brooks's crew attended to urgent works delayed by the prospect of fighting, overhauling furnaces, "sweeping connections," and "keying up" crossheads and main bearings before refilling her boilers. By March 28, Page's bunkers were brimming with coal, her powder was fresh, and every nook and cranny master's mates J. B. King and William H. Savage could identify was crammed with supplies.

Captain Page remained vigilant. "It cannot be doubted that the *Niagara* and *Sacramento*, while lying in the port of Corunna, were making that neutral port a 'base of naval operations'—a point of departure—where they lay in wait for and whence they designed to issue and attack the *Stonewall* on her going to sea."[34]

Stonewall was vulnerable in port. The Union's superior firepower remained. Under their international obligation to protect her, the Belem Tower's gun crews stood to, day and night, trained on Union warships that considered *Stonewall* a pirate. With all available hands, coaling in fair weather could take as little as seven hours. In poor conditions or with limited facilities, it could take twelve hours of heavy labor. Brooks records 170 tons of coal being taken on, demonstrating they'd been at full speed to try and put Union forces behind them. Unsure if the Union would observe international law, Page requested a nighttime departure as soon as coaling was complete. The port declined. *Stonewall's* crew was utterly exhausted after six weeks of constant battle stations and heightened watches. The Belem Tower burned with light. The Union warships were almost as bright. Every gathering of voices was suspected. Every lighter and davit boat was a threat. A long night passed.

When *Stonewall* steamed west the next morning, drifted with coal dust, the Union vessels were anchored a kilometer away, close enough that Page's spyglass picked out "his quondam shipmate and friend, bearing the rank of commodore" who had cruised in the West Indies on board of the same ship, the "old Erie," when one was "sailing master," the other a "green midshipman."[35]

Niagara and *Sacramento* were silent and still as the rebel ship's smoke trail shrank toward the horizon. Just hours later though—well short of their twenty-four-hour rule—the *Niagara* slipped her anchor. Before it was clear she did so to move to an anchor point deeper in the harbor, the Belem Tower opened fire on her—the first and last time a foreign nation fired on a recognized U.S. warship through the American Civil War.[36] Portugal had fired on the United States.

On the *Niagara*, Gould's diary notes, "At 11am the rebel ram *Stonewall* went to sea. . . . At 2pm . . . we got ready to get underway." He was in no doubt why the fort was mistaken, "we were obligated to go do[wn] river in order to turn around. . . . At 3.15 pm got underway and stood down in the river . . . the fort opened up on us and fired 9 shots, and continued to fire on us after we had turned and dipped our colours several times . . . one shot st[ruck] us forward of the Beam and an[other] struck our smokestack."[37] Craven offered no fire in return. The fort had offered no warning shot—they were not obligated to—and it was sheer luck no one was harmed. After outraged diplomatic exchanges, the Portuguese issued an apology, the fort commander was stood down, and a twenty-one-gun salute was fired as the U.S. flag was symbolically raised. After the precarious Trent Affair, a Union government with no appetite for another international incident accepted it quickly, and efforts were made to hush the episode. None of it brought the *Stonewall* back.

Page records, "the Stonewall stood out to sea, touched at Tanariffe, the most eligible point from which to cross the Atlantic, and filling up with coals, shaped her course so as to reach the latitude of the 'trade winds' in the shortest possible time, where her sails would come into requisition. It was advisable to avail of those winds in order to economize coals, as she could not carry enough to steam the whole way across."[38] His last orders from Commodore Samuel Barron directed that she capture gold aboard Californian passenger steamers en route to Europe and strike Union ports in New England as a "heavy blow in the right place." She was further ordered to strike the Union naval base 2,735 kilometers away at Port Royal, South Carolina, to disrupt operations "where an immense fleet of transports must be collected without adequate defense."[39] It was bold and ambitious but very, very late.

The *Niagara*'s Commodore Craven wrote, "After 45 days of constant watchfulness, at times buoyed up with the hope that she might be detained definitely at Ferrol . . . I have now been compelled to lose sight of one of the most formidable ironclad vessels now afloat. It may appear to some that I ought to have run the hazard of a battle, but according to my judgement I shall ever feel that I have done all that I could."[40] The *New York Times*, in an article dated April 13, 1865, was outraged at the *Stonewall*'s twenty-four-hour head start: "this new scourge is on the high seas, and will dauntless prove to us still further the advantage of European neutrality at this particular crisis. They have been guilty of an essentially unfriendly act; and their joint action—for such we must call it—of letting loose this pirate at this time, is particularly foolish and criminal."

Craven was tried by courts-martial at the order of Gideon Welles on the basis that he "did fail to use any exertions or make any effort whatever to overtake and capture or destroy the said vessel of the enemy as it was his duty to have done."[41] Welles had convened the first ironclad board in the North before the Civil War and watched their development with a paternal eye. He was adamant that his warships could not be doubted, and how concerned his men could be.

Craven's former commander was president of the panel of review. His peers sat in judgment, among them Charles H. Davis, who'd fought alongside him at Vicksburg; John A. Dahlgren, who'd commanded at Charleston; and Captain S. Phillips Lee, who'd led the North Atlantic Blocking Squadron. Their reluctance to deny a field commander discretion saw them return a mixed verdict with a recommendation for two years' leave with pay. Welles demanded a clearer position. "I should not be surprised if Farragut's kind and generous heart acquiesced against his better judgement."[42]

A conviction was duly recorded, with the qualification, "except the words 'as it was his duty to have done'" to allow clemency. When the same punishment was recommended a second time, Welles preempted them again, arguing, "the inference is that the General rule with a commanding officer of the Navy should be, 'Do not fight if there is a chance of defeat,' rather than the converse rule, 'Fight if there is a chance of victory.'"[43] Though he railed against a fraternity of brothers protecting one another, Welles ultimately deferred to the panel's direct experience. The conviction was overturned. Craven was freed, was restored to duty, and went on to become a rear admiral and commander of the postwar Pacific Squadron.[44]

The conduct of *Sacramento* was not above question either, despite claims of outstanding engine repairs dating back to her previous months in port in Cadiz. Horatio J. Perry, writing on behalf of the secretary of state, tried gamely not to judge his captain: "I have been unwilling to give credence to reports which have reached me to much improper, if not positively disloyal, language used by some officers of this ship in the cafes and public houses at Cadiz. . . . I trust the delay of the *Sacramento* can be satisfactorily explained to the Navy Department, but happening in connection with these antecedents, it has made me fear that the heart of that ship is not in the work she has to do."[45]

Behind them, *Stonewall* disappeared from Union view, "steaming rapidly southward" in search of the Atlantic trade winds that would carry her to war.

IF THE THING IS PRESSED 17

*N*iagara and *Sacramento* found no trace of her after their twenty-four-hour delay elapsed. No merchants reported unknown smoke trails on the horizon. The challenge *Stonewall* now presented to the Union navy would have echoes generations later when the *Bismarck* (50,300 tons; sixty-four guns) broke into the Atlantic in World War II. The North's blocking squadrons were alerted. Planners speculated on ports and routes.

After three days, Thomas J. Page was confident enough of their escape for William P. Brooks to cut their engines for ten minutes at a time to test her performance under sail and drill his men on fast restarts. Experiments at different revolutions per minute went on for days, trading speed for coal consumption.[1] There was little more the Confederacy could do for her. At home, the South's war goals were unraveling. Communications were breaking down. Her attempts to assemble an onshore fleet were in tatters.

Even then, rebel agents in Europe still sought new acquisitions. Their last raiders were still at sea. Runners continued to get through. Subterfuge continued. On March 10, the Confederate Congress leaked false papers promoting *Stonewall* as a wonder weapon and suggesting a wave of further ironclads would follow.[2] By late March 1865 the Confederate navy secretary hadn't heard from James Dunwoody Bulloch for weeks. He alternated between resignation (ordering Raphael Semmes to destroy his nine makeshift river gunboats and make for wherever Robert E. Lee reset his headquarters) and hope (checking every day for a telegram from a *Stonewall* that was at sea, some 5,700 kilometers away).[3]

Captain Page was now so at ease with his command moving into the waves like a porpoise and hurling vast plumes of water down her flanks, he simply referred to her "fantastic tricks" in his diary.[4] His confidence was about to be tested. No ironclad comparable to the *Stonewall* had ever completed a transatlantic crossing.

After battling the worst Spanish weather had to offer for more than a month, *Stonewall* finally caught the mild conditions they'd hoped for and began a slow and monotonous passage.[5] No further distress was recorded in the rudder bolts, and bracing was repaired in Spain and Portugal. Page could finally resume a tiny cabin whose water stains spoke of repeated flooding. The larder stayed dry for the moment. Brooks focused on a small series of running repairs to the condensers of their water purifying "donkey." His direct staff of two oilers, six firemen (including James Stewitt), and three trimmers was below her full complement, so further recruiting would be a priority when they reached the South to alleviate unrelenting six-hour alternative watches in hot, loud, and trying conditions.

Hidden in the vast Atlantic, she laid on all the sail she had and spelled her engines to conserve coal and maintain her pumps and "countershaft in-gear." When sails were first spotted on the horizon, Brooks rushed to restart her boilers, quarters were sounded, and every man on deck tracked the approach of a clipper-rigged barque sailing from Baltimore to Rio de Janeiro with a cargo of flour, remarkable for her beauty. Still wary, *Stonewall* ran up a deceptive French flag. An American flag was raised by the barque in reply. Page takes up the story.

"When she had come within a suitable distance, the French flag was hauled down, the Confederate hoisted in its place, and a 'nine inch' shell thrown across her bow. The music of such a projectile, flying through the air with ignited fuse, is not that of the Aeolian harp. With 'flowing sheets,' the bark 'came up into wind' as gracefully as are the movements of the swan when gliding through the waters of a placid lake. Here was presented an unpleasant conflict of duty and inclination. To destroy such a craft was repulsive; and yet duty might demand it."[6] Here, Page had the *Alabama*'s reputation of chivalry to uphold.

Stonewall's aft guns were moved from one firing port to another until they came alongside, and the barque's captain was summoned aboard. Page had tremendous empathy for the man. "His troubled appearance may be more easily imagined than described. In great anguish he declared that he had been in that trade many years, and this was the first time he had brought his wife and little daughter with him. Here was an appeal that added to the embarrassment of the situation, not easily disregarded. The *Stonewall* had no accommodations for such passengers, and moreover this was not the kind of game she was in pursuit of. The captain of the barque was given to understand that a bond would be required of him for the release of his vessel, and that he should assure his owners they were indebted solely to his wife and daughter for the rescue of their vessel and cargo from the flames." Page refused to plunder his cargo.[7] The *Stonewall* was not a raider or a runner. Her holds were full, and this beauty had no coal to seize. *Stonewall* was a warship, and her business was sinking her kind. The captain and ship were released and watched with admiration to the horizon. *Stonewall's* long transit resumed.

Fragmentary records indicate the sudden death of an assistant paymaster, potentially the Alabama-born paymaster's clerk, William Boynton, which by the standards of the day reflects well on the discipline and hygiene instilled by Captain Page.[8]*

This was not to say ships were necessarily sanitary. The Civil War diaries of Ensign Symmes Brown of the *Tyler* are typical, "The boat is actually alive with roaches and rats, mosquitoes and flies, knats and bugs of every description. . . . While I am writing, the roaches are running all over my patent desk. I never saw a place like it. The boat is awful dirty."[9] One saving grace was that rebel surgeons, such as Bennett W. Green or the Hampton Road veteran James H. Herty, had a strict naval screening process to pass. Doctors in volunteer army units had no minimum standard to meet at all. U.S. Army soldiers stood a one in ten chance of dying from disease and ill health off the battlefield. Their naval peers recorded such deaths for one in thirty.[10]

Their time at sea began to blur. A typical day might start at 4:00 or 5:00 a.m. with reveille being shouted or bugled. The master at arms, Sergeant John Prior, would lap the sleeping quarters and slap the hammocks of his sleeping crew, which were so tightly bundled together that G. P. Schönheyder had mused it may be grounds to decline delivery to Denmark, and were then stowed on deck behind netting along the ship's armored bulwarks. On a clear day, they'd return dry. In bad weather, you served wet and slept wet, whatever naval regulations said to the contrary. At dawn, her flag was run up. They'd wash down decks painted white with salt using seawater and holystones. Brass was polished. Gun tracks were burnished. Guns were cleaned, inside and out. Sails and rigging were checked. Rope splices were inspected. Every shackle holding blocks and lines was eyeballed. A few minutes were allowed for each man's ablutions, which was adequate given that it amounted to nothing more than the head and a bucket of water.

Inspection wasn't the dress uniform preening of a graduation ceremony. It was the practicality of clean hands, clean faces, and pants rolled to prevent tripping. Repetition was everything. Many captains would have their ship boys race to the topmast and back down, sending the last-placed finisher up

---

*Despite an account attributing the death to his role, he is not listed in the honor rolls that (mistakenly) recorded George A. Borchert's death.

again to quicken their hands.[11] The division between sailor and landlubber began to break down.

Breakfast was at 8:00 a.m. and divided into different messes. No space aboard was fit for the crew to stop work and eat at once. Cooking was typically rotated. Even with the stove gimballed to swing in the opposite direction of the ship's rolling, heavy weather meant fires were extinguished and food was served cold. Coals were carefully rationed and recorded by chief engineer Brooks. Crews could choose to pay for special foods, but the navy would not, and there is no record of them doing so. There was so little variety, crews learned to judge their distance from port from the menu. An appointed orderly managed the food and serving utensils. Each man's cutlery was his own. While most of the South had been reduced to ersatz substitutes like chicory or dandelion root, *Stonewall*'s men still started with coffee and salt beef, supplemented with fresh food in port.

By 9:30 a.m., everything was stowed, quarters were sounded, and the readiness of key equipment—starting with the guns—was checked. If no remedial work was required, downtime was allowed for conversation, diaries and letters, personal sewing and repairs, or the smattering of reading material, often months out of date and read until they disintegrated or joined them in the head.

Lunch was at noon, back in assigned messes, with vegetables joining salted beef or pork. Water was stored in wooden barrels, with a typical allocation of half a gallon per man per day for all uses.[12] Confederate ration policies stipulated luxuries like cheese, butter, and raisins were rarely sighted; however, by this point, sailors ate better than soldiers, with as much as one and a quarter pounds of meat a day, when soldiers might be lucky to see it three times a week. Everything was regulated with watches of four hours on and four hours off. Afternoons began with duties assigned by paymaster Richard W. Curtis, chief surgeon Green, chief engineer Brooks, Sargeant Prior, and so on for their teams. Weather permitting, next came drills executed by first officer Robert Randolph Carter that seemed never ending: drills for fighting fires (every sailor's dread in the lonely ocean vastness), for a man overboard, for dispatching boats, for shifting casualties, for shoring up a breach, for this piece of gear failing or that, and, as ever for the *Stonewall*, for finding and addressing leaks. Two to three times a week, again, when the Atlantic permitted it, bathtubs were taken on deck to wash clothes and linen. Absent a priest, if there was a religious service, it was a brief reading from Captain Page on Sunday.

An evening meal was served as early as 4:00 p.m., subject to the sea state.[13] At 5:30 p.m., men were called to their quarters, and inspections were made of all spaces. Attention to detail mattered as misplaced items, darkness, and the moving ship could mean breakages or injury. Once satisfied, the boatswain

John M. Dukehart's pipe announced that the hammocks could be retrieved from the deck nettings. Aside from watches, and specialized assignments such as engineering, it was then free time. Smokers—and most of them were—did so on deck. Friction matches were strictly forbidden for fear of fire, and hand-rolled cigarettes were still years away, so cigars and pipes were lit with a small taper from a whale oil lamp.

Cards and gambling were officially forbidden—but common—fleet wide. Dominoes were popular. A musician with banjo or fiddle was a welcome addition. Some whittled. Some repaired clothing. Nothing was prized more than mail from home, but it was *Stonewall*'s fate she'd never receive any. At sunset, her flag was lowered again. Some rebel captains encouraged minstrel shows. Some readings or religious services. Some boxing. Some nothing at all. Merchants knew the sailors' love of a drink. In most savvy ports, grog could be smuggled aboard in mislabeled tins; however, drunkenness was still a serious matter, and it meant irons at least for any man unfit for duty. Tattoo marked the end of the day—three hours after sunset if it fell before 6:00 p.m. or two hours otherwise. The flag was raised when she made port, encountered a vessel, welcomed a dignitary, or marked the anniversary of the confederation. In all of this, fatigue management was crucial. Brooks continued to stagger his shifts, so that he, William Hutcheson Jackson, and C. J. Kolsh traded supervision of her machinery seven times a day.

Though Page had intended to make for Bermuda, northwest winds and a "heavy head swell" after leaving the trade winds upped her coal consumption and forced her to change course. It was heavy going. The prevailing westerly winds and gulf stream made going to Europe faster than returning. Page deferred to Brooks's engineering needs, on April 7, for example, shutting down her engines so he could work on uncoupling and recoupling her main shaft with jackscrews and levers. Page carefully stretched out her coal consumption under sail, with Brooks recording extended periods with "her engines disconnected from screws." Even when under steam, Brooks alternated her boilers on and off to minimize wear and coal consumption. When they reached home waters, he was damned if it wouldn't be in fighting-fit condition.

The last domestic naval bastion for the South was the Richmond fleet, with the steam ironclad ram *Virginia II* (four guns)—with 8-inch armor to her port and bow and 6 inches on her flanks—leading the smaller ironclads *Richmond* and *Fredericksburg*. They'd played an important part in the defense of Richmond in 1864–1865, but when the city fell on April 2, 1865, the coastal navy of the Confederate States of America had reached its end. The last class of the Naval Academy sank their beloved training vessel, the *Patrick Henry*, a veteran of the Battle of Hampton Roads.[14] The North never came close to the number of rebel vessels that rebels sent to the bottom.

On April 9, the *Stonewall* reverted to form, and Brooks's methodical handwriting records serious seawater leaks into her aft magazine through corroded bolts on the port delivery pipe. There are few accounts of the *Kearsarge* sinking the raider *Alabama* that don't speculate about the quality of her powder. This was potentially debilitating to her firepower, but with stores at a premium, Page elected not to test fire his powder at sea, making his first combat action a test of faith. The starboard screw shaft had to be uncoupled, and she labored on with one engine as lasting repairs with a reinforcing band of iron replaced emergency caulking. The resulting strain on her bilge pumps then required their overhaul, illustrating the tight tolerances under which she worked. The stress on Brooks himself went unspoken, but for several days, he stayed on station without any rotation to Jackson or Kolsh, recording no sleep at all. The importance of Brooks's work is hard to overstate—with such notorious seakeeping, in a beam sea with waves crashing into her sides, an engine failure could be fatal.

Through thousands of lonely miles, no ship reported her, and she reported no smoke or sails on the horizon. The *Stonewall* was next seen 5,992 kilometers away approaching Nassau in the Bahamas on May 6.[15] The American Civil War raged on, more and more on the North's terms. President Jefferson Davis vowed to fight on. *Stonewall* came into port hot, with her sails trimmed, both engines at high throttle and her guns manned, ready for anything. No one seemed to care. Nassau was a bustling redout for Southern blockade-runners and European merchants just forty-eight hours and 901 kilometers from Charleston. While port officials allowed *Stonewall* to reprovision with more than 150 tons of coal—all of it moved by hand—they insisted she do so offshore. Doing so was a calculated risk, immediately taking her at least 120 tons over the fighting weight Page chose to confront *Niagara* and *Sacramento*.

Page could only speculate on their austere reception. On reaching their docking station, depth soundings were made, chains were loosed, and her anchor was dropped. She banked her fires by 2:30 p.m. Only once her fires were "hauled" could Brooks service his pressure tubes and address a loss of maximum revolutions per minute. Preventative maintenance on his air pumps and other systems followed, with the expectation that enemy contact would prevent it in future. Making ports after weeks at sea was a relief to all. Even Brooks, the stoic chief engineer, had references to pleasant winds and smooth seas creep into his logs, an absolute flourish by his standards. There was no break in the workload. Docked, command passed to first officer Carter. Now was the chance to pull down rigging under a watchful eye from the second mates, George A. Borchert and Edmund Gaines Read; scrape and grease spars; and, unendingly, holystoning decks stained with coal powder.

Stores were inventoried and replenished through her pantries with master's mates J. B. King and William H. Savage.

First officer Carter expanded watches, twenty-four hours a day. Her flag was raised each dawn and lowered each dusk with the same reverence as it first had been in Spanish waters. The following day, she shifted her anchorage closer, and it was May 9 before she eased her way out with frequent depth soundings. Nassau's authorities had followed the South's decline as closely as anyone and had long since started hedging their bets. When the *Stonewall* was recorded in their logs, it was simply called a "steamer," with a cargo of "ballast."[16] America beckoned.

While Union captains were not uniformly supportive of Commodore Thomas Craven, many shared his fear of the rebel flagship. Clipper ships and telegraph wires hummed with rumors of her location. A whole squadron of warships was dispatched to the Gulf of Mexico to try and prevent an assault on Galveston, Texas, that never came. Ambassadors in Canada passed on frantic reports on an imminent attack on New York. New England captains diarized the danger. Ships up and down the coast were ordered to stand ready for her assault, among them, the *Nantucket* under Commander R. F. R. Lewis, who was (correctly) convinced she'd be ordered to strike the vulnerable Port Royal in South Carolina.[17] Leave was canceled. Repair works were delayed. Union secretary of the navy Gideon Welles ordered that port squadrons be reinforced. Harbors from Florida to Maine were to prepare for attack.

In January 1865, the capture of Fort Fisher, North Carolina, by Union forces at the entrance to the Cape Fear River had closed one of the last seaports still open to blockade-runners. In February, Columbia, South Carolina, had been the next to fall into Union hands, followed by Charleston, South Carolina. Only the *Stonewall* could reopen them. Southern papers speculated on where she would appear. Ships like the *City of Richmond* spread new stories as they docked in Bermuda. By March 1865, the ambassador there wrote that *Stonewall* was "hourly expected." There was still fight in the South as long as there was hope. The rebel attack on Fort Stedman, Petersburg, launched Lee's last offensive.

Brooks recorded erratic coal consumption as they passed in and out of heavy weather. Some twelve-hour periods used no coal at all under sail. Some days consumed as much as 10 tons as they pushed on aggressively. Running repairs continued, including fashioning "plummer block binder bolts," an impressive level of workshop performance at sea.

On land, there was a growing disconnect between the orders flowing from the Southern capital and reality on the ground. Discipline was eroding. Desertions were up. Speculation on new Southern refuges spread. Government offices were being packed up and stripped out. Safes were being emptied. Opportunists stepped in. In London, Confederate agent Duncan Kenner pitched the British prime minister, Lord Palmerston, a plan for England to enter the war on their behalf if they renounced slavery, which contradicted every dictate Jefferson Davis made before and after. After years of war, Palmerston likened it to "preaching to mad dogs" and rejected it out of hand.[18]

The defending squadrons ahead of Page were a polyglot of ships. The Union's monitor ironclads were strictly riverine craft when *Stonewall* was conceived. By April 7, 1865, the first of four Miantonomoh-class ocean-going monitors, the *Monadnock* (3,348 tons; two guns), a twin-turret warship two and a half times *Stonewall*'s displacement, had been assigned to Acting Rear Admiral Sylvanus Godon's Special Hunting Squadron to buttress side-wheelers like the *Wasp*.[19]

No thought was given to sparing wooden-hulled ships any confrontation. With Northern pride at stake, Welles set a clear expectation that the Union navy should fight on any terms. Regardless of the *Niagara* and *Sacramento*'s failings, modest gunboats like the *Chippewa* (691 tons; five guns) and wooden screw steamer *Monticello* (665 tons; three guns) were pressed. The monitor *Canonicus* (1,034 tons; two guns), which had captured several blockade-runners off South Carolina's coast in recent months and had seen off the domestically built ironclad *Tennessee* in the run to Mobile, was deployed despite being so rundown she needed a tow from the supply steamer *Fahkee* (670 tons; three guns), though she later became the first monitor to enter a foreign port and survived as the last of her kind until 1908.[20]

Any gentleman's agreement on naval warfare was long gone. After torpedo-mines had shattered monitor ironclads like the *Tecumseh*, Union forces began to deploy them in turn. Already, the *Albemarle* had been sunk by Screw Picket Boat Number One's Lieutenant William Cushing with a pole charge. Picketboats headed by the *Monticello* finalized preparations for using newly patented Wood/Lay 100-pound underwater mines to try and close their river mouths to the *Stonewall*.[21]

A gathering of ironclads was a different proposition to the *Niagara* and *Sacramento*. If they were able to form a connected battle line, especially in unfavorable weather, while *Stonewall* could pierce them with her 10-inch, 300-pounder and certainly destroy them by ramming, there was a strong chance they could hole *Stonewall* in return. No comparable ironclads had been destroyed outright in battle. One way or another, one soon would be.

Admiral Godon didn't have the intel required to meet *Stonewall* at sea. Deploying his forces at every possible port meant he couldn't guarantee local superiority. His nightmare scenario was *Stonewall* being free to simply move offshore to avoid his coastal monitors and pick off his wooden vessels when conditions suited her. Contradictory reports on her whereabouts had her across a 3,220-kilometer arc. Stories abounded. *Stonewall* was leading a fleet of blockade-runners. She would raid Florida to rendezvous with Jefferson Davis. She'd somehow manage the shallow port channels to battle the Union fleet at Galveston. *Stonewall*'s sister ship (still serving in Prussia and entering her last short years of service) would join her. She would leave in twenty-four hours to attack Texas.[22]

Even this late in the day, Confederate blockade-runners continued to supply frontline rebel forces. Edmund Kirby Smith's forces, for example, received more than ten thousand small arms, powder, cartridge paper, uniforms, and a full battery of modern breech-loading Whitworth field artillery from a single voyage of the *Denbigh*, which was the second-most successful of the Southern runners after the S*yren* in the war's last year (though she grounded herself shortly afterward and was destroyed in place by Union forces[23]).

The commander of the Northern East Gulf Blockading Squadron, Admiral C. K. Stribling, dispatched personal notes addressed to Captain Page to a range of possible ports offering terms of surrender. The former slave, William B. Gould, aboard the *Niagara*, who'd watched her steam past unopposed, was still convinced of her threat. "I heard of the arrival of the *Stonewall* at Havannah. She no doubt will try her hand on the Texan Coast."[24] Gould had worked himself up to landsman and then wardroom steward, despite all obstacles, and some crewmen refusing to share tasks or tools with one of his race. As an onboard servant, it was as much as he could achieve. He finished his war providing officers silver service.

Havana, Cuba, would be Page's last chance to fill his coal bunkers and provision before his assault on the mainland. He'd run the gauntlet of Union pickets this far; however, it was a predictable move, so he prepared his crew for action. Down went the sails. Up went the boiler pressure and gun crews.

If Nassau had refused to accommodate him in port, what welcome could he expect? He approached Havana, Cuba, on May 10, cautiously under clear blue skies with the water mirror smooth and perfectly suited for his ram. To his great surprise, he passed no pickets, no opponents steamed out to meet him, and even the merchants around him showed little interest.[25] He docked alongside the Confederate side-wheeler *Harriet Lane* (600 tons; seven guns) and handed over acting command to First Lieutenant Robert R. Carter once again.

The *Harriet* had had a storied war. The copper-sheathed revenue cutter–turned–gunboat had been part of the Paraguayan fiasco that was the culmination of Page's explorations with the *Water Witch*, participated in the war's opening attack on Fort Sumter, and survived the Battle of Pig Point, Virginia, and attacks on Fort Clark, Fort Hatteras, Shipping Point, New Orleans, and Vicksburg. She'd sunk the rebel ship *Neptune* and served as Admiral D. G. Farragut's flagship before being captured with her code books intact by Southern cavalry after the Battle of Galveston in an action that showcased the war's cruelty and reach. After shore-based fire killed her Union commander Jonathan M. Wainwright and mortally wounded Lieutenant Commander Edward Lea, the first rebel aboard was Lea's father, Confederate major Albert M. Lea, too late to do anything but hold him as he died. Among the defenders was Captain Wainwright's ten-year-old son, who'd emptied two revolvers from the bridge standing over his body. Among the attackers had been the Texas Maritime Service's oldest member, sixty-nine-year-old Captain Levi C. Harby.[26]

Page was barely ashore when the *Harriet*'s captain, Leon Smith, stopped him in his tracks. On April 6, 1865, Confederate sailors reduced to fighting as infantry were part of battles along tributaries of the Appomattox River, including, ironically enough, Sailor's Creek, that prevented President Davis from decamping to the "lower Confederacy" in Texas. In a trio of Union victories, eight Southern generals and more than eighty-eight hundred men were captured—almost a quarter of Lee's army. "If the thing is pressed," wrote Union general Philip Sheridan to General-in-Chief Ulysses S. Grant, "I think that Lee will surrender." When Sheridan's report reached President Abraham Lincoln, he was resolute that they "[l]et the thing be pressed."[27] General Lee wrote to President Jefferson Davis, "a few more Sailor's Creeks and it will all be over." Within three days, it was.[28] April 9 opened with a desperate breakout attempt by Lee's Confederate army toward General Joseph E. Johnston in North Carolina. It ended with General Grant accepting the surrender of the Army of Northern Virginia from General Lee at Appomattox Courthouse.

Page and the *Stonewall* were too late.

By the time he'd steamed south from Tenerife, Richmond and Petersburg had fallen. Their armies were in disarray. The government was in flight. Their governors, gold, and documents had been evacuated from Richmond for Danville.[29] On April 26, the primary remaining Southern force under General Johnston surrendered to William T. Sherman. General Richard Taylor followed in surrendering his forces in Alabama, Mississippi, and East Louisiana on May 4. Scattered forces followed suit as word spread. Page gave Brooks permission to bank their fires, though running repairs to her pumps and valves continued and a twenty-four-hour vigil was maintained.

Lincoln didn't live to see his victory. On April 14, he was shot by John Wilkes Booth while watching *Our American Cousin* at Ford's Theatre, Washington. When his usual bodyguard was too ill to serve, John Frederick Parker had been called in. After seating Lincoln and his wife, he found he couldn't see the play from his station in the hallway outside, so he'd gone downstairs instead. At intermission, he left for the bar next door, crossing paths with

John Wilkes Booth leaving it in return, to simply walk up to Lincoln's balcony seats and shoot him at 10:00 p.m.[30] Lincoln passed away at 7:02 a.m. the following morning. Bizarrely it was later realized that the man who the assassin's brother Edwin had saved from falling under a railcar the year before had been Lincoln's son, Robert.[31]

With bitter poetry, the civil war that had opened with rebel aggression at Fort Sumter, closed with Union forces storming it. On April 23, the side-wheel ram *Webb* made a desperate run down the Mississippi to try and reach the sea. She made it no further than New Orleans before being trapped and later torched by her crew.

The outcome of the war between the states had been decided. The Confederacy's President Davis was captured May 10, either safeguarding his family or in his wife's clothes depending on who was telling the story. In a bitter postscript, on May 12, rebel forces prevailed in a final battle at Palmito Ranch that meant absolutely nothing. On May 26, General Simon Bolivar Buckner surrendered the last Confederate army. While some smaller units such as Kirby Smith's held out until June 2, and there were actions in Galveston, Texas, and elsewhere as late as June 22, President Andrew Johnson had formally proclaimed the war at an end on May 10, shortly after *Stonewall* left the Bahamas. The last general to surrender was the Cherokee Stand Watie on June 23, whose Cherokee, Muskogee, and Seminole warriors fought in opposition to Union plans to carve out Oklahoma from their lands, despite having emancipated their own slaves in 1863.[32] Confederate troops stacked their weapons, signed a pledge not to take up arms, waited for final payments that would never come, and went home.

Captain Page records, "The sad intelligence here received, which I need not describe, was not to be questioned, and the feelings of both officers and men may be imagined, but not expressed." The so-called war of Northern Aggression had ended decisively in the Union's favor. He continued, "Arrived at Havana, the usual visits of ceremony made, the vessel was admitted to the customary hospitalities of the port, with no limitation as to the time she would be permitted to remain." "The little craft that had so bravely breasted the storms of tempestuous seas, to do her duty in a holy cause, found herself a useless hulk, an encumbrance."[33]

There was no time for indulging his disappointment. "The political state of affairs in the Confederacy had not been as yet officially announced to the authorities of Cuba. When that shall have been done, the *Stonewall* would no longer be entitled to the flag she so proudly bore off Ferrol."[34]

It was Page's legal arguments that kept *Stonewall* from Union hands in Spain. Once again, it fell to him to act, weeks away from the authorities he served. Unaware of *Stonewall*'s whereabouts, Bulloch lamented, "Manifestly he could now venture upon no offensive operation." Paymaster Curtis confirmed the last of the gold bullion he'd taken on in El Ferrol had been spent. Major Helm, the leading local Confederate agent, could do nothing for him. "The position was perplexing, and quite exceptional."[35]

Page wasn't alone.

Aside from Captain Smith's gunboat *Harriet Lane*, the Scottish blockade-running Captain William Watson was trying to salvage what profits he could for the schooner *Rob Roy* when the *Stonewall* was sighted. No one was in charge. Ships under rebel contracts were scattered around the world. IOUs, Confederate dollars, and cotton futures instantly became worthless. No one could account for a fortune in gold and bonds. It was every man for himself. Watson conceded, "As for the large fleet of blockade-running steamers thrown idle at Havana, it would be difficult to say what became of them all."[36] The reconciliation of just how little they'd been left with settled in; Watson, for example, found his final share of blockade-running bounty whittled down to an average ship master's wage by onerous fees and taxes.

Though her fires were out, *Stonewall* continued to man her guns and post pickets. They were Confederate until Page said otherwise. On word of her arrival, the commander of the East Gulf Blockading Squadron, Admiral C. K. Stribling, deployed the side-wheelers *Powhatan* (2,415 tons; sixteen guns), *Mahaska* (1,070 tons; six guns), and *Tallapoosa* (974 tons; eight guns), with the screw steamer *Aries* (820 tons; six guns) to blockade Havana harbor. When Page didn't respond, the *Powhatan* was ordered to dock nearby, one of whose officer's recorded, "we lay in Havana, side by side, so near that one could have tossed a biscuit from one deck to the other. . . . In the morning, at sunrise, the brand-new Confederate flag of the ram was thrown to the breeze at the same moment as our own, and the dip of the setting sun was the signal for a similar roll call and salute, as the two flags were simultaneously lowered."[37] The Union squadron's orders were explicit—if *Stonewall* got underway, they were to fight to their destruction, or hers.

Powhatan relayed a message to the captain general of the Island of Cuba, as the Spanish Crown's representative, that with the war ended, the *Stonewall* was a pirate, not a ship-of-war, and any intervention on her behalf would be judged accordingly.[38] Union rear admiral S. W. Godon wanted Page to understand his situation—when he offered a mild parole offer, it was Captain William Ronckendorff's freshly arrived heavy ocean-going monitor *Monadnock* that delivered it.

Page noted wistfully, "among the arrivals which soon followed her into Havana was an imposing looking American man of war steamer. She anchored only a very short distance off. One morning a letter was handed to the commander of the *Stonewall*, which bore the signature of an old acquaintance—the captain of the man of war close by. The purport of this communication was suggesting the propriety of surrender of the *Stonewall* to him. Its receipt was promptly acknowledged, and although its kind suggestions were fully appreciated, they were politely declined."[39] *Monadnock* wasn't necessarily the trump card Godon hoped. While she was one of only four ocean-going monitors and twice *Stonewall*'s size, she was 3 knots slower, so Page could choose to ram or run. Page agonized about surrendering, undefeated.

Her crew were his. The vessel, too. For Page, there were no good choices. His men had fulfilled their duties and were owed their due. If he made a run for a Southern port, it would be through a whole Union squadron as a pirate, liable to be hung, even if he survived. Page lamented, "I have no country to fight for, and no flag to fight under."[40]

No orders covered this eventuality. Instead, Page's sense of honor guided him.

Was the vessel his to sell? The Spaniards came in hard with an offer for $100,000, which Page felt he must decline. A second offer for $50,000 followed.

The United States was not Page's America. No Union treatise could be fair or fitting. He concluded instead, "The *Stonewall* was in a position to present herself to the Captain General, or, through him, to the Queen of Spain." He didn't do so out of any love for the Spanish Crown; the gesture seemed to be the lesser of two evils. He thought Spain's "language was indecipherable" and was keen to depart Cuba, noting, "a man could cook an egg on the iron plating in that kind of heat." "Negotiations were entered into with the authorities of Havana, which resulted in the acceptance of the Stonewall as a present, subject to the decision of the Queen of Spain."[41]

Page resolved, "By the terms of the agreement, there was advanced to the *Stonewall* the sum of $16,000 in order to pay the officers and crew what was due them, as set forth in the books of the paymaster [Curtis]. A much larger sum would have been advanced, and was suggested, but her commander was in honor bound to the crew for the payment of what was due them—the vessel being fully responsible—and he would receive nothing more."[42]

By May 19, 1865, it was done, just as Commodore Craven's court-martial for failing to fight him was coming to a close in Washington. It was a relief to all sides. The Spanish position if the Union had tried to storm her was unclear, and contemporary reports noted, "a considerable display of activity on board of the Spanish war-vessels, which consisted of three large frigates and some smaller vessels," alongside *Stonewall*.[43] The Spanish promptly turned her over to the victorious U.S. government for the same $16,000 Page had accepted, ensuring no money passed directly from Union to Confederacy.

The discretion of Spanish officials throughout left a lasting impression on Page, who noted, "An Admiral, with his attendant staff of officers, came on board to formally receive the *Stonewall*. He appreciated the painful position of the commanding officer, and before proceeding to the details involved, remarked to him, 'My barge is at your service, and Captain will attend you to the arsenal, and thence to your quarters on shore.' Officials of some governments would have avoided a Confederate officer at that time as they would have done a contagious pestilence. Captain performed the duty assigned him with all that courtesy for which the Spanish race has ever been preeminently distinguished."[44]

The U.S. secretary of state, William H. Seward, also noted that his "[g]overnment appreciates equally the promptness, the liberality, and the courtesy which have marked the proceedings of her Catholic Majesty's Government on this interesting subject."[45]

Northern newspapers, some of whom declared Portugal, "foolish and criminal" for upholding international law in the Fort Belem standoff, commended the conduct of Spain as "judicious, dignified, and in entire conformity with amity toward the United States."[46] Scarcely thirty years later, the Spanish-American War would see Cuba pass into American hands.

Marine Sergeant Prior locked all small arms in their armory and surrendered their keys. Officer King dispatched his powder monkeys from deck to magazine one last time, ordered her guns cleaned down, and ignored any suggestion to hurl her guns overboard. With the crew paid in gold and coin for every dollar they were owed, but not a penny more, paymaster Curtis closed their books on May 19. Last to finish work were Brooks's men, who methodically cleaned down and lubricated her machinery for whichever engineers took their place. Brooks's austere log simply notes, "paid off and discharged crew." With their legal situation resolved, Page accepted the *Monadnock*'s captain aboard, who, ironically, had also commanded the *Water Witch*. Their subsequent tour of the now-Spanish ship left Ronckendorff convinced he'd prevail in battle despite *Stonewall*'s greater maneuverability and with an apparent misapprehension on how thickly armored she was. Rear Admiral S. W. Godon, commanding the aging wooden side-wheeler flagship *Susquehanna* at Havana harbor, was impressed when he inspected the *Stonewall*, but he was confident *Monadnock* "would be more than her equal" as "the *Canonicus* would have crushed her, and the *Monadnock* [with two turrets] could have taken her beyond doubts."[47] Perhaps, but it's far from certain.

Although the Crimean War had seemed to signal the supremacy of new explosive shells, five years of warfare had instead showed the supremacy of armor. Of all the South's ironclad losses, only one was to direct fire. Given fair weather, while *Stonewall*'s primary 300-pound Armstrong gun was formidable, it was her ram that would most likely have given her an edge.

Page wasn't the last Confederate captain at sea. The final shot of the war was fired by the *Shenandoah* across the bow of a Union whaling prize in the Sea of Okhotsk on June 28. Her captain, James Waddel, was unmoved by a newspaper the Union prize ship produced confirming Lee's surrender, which also noted, "Mr. [President] Davis had issued a proclamation informing the Southern people that the war would be carried on with renewed vigour." [48] It was not. It would be August 2 before Waddel learned the war was over from a British merchantman. Resolving to surrender on his own terms, he made for England with his guns stowed and hull repainted. By the time he reached Liverpool on November 6, 1865, and handed himself over to the British, it had been half a year since Appomattox.

On May 29, Lincoln's successor, President Andrew Jackson, issued a proclamation of Confederate amnesty so sweeping there were as few as a dozen exclusions, including Robert E. Lee. This was still problematic for rebel agents in Europe. They might have been easily picked out by Scottish temperance campaigners for their hats and sidearms at the Little White House, but they hadn't worn a uniform, and their legality as spies was murky.

On Christmas Day 1868, President Andrew Johnson proclaimed a final amnesty for all former Confederates. Officially, only the commander of the notorious prison camp at Andersonville, where as many as thirty-two thousand Union troops were held in brutal conditions and nearly thirteen thousand died, was executed for war crimes. [49]

The Union had prevailed. America was bloody, but whole.

AFTERMATH 18

One and a half million men had served the North. At least 360,000 died. More than 800,000 had served the South. At least 260,000 died, and likely a good deal more given the paucity of records that survived the war. One in three Southern families lost a family member. It was a greater loss of life than America would bear in World War I, World War II, the Korean War, and Vietnam War combined.[1]

These losses were cruel and arbitrary. A single class of Ole Miss University recruited to A Company, Eleventh Mississippi took 100 percent casualties at Gettysburg. The Twenty-Sixth North Carolina Regiment raised across seven local bordering counties, took 714 casualties among their 800 men in a day. The Christian family of Christianburg, Virginia, alone suffered 18 killed in the war. One in thirteen went home with missing limbs, risking destitution for their families. Mississippi spent more than one-fifth of its first postwar budget on artificial limbs and care for amputee veterans.

It was a harbinger of the warfare to come, with its ironclad warships, rifling, mines and submarines, dueling artillery, automatic weapons, telegraphs, reconnaissance from the air by balloon, transport by rail, mass media coverage, and systematic medical care.

The South would never be the same again. Only Texas was largely spared direct destruction. A new Bureau of Refugees, Freedmen, and Abandoned Lands helped more than three hundred thousand former slaves with literacy and other support. Ten thousand families received land allocations most would lose to a sharecropping system that reduced them to little more than indentured laborers in the years to come. Most of America's postwar investment was in the victorious North, which laid 72,420 kilometers of railway in the following fourteen years while just 7,000 kilometers went down in the South. The plantation-based economic model was broken. Five years after the war's end, the South's cotton production was still half what it had been, and its price would plummet more than 75 percent before the nineteenth century was out.[2] With victory came occupation. The last Northern troops didn't leave until 1877.

The Thirteenth Amendment (1865) abolished slavery, the Fourteenth Amendment (1868) granted equal rights and citizenship to all men, and the Fifteenth Amendment (1870) granted black men the right to vote. Briefly, men of African heritage served as secretaries of state, mayors, congressmen, and, in at least one case, state governor in the South until instruments like poll taxes and literacy tests were weaponized against them.[3]

The African American experience would prove radically different in the North and South. The Klu Klux Klan (which would peak with more than 4 million members) was founded in Tennessee in 1866.[4] African Americans were systematically disenfranchised throughout the former Confederacy. By 1910, more than 99 percent of black men had been stripped from electoral rolls in North Carolina, for example.[5] Jim Crow laws embedded segregation. For the capable but unrepentant James Dunwoody Bulloch, it was a resumption of the natural order. "As the political dis-abilities of the whites were removed, or the disqualifying Acts were permitted to lapse, the superior race assumed its natural ascendency, and the pliant blacks were taken like sheep to the polls, and voted against the very Party who claimed their gratitude for giving them their freedom and the protection of the franchise."[6]

On June 22, Secretary Gideon Welles announced that France and Great Britain had "withdrawn from the insurgents the character of belligerents," and that their blockade was lifting. Some with the money to do so fled to England, like Judah Benjamin, the former Confederate secretary of state, who reached England on August 30, trailing rumors of missing gold and treasure.[7] At least ten thousand to twenty thousand die-hards fled the rebel states within weeks, primarily for Mexico. The rebel diaspora was recorded in Australia, Japan, Britain, Cuba, Egypt, Canada, and throughout South America where they farmed in Venezuela and Brazil, felled timber in Honduras, and served in Argentina's navy.[8] Brazil alone recorded twenty thousand U.S. immigrants over the next two decades. Within years, dreams like the Confederate colonies of New Texas and Americana were over, and a steady inflow of returnees began.[9]

The Civil War cost the federal U.S. government more than $6.8 billion. Around a twelfth of it was invested in a navy that had become the largest in the world. The Union navy had begun the war with just 90 ships, just 40 of which were in service. She finished it with 672 warships with more than 4,610 guns and more than fifty-nine thousand sailors. Of the warships, 112 were sailing ships, 560 were steamers, and 71 were ironclads; 418 had been constructed by third parties, with the remainder from their burgeoning domestic shipbuilding industry, much of it owed to "Father Neptune," the U.S. secretary of the navy, Gideon Welles. The Royal Navy of the day had fewer ships or guns, despite Britain allocating more than 17 percent of her GDP to the military.[10] The South knew they could not and should not build a mirror force to oppose them. Under Stephen Mallory, they built one of the world's most advanced—and certainly the most innovative—fleets. At their height they commanded 121 warships with more than four hundred guns, featuring all-new ironclads such as the *Stonewall*, eight torpedo boats, and two submarines.

For the most part, Southern innovations were negated by the North's greater capabilities.

While the seizure or sinking of 242 Northern merchants, whalers, and fishing vessels by the South represented a small percentage of the Union fleet, it diverted crucial resources away from the war on land. Every ship out hunting raiders was one less for rebel blockade-runners to face. The Union's commercial fleet halved during the war from more than 5,000 vessels to 2,500, though most of this is attributable to owners serving other destinations or simply adopting different flags of convenience.[11] There was only so much the 20 leading raiders raised in the South could do.

The end of the war was not the end of recriminations for the Confederacy's European collaborators. John Bigelow pursued the Arman works for years through the French legal system with appeal after appeal until the illegality of their actions was beyond doubt and 450,000 francs in damages were awarded.[12]

As the true extent of Great Britain's violation of their neutrality pact came to light, American sentiment hardened. In separate actions, reparations were sought for private damages caused by English-built ships like the *Alabama* and public damage inflicted by prolonging the war. Unsatisfied with the Crown's initial response, America pressed for an international court of arbitration. Germany and Italy had both unified as America fought. Japan was about to enter her own civil war with the *Stonewall* prominently cast. The notion of nations acting like citizens of a rules-based international community was intriguing, fifty-four years before the post–World War I League of Nations was convened.

Secretary William H. Seward summarized America's position for Minister Charles F. Adams, "It seems to the President an incontestable principle, that whatever injury is committed by the subjects of Great Britain upon the citizens of the United States, either within the British dominions or upon the high seas, in expeditions thus proceeding from British ports and posts, ought to be redressed by her Majesty's government."[13]

Great Britain's initial response wasn't just to defend these charges, but to counterclaim for the seizure of goods and damages done to British shipping as part of the Union blockade. Together they were termed the *Alabama* claims, after the South's most notorious raider. Estimated U.S. claims ranged as high as $8 billion. There's no doubt that European commercial interests prolonged the war. Some estimates, such as those of maritime historian Dr. Eric Graham, suggest it could have added as much as two years and four hundred thousand deaths to the Civil War that might otherwise have been.[14] In 1868, a package arbitrated with the new minister to the Crown, Reverdy Johnson, stalled in the U.S. Senate because it didn't cover the costs of prolonging the conflict. Whatever the true figure, these claims had to be balanced against other national goals. America wanted France out of Mexico. British claims in Canada were unresolved. At one point, land swaps were discussed for British West Indies and Canadian territories.[15] In 1870, five commissioners on each side resolved land and sea boundaries between the United States and Canada and turned to the *Alabama* claims. Britain expressed regret for treaty violations that ranged from Scottish warship production on the River Clyde to *Shenandoah*'s shelter in her Australian colony. The tribunal awarded the United States $15.5 million in damages, which Great Britain paid in full, but without apology, on September 13, 1873.[16] To administer the resulting Treaty of Washington, a Joint International Tribunal of Arbitration was raised in Geneva, Switzerland, with unprecedented support from its five founding seats: the United States, Great Britain, the Kingdom of Italy, the Swiss Confederation, and the Empire of Brazil. It sat where the Geneva Convention for the Treatment of Wounded in War had been developed in 1864, after the horrors witnessed in European and American theaters.

There would be no reunions for the men of the *Stonewall*. Paymaster Richard W. Curtis was there as each crew member signed on. He was there as they signed out, were paid off, and began to scatter around the world. *Stonewall*'s Lieutenant Barron, who'd served on the *Virginia* at Hampton Roads, made for Argentina. Lieutenant William Whittle later joined him there after the *Shenandoah* cruise, though both ultimately returned to the American South.[17]

South Carolina's chief engineer, William Param Brooks, a veteran of the *Sumter* and an *Alabama* survivor, whose records document the *Stonewall*'s passage to the United States as the *Nuetsra Salud del Carmen*, headed to Spain, where he served as an engineer in the navy for eleven years before returning to Savannah, Georgia, and the merchant marine with the Ocean Steamship Company. He died on April 19, 1889.[18]

First lieutenant George A. Borchert found his brother had died a prisoner of war, and his father was mired in compensation claims for their family's bakery with the Union. There seemed little to return to. He made for Mexico instead, meeting up with his friend, and applying for land. Both went on to serve first in the Mexican navy, then Colombia's, before they met a bloody end on September 1, 1867, shot and stabbed by thieves, when sent by General Gutierrez to investigate thefts from the steamer *Rayo*. Borchert's remains were initially buried locally, before repatriation home for his final resting place in the American South.[19]

Paymaster Curtis returned to England on the former blockade-runner *Ptarmigan*. With the question of whether rebel crews were pirates running hot in the press, in November, he sailed for Queensland, Australia, on the *Legion of Honoras*. When he purchased the 1,100-acre Endcliffe Vale Estate shortly after his arrival, he paid cash and lived near Union veteran James Latimer.[20] Indigenous relations were fraught at the time. When a native man murdered another on Curtis's land in 1868, it was such a stain on his reputation that when he sold his land to a winemaker and moved to Clayfield, Brisbane, his children chose to stay behind. He remade his life in government service as the first agent appointed to accompany vessels to the South Sea Islands in 1871. His was a rare story of reform, working honorably to see that South Seas labor for Queensland, Australia was paid fairly and not exploited with so-called black-birding abductions and indentured labor. Still under thirty, he returned to Brisbane and married Coroline Amelia Bolden in 1872. He had four further children he supported by working with Queensland Fire Insurance, the Mutual Assurance Society, and, finally, as a railway arbitrator before his unexplained death in 1905, drowning in the Brisbane River.[21] Even half a world away, he remained a son of the South. When he was buried in Toowong Cemetery, it was alongside six other rebels.[22]

Matthew Fontaine Maury, who'd leveraged his social and scientific standing with mixed results as a rebel agent, made such as impression on Emperor Maximilian in Mexico postwar that he was appointed director of the Astronomical Observatory in Mexico City, and later, as Imperial Commissioner of Immigration and Honorary Counsel of State. He regretted nothing and went as far as placing a notice in the Mexican *Times* on November 4, to boast, "I have neither directly or indirectly asked pardon nor other favor from the President of the United States."[23] Men like Brigadier General James E. Slaughter, and the former governors of Louisiana and Texas, followed him south, but grand schemes to have Brazil buy the South's slaves or to accommodate one hundred thousand Southerners (and their slaves under seven years of indentured labor) amounted to nothing. When Emperor Maximilian's largesse waned in 1866, many Southerners decided that they could face a united America after all. Maury spent two years in England before quietly returning home in late 1868.[24]

Maximilian, a former vice admiral of the Austrian navy, had been wise enough to turn down an offer to assume the Mexican monarchy in 1859, in the aftermath of war and default. After France invaded Mexico in 1862 in pursuit of its debts, Maximilian was unwise enough to accept a repeat offer, and was installed in 1864, trying, and failing, to find a middle ground between the country's factions, despite a modernizing agenda that delivered new currency, highways, education, hospitals, and (incomplete) indigenous reconciliation. His reign was brief. By 1866, the U.S. government was shamelessly raising bonds, funding mercenaries, supplying arms, and securing themselves mining leases and more despite claims of neutrality in Mexican affairs. When French forces withdrew under pressure from the United States and Prussia, Maximilian's wife and advisors followed, but he chose to stay. After he was handed over by his remnant army near Querétaro without a final battle, the victorious insurgent Benito Juarez ended the country's regal experiment by lining him up against a wall, aged just thirty-four. His final words were fatalistic, "Men of my class and origins are appointed by God to be the happiness of people or their martyrs."[25]

The escaped slave and *Niagara* crewman, William B. Gould, who lamented not engaging the *Stonewall* in Spain, wrote of the final Union victory, "On my return on board I heard the Glad Tidings that the Stars and Stripes had been planted over the Capital of the D—nd Confedercy by the invicible Grant." "While we honor the living soldiers who have done so much we must not forget to whisper for fear of desturbeing the Glorious sleep of the ma[ny] who have fallen. Mayrters to the cau[se] of Right and Equality." After an honorable discharge from the navy, he married the former slave Cornelia Williams Read in Nantucket; he settled in Dedham, Massachusetts, working as a plasterer. Together they had eight children, six of which followed his service in the military. He became a town elder and commander in the veteran's organization Grand Army of the Republic. He spoke at town festivities in what is now commemorated as William B. Gould Park until he passed away at eighty-five in 1923.[26]

The Confederate secretary of the navy, Stephen Mallory, served out the war with achievements out of all proportion to Southern naval resources. He was imprisoned for a year after the conflict before being pardoned by President Andrew Johnson in 1866, but he was barred from holding public office. He remained a vocal opponent of black suffrage and returned to Florida to practice law until his death in Pensacola, Florida in 1873.[27]

Northern shipwright and inventor John Ericsson went on to develop a series of naval concepts, including the caloric engine (which used air instead of steam), the torpedo, and John Phillip Holland's submarine experiments.[28] Monitor-class ironclads were his legacy. He returned to his native Sweden to evolve their design at Motala Warf in Norrköping, with a lead ship named for him. Three further designs followed, including the *Kanonbåten Sölve*, which can be seen in the maritime museum in Gothenburg.[29] Brazil, Norway, and Russia also pursued their design principles.[30] Ericsson lived to the age of eighty-five, and even on his deathbed, he was still working on a final design for a revolutionary solar "sun motor."[31]

The new South—the defeated South—was not for *Stonewall*'s Captain Thomas J. Page. He moved to Argentina with his sons Philip Nelson and Frederick, where he was welcomed by a growing Confederate community, befriended President Bartolomé Mitre, and moved in the highest circles. While he often spoke of the simple pleasures of running a plantation, he missed command and longed for the sea. When General Urquiza offered Page the opportunity to reshape their navy, he accepted.

He proposed a defensive system spanning the capital Buenos Aires, the island Martín Garcia, and as far as Ensenada, backed by two new ironclads and twin corvettes. He even reached across Civil War lines to advocate for the electric torpedo ship developed by Swedish American John Ericsson. President Mitre's successor, Domingo Faustino Sarmiento, said yes to it all. Page returned to England to supervise the construction of what would become the *El Plata* and *Los Andes* and gunboats *Paraná* and *Uruguay*. While he published a strangely ghostwritten or coauthored account of his war, he wasn't given to poetic license, and made no comparisons between the two nations he served. With his projects delivered, he finally retired to ranch with his son, Philip Nelson, who'd matriculated from the Virginia Military Institute, fought in the Battle of New Market, and served out the war in the army.

Page remained a sheep and cattle farmer in Concordia, Argentina, until he was coaxed into following his mother's heritage and relocating to Florence, Italy, as secretary to the Argentine diplomatic mission in 1884. He retired to farm contentedly once again outside Rome in a community sprinkled with Americans who knew him as "the Commodore." His service was complete. When Italy offered him an admiral's commission in the navy, he turned them down. He farmed peacefully until his death, aged eighty-one, in 1889.[32] Though he'd never set foot on American soil again, he distanced himself from his more bitter contemporaries with a dying wish that he be buried with the stars and stripes. He was laid to rest in a Protestant ceremony with the simple epitaph, "Thomas Jefferson Page of Virginia; Captain, U.S.N. and C.S.N., Explorer, Christian Gentleman."[33]

By war's end, Prussia's Otto Von Bismarck was a man on the rise, and Emperor Napoleon III, who worked with Arman to make *Stonewall* possible, was a sick man. His efforts to extract concessions from Prussia after she defeated Austria in 1866 started a clock ticking down to his own defeat in the field in the 1870 Battle of Sedan in the Franco-Prussian War, where some suggested he'd sought a glorious martial death. Instead, he was deposed to enable the Third French Republic, and he died a quiet death in England later that year.[34]

As a spy, Bulloch was excluded from the postwar amnesty afforded to most Confederate officers. He settled across the channel in Liverpool, close to the yards that had built the Laird rams and the offices of Confederate financiers where he'd signed papers to build or modify almost two hundred ships, hat on, cigar in hand. Spycraft had become second nature to him. He made a number of clandestine trips to the United States to visit family and complete a naval history of the War of 1812 with his father. He never forgot the cause. When he died in 1901, his occupation was listed as "Naval Representative of the late Confederate States of America (retired)." His estate passed to his nephew Theodore Roosevelt who became president of the United States later that year.[35]

John Slidell, who'd commissioned six ships for the Confederacy in Europe, stayed in Bordeaux, France, after the war before shifting to England after the Franco-German War for a final year at Cowes, on the Isle of Wight, before dying aged seventy-eight in 1871.[36]

Lucien Arman, who contracted with Bulloch to build the *Stonewall* and returned it to Confederate hands after Danish service, found himself hopelessly overextended by his shipyard and steam engine production at Le Havre and under siege by those seeking reparations. The paper trail from his desk to at least six rebel vessels is irrefutable, and rumors abounded of payments on others. To Lucien, it had never been personal or ideological. It was just business. By 1868, his former ties to Napoleon III meant little, and his creditors couldn't be stalled any longer. Bankrupt, he resigned from all public offices and had his name brought so low in the press that his son changed his family name to Arman de Caillavet. He died in Bordeaux in 1873, aged sixty-one.[37] Arman wasn't alone. The collapse of Southern dollars, IOUs, and futures dragged a series of firms under in the aftermath of the war, their primary financial partner Trent, Trenholm & Company among them.

Confederate president Jefferson Davis finished the war with a greatly diminished reputation. It was only in April 1865 that he surrendered control of the army to General Lee. General P. G. T. Beauregard wrote, "Davis was loathed by much of his military, Congress and the public—even before the Confederacy died on his watch. If he were to die today, the whole country would rejoice at it."[38] He was a man of contradictions. While he'd humbly telegraphed Governor John J. Pettus, on the outbreak of war to "judge what Mississippi requires of me and place me accordingly," he maneuvered himself into the rebel presidency with such unseemly haste that Texas was excluded from the vote. His wife, Varina Davis, claimed when he was appointed president, "Reading that telegram he looked so grieved that I feared some evil had befallen our family." When Abraham Lincoln offered to resupply the Union-held Fort Sumter but not reinforce it to prevent any escalation, however, it was Jefferson who calmly ordered the Southern assault on April 12 that started the war. He moved in elite circles, never traveling as widely or consulting as deeply as Lincoln, though he expressed deep regret at his assassination. Davis feuded with Vice President Alexander H. Stephens, with Congress, and with his generals. Once his mind was set, it stayed that way in the face of all advice, for example, in his inability to grasp the cause and effect of money printing on inflation. He dissolved the Confederacy on May 5, 1865. When he was captured fleeing south on May 10, caricatures of the time claimed he was hiding in his wife's shawl. Someone had to be responsible for all this. By May 19, he was briefly in irons, before being reunited with his wife and daughter. Though the House of Representatives voted 105–19 to take him to trial June 11, 1866, it never happened. Within two years, his parole was paid by wealthy patrons, and he moved back to the finest circles of Lennoxville, Quebec.

Travel suited him. He toured Cuba and Europe, dining with sympathizers and suppliers. Work did not. He refused university roles and commercial offices he thought below his station and pursued a string of prestigious European offices for which he was never considered. His pardon was included in Johnson's Christmas 1868 proclamation, and his treason case was finally dismissed on February 15, 1869. Failure left him embittered. Bitterness inured him to success. He outlived his brother and sons, backed failed ice-making ventures, and exchanged lawsuits with developers, investors, his brother's investors, and even the family of the widow at whose estate he wrote his memoirs, who were cut out of her will in his favor. He too remained unrepentant. His claims the South was "cheated not conquered" make uncomfortable reading for their similarity to Germany's claims they were not defeated in World War I but "stabbed in the back." He deemed "Yankee and Negroe" rule "oppressive" and raged that the postwar "night of despotism" gave rights to blacks that made them "more idle and ungovernable than before." His self-serving "The Rise and Fall of the Confederate Government" speaking engagements and the revisionist work of the Southern Historical Society, among others, went some way to rehabilitating his name. He died holding his wife's hand at his Brierfield plantation on December 5, 1889. Perhaps nothing sums Davis up better than a burial where an American flag-draped coffin hid his Confederate uniform and a sword he'd worn in the Black Hawk War. Men like Davis knew that the South had fallen but dreamed she would rise again.

After her pseudonym *Sphinx*, Danish service as *Stærkodder*, a second nom de plume as *Olinde* as she was transferred to Confederate hands and recommissioned as the *Stonewall*, chief engineer W. P. Brooks's steam log finally documents the five-nation ship being recommissioned as the *"Fragata H. Nuestra Salud del Carmen"* (Carmen's health) by Spanish forces postwar.[39] Notionally a Spanish warship from July 1865, she sailed for America's shores escorted by two ships that might otherwise have confronted her—the side-wheelers *Rhode Island* (who had the original *Monitor* under tow when she foundered) and *Hornet* (835 tons), a captured Confederate runner that would support rebels in Cuba ten years hence—departing October 21 and arriving November 23.[40]

In an unfortunate demonstration of the five-nation ship's ram, she failed to spot a coal schooner off Smith Island overnight on October 22 in Chesapeake waters reputedly home to a serpentine monster, and sheered it neatly in two, though thankfully without loss of life. The *Stonewall*—which had shed the name *Nuetsra Salud del Carmen* like a skin as soon as it was home—was taken under tow to Port Royal, South Carolina, where she was described as being in poor condition and compromised by leaks.

She was decommissioned in the same Washington, DC, Navy Yard where the *Monitor* had been repaired after the world's first ironclad battle, and where Abraham Lincoln's assassin would later be held. Countless Northern naval officers, many of them who'd served aboard the *Monitor*'s successors, toured her enviously. The yards, already home to the Potomac Flotilla, were packed with warships big and small, wood and iron, so tightly bound you could almost walk from one side to the other across them in a show of force—redundant now, with the war over—the Confederacy could never equal.

Stonewall remained one of the most powerful warships afloat, but the Union's focus was on demobilizing more than seven hundred thousand troops in barely twelve weeks.[41] For two years, she waited at Washington Navy Yard while the Union navy worked through the organization, retention, or disposal of the world's largest naval fleet. Debate raged over *Stonewall*'s place—if any—in a U.S. navy dominated by monitor derivatives. Secretary Welles was against hurried fleet disposals, arguing, "It is still wise—the wisest—economy to cherish the navy, to husband its resources, to invite new supplies of youthful courage and skill to its service, to be amply supplied with all needful facilities and preparations for efficiency, and thus to hold within prompt and easy reach its vast and salutary power for the national defence and self-vindication."[42] President Johnson was not persuaded, and American warships were laid up, paid off, sold, and scrapped at such a rate that it would be World War II before America's fleet was world-leading again. It was 1867 before the decision to sell *Stonewall* was made. America's debts at the time were formidable. In 1860, the nation owed less than $60 million. By 1863, it was more than $1 billion. At war's end, national debt exceeded $2.7 billion.[43] A European buyer was expected. England had acquired the twin Laird rams so France could not. France took Dunderberg so Prussia couldn't, and so on. In the end, her future lay in Japan.

Could the South have won? Speculation and counterfactuals started as soon as the war stopped. What if this order was given, or that action taken? Most focused on individual decisions, leaders, and battles, which failed to account for the economic fundamentals that shaped the conflict. Many framed the war in terms of the United States having won their independence from the British Empire at an arguably greater disadvantage. Stalemate would have been a rebel victory, in effect, or as James McPherson put it, "The South could 'win' the war by not losing," but "the North could win only by winning."[44]

There is a strong case Confederate president Jefferson Davis should have exported more cotton on neutral shipping earlier, and that iron diverted to domestic warships would have been better used on railways to offset the loss of their rivers. Could the Trent Affair have dragged Britain into breaking the North's blockade? Was there a greater role for guerilla warfare? Could slaves in their hundreds of thousands have fought to win their emancipation? Perhaps their greatest chance was if Lincoln had been defeated in the 1864 election. By June 1864, General Lee conceded to General Jubal Early, "We must destroy the Federal army before they get to the James River. If they get there, it will become a siege, and then it will be a mere question of time." When the river was crossed before the month was out, he fought on regardless. After that point, with Lincoln committed to victory and General Grant willing to stay in contact with the South no matter the cost, the die was cast. "You must endeavour to enjoy the pleasure of doing good. That is all that makes life valuable," Lee wrote to his invalid wife, adding, "When I measure my own by that standard I am filled with confusion and despair."[45]

Single actors or actions could be more impactful at sea. *Stonewall* was the focus of many what-if scenarios. Had the rebel's European-built fleet been realized, the *Stonewall*, her sister ship *Cheops*, and their four escorts, together with the Laird-build ships that became HMS *Scorpion* and HMS *Wyvern*, had the potential to inflict major damage on the Union navy and potentially the war at large.

While their very existence was a remarkable achievement, the South's domestically built ironclads consumed far more resources than they won. Without the rotating-turret technology of the North, the South fought at a further disadvantage. Some of their improvised ironclads, like the *Memphis*, were simply not viable. Cruelly, most were destroyed by their own forces, like the *Atlanta* (who grounded herself attacking the monitor *Weekhaven*), the *Columbia*, the *Texas*, and so on. Some were destroyed while still under construction by accidents or enemy action like the *Mobile*. Only one was ever lost to direct Union action. Worse still, a number were captured and went on to serve their enemy, like the *Columbia*, *Tennessee II*, and *Texas*.

For all their shortfalls in experience, the South showed her crews could match the North under favorable circumstances, as with the *Chicora* (four guns, spar torpedo) and *Palmetto States*, which severely damaged the *Keyston State*, drove the *Mercedita* to surrender, and forced remaining Union vessels to retreat.[46] There can be little question that *Stonewall* had the potential to sink any single ship in the Union fleet, though she would have done so outnumbered and at great risk, depending on the weather state and her opponents, and arguably far too late in the day for it to matter on a strategic scale. Union secretary of war Edwin Stanton's reaction to the less-capable *Virginia* suggested a single ship could change the "whole character of the war."[47]

The ram ship concept was certainly proved. The cotton-clad *General Bragg* rammed the *Cincinnati*, and General Van Dorn struck *Mound City* in the early Battle of Plum Point Bend in May 1862, marking the first instance of ironclads being sunk.[48] The tactic was employed throughout the war, as with the *Virginia* against the *Cumberland*, *Monarch* against the *Queen of the West*, the namesake *Stonewall Jackson* against *Varuna*, or the subsequent sinking of the U.S.-built Italian *Re d'Italia* in 1866 by the Austrian SMS *Erzherzog* at the Battle of Lissa on the other side of the world.

Despite the confidence of the Union captains who toured *Stonewall* in Havana, it's clear she could potentially destroy any of her blocking ships individually, and break through their lines. From there, projections become more clouded. Would conditions have enabled her to operate her forward 10-inch gun? Would she survive each major collision—likely a deathblow for her victim—with her key machinery, sternposts, rudders, and screws intact? Here, chance would play her part. Even a vessel she'd fatally wounded could check *Stonewall* if their rigging fouled her screws, or if a stern shot compromised her rudders.

The 7,000-ton ironclad ram *Dunderberg* (fourteen guns) had started construction before the *Stonewall*, but it was only completed after the war. Refused acceptance by the Union navy, she was acquired instead by Napoleon III of France over his navy's objections, where she was relegated to the reserve before brief and uneventful service in the Franco-Prussian War.[49]

The ram ship's window was closing fast. Its last comparable expression was 1865's 1,900-ton, four-gun ironclad *Huascar*, which served the Peruvian navy in her war with Spain and, later in the War of the Pacific that set Peru and Bolivia against Chile.[50] As shipborne firepower and accuracy evolved, no further rams followed, though there'd be echoes of them in World War

I tactics against surface submarines, like HMS *Dreadnought* sinking U-29 or tragic accidents like the HMS *Camperdown* sheering through the HMS *Victory*, the pride of the British fleet, with the loss of 358 lives.[51]

Union forces were not idle while *Stonewall* was developed. If *Stonewall* had attempted to confront them directly, the heavy ironclad *New Ironsides*—with a reinforced bow of her own and vastly superior firepower, though with lesser maneuverability—would have faced her. *Stonewall* would have been on surer footing against successive Union monitor designs, which ultimately proved to be a design dead end. Five inches of hot-rolled European armor—significantly stronger than that cast in the South—would likely have held up to their turreted guns. *Stonewall*'s ability to turn almost within her own length meant she had every chance of striking them with her ram, and their low seaboard meant once they were holed, they were lost. The French *Gloire* and English *Warrior* remained the reference designs for what would follow, ignoring monitors and rams alike.

The Northern blockade worked. J. Thomas Scharf, in his *History of the Confederate States Navy*, concludes it "shut the Confederacy out from the world, deprived it of supplies, weakened its military and naval strength."[52] The fact that more than 80 percent of Confederate goods put to sea successfully ran the Union blockade is somewhat misleading. In the four years before the Civil War's outbreak, Southern ports averaged more than twenty thousand merchant ships per year. Only eight thousand—smaller but faster than their predecessors—could do so through the Civil War. The South smuggling a million bales of cotton to foreign markets pales against the 10 million that had shipped before.

If the Laird rams, or their French-built successors *Sphinx* and *Cheops*, had opened a window in the blockade, larger, slower, and more efficient ships could have steamed through. Every inbound ship would add to supply. Every outbound ship would raise her income. Regional hubs like Nassau could have been bypassed altogether. More iron could mean more rail. More rail could mean less wastage and could free more agricultural workers to fight. In January 1863, when rebel forces captured *Westfield*, *Morning Light*, and *Velocity* and sank *Harriet Lane* and *Hatteras* in quick succession in Texan waters, it provided a significant window for resupply, for example.[53]

Ultimately, the Confederate navy's successes—like *Palmetto State* and *Chicora* over Union forces at Charleston Harbor, South Carolina—were tactical, not strategic. Even if a breakthrough Southern design had sunk or scattered Union forces at the mouth of the Mississippi, it couldn't silence the forts now in Yankee hands or force the retreat of the bluecoats on her banks. Ports further south were a greater opportunity. The earlier we imagine new European-built warships arriving for the South, the more impact they could have had, for example, sinking the *Southfield* forced the Union blocking squadron to withdraw and secured Plymouth and a pool of resources that the South drew on for years. Their window of opportunity was arguably still open when the Laird rams were lost to Clarence Yonge's testimony, but by April–May 1865 as *Stonewall* approached the United States, there were no material land forces left to exploit any success on the coast.

When Lincoln held a conference with Rear Admiral David Dixon Porter and generals Grant and Sherman on the steamer *River Queen* at City Point, Virginia, on March 28, 1865, it wasn't the *Stonewall* they discussed, it was already how to manage the South's surrender. The end was in sight. While inspecting a trio of battle-damaged monitors at Fort Fisher, North Carolina, in the Washington Navy Yard later that month, Lincoln was already musing about a quiet retirement in Illinois.

The South's crash course of domestic shipbuilding failed. More Union monitors were destroyed by mines and shore fire than by any Confederate warship. More Southern ships were destroyed by the Confederacy in retreat than by the Union in battle. Bulloch—the father of the Confederates' European shipbuilding—was sanguine about *Stonewall*'s potential by 1865: "They had got such a firm grip of the passes of the river, and of every approach to New Orleans, that an attempt to displace them, or even to make such a naval demonstration in that quarter as would cause them serious apprehension, would have required a far greater force than one small ironclad ram."[54] If there is a counterargument to this, it's the defining influence *Stonewall* had on Japan's civil war.

So-called torpedo mines destroyed *Cairo*, *Commodore Jones*, and *Albemarle* and severely damaged others like the *Commodore Barney* and *New Ironsides*. Mines could be made in a wider range of locations, with fewer resources, and do as much to hold Union forces at arm's length as any gunboat. Even then, they could slow the Union, but they couldn't stop her. The South's relentless innovation—the submarine, balloons, torpedo mines, or the Hall's rockets envisaged for smaller warships—were a concession of weakness.

It is hard to build a case for any Confederate warship having the kind of fever-dream impact Samuel Barron, or a more moderate Bulloch, had imagined. The numbers against them were overwhelming. If *Stonewall* had shattered the Union squadron at Port Royal, she'd be focused on re-coaling while the North moved whole squadrons toward her.

At war's end, the *Niagara*, which let Stonewall pass her twice, was in Japanese waters that *Stonewall* would one day dominate. Like so many others, she was promptly decommissioned postwar, idling until 1885 before she was broken up. Her partner in ignominy, the *Sacramento*, steamed home from Ireland postwar and was recommissioned in 1866 for service in Chinese and

Japanese waters that partially overlapped with *Stonewall*'s, before her grounding and destruction in India in June 1867.[55]

The Laird rams HMS *Wyvern* and HMS *Scorpion*, the would-be *Mississippi* and *North Carolina*, served the English Channel fleet until they were derigged from barques to schooners and dispatched to guard Hong Kong and Bermuda, respectively. Neither fought, and both proved even more difficult to handle than *Stonewall*. So much so, naval architect Edward James Reed recorded of *Wyvern*, "on one occasion her behaviour at sea was so bad that she had to be brought head to wind in order to prevent her shipping large, and, of course, dangerous, quantities of water, the extreme angle of roll rising to 27 degrees each way."[56]

Ultimately, while the *Stonewall* could have impacted the war, even changed it at a tactical level, as the one surviving element of a whole ironclad fleet conceived in Europe's leading shipyards, there was little she could do at a strategic level.

The irony of the Confederate navy's last flagship wasn't that she would dominate her nation's waters and determine the outcome of a civil war that had waged for years.

It was that exactly that would happen, in of all places, Japan.

WAR-TORN MAPS 19

All over the world, maps were being redrawn, not with what was right, but with what was possible.

Italy's wars of independence carved a new nation from the Austrian Empire. Prussia's rise came at the expense of Denmark, and displaced Austria as the leader of the German people. After the Opium Wars, China was being ruthlessly exploited by English business interests. Mexico's independence was carved out from the French Empire. The American plains wars opened the west, at the cost of America's first nations. The Ottoman Empire held herself together with the suppression of revolts in Greece and elsewhere.

Stonewall had flown four flags and served two navies without firing a shot. Despite her inauspicious start, the five-nation ship was about to take on the defining role James Dunwoody Bulloch and Samuel Barron had dreamed for her. It was in Japan that she rammed and was rammed. It was in Japan she was the fool to fight a fort, and win. It was in Japan she was stormed. And it was in Japan that she settled a civil war and set a nation on a new path. The five-nation ship's story was just beginning.

Nineteenth-century Japan was the child of three revered national unifiers. Before them, in the Sengoku ("warring states") period from 1467 to 1573, Japan was wracked by division and conflict. After Oda Nobunaga, Toyotomi Hideyoshi, and Tokugawa Ieyasu, a unified Japan, massively influenced by previous high-Chinese culture, was ready to carve out her own path.[1] It would later be said of them in verse:

> If the cuckoo does not sing, kill it. This was Nobunaga.
> If the cuckoo does not sing, coax it. This was Hideyoshi.
> If the cuckoo does not sing, wait. This was Ieyasu.[2]

The first was Oda Nobunaga.

Sixteenth-century Japan was comparable in many ways to China's own "warring states" period. The shogun, Ashikaga Yoshiteru, controlled little beyond the reach of his direct forces, and the country was a patchwork of divided loyalties, conditional support, and unacknowledged independence. Religions and philosophies rose and fell. The chaos was symbolized with Japan's equivalent strategy game to chess, Shogi, which changed so all pieces were a single color and could switch sides, dead pieces could return, and whose side they were on depended on which way they faced.

Nobunaga hardly seemed to be the answer. He was an erratic youth, dismissed as "the Fool of Owari" who ran with children below his station. On his father's death in 1551 when he was sixteen, what should have been his formal entry from the isolated palace to public life was marred by him arriving late in inappropriate dress, to hurl incense at his father in state and upend the offertory table. It was said his father-in-law first saw him dressed like a peasant, seated backwards on his horse, eating fruit from a bag. Although he was the clear heir, his reputation saw multiple rivals express their claims. If his critics were surprised when he raised a thousand men to back his, they were shocked when he overcame invasion by the rival daimyo lord Imagawa Yoshimoto and won the ensuing peace with shrewd prisoner exchanges that included Tokugawa Ieyasu, a dynamic figure raised as a hostage, who later founded the Tokugawa line of shoguns. In 1552, Nobunaga fought off an alliance of his younger brother with the rival Owari province. It was becoming clear he was a man who could gather power. All that remained was to show he could be worthy of it.

In 1553, in a great personal blow, his confidant and mentor Hirate Masahide, a warrior-advisor to the shogun and emperor, composed a letter defining the man Nobunaga should be and committed ritual suicide—*seppuku*—as the ultimate demonstration of the honor he demanded. It was a lightning bolt. No story from that day on is anything like those before it, and the temple he founded in his honor became the place Nobunaga contemplated his hardest tasks.

In 1554, he defeated the Imagawa clan, who'd seized Owari province as soon as they'd sensed weakness. Still just twenty, he learned to be ruthless. When he broke the siege of his rebel uncle at Muraki castle, he forced his suicide. One by one he flushed out conflicts with his father-in-law, his younger brother—who dragged down the Oda clan with him—and his son. It was 1559 before his rule in Owari was absolute and he could contemplate Japan's future. He wasn't just a refocused man; he was an ambitious one. His father's kingdom wasn't his goal; Japan itself was. On he went, isolating enemies where he could, defeating them where he must, creating ever-more complex webs of influence.

Nobunaga didn't just find his voice. He found gunpowder.

As Japan's de facto military leader from 1568 to 1582, Nobunaga was known for his pioneering use of firearms, which broke the line of Ashikaga shoguns and consolidated his power in Kyoto. The general then turned statesman, launching a new currency, opening limited Western trade, and even permitting limited Christianity as a possible bulwark against growing Buddhist influence. He continued to look for talent, not status, going as far as recognizing the African-born samurai Yasuke. His leading general, Toyotomi Hideyoshi, had been born Hiyoshimaru in 1536 as a peasant's son and rose the hard way, as a page to a lesser retainer of the Tōtōmi daimyo and foot soldier, before his recognition as a samurai. As the first great unifier displaced daimyo after daimyo, he created a wake of new lords behind him. In 1568, Hideyoshi joined their ranks, and adopted a third name, Hashiba, Lord of Chikuzen.[3]

Just as American Civil War ironclads built on lessons from the Crimean War, Asia's first ironclads were shaped by what came before them. Well before their nineteenth-century expression in Europe, the ironclad was born in Japan and Korea. In sixteenth- and seventeenth-century waters, their last world in naval technology, albeit close to shore, was the atakebune ship.

With no strong central authority, Japan's profile at sea for much of the sixteenth century was shaped by the Wakō pirates plundering China's coastal trade. As power began to consolidate approaching the seventeenth century, these forces had become a polyglot Asian fleet, with fewer and fewer Japanese hands. If gunpowder had helped Nobunaga dominate on land, he was as convinced it could at sea. He commissioned six upscaled Ō-atakebune ("great atakebune") or Tekkōsen (ironships) that rose, story by story like a floating castle, with unprecedented plate armor and gun power.[4] While formidable, their ponderous seakeeping and tremendous weight made them hard to maneuver and poor gun platforms when they did. On this scale, their actual performance was almost secondary to the message they sent to Japanese pirates and opposing forces in Korean waters.

Portuguese missionaries reported, "Their structure above the surface is fully covered by iron, and there is a tower on the deck. Bridges are covered by iron, and no wood is exposed. And whole parts are gilded very beautifully. These were worth admiring, I sometimes entered in the ships. I measured the length of one there, it was 19 jou (36.3 meter[s]) long. These ships astonished several Portuguese who looked inside."[5] Like the Union's monitor classes, while they were potent in their day, they represented a dead end in design. The future was not with ships with rowing decks that had to be towed into battle.

In concept they were like overscale hyperextensions of medieval Euro-pean ships with raised forecastle and aftercastle that applied land-based con-cepts to the sea. Just as the Confederacy and Union applied very different ironclad concepts, Korea took a different line with answering Geobukseon warships that bore an uncanny resemblance to the low-slung improvised Confederate ironclad *Manassas*. These smaller oar-and-sail turtle-shell-shaped ships, complete with sulfur smoke billowing from ornamental bow dragons, featured hammered iron over their roof, variously described as in plates, hexagons, or spikes, and featured prominently in Admiral Yi Sun-Sin's later defense of Korean Joseon against Japanese invasion.

Just when the region seemed Nobunaga's to shape, in 1582, his samurai general, Akechi Mitsuhide, turned on him for reasons lost to history. When ordered west with thirteen thousand troops against the Mōri clan, he instead declared, "The enemy is at Honnō-ji," and led them to surround Nobunaga at a tea ceremony. Did Nobunaga think of Masahide's example almost three decades earlier? Nobunaga did not beg or plead or threaten. He asked noth-ing from his bodyguards, instead directing his retainers to burn the temple and prevent his head being taken, before drawing his sword and committing *seppuku*.[6] While his son escaped, he was later surrounded at Nijō castle and killed. Nobunaga's line had ended, but others would achieve his vision.

Though Mitsuhide rewarded his troops by sacking Azuchi castle, the imperial court was horrified, and his efforts to find patronage were rebuffed. When word of his lord's death reached General Toyotomi Hideyoshi, he signed an immediate peace deal with the Mōri, and after a four-day force-march, his twenty thousand men scattered rebel forces anchored between Shōryūji castle and Mount Tennozan on the Yodo River. Mitsuhide was killed ignobly by the bandit leader Nakamura Chōbei.[7]

There was no rest for Hideyoshi as Nobunaga's sons splintered into fac-tions. Hideyoshi pledged allegiance to his grandson. The daimyo Tokugawa Ieyasu was for his second son. Others, bordering him, rallied to his third. Within a year, he'd driven the defeated lord-sponsor of the third son to *sep-puku*. In 1584, after inconclusive skirmishing, he concluded an alliance with the damiyo Tokugawa Ieyasu, and they campaigned together thereafter faithfully. He ruled, not through any son at all, but by amassing the greatest military force seen to that time. To win the ensuing peace, Hideyoshi set about rebuilding symbols of power like Osaka castle, and invested heavily in naval forces.

Officially, even then, he was subordinate to the semi-divine emperor, and notionally held the role of chancellor to the emperor. The emperor blessed him with the new family name Toyotomi, so his primacy would survive him.

When Moti Terumoto resumed hostilities, he did so alone, and his defeat was quickly followed by those of the Shikoku and Kyushu islands. The emperor acquiesced to it all.

In contrast to the European model of the divinely appointed king (or queen) for life, Japanese power was often exercised from behind the throne. Having consolidated power, Hideyoshi notionally stepped down to the role of taikō, a title implying retirement, and installed his nephew, Toyotomi Hidetsugu, as the new kampaku chancellor. In practice, rule was still his, and preparations for new ambitions in Korea, Ming China (1368–1644), the Philippines, and even India quickly began.

If anything, Hideyoshi was more ambitious than his predecessor. After his subjugation of the eastern Kantō and Ōu districts in 1590, he launched a new daimyo council, and began raising 158,000 troops and 9,200 sailors, many of them former Wako pirates, for his ambitions in Korea. Advocates said it was a divine vision. Detractors said it was a diversion to prevent revolts like Mitsuhide's.

His 1592 invasion of Korea started brightly with the seizure of Port Busan's forts, and a defeat of Korean general Sin Ip at the battle of Chungju with gunpowder the Korean's lacked, sending Korea's King Seonjo fleeing northward. Another one hundred thousand troops were marshalling in northern Kyushu. Vast supply depots had been assembled. Accessing either required control of the 193-kilometer strait between them, and here, his troubles began.

Every time Japan's fleet gathered to sweep a Korean navy, reduced at one point to as few as five turtle ships, from the Yellow and Southern seas, Korean admiral Yi Sun-shin overcame them. In the cataclysmic Battle of Hansan Island (August 14, 1592), Korean forces shattered the Japanese instead, sinking fifty-nine out of seventy-three enemy ships with more than nine thousand sailors lost. Not all of it was down to the Korea Geobukseon turtle ships' more practicable and maneuverable application of iron. Sun-shin's "crane wing maneuver" used a fake retreat to lure the Japanese into devastating preranged gunfire. Though little known, together with the Battle of Salamis, the Siege of Calais, and the Battle of Trafalgar, many consider it one of the most influential naval battles of all time.[8] Japan's advance stopped. Dwindling supplies, local uprisings generated by their brutal occupation, and Chinese reinforcements for their Korean vassal-state forced Japanese troops to consolidate their occupation in a line below Seoul.[9] Five years of stalemate followed as neither side could displace the other.

Europe's great powers were aware of the Asian dragons. Those who led their approach to them with Christianity failed. Those who led with guns succeeded. It was Western firepower that defined the Battle of Nagashino in

1575, where Nobunaga defeated Takeda Katsuyori, and his General Ieyasu would be hailed as the "Japanese Napoleon."[10]

Hideyoshi launched a renewed Korean invasion in 1597, with nine thousand ships conveying one hundred thousand men. Most were light Kobaya ships that moved like a school of fish, landing boarding parties of samurai ship to ship. Their design was generations behind their European counterparts, with board-and-iron nail construction that meant low sea-boards, saltwater corrosion, and short lifespans. Their pentagonal hulls made them susceptible to heavy weather, and they were such poor gun platforms that they either mounted no cannon or did so with light weapons suspended from beams with ropes.

Once again, the invasion started well, overcoming Korea's General Won Gyun, who assumed leadership amid political maneuvering that saw the crane wing maneuver's Admiral Sun-shin reduced to fighting as a common man. Within months, though, Japanese forces were struggling to advance against a coalition of Korean, Chinese, and ubyong guerrilla forces.

While on paper, Japan controlled an army powerful enough to overcome them, as long as Korea controlled the sea in between, they remained checked by supply. Japan put everything they had into reducing the Korean navy, yet again, with initial success. With just a dozen principal warships remaining and disaster looming, the Korean Joseon Dynasty's King Yi Yeon recalled Sun-shin in desperation.[11] Sun-shin found a solution, not in how he would fight, but where.

Once again, he took a vastly outnumbered fleet out to meet his enemy. Once again, he faked a disordered retreat. Once again, Japan chased him headlong for a decisive final battle, this time into the Myeongnyang Strait (the "strait where stones cry," so named because the tide was so strong it could be heard moving boulders on the bay floor). Only once the first Japanese ships had crossed the chains he'd positioned across the narrows did he raise them. Japan's lead ships found themselves sailing into massed gunfire while the balance of their fleet struggled to turn, rammed one another, grounded, or were reduced by Korean fire. Japan lost thirty-one ships. Korea lost two men.[12]

Hideyoshi never surrendered his claims on Korea, though cynics suggested he'd met his goals by spilling his soldiers' blood on their soil instead of Japan's.

Hideyoshi thought Japan's ascendency was destined. He thought peace at home would last. He thought he'd have more time. Within two years of his second failure in Korea, frustrated and embittered, the second great unifier died after a three-month illness.[13] When news of his death reached Korea in 1598, the armistice among Korea, Japan, and China quickly broke, and beleaguered Japanese invaders had to fight their way to the coast for chaotic withdrawals that echoed those of Dunkirk in World War II and claimed the life of the victorious Sun-shin with a stray shot.

Without an official heir, Hideyoshi's office would be split across five regents, the most powerful of which was the former Nobunaga ally and third great unifier, Tokugawa Ieyasu, until his five-year-old bastard son came of age.

The complicated allegiances of his samurai-father, Matsudaira Hirotada, saw Ieyasu lose his mother at two, abducted by the Oda at four, and hostaged to the Imagawa at six, before his father was murdered. With his family's fortune gone, he served Imagawa Yoshimoto faithfully until his defeat by Nobunaga's forces, to whom he transferred his loyalty and for whom he won control of the Imagawa clan.

While Nobunaga consolidated power nationally, Ieyasu did so locally, crushing rebellious Buddhist groups and expanding east. Upon Nobunaga's suicide, his holdings from Okazaki to Hakone made him second in power only to General Hideyoshi. Though they initially clashed, the more conservative Ieyasu swore his loyalty to Hideyoshi, and proved it in their joint conquest of house Hōjō. Surrendering his five home provinces (Mikawa, Tōtōmi, Suruga, Shinano, and Kai) at Hideyoshi's request in exchange for eight in Kantō from the Hōjō shifted Ieyasu's power base to include present-day Tokyo.[14] It was later said, "Ieyasu won the Empire by retreating."[15]

He proved a wise and capable administrator. By keeping his forces out of the second unifier's failed Korean ventures, he was able to expand his forces, tax base, and productivity with major water projects.

When the shogun's eldest regent died a year later in 1599, Ieyasu moved on Osaka castle in Fushimi to either protect or control the six-year-old shogun. Months of political machinations split the council of regents into two factions in the east under Ieyasu and the west under Terumoto, who'd been repeatedly checked by Nobunaga and whose commander, Ishida Mitsunari, had previously been saved from assassination by Ieyasu. By July 1600, they were in open conflict. A series of clashes, including Ieyasu's son leading thirty-eight thousand men along the Tōkaidō road and Mitsunari recapturing the former shogun's Fushimi Castle, culminated in a final confrontation at Sekigahara, comparable in importance to the Battle of Hastings in Britain. Mitsunari's western forces focused on military scale. Ieyasu focused on political maneuver.

Neither side selected the ground for the largest battle ever fought on Japanese soil, with both armies stumbling across one another in torrential rain, on October 20, 1600. At 8:00 a.m., the next morning, the fog burned away to reveal Mitsunari's 120,000 men heavily outnumbered Ieyasu's 75,000.

After indecisive early clashes, the western force's Kobayakawa Hideaki, who had wavered over Ieyasu's offers of favorable posts for weeks, switched sides. Both sides converged. Western forces centered on house Ōtani held until the further daimyo Wakisaka Yasuharu, Ogawa Suketada, Akaza Naoyasu, and Kutsuki Mototsuna also switched their allegiance to Ieyasu. When the Ōtani retreated, Ieyasu's forces began to roll up their opponent's flank. Mitsunari's force's last hope were undeployed elements of the Mōri clan, who held up the Chōsokabe clan's army behind them. Under Kikkawa Hiroie, while they didn't switch, neither did they engage. The western retreat quickly became a rout.[16]

Within hours, it was done. Ieyasu rewarded his loyalists, preserved those who had switched sides, and drove his opponents to suicide, execution, or penury. The emperor demurred and recognized Ieyasu as shogun in 1603.

Among the defeated were two clans that would have an outsized influence on Japan's future Boshin Civil War. The Mōri clan were relocated to strengthen the Chōshū Domain, despite them not having fought for either side. The Shimazu clan of Satsuma province used the distance to their island of Kyūshū to build a lucrative autonomy. By the time Bulloch's men were actively tapping Europe's shipyards for a new Confederate navy, both clans were pursuing warships of their own.

Japan, now under the third of her great unifiers, Tokugawa Ieyasu, turned her back on dreams of an East Asian Empire for a period of profound introspection.

It would take America's black ships to pull Japan's gaze back to the Pacific.

BLACK SHIPS AND BARBARIANS 20

With absolute power consolidated after two centuries of fractious conflict, the third great unifier, Tokugawa Ieyasu, laid down five policies to define a peaceful, ordered, and prosperous Japan.

- Bloodshed must stop. Katana kari (sword hunting) disarmed famers, merchants, and monks.
- Land must be open. Shiro wari sharply reduced the number of castles standing.
- People must know their place. Strict shi-nō-kō-shō class distinctions divided warriors, farmers, artisans, and tradesmen.
- Money must flow. Kenchi (land surveys) swept away rent-seeking road checkpoints and re-baselined taxation.
- New mining underpinned a new national currency.[1]

As the old Japanese saying goes, "Nobunaga mixed the cake, Hideyoshi baked it, and Ieyasu ate it."[2] The newly pronounced Tokugawa shogunate would rule for centuries.

The emperor remained a distant figure on the Chrysanthemum throne, in a line not just from Emperor Jimmu in 660 BCE, but from Amaterasu, the foremost deity in Shinto mythology, who gifted them semidivine status of their own. Amaterasu's symbol was the sun. It would be the end of World War II before this claim to divinity was renounced.

No shogun ever sought the emperor's title for themselves. Emperors ruled by blood right. It was a religious role, steeped in tradition and ceremony, and far removed from the trade and land that generated wealth. Shoguns could still marry into the emperor's line in any case, as Tokugawa Masako and others did.

The first Europeans that Japan encountered were Portuguese traders operating Chinese junks from ports like Goa as early as 1543. While trading metal and gunpowder in and luxuries like silk and porcelain out was hugely profitable, it had to be, as it meant running the gauntlet of the Wako pirates. It was also at the indulgence of the coastal daimyo, who dismissed early Portuguese traders as Nanban ("Southern Barbarians"). As the Japanese footprint of the Wako eased, and especially after Portugal's acquisition of Macau in 1576, trade boomed with massive Carrack ships of 1,500 to 2,000 tons that dwarfed their Japanese peers.

By 1607, as the first English colony in America settled at Jamestown, Virginia, the three great Japanese unifiers' work was done. The emperor was enshrined in the imperial palace in Kyoto. Shogun Ieyasu chose the small fishing village of Edo as his capital. Like Hideyoshi before him, he ruled directly for two years then publicly abdicated in favor of his son Hidetada, while retaining absolute power.

While loyal to allies, he was cold, driven, and unforgiving. One of his first acts as shogun was ordering the execution of a man who'd crossed him in his youth, who he'd not seen since. He ordered the killing of Hideyori's infant son, Kunimatsu. He ordered the death of every defender who held Osaka castle against him and lined the road from Kyoto all the way to Fushimi with their heads. His passions were swordcraft, swimming, and hawking. He wanted a noble, strong, and unbroken line of rulers to follow. This was a man used to thinking about the long game—he'd shed his birth name—Matsudaira Takechiyo—to imply a totally fabricated connection to the Shogunate Minamoto clan a full thirty-seven years earlier.

"The strong manly ones in life are those who understand the meaning of the word patience," he wrote. "I am not as strong as I might be, but I have long known and practiced patience. And if my descendants wish to be as I am, they must study patience."[3]

Nobunaga had diverted his samurai classes with Korean campaigns. Ieyasu was more direct. Many were dispossessed of land as a new network of more than three hundred daimyo were carved out for the clans that pledged to Ieyasu before the battle of Sekigahara (the "fudai daimyo" hereditary lords) and those who'd pledged afterward (the "tozama" outside lords). While they'd lost out materially, the samurai class remained prestigious, and the sword hunt dictated that peasant and merchant classes couldn't rise against them.[4] The samurai permitted to retain their swords shifted to new seats of power. Those forced to surrender theirs lived and died as bureaucrats, line troops, and peasants.

This construct ensured a larger number of weaker daimyo were prevented from amassing power on a national scale. In line with a long-standing tradition

of familial hostage taking, each daimyo (bar the Satsuma, by decree) had to al-
ternate a year living in Edo for every year in their house's base of power.

Society was stratified into four ridged tiers, with samurai, craftsmen, and
merchants all leveraging the 80 percent of people pinned in the peasantry.
It shaped what they ate, what they wore, and who could access luxuries like
silk at any price. Merchants, craftsmen, and samurai lived in strictly defined
quarters radiating out from each daimyo's castle.[5]

While Ryūkyū (modern Okinawa) was invaded in 1609, Ieyasu went no
further. He knew the world beyond, but he chose isolation.

In 1610, the small Japanese warship *San Buena Ventura* (120 tons), built
under guidance of English adventurer William Adams, was tasked with sailing
a shipwrecked Spanish crew back to New Spain (Mexico), making Tanaka
Shōsuke the first Japanese man to set foot in the Americas.[6] William Adams
later wrote, "The people of this Land of Japan are good of nature, courteous
above measure, and valiant in war: their justice is severely executed without
any partiality upon transgressors of the law. They are governed in great civility.
I mean, not a land better governed in the world by civil policy. The people be
very superstitious in their religion and are of diverse opinions."[7] It's likely their
divided opinions would have been over his presence as a foreigner.

New Spain hoped it would be the start of a new relationship, but their
offers of assistance in mining and metallurgy were declined. The only traders
to secure a toehold were the Dutch, who provided the weapons Japan desired
without entangling them in Christianity. By 1614, the fledgling community
of Japanese Christians was subjected to Ieyasu's Christian Expulsion Edict,
which required all citizens to be registered with Buddhist temples. Any who
refused were denounced. Some renounced their conversion. Some took their
practices underground.

Despite outlandish proposals to strike as far away as the Philippines, Ieyasu
resisted any drive for expansion. After the four-month Christian Shimabara
Rebellion in 1637–1638 led by fourteen-year-old Amakusa Shiro, whose head
ended up on a pike in Nagasaki, foreign trade was curtailed even further.[8]

The Dutch (who remained happy to separate the wallet and the soul and
were now known as Kōmō "Red Hair"), were confined to a single port on
Dejima island in Nagasaki harbor. Japanese citizens were forbidden from
traveling overseas except for a 350-ship red seal fleet. Even this was canceled
in 1635. Only two ports were authorized for Korea via Tsushima Island and
Qing China via the Ryūkyūs. The flaw in the system was the ensuing concentration of wealth through just three clans including the Satsuma.

The death knell for any remaining free trade advocates was 1808's humiliating Nagasaki harbor incident. Napoleonic France had annexed the Dutch
Republic and turned her resources on the British, who responded with at-

tacks on Dutch shipping. On October 4, the third-rate British Minerva-class warship HMS *Phaeton* (944 tons; thirty-eight guns) entered Nagasaki under a false Dutch flag and took the Dutch officials who came to greet her hostage, while their Japanese escorts swam for their lives. The *Phaeton* demanded re-provisioning for their release.

Japan was unprepared. The Saga clan tasked with the harbor's defense were found to have a hundred men where a thousand should be until the annual spring-to-autumn Dutch trading season.[9] Their fort's guns were dated or unserviceable. While orders were immediately dispatched to raise eight thousand Samurai and a flotilla of forty lesser ships, the local Nagasaki magistrate could only capitulate. Even once she was restocked, the *Phaeton* waited a few days in case any Dutch ship arrived and left in her own time. Japan's humiliation was absolute.[10]

While magistrate Matsudaira committed *seppuku*, the shogun's response was tempered. Interpreters were ordered for English and Russian. Dictionaries were commissioned. While new coastal defenses were funded, it would be a decade before Tokugawa Ieyoshi had the confidence to pass laws prohibiting foreigners coming ashore on pain of death.[11]

People knew their place. Foreigners were a distant contagion. The emperor was on a Chrysanthemum throne. The gods smiled on them. In time, the Nagasaki harbor incident began to seem distant and isolated. Even if it recurred, there was a belief that righteous "kamikaze" storms would protect their islands, as they had from Mongol invasion fleets in 1274 and 1281. All was as it should be.

While Japan was cutting herself off from a wave of global industrialization, she was self-sufficient. Her paddies, forests, and fisheries were well managed. Literacy was climbing. Art, culture, and printing flourished. Credit notes for rice harvests underpinned a proto-mercantilist system.

No other foreign sailors would be saved and transported. Those few traders or whalers that wrecked on Japanese shores were imprisoned or killed. While Western governments were aware of such incidents, no single example escalated. In 1837, when the merchant ship SS *Morrison* used the pretext of returning Japanese castaways to try and open trade talks, it was battered by fire from port forts. Before it had limped back to the United States, new coastal forts were commissioned.[12]

The first Opium War (1839–1842), in which the British humiliated Qing China, prompted a Western reevaluation of Japan's potential. If China had wealth to offer and souls to save, why not Japan?

America's merchant networks had blossomed throughout England's war from 1842. On the resumption of peace, when Britain found America had become a significant competitor, they passed a series of new navigation acts from 1851 that barred foreign vessels trading between empire ports and monopolized the export of manufactured goods, furs, tobacco, and more to England. America sought more non-empire ports in the Americas, Asia, and the continent as a result.

Though America's Asian presence was small, her captains sailed with almost total discretion. In 1845, the round-the-world voyage of the *Constitution* (1,576 tons; fifty-two guns) paused in Turon Bay in Cochin China when Captain "Mad Jack" Percival took it upon himself to free a French Christian missionary held under a death sentence. In a classic piece of gunboat diplomacy, he backed his demands for his release by kidnapping three local "mandarin" officials and seizing three of the Cochin emperor's small square-sailed war junks. A series of skirmishes—including the escape and recapture of the junks—resulted in local casualties. When the Cochin gathered a flotilla of junks, reinforced their forts, and cut off any supplies to *Constitution*, it was finally enough to break the deadlock. By May 26, the junks were released, Mad Jack was victualed, and he quietly sailed for China and a reprimand on his return home. An apology was issued by President Zachary Taylor. One of the *Constitution*'s officers put it in a larger context: "It seems . . . to have shown a sad want of 'sound discretion' in commencing an affair of this kind, without carrying it through to a successful conclusion."[13] The capitulation was music to Japanese ears. America was becoming a major power, but far from invincible.

While the emperor was the titular head of state, the shogun ruled Japan through his control of the military and bureaucracy. Foreign policy—what little there was—was his. Ieyoshi's resistance to Christianity escalated to crucifixion.

In 1846, after the U.S. East Indies squadron's James Biddle concluded a treaty with China, he entered Edo Bay with the ship-of-the-line *Columbus* (2,480 tons; ninety guns), sloop *Vincennes* (700 tons; eighteen guns, which had been the first U.S. naval vessel to circumnavigate the globe), and a treaty of friendship that Japan gave a hard "ee-ya" (no). The two ships had been chosen to impress. *Columbus* was one of America's two leading warships, together with the *Ohio*. They did not.

As many as a hundred small vessels swarmed Biddle in the capital's harbor, first blocking any attempt to leave the ship, then permitting him only as far as an anchored junk ship. Even then, a misunderstanding while Biddle tried to embark saw a samurai unsheathe his sword, and Biddle make a swift exit. With prevailing winds against them, *Columbus* then had the ignominy of having to be towed by shogunate guard boats to exit the bay. The former flagship had no chance at redemption, sitting out the intervening years until she was sunk by the Union in 1861 in the Norfolk Navy Yards, a stone's throw from the *Merrimack* that was reborn as the ironclad *Virginia*.

Japan's rejection was so emphatic it would be three years before the American sloop *Preble* (sixteen guns) returned to Japan at Nagasaki, and even then, with limited orders for the U.S. Far East Squadron's Commodore David Geisinger to secure the release of American whalers from the shipwreck *Lagoda*, whose imprisonment was so harsh that several died of exposure and at least one had hung himself in desperation and been left in place. There was no talk of trade, treaties, or friendship.

Guard boats initially blocked the *Preble*'s way but held their fire as she pressed her way through their lines. No American aboard spoke Japanese, so Dutch interpreters interceded. Fourteen *Lagoda* crew members were freed. Their treatment was met with an outraged American press, disinterested in them being deserters and not wreck survivors at all. Captain James Glynn's after-action report concluded that any future engagement would need to be accompanied by a show of force.

A U.S.-Japanese confrontation continued to edge closer. America's victory over Mexico in 1848 expanded her borders from sea to shining sea and fed the notion of a "manifest destiny" to grow. In 1851, while the Confederate ironclad *Sphinx* was still thirteen years away, President Millard Fillmore signed a letter from Secretary of State Daniel Webster offering the emperor of Japan "friendship and commerce."[14] Command of the U.S. East Indies Squadron was passed from Commodore John Aulick to the more diplomatic Commodore Matthew Calbraith Perry (the younger brother of the Independence War hero, Commodore Oliver Hazard Perry).

In 1853, the American black ships came, and nothing would ever be the same again. Two lessons had been learned. Both were applied. When Perry steamed for Japan, he did so with trading quantities of arms including one hundred Colt pistols. And he did so with overwhelming force.

Perry was a career officer who had made his name in the Mexican-American War and championed the U.S. navy's transition to steam power. The navy he served was replete with names the American Civil War would immortalize. His brother-in-law, Senator John Slidell of Louisiana, would serve as the Confederacy's representative in France during the war between the states and have his fingerprints all over the *Stonewall*'s first contracts. On the flagship *Powhatan* was Lieutenant James D. Johnston of Kentucky, a future Confederate commander, and executive officer when the first delegation from the Tokugawa shogunate later steamed to the United States. *Powhatan* was commanded by Captain Josiah Tattnall of Savannah, Georgia, who would trade leadership of America's East India Squadron for a captaincy and command of rebel naval forces in Georgia and South Carolina.

Also aboard was Lieutenant John M. Brooke from Tampa, Florida, who'd develop the ironclad *Virginia* and his namesake heavy cannon, who'd later serve as an instructor to the shogun's navy, and who was onboard the Dutch-built Japanese warship *Kanrin* when she became the first to transit the Pacific with a delegation to the United States.

Also serving with Lieutenant Brooke was the former Japanese citizen and now baptized and naturalized American, Joseph Heco, who'd been taken to San Francisco as one of seventeen shipwreck survivors aged thirteen (who were actually the second Japanese crew thus taken to the United States). His distinguished career later included translation for the American consul in Yokohama, meeting Abraham Lincoln in a brief return stateside, publishing *Hyōryūki* (Record of a castaway), and founding the first Japanese-language newspaper. Today, he is widely regarded as the father of Japanese journalism.[15]

Perry first reached the Ryūkyūs and the Bonin Islands south of the main Japanese islands where he made territorial claims that were simply ignored and was replenished without incident. Biddle had approached Japan with two warships. Perry had nine, led by the three side-wheel frigates *Mississippi*, *Susquehanna*, and *Powhatan*. *Mississippi* boasted eight 8-inch Paixhans guns. *Susquehanna* had a battery of two 150-pounder Parrott rifles and twelve 9-inch Dahlgren smoothbores. *Powhatan* had an 11-inch Dahlgren gun and ten 9-inch Dahlgrens. They were supported by the three lightly armed store steamships *Lexington*, *Supply*, and *Southampton* with a complement of marines and a further trio of sailing sloops, *Macedonian* (1,341 tons; thirty-six guns), *Plymouth* (989 tons; twenty-two guns), and *Saratoga* (882 tons; twenty-two guns, who was decommissioned an incredible thirteen times before the American Civil War's outbreak).

No one who saw it forgot Perry's fleet entering Edo harbor on July 8, 1853. What started as a faint haze of smoke on the horizon grew larger, darker, and thicker until it split into four shapes—his flagship *Susquehanna*, the *Mississippi*, *Plymouth*, and *Saratoga*. On they came, against the tide, despite their sails being furled, with a sound no one in Edo had heard before. These were the black ships, named for their dark antifouling paint; each one an order of magnitude more powerful than the ships Biddle and Glynn reported confronting them. They steamed past the harbor's light guard ships with their guns trained on the fortified village of Uraga. Gun crews swarmed along their lengths, until, in what they called a belated celebration of the Fourth of July, they fired a mass volley of shots that painted them all in thick, dark smoke. Japan's ponderous Ō-atakebune and Tekkōsen warships had been shattered on Korean shores without replacement. The largest American warship was now ten or more times bigger than any Japanese ship afloat. Breathless accounts across the city portrayed them as being as big as mountains or castles, yet swift as birds.[16]

Nothing was left to chance. They'd learned to spurn Japanese emissaries who were too junior and to ignore signs—written quite uselessly in French— to turn away. Perry demanded his letters be presented to Japan's highest officials immediately. Once again, the Japanese were not in a strong position to respond. The Dutch had tipped off Shogun Tokugawa Ieyoshi of their approach and provided him with a globe putting Japan into a slender perspective in the Pacific. These black ships, he was told, were commanded by the "barbarian-suppressing supreme General" who had dominated Mexico. Nothing he could muster could oppose them, and as luck would have it, they found him in poor health.

The desire for isolation in Japan was dominant, but not universal. Sakuma Shozan, for example, had advised the shogun to embrace the West three years before, but the central Japanese concern was cultural not mercantile. "Military power depends on the clarity of moral principles, and not on military training or machinery," Nakaoka Shintaro wrote, "Without the right people, regulations and machines are useless."[17]

These black ships were immeasurably worse than the English humiliation inflicted in 1808. This was foundational. Japan is indivisible from its seas. Even in its alps, no point is more than 100 kilometers from them.

A frail Ieyoshi consented for the Americans to land at Kurihama, near Yokosuka, to present their demands. That America addressed them to a figurehead emperor, and not the ruling shogun, reveals the United States' limited grasp of Japanese culture. Perry granted them time to consider their response and steamed out on July 17, with a promise to return. The shogun was in an impossible position. Granting Americans coaling ports, trade access, and protection for whalers meant irreversible change, but he was powerless to oppose it.

A month after Perry had demonstrated his Paixhans guns, Russian admiral Yevfimy Putyatin arrived in Nagasaki and staged demonstrations of his steam engines aboard the *Pallada* (2,090 tons; fifty-two guns). Ieyoshi promptly added them as a requirement from his Dutch suppliers. When the *Pallada* later sank off Miyajima, the crew were not seized or killed as they would have been prior; instead, local shipwrights in Heda helped them build a modest new vessel for the return journey to Russia in March 1854. In gratitude, a Russian vice admiral gifted it to the shogun afterward, together with fifty-two cannon the following year. Six copies of this diminutive warship were immediately ordered by the shogun. These insights into European designs were disseminated via Rangaku schools, and Tanaka Hisashige, founder of what would become the Toshiba Corporation, was soon at work on Japan's first domestic steam engine.

Ieyoshi didn't live to see the results, passing away at the age of sixty on July 27, 1853, of a heart attack attributed to heatstroke. While he acknowledged fathering an extraordinary twenty-seven children with Princess Takako (1795–1840) and eight concubines, only his successor as shogun, Tokugawa Iesada, lived past twenty.

When Perry returned to Edo Bay with the warships *Susquehanna*, *Mississippi*, and *Saratoga*, they were joined by the *Powhatan*, *Lexington*, and *Macedonian*; the sloop *Vandalia*; and the store ship *Southampton*. Their marine complement had been expanded to more than sixteen hundred men. If Iesada needed time to bed down his ascension, he didn't get it. When Perry felt he was being stalled by the shogun's representatives, he threatened to summon a mythical one-hundred-ship American fleet that would have been larger than the actual U.S. Navy of the day. When a shift to Yokoyama didn't hasten talks, Perry landed five hundred sailors and marines.[18] There was carrot as well as stick. Perry lavished the new shogun with demonstrations and gifts including a working scale model of a steam locomotive, a telescope, a telegraph, and luxury goods like wines and liquors.

The resulting Convention of Kanagawa on March 31, 1854, was derided locally as the "unequal treaty." America gained official consuls and trade ports at Shimoda and Hakodate and guarantees for shipwrecked sailors. Its most-favored-nation clause dictated that any concession granted to European powers (as ever, led by the Dutch) would be automatically extended to the United States. Extraterritoriality ensured Americans could only be tried in their own courts. No Japanese signature was ever added to the English-language version, with Perry claiming, "It will be observed that the practice usually pursued in affixing signatures to treaties was departed from on this occasion, and for reason assigned by the Japanese, that their laws forbade the subjects of the Empire from putting their names to any document written in a foreign language."[19] It made no difference and, as feared, was just the start.

Shogun Iesada struggled to reconcile Western encroachment with Japanese identity. He was not a warrior, nor an orator, and what statements he made, he made through intermediaries over whispers about his health, recording, "Because of my illness, I can not participate in ruling politics, so I stay inside the palace and was trying slightly not to lose my manner."[20] Some accounts speculate he may have had cerebral palsy, which is supported by accounts from an American envoy who described him taking preparatory physical actions before replying in conversation, though it's not universally accepted. What is known is that he was heavily scarred by childhood smallpox and was unexceptional in the skills that remained to him. The Fukui daimyo,

Oshinaga Matsudaira, dismissed him as "the lowest grade among all mediocre people." In trying to defend him, his vassal Masahiro Asahina pleaded, "There must be many daimyo that were more inferior to Iesada Shogun among the three hundred lords," which isn't exactly high praise.[21]

He, however, did have a sense of urgency. In 1855, two years after the black ships, Dutch king Willem III gifted Japan the barque-rigged third-class side-wheel steamship *Soembing*, which was promptly relaunched as the *Kankō* (769 tons; four guns), named for a line in the I Ching "to view the light of the country." With her came a marine detachment led by G. C. C. Pels Rijcken (1810–1889), who commenced instruction in Japan's first naval academy.[22]

Marriage was the last card he had to play. After the death of his first and second wives, Iesada married the sister of the emperor-aligned Satsuma daimyo, Shimazu Nariakira. When this also failed to produce an heir, he adopted a cousin whose line could be traced back to the eleventh shogun, Tokugawa Ienari, who was renamed Tokugawa Yoshinobu. None of it was enough. When Iesada became the first Tokugawa shogun to grant his daimyo council limited decision-making, it wasn't a solution, it was a precedent. The great houses immediately fell out with one another and gridlocked the court. Clans without an invitation watched with growing horror. This was weakness. This was not Japanese. This could not be what the emperor wanted.

Some were prepared to do something about it. By the time Russia added treaty demands of her own, every major power in Europe was represented. Russia shared America's use of Shimoda. England and Holland had Nagasaki opened to them.[23] Foreign faces were seen more and more, some of them openly wearing crucifixes that could have meant death months before. American Christians eyed an opportunity to spread Protestant faiths in soil where Catholicism had failed to take root.[24] After 260 years of blessings, it seemed the gods were angry. Within months, the Great Nankaidō and Tōkai earthquakes and tsunamis killed as many as eighty thousand citizens.[25]

As Iesada made concession after concession, resentment grew.

Within the bushido code, samurai could and did kill those below them for causing offense. Though this was limited to certain scenarios and required the samurai to submit themselves to their daimyo's judgment, it was inevitable that it would result in Western deaths, at least one of which was answered by Western warships.

When France's treaty was concluded, a Chinese consular staffer was murdered overnight. An American consular secretary and an English merchant named Richardson quickly followed.[26] Two Russians died onshore within six weeks of their country's treaty. The English consul-general Rutherford Alcock's translator was murdered in the entrance to their legation. Two Dutch merchants were killed in the street. The building housing the French ambassador burned down. The following year, in the Tozenji incident, four "idle and warlike" ronin Mito samurai and at least one guard died in a bloody assassination attempt on the shotgun-armed head of the British legation, Sir Rutherford Alcock.[27]

Emperor Kōmei maintained his silence. While he'd agreed to Dutch trading concessions before the black ships, he saw it as a pragmatic step to the weaponry his shogun sought. Now hard-line conservative daimyo, adamant that a reformed Japan would no longer be Japan at all, looked to him. Shogun Iesada played for time, ending the Sankin Kotai system obligating daimyo to spend every second year in Edo, which just freed their hands. In all, he stalled a further four years before concluding an expanded full trade treaty with the U.S. consul, Townsend Harris, in 1858 that met all of their demands and none of his.

One thing all Japanese leaders could agree on was their weakness at sea. No further resources would be poured into traditional Fune boats with banks of rowers and lattice sails, or coastal defenses with dated cannon. Laws forbidding the daimyo lords from constructing large vessels were repealed. A major cannon foundry was established by Egawa Hidetatsu in Nirayama based on Dutch plans. Japan was entering an iron world.

The Western-style sail frigate *Hōō* (610 tons; ten guns) was laid down with Uraga bugyō port authorities using Dutch reference materials, the testimony from the (very few) travelers like translator Nakahama Manjirō who'd traveled to western ports, and direct observations of Perry's American black ships. Though obsolete when she launched, she represented an important stepping-stone, and others quickly followed. Work on early copper-sheathed warships including the Satsuma clan's *Shōhei* and Mito's *Asahi* drew on previous (illegal) design work and represented a significant shift in military infrastructure from the state to individual clans that would have serious implications in the future. The *Kanrin* followed in 1857 as Japan's first sail and screw-driven steam corvette, which, as the nation's new face to the world, went on to escort their first delegation to the United States and assert their claims to the Bonin islands against English interests.

As each clan stepped up their response, Iesada's voice continued to diminish.

In 1858, at just eighteen years of age, Iesada died such an isolated figure that only a handful of his most trusted confidants knew he'd been unable to eat for seven days or sleep for five.[28] His five-year reign under the shadow of the black ships was marked by insurgency, earthquakes, tsunami, and cholera epidemics that killed hundreds of thousands.

His selection of a successor was even more fraught than his had been. His first wife, Princess Takatsukasa Atsuko, died of smallpox without providing an heir. His second marriage to Princess Ichijō Hideko lasted barely a year before she too passed away. His third marriage to the adopted daughter of the Satsuma daimyo, Princess Atsu, remained childless. As a pragmatic choice, he adopted his cousin Yoshitomi, who had built a strong reputation as an administrator.

The Satsuma, Mito, and others emboldened with new powers on the daimyo council, wanted the adult Tokugawa Yoshinobu (who became one of the new shogun's guardians until he came of age) or Matsudaira Naritami as his successor. Instead, thirteen-year-old Yoshitomi was elevated as the Tokugawa shogun Iemochi. Too young to impose himself on the battlefield, Iemochi was shrewdly advised to marry Princess Kazu, daughter of Emperor Ninko, to indicate their lines were joined and inseparable. Contemporaries remarked on his accommodating nature. Servants recorded their pleasure to serve him.[29] His advisors doubled down on shows of pomp and ceremony to reinforce his station. The following year, when he became only the second shogun to call upon the emperor directly, he did so with three thousand retainers. The Tokugawa line's frailty remained a red flag, though. A later procession that it's claimed had ten thousand men was undercut by his absence with a fever.

Iemochi's shogunate was desperate to show an upside to this disruption. Iemochi sent their first delegation to America in 1860, headed by a trio of samurai; an entourage of 745,000 cheering spectators greeted them in the Washington Navy Yard on May 14, where they were escorted by the secretaries of state, war, treasury, and navy. Detailed inspections were made of anchor, boiler, engine, and ordnance workshops. A further twenty thousand Americans lined the route to their accommodation in Willard's Hotel. The Japanese delegation was shocked by local informality, "ragged urchins . . . boys, . . . dirty, black and white, poked their filthy digits into the carriage for the Ambassadors—Princes, be it remembered—to shake hands with them, while the Police, whose business it was to prevent such an insult, indolently lolled."[30]

Vice President John C. Breckinridge strolled over with invitations to Congress and dinner. Pianos, indoor plumbing, and Washington's gas lighting impressed. Attempts at rice dishes swathed in butter and sugar did not. Seventeen-year-old interpreter Tateishi Onojiro, who waved emphatically at the crowds while his peers sat impassively, became a favorite. By the time he departed Washington, crowds chanting "Johnny! Johnny!" were rewarded with him performing impromptu magic tricks. After being showered with $50,000 in engagements and tours, the Japanese delegation left with custom cast medals, and they gifted exquisite black lacquer sho-dana cabinets to their American hosts in return. Among them, Katsu Kaishu, the captain of the

Dutch-built *Kanrin*, had been impressed by the scale of U.S. industry and the industriousness of their workers. His report greatly influenced Ryoma Saka-moto, who would write the Five Article Oaths that helped define the Meiji era to come. The American Civil War that would give rise to the *Stonewall* was less than a year away. None returned.

Japan's clans were coalescing into two factions. The Jo-I were for the emperor and against foreigners. The Kai-Koku shogunate supporters saw themselves as part of a wave of change breaking over long-standing empires like the Ottomans in Turkey, the Qing in China, or the Romanovs and Hapsburgs in Europe.

Both sides tried to ground their view in Japan's warrior tradition. The first great unifier, Nobunaga, had said two centuries before, "Let us have inter-course with foreign lands, let us learn their drills and tactics, then when we have made our nation united as one family, we shall be able to go abroad, and give lands in foreign countries to those who have distinguished themselves in battle."[31] Kanagawa, Ni-igata, Hyogo, and Yokoham trade ports opened to the West in 1863. Foreigners were not the only targets of protest and vio-lence. When Ii-Kamon-no-kami, head of the Kai-Koku party, imprisoned the conservative daimyo of Mito, he was assassinated. Japan's daimyo began marshaling troops and gathering resources.

Permission to spend less time in Edo, retain more castles, and earn vastly more from the island Ryukyu Kingdom that was paid in tribute to the Chi-nese Manchu emperor meant the Satsuma were amassing the kind of power no clan had held for more than two centuries.[32]

Across the nation, daimyo remilitarized a samurai class who'd been ebb-ing into administration. A growing number, including the future admiral Enomoto Takeaki, were sent to study in the Netherlands. While all were sworn to their clan, more and more began to identify with a national agenda. Merchants, led by the Dutch, but joined by a growing number of flags, found an ever-more lucrative market for weaponry.

Battle lines were being drawn, figuratively and literally.

Imperial clans like the Mito rolled out a new Dainihonshi (Great History of Japan) education system that reframed the emperor from spiritual figure to direct leader. Scholars like Aizawa Seishisai called for action, citing daimyo Nariaki's tome *Japan, Reject the Westerners*. When the shogun's regent, Ii Naosuke (1815–1860) tried to put down pro-imperial dissent with the violent Ansei Purge (1858–1860), his assassination was openly attributed to the Mito or Satsuma without any reprisal.[33]

For a time, it seemed like enough. In 1861, with the outbreak of the American Civil War, the far-flung U.S. fleet was urgently recalled to block-ade the Confederacy. Only the side-wheel *Saginaw* (453 tons; four guns)—

who'd leveled a fortress at Qui Nhon Bay, Cochin China (in present-day Vietnam), when pursuing missing sailors from the U.S. barque *Myrtle* (60 tons)—remained on station in the Far East.[34] In 1862, the *Saginaw* was ordered away to protect whalers in the eastern Pacific from Confederate raiders.

When reports of a Confederate ship in far eastern waters reached the naval secretary, Gideon Welles, he ordered the screw sloop *Wyoming* (six guns, which predated the state of that name) under Commander David Stockton McDougal, a lifelong navy man and veteran of the Mexican-American War, to uphold an Asian presence. Though extensive repairs were required after a grounding near Swatow, China, she patrolled the Sunda Strait between Sumatra and Java in the Dutch East Indies where Japanese forces would sink the Australian HMAS *Perth* and American USS *Houston* in World War II and narrowly missed intercepting the *Alabama* as she transited back from repairs in Melbourne. Confederate captain Raphael Semmes knew he was being hunted, declaring, "Wyoming is a good match for this ship," but "I have resolved to give her battle."[35] In the end, they never crossed paths, and all *Wyoming* had to show for it was the *Alabama*'s mail they'd been given in error in Singapore.

She was about to return home when Japan erupted.

On March 11, 1863, the emperor gave Shogun Iemochi just eight weeks to enforce an "Order to Expel Barbarians." Doing so simply wasn't possible, so his intentions were unclear. Kōmei took no actions to help, nor did he ask his petitioners to.

Accelerating change was creating winners and losers. Mavericks emerged, none more important than the man they would come to call the "last samurai." Saigō Takamori watched his father fall from esteemed samurai to impoverished tax official as one of seven children sharing a single bed. He trained at a goju samurai school from age six to his graduation at fourteen, when he was formally introduced to the Satsuma (Kagoshima) clan. At more than 6 feet tall, and weighing 200 pounds, he was a veritable giant for the age. By the time he joined the local bureaucracy as an agricultural advisor, his parents had died, his marriage was childless, and he had an extended family of twelve to support. His break was distinguishing himself as an attendant, spy, and advisor to the daimyo, Shimazu Nariakira. When his lord died suddenly, heatstroke was blamed, and poison was suspected. Takamori was dissuaded from committing *seppuku* to join him by the monk Gessho, who he saved in turn, before he was killed fleeing from shogunate forces for advocating rebellion. After a cycle of exile and escape, he was recalled by an imperial faction rallying around the cry "sonnō jōi" ("Revere the Emperor, expel the barbarians").[36] Despite a second period in exile for alleged activism, by 1864, shogunate forces could not or would not police their opposition, and he returned for the simple reason the Satsuma were stronger with him, than without. By forty, he was Satsuma's military commander in the imperial capital Kyōto.[37]

While the sea was the shogun's strongest area of operations, it was where matters then worsened.

Prince Mori's Chōshū controlled the east-west Shimonoseki Strait between Honshu to the north and Kyushu to the south where the Japanese had seen off Mongol invasion fleets in 1274 and 1281. The East China Sea bounded him to the west. The Japanese Inland Sea defined his east with six forts armed with early cannon and a growing number of the latest American 8-inch Dahlgrens.

When the emperor's June 25 midnight deadline for the expulsion of foreigners expired, the Chōshū took it upon themselves to act in his name. Within the hour, two of their ships, flying the shogun's colors rather than their own, opened fire on the Western merchant ship *Pembroke*, which was anchored in the strait awaiting a pilot and favorable tide to depart. *Pembroke* managed to break out through the Inland Sea and Bungo Strait with minimal damage and made for Shanghai.

Chōshū attacks continued in the days that followed, notably with the near-sinking of the French dispatch boat *Kien-Chang*, a former Opium War hospital ship purchased in China in 1860. The Dutch *Medusa* (1,808 tons; sixteen guns) under Captain Casembroot might have thought themselves an exception, given their two centuries of trade on Japan's terms, but also came under fire. When she finally extricated herself, four of her crew were dead, sixteen were wounded, and the hull had been pierced thirty-one times.[38]

The young shogun Iemochi remained poorly placed to respond. His private physician documented symptoms ranging from "an extremely sickly constitution" to "a lack of interest in women."[39]

It was July 10 before exaggerated reports that the *Pembroke* had been sunk with all hands reached the U.S. consul in Yokohama, and the following day before new mail from Shanghai confirmed *Pembroke* was safe, and the Wyoming had arrived from Hong Kong. Ambassador Robert H. Pruyn and Commander McDougal delivered a diplomatic protest to the Tokugawa minster of foreign affairs, who expressed his regret, explained the attacks were unsanctioned, and asked for time to resolve the situation. It was enough for Pruyn. It was not for McDougal, who disregarded his prior orders to take *Wyoming* home and secured permission to retrace the *Pembroke*'s escape and take action at "the scene of the outrage."[40]

For the U.S. Navy, the time for diplomacy was over. While British, French, and Dutch forces conferred on how they would respond, the *Wyoming* steamed into what would become the Battle of Shimonoseki Strait.

USS *Monitor*, the first ironclad commissioned by the U.S. Navy. U.S. NAVAL HISTORY AND HERITAGE COMMAND

Crew of the USS *Monitor*, July 1862. U.S. NAVAL HISTORY AND HERITAGE COMMAND

John Ericsson, who designed the *Monitor*.
LIBRARY OF CONGRESS

Franklin Buchanan, captain of the *Virginia*.
LIBRARY OF CONGRESS

The Confederate ironclad *Virginia* (often known as the *Merrimack*, based on the Union hull used to build it). U.S. NAVAL HISTORY AND HERITAGE COMMAND

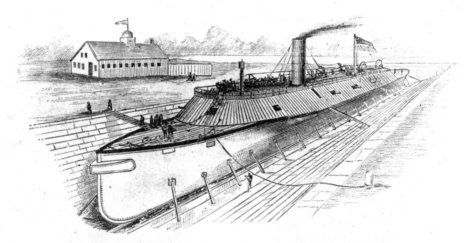

THE VIRGINIA (MERRIMAC) IN DRY-DOCK, AFTER BEING ARMORED.

Drawing of the CSS *Virginia*, as seen in drydock in early 1862. U.S. NAVAL HISTORY AND HERITAGE COMMAND

John L. Worden, captain of the *Monitor*. LIBRARY OF CONGRESS

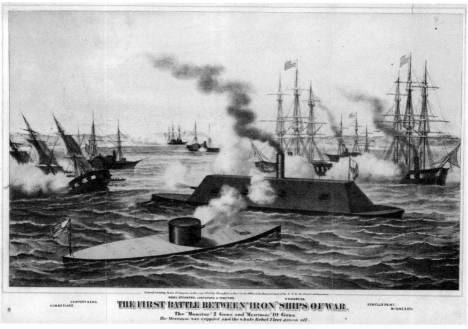

Battle of Hampton Roads, March 1862. LIBRARY OF CONGRESS

The *Monitor* and *Virginia* clash at Hampton Roads, as seen in a lithograph based on a painting.
U.S. NAVAL HISTORY AND HERITAGE COMMAND

Confederate diplomat John Slidell, famous for his role in the 1861 Trent Affair, approached France about building warships for the Confederacy. LIBRARY OF CONGRESS

Emperor Napoleon III. LIBRARY OF CONGRESS

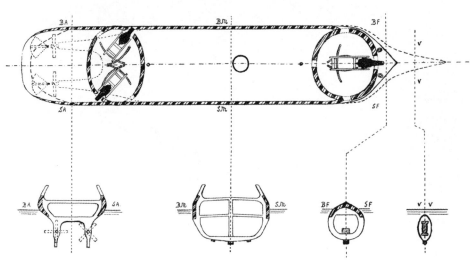

Plans for the ironclad that became the *Stonewall* and later *Kotetsu*. AUTHOR UNKNOWN

CSS *Stonewall*—named *Sphinx* at the time—under construction at the Arman shipyard in Bordeaux, France. GRAVURE DE M. DUFFET FOR *LE MONDE ILLUSTRÉ,* 1864

CSS *Stonewall* at Ferrol, Spain, March 1865. LIBRARY OF CONGRESS

Confederate general Thomas J. "Stonewall" Jackson, namesake of the new ironclad. LIBRARY OF CONGRESS

Thomas Jefferson Page, captain of the *Stonewall* (seen here in his prewar U.S. Navy uniform). U.S. NAVAL HISTORY AND HERITAGE COMMAND

Confederate secretary of the navy Stephen Mallory. LIBRARY OF CONGRESS

Union secretary of the navy Gideon Welles. LIBRARY OF CONGRESS

USS *Niagara*. LIBRARY OF CONGRESS

Thomas T. Craven, captain of the *Niagara*.
U.S. NAVAL HISTORY AND HERITAGE COMMAND

Commodore Matthew Perry, who led American expeditions to Japan in the 1850s. LIBRARY OF CONGRESS

The *Stonewall* at the Washington Navy Yard, June 1865. The U.S. Capitol is visible in the background.
LIBRARY OF CONGRESS

Another view of the *Stonewall* at the Washington Navy Yard.
LIBRARY OF CONGRESS

Washington Navy Yard, June 1866. The *Stonewall* is at anchor at the center of the photograph.
U.S. NAVAL HISTORY AND HERITAGE COMMAND

Ships at the Washington Navy Yard, as seen from the USS *Minatanomoh*, 1865–1866. The *Stonewall* is in the background at center. U.S. NAVAL HISTORY AND HERITAGE COMMAND

Drawing of the *Stonewall*. U.S. NAVAL HISTORY AND HERITAGE COMMAND

BATTLE OF HAKODATE, 1869.

圖之戰海館函年二治明

Battle of Hakodate, June 1869. The *Kotetsu* is at center. U.S. NAVAL HISTORY AND HERITAGE COMMAND

The *Kotetsu*, later *Azuma*. U.S. NAVAL HISTORY AND HERITAGE COMMAND

Another look at the *Kotetsu/Azuma*. U.S. NAVAL HISTORY AND HERITAGE COMMAND

THE BATTLE OF SHIMONOSEKI STRAIT

21

Western maps called the Chōshū bottleneck the Straits of Van der Capellen. To the Japanese, these fast-silting, fast-flowing waters split two of Japan's four home islands with Shimonoseki to the north, and Kitakyushu to the south.

Thought to have separated just six thousand years ago, the sea doesn't just pinch close here, it twists, so ships must carve a tight *c*-shape though them. Shoguns had risen and fallen here in the 1185 Genpei War that led to Japan's first feudal military government under Minamotono Yoritomo. In 1612, the revered samurai Miyamoto Musashi and Sasaki Kojiro chose it as worthy of a fight to the death.[1]

On July 13, 1863, the five-year-old screw sloop *Wyoming* anchored off Hime Shima island, east of the Shimonoseki Strait for a meeting with the Tokugawa foreign minister, which was cancelled due to illness. Two days later, a Japanese employee to the American legation advised that the Chōshū were coming for them. Neither Captain David Stockton McDougal nor his crew had fought before. He ordered preparations for battle. They were about to fight.

He raised anchor early on July 16 with local pilots and sounded general quarters at 9:00 a.m. with his guns draped under tarpaulins but loaded. At 10:00 a.m., the American warship approached the channel and sighted three Chōshū ships, two with smokestacks, and one simply under sail. The shogun's colors were gone. These flew the Chōshū's, who he knew to be "bitterly opposed to foreigners."[2] *Wyoming* entered the channel at 10:45 a.m. A building storm gusted about them, whipping the water into whitecaps.

Japanese shore forts with U.S.-made Dahlgrens fired first, guided by stakes they'd planted in the channel and zeroed their guns on. A local eyewitness reported their fire intensified when *Wyoming* raised U.S. colors. Despite his inexperienced crew being "quite pale" under such fire, McDougal steered a surprising line toward the forts, inside their fall of shot and below the depression angle of most of their guns. McDougal noted that their "aim was wild" and "mostly went ten to fifteen feet overhead," shredding their rigging.[3]

At the tightest point of the channel, McDougal opened fire on the trio of Chōshū warships anchored in a blocking line but trying to get underway. The Chōshū's first sail barque was nearest the town of Shimonoseki. The former American brig *Lanrick*, now renamed the *Kosei*, was about 50 meters further on. The heavier *Koshin* was farthest from them. McDougal steered between them with the steamships to port and sail ship to starboard, so close their marines brought down Japanese crewmen with rifle fire and her 11-inch guns were almost point blank. The Japanese barque returned three broadsides, despite a series of penetrating shots. The brig did likewise.

Six sailors were cut down on the *Wyoming*'s forward battery, one dead. A marine was killed by shrapnel. As she cleared the sail ships at what McDougal called "pistol range," the barque was still firing, even as it began to go down. *Wyoming* gave the Chōshū's larger steam ship a port broadside and turned aggressively to make a second pass. Too aggressively for such a tight channel as it happened, which left her grounded and vulnerable. The *Koshin* charged in to either ram or board her.

While *Wyoming*'s rate of fire was dropping away, a single round struck the *Koshin* at the waterline and pierced her boiler explosively. The blast threw every American crewman to the deck from hundreds of yards away. When the smoke cleared, *Koshin* was plunging down at her bow. *Wyoming* fired on, achieving two further penetrations. In less than two minutes, the Chōshū flagship was gone. Finally able to reverse herself back into the channel, *Wyoming* lined up the brig *Kosei*—already sinking—with her 11-inch guns and repeatedly pierced her above the waterline. *Kosei* disappeared. The last remaining Chōshū sail ship took a fearsome beating, with so many hull penetrations she was little more than a floating hulk, close enough for McDougal to hear the screams of the dying over the storm as she drifted away.

Wyoming then positioned herself against the forts that opened the engagement and fired until each was silenced in turn, stopping only to conserve her shot and powder for any Confederate raiders on her journey home. Captain McDougal was so certain of the moment's importance that he ordered a shore party to souvenir an ornate bronze-cast Japanese cannon that was later prominently displayed in the Washington Navy Yard that would host the *Stonewall*.[4]

At 12:20 p.m., *Wyoming* steamed to a sheltered point in the lee of Skara-jima against what were becoming typhoon-strength winds. Behind them onshore, fires started by overshots burned so fiercely that they could be seen through 8 kilometers of driving rain. Watches were posted. Fresh powder and shot were readied. The wounded were carried below decks. *Wyoming* steamed back in the following dawn to shatter the lesser forts of the west side of the bay, which did not reply.[5] It was over.

The Chōshū had hit the Union ship twenty-two times. fourteen were penetrations. Her rigging and smokestack were riddled with holes. *Wyoming*, in fifty-five minutes, and with just fifty-five shots, had destroyed everything that opposed her. Four Americans were buried at sea. A fifth followed shortly after. Seven were wounded.

Despite their total defeat, the Chōshū had closed the straits to foreign shipping, and the blowback was directed at the shogun they opposed. European missives to his court were blunt. "The outrages and insults which the Prince of Chosiu has ventured to undertake . . . is looked upon as an attempt to carry out the edicts of the Mikado [emperor]. No reasonable man in Japan can doubt as to what must be . . . the fate of the country if the outrageous and lawless attempt to cancel solemn treaties by treacherous and violent acts is not immediately abandoned."[6]

The U.S. Naval Institute would later record, "Had this engagement occurred closer to home and at a different time, it might well have entered the annals of famous battles." As it happened, it was just three days after the Confederate defeat at Gettysburg that proved a turning point in the United States. McDougal's after-action report to Gideon Welles is confident, "the punishment inflicted . . . will I trust teach him a lesson that will not be forgotten."[7] It did not.

French forces followed within days, with French admiral Constant Jaurès's flagship steam frigate *Semirami* (thirty-four guns) and gunboat *Tancrede* (four guns) battering the same channel forts and landing troops who destroyed their magazines and fired the nearby village. By the time Shogun Iemochi appealed to the emperor in person to call off the Chōshū (only the third time any shogun had called upon the emperor directly), he'd paid £25,000 in compensation to the British. The Chōshū, owing a further £25,000, paid nothing.

The English response—ordered in retribution for the killing of a British merchant by samurai serving the Satsuma—was even larger. Without the conflicting priorities of a civil war, the British deployed a sizable fleet under Acting Vice Admiral Augustus Leopold Kuper. On the August 15, 1863, they entered the harbor of the Satsuma capital, Kagoshima, and bombarded the city systematically until more than five hundred buildings were destroyed. Satsuma shore batteries maintained sporadic fire throughout, including a single shot that beheaded Captain Josling and Commander Wilmot. In all, thirteen English lives were lost. Samurai screamed challenges at them, standing waist deep in the water, and counted themselves victors as the British hadn't landed.[8] The Satsuma paid their dictated compensation by borrowing it from the shogun and never repaying him.

Western forces had succeeded at every tactical level, but the larger strategic victory belonged to imperial Japanese rebels. Nothing had been conceded, except their rival shogun's money. It lit a fuse. Anti-foreigner riots fanned out from Edo, where the American legation was burned to the ground.

Coverage in England's *Times* newspaper showed a remarkable awareness of the shogun's vulnerability, "It is believed that his Government would gladly see a British force employed in chastising the insolence of the anti-foreign Daimios, whom he is quite unable to curb, and whose hostility is very dangerous to his throne." It also acknowledged that no decisive change could be effected by Western power from the sea. "Japan is an entirely self-supporting country; until the arrival of foreigners it had no trade and desired none; the destruction of all its ports by our fleet and the cessation of trade would, therefore, have no other effect than to cause the inhabitants to withdraw into the interior and revert to their old habits."[9]

Militant imperial clans were not deterred. Work began immediately to raise the ships sunk by the *Wyoming*. Coastal forts were first repaired, then expanded. Foreign vessels continued to be attacked and would be for more than fourteen months. New agents were dispatched for European warships.

The paradox remained that opposing Western interests required Western weapons. Some foreigners fled. Most didn't, given the amount of money changing hands. English trader Charles Lennox Richardson was killed in the Namamugi incident when he dared overtake the Edo-bound procession of the proud Satsuma daimyo, Hisamitsu Shimazu. The shogun offered England a £100,000 apology. The Satsuma offered nothing.[10]

Despite the British incursion in Nagasaki Bay setting so much unrest in motion, the Satsuma signed new supply agreements with them.[11] As the American South had noted, Scottish shipyards were producing warships at an unprecedented rate. Her munitions plants hummed, too. Scottish arms dealer Thomas Blake Glover staged a series of (illegal) European tours for Chōshū and Satsumi samurai and sold the Chōshū seventy-five hundred Minié rifles in 1865, whose spiraled barrels and bullet-shaped rounds increased range, accuracy, and damage so profoundly that amputations became a battlefield staple in Japan, too. Some thought Glover sided with the emperor because France was with the shogun. Others thought he sold to whomever could buy.

Glover recorded, "The Bakufu had made 'a pointed request' to the British Queen not to allow the illicit trade. The Shogun himself sent her a personal letter." Neither Glover nor Her Majesty replied. Nakaoka Shintaro noted of their new Western-style army, "in every way the forces of the han have been renewed; only companies of rifle and cannon exist, and the rifles are Miniés, the cannon breech loaders using shells." Imperial clans became more discerning buyers after the lessons of Shimonoseki. The Shintaro, for example, rejected the delivery of a 60-horsepower warship when 120-horsepower was contracted for the former Union ship *Otchu*, declaring, "The greatest value of a gunboat lies in the fact that it is powerful and fast, even though it is small. To take an analogy from the flight of birds, it can be compared to a great hawk or a falcon. A falcon which lacks quickness has little value."[11]

In reply, the shogun doubled down on new French ties that stretched all the way to the court of Emperor Napoleon III, whose prestige had risen after the Crimean War, and who would soon contract for the *Stonewall*'s construction. Dutch traders switched their cargos to military goods for both sides.

Worse was to come.

When the shogun inevitably failed to deliver on the emperor's deadline to expel all foreigners and the Chōshū battled Western forces at sea, the Mito clan split into factions, one of which under Fujita Koshirō marched southwest to Mount Tsukuba in early May in defiance of their lord's orders. As word spread, it swelled with hundreds of men under the reluctant leadership of Takeda Kōunsa. By the time the shogun proclaimed it the Mito Insurrection, houses including the Tengutō and Shishido joined an uprising as incendiary as Schleswig-Holsteinian prince Frederick's volunteers seizing Rendsburg or the Confederacy besieging Fort Sumter.

Loyal Mito forces joined a six-clan, 6,700-man shogunate army defeated at Nakaminato on October 10. The rebels marched on, living off the goodwill of those they passed. Despite tactical success, the contagion spread no further, and the shogun's army swelled with new pledges. By December, the remaining thousand rebels were shattered by shogunate forces ten times larger. In all, more than 1,300 rebels died on the battlefield. Along with their leaders Fujita Koshirō and Takeda Kōunsai (whose wife, sons, and grandchildren were killed with him), 353 followers were beheaded. A further 100 did not survive captivity in bitter winter conditions. The loyal Mito faction awarded control of their house to the heavy-handed Ichikawa Sanzaemon for three years, until they faced a brutal retaliation from the Tengutō they'd punished, and the Mito once again switched sides.[12] There had been localized violence with the Yamato Tenchūgumi or Tajima Ikuno incidents previously, but all were unsanctioned or deniable, and it was masterless samurai who paid the price.[13] This was different.

While clashes continued in August 1864, the Kinmon incident exploded 500 kilometers away. Kyoto, seat of the emperor's Chrysanthemum throne, was one of Japan's three largest cities. After extensive damage in the Onin War (1467) and a lengthy period of deep divisions among samurai, religious factions, and court nobility, it had been transformed from individual fortresses and factions to a city of order and beauty within impressive "Odoi" city walls.

The previous month, when masterless ronin from Chōshū, Tosa, and Higo domains were discovered plotting to supposedly "free" the emperor by the shogun's sky-blue-coated Shinsengumi special police, their Ishin-Shishi leaders were summarily executed.[14] Though the plot was unsanctioned, and despite being bloodied at sea by Western forces, it was a response the Chōshū would not bear. While the emperor's silence continued, the troops they landed in Osaka Bay to march on his palace claimed to do so in his name. Worse still was the presence of other flags for the Mototake, Kanenobu, and Chikasuke houses alongside them.[15] The shogun summoned a second army of loyalists to meet them. Across the nation, men were marching. Peasants left their fields, weapons in hand. Samurai renewed their oaths. Old alliances were thrown out or restored. Men like the twice-exiled "last samurai" Takamori who had been too radical months before were suddenly thrust into command.

On came three thousand troops in traditional garb. The Chōshū's long-standing enemies (though fellow emperor-aligned imperialists), the Satsuma, who maintained a stranglehold on the emperor's security, met them together with the Aizu at the city's Hamaguri Imperial Gate, with the future shogun, Tokugawa Yoshinobu, in the thick of it on the city walls.

When the bloodshed began in such close quarters, surging to and fro through the city gates, it quickly degenerated into skirmishing bands, some with rifles in hand, others with swords and polearms. In the chaos, it was unclear who started a fire in the Takatsukasa family compound that spread quickly, forcing the rebels to withdraw.[16] Each side blamed the other.

Among close-standing wooden buildings, fire had devoured hundreds of buildings at Shimonoseki. Here, even the emperor could only watch as it consumed more than 30,000 buildings.[17] The city was never the same, and within five years the court had passed to Edo (present-day Tokyo). Four hundred rebels died, and with them sixty of the shogun's defenders.

It wasn't the shogun who tested the Chōshū's resolve. After the *Wyoming*'s victory, nor would it be America. While the young shogun Iemochi labored to clarify the Chōshū alliance as rebels, Western accounts failed to make the distinction, often using the terms *shogun* and *mikado* (or emperor) interchangeably.[18]

Europe's great powers were about to teach both why warships are the best ambassadors.

THE SECOND BATTLE OF SHIMONOSEKI STRAIT

22

In civil-war America, the Union Anaconda Plan was squeezing the South. Atlanta had fallen. The Confederate submarine *H. L. Hunley* became the first to sink an enemy warship—the *Housatonic*—with the loss of all hands. The Union's thirteen-monitor Red River campaign failed to sever Texas from the Confederacy. At Mobile Bay, D. G. Farragut said "damn the torpedoes," ran a minefield, and destroyed a rebel fleet headed by the iron-clad *Tennessee*. Elsewhere, the ill-fated archduke Maximilian I of Mexico was installed as Mexican emperor.

In Europe, an Austro-Prussian army defeated Denmark at the Battle of Dybbøl while the warship *Stærkodder*, less than a year from becoming the Confederate *Stonewall* and three years from becoming a Japanese flagship, went back on her slipway for repairs. In the Second War of Schleswig, the Danish navy defeated a largely Austrian fleet in the Battle of Heligoland. Russia prevailed in the Russian-Circassian War. Italy had fought two wars for independence and would soon win it with a third. Twelve nations signed the first Geneva Convention.

In China, with the Third Battle of Nanking, the Qing dynasty finally defeated the Heavenly Kingdom Taiping Rebellion. The Māori Wars raged in New Zealand. From one end of the globe to the other, arms merchants sold, and armies bought.

Despite the *Wyoming*'s punishment of the Chōshū fleet, merchants continued to be fired on. Britain, France, and Holland agreed on a coordinated and overwhelming response. America was part of the dialogue, but with the *Wyoming* forced home for boiler repairs and only the anachronistic sail ship *Jamestown* (1,168 tons; twenty-two guns) available to replace her, her Captain Cicero Price was forced to charter the steamship *Ta-Kiang* and wrangle a single 30-pounder Parrot gun aboard to even keep up as an observer.[1]

The punitive European fleet was led by eleven British steam warships under Admiral Augustus Leopold Kuper on the screw frigate HMS *Euryalus* (2,371 tons; fifty-one guns), including the first-rate two-decker ship-of-the-line HMS *Conqueror* with a large complement of marines (2,694 tons; eighty-nine guns), the screw corvettes *Tartar* (1,997 tons; twenty-two guns, built for the Russian navy but seized) and *Barossa* (1,700 tons; twenty-two guns), the paddle wheel frigate *Leopard* (1,406 tons; eighteen guns), and sloop *Bouncer* (six guns), together with the gunboats *Perseus*, *Bouncer*, and *Coquette* (all 409 tons; four guns). They were joined by a trio of French steamships—the screw frigate *Semiramis* (2,497 tons; eighty-six guns), the gunboat *Tancrede* that'd engaged land batteries and landed troops in the First Battle of Shimonoseki Strait, and the screw corvette *Dupleix* (1,773 tons; twenty-four guns). The Dutch added the frigate *Medusa*, who had her recent dead to avenge, along with the screw corvettes *Amsterdam*, *Djambi*, and *Metal Cruyis* (1,083 tons; sixteen guns).

At dawn, September 4, 1864, the combined fleet was revealed at anchor in three national columns (with the American-chartered *Ta-Kiang* attached at the rear of the French contingent) directly opposite the freshly rebuilt shore forts of the Shimonoseki Strait, who watched them in silence.

On September 5, they rearranged their forces around the heavy *Euryalus*, *Semiramis*, and *Conqueror*, with medium ships arcing out from them and their lighter elements shifted to their flanks. Demands for the Chōshū's capitulation were presented in English, Dutch, and Japanese.[2] Once again, stormy weather greeted a confrontation, greatly complicating shipborne gunners targeting land forces. When the rebel silence continued, there was no hesitation.

Euryalus boarded three British-built Satsuma warships, the screw ship *England* (1,150 tons, purchased for $125,000), *Sir George Grey* (492 tons, purchased for $85,000), and *Contest* (350 tons; $95,000). At 2:00 p.m., their ultimatums were repeated. Within an hour, an unidentified Japanese "vice-minister" was taken aboard with a party of forty guards but recalled by other officials before any meaningful discussions began.

The Japanese journalist, Joseph Heco, reported that the imperial rebels sent an explanatory letter noting any murderers of Europeans would face severe justice, that they sought genuine perpetrators, and that they were not tempted "in an instant [to] take some condemned criminals out of prison and hand them over to the Admiral as being the murderers of Mr. Richardson" [killed in the Namamugi incident]. They claimed the shogun was ultimately responsible for their violence, "as he had permitted foreigners to come into Japan contrary to law and custom, and granted them liberties which permitted them to interrupt and impede the movement of Japanese Princes on the high-roads," and concluded that they were "not bound by the Treaties of the Tycoon with foreigners."[3] For the Europeans, nothing less than unconditional surrender could be accepted.

British accounts claim that Chōshū shore batteries were the first to open fire, raking the *Euryalus* while her band played "Oh Dear, What Can the Matter Be?" Japanese accounts suggest *Euryalus* fired first. Either way, "the Admiral immediately made the signal 'burn prizes,'" and the three seized ships were set ablaze and drifted brightly through the rain-lashed battle that followed.[4]

When *Euryalus* fired her first broadside, at least eight shore batteries opposed her, some just 500 to 600 yards off. Five smaller junks were destroyed outright. Their three-hour gunnery duel was indecisive despite the spectacular explosion of one of the English warship's Armstrong guns, recorded by a deck officer in correspondence with historian William Laird Clowes. "In the forecastle we had a 7-in. B.L. 110-pr. Armstrong. Whether the men in the heat of the action became hurried I cannot say; but certain it is that the breech piece of this gun blew out with tremendous effect, the concussion knocking down the whole gun's crew, and apparently paralysing the men, until Webster, captain of the forecastle and of the gun, roused them."[5]

Despite torrential rain, numerous Western shots overflew their targets and set the overlooking township alight again, throwing the shore forts into hellish silhouettes. Hundreds of wooden homes burned. When the Japanese guns ceased fire in the late afternoon, it was too near darkness for a full European landing, though *Perseus* reported spiking a number of guns with a small shore party.[6]

Incredibly, English ships received "a request from Buzen, on the side of the strait opposite to Shimonoseki, that the people there should be permitted to fire blank cartridges at the [European] squadron during the attack, and yet not be molested. They desired to keep in the good graces of both parties, with a diplomatic view to the future."[7] Despite everything, it seemed they had more to fear from their countrymen.

No one disputes that the Satsuma fired first at dawn on September 6. While at least two vessels were struck, they faced overwhelming counterfire from the superior European fleet. As the volume of Japanese fire declined, the *Ta-Kiang* and seven of their smaller vessels rowed in a thousand-strong wave of Royal Marines and armed British, French, and Dutch sailors. Japanese gunners were swept from their positions, and the remaining guns were spiked. Japanese magazines were set alight. Despite a brief grounding of the corvette HMS *Perseus* (seventeen guns) and a late counterattack on the Marines after French and Dutch forces withdrew in good order, the day was theirs. By September 7, shore fire was sporadic, and allied forces had either destroyed or removed sixty-two Chōshū cannon.

Remaining Chōshū forces surrendered on September 8. The allies sustained seventy-three casualties. The Japanese had forty-seven. Eight Victorian crosses were later awarded for actions in storming the coastal forts, including the first to an American, Ordinary Seaman William Seeley, then serving in the Royal Navy. A Chōshū representative was rowed to the *Euryalus* with an offer for a two-day truce and reopening the strait that was immediately accepted.

The West continued to show a fundamental misunderstanding of domestic politics. The Buzen's extraordinary outreach went unremarked. While a number of Chōshū leaders were beheaded, European delegates presented their claim for $3 million compensation to the shogun, who had nothing to do with either confrontation—a sum so large, some felt it was chosen to be impossible to pay. A further treaty was demanded with access to additional ports. European troops were posted ashore to enforce them. While the shogun burned goodwill calling in debts and raising taxation to respond, the Satsuma joined the Chōshū in dispatching agents to Europe and placing military orders with traders like Scotland's Scott Thomas Glover in Nagasaki.[8]

Once again, it had been a tactical victory for the West, and a strategic loss for the shogun. Humiliation followed humiliation. Communications with London were so slow, even when they switched to telegrams after India, that new demands for a public apology and a further £100,000 compensation straggled in more than twelve months later. Shogun Iemochi provided both, and tried to balance them with decrees limiting Western conduct that were largely ignored. A wave of recrimination exiled everyone from the emperor's special consultant for national affairs to the emperor's favorite concubine, and the mother of the future emperor, Meiji, from court.

These capitulations pushed more daimyo into the emperor's "sonnō jōi" orbit. While they had lost a further battle for Japan's future, the Chōshū and allied clans had not lost the war. Both imperial and shogunate forces redoubled their imports of Western arms, though only the shogun's efforts were compromised by spiraling debts.

Emperor Kōmei's silence continued.

The shogun assured the emperor their roles were unchanged and unchanging. British consuls intercepted a missive from shogun to emperor, stating he "received marks of the Mikado's favour, and, at the same time, promised to confine his functions to those of a military vassal, and to endeavour, by improving the military resources of the country, to enable Japan to hold her own against other powers."[9] Too late. Hard-liners on each side had begun to outpace them.

While Takamori had the emperor in his heart, a samurai lived to serve. When the shogun Iemochi set about raising an army in 1864 to punish the

Chōshū, it was Takamori he chose to lead it.[10] By September 1, 1864, his multiclan forces were underway. The goal wasn't just to crush the rebellion, but also the idea that the shogun and emperor were a choice, and not a divine partnership.

The Satsuma had been long-standing rivals to the Chōshū. Takamori had performed selflessly at Kinmon gate for his shogun. Only a handful of rebel houses declared against more than three hundred for the shogun. Confidence was high. Progress, however, was slow.

The Satsuma-led army, bolstered heavily with the Aizu, grew en route as new clan pledges joined them. Was Iemochi worthy of the great unifiers? Whispers about his health were growing louder. Even benign actions—like the sudden departure of chamberlain Tadamitsu—were rumored to be signs of an imminent assassination attempt.[11]

When the shogun's 150,000-man, thirty-six-clan Seicho-gun army ("conquering army of Chōshū") deployed outside their capital, the Chōshū proved as committed in politics as they were in battle.[12]

No rebel army awaited Takamori, not because their leaders opposed armed insurrection, but simply because it was too soon. By the time Tokugawa Yoshikatsu, Prince of Owari, led the shogun's army to the Chōshū gates, rebel leaders like Masuda, Kunichi, and Echigo already had their heads on spikes and the imperial Chōshū daimyo Mori Yoshichika and his son were imprisoned in a temple. It was unclear what was left for Takamori's shogun's army to do. Denied the opportunity to show strength, Iemochi instead opted for magnanimity. Noble rebel leaders like Sanjo Satenomi were lucky to be exiled to other domains. Rebel promises that their Kiheitai troops would be disbanded were made and believed, even as the Chōshū's fleet commander, Takasugi Shinsaku, worked with the Scottish merchant Glover on new armaments.[13]

By January 1865, the shogun's army had been checked with no bloodshed the Chōshū hadn't chosen. Just as the obligation of daimyo to shogun was fraying, so was the relationship of samurai to their daimyo. New European voices reinforced the notion that a man's loyalty should be to a national identity, cause, or leader, more so than to his direct patron. Maverick samurai began to have an outsize influence on events.

When rebel leaders reached out to the shogun's general Saigō Takamori privately, his even meeting them in a Shimonoseki still rebuilding after being fired by Western reprisals, would have been a betrayal of his office. Trusted former shogunate Tosa officers quietly facilitated talks elsewhere. Just six years after being exiled for his imperial advocacy, he decided he could bear being a traitor to his shogun if he was a servant to the emperor. The result was a military alliance between the Chōshū and Satsuma with six articles committing them to controlling Kyoto and Osaka, calling for direct emperor rule, the destruction of the "Hitotsubashi, Kuwana and Aizu (the allies of Bakufu)" if they "continue to commit the sacrilege of utilizing the Imperial Court," ending with the pledge, "God knows the alliance will never change in the future."[14]

The shogun's spies—though not aware of the pact—alerted Iemochi to the Satsuma's resulting diversions of rice and arms. His attempts to reimpose mandatory daimyo residencies in Edo were ignored. Iemochi felt the tide turning against him, at one point feeling so powerless that he threatened to resign, which left the Edo castle in such an uproar that it's said men and women ran through the corridors, with at least one figure crying it would mean "life is no longer worth living" and hurling himself down a well before he was dissuaded. Emperor Kōmei's silence continued, though he declined Iemochi's offer to resign over the opening of Hyogo Port and had two leading doctors from the Tenyakuryo (Bureau of Medicine) dispatched to aid his shogun on reports of his ill health.

With the rebellion's weaknesses at sea exposed, the shogun continued his efforts to make his navy unassailable. Rebels could pick up a gun, but only a nation's true leader could deploy a fleet. By 1865, Japan's first modern naval arsenals at Yokosuka and Nagasaki were under construction with French naval engineer Léonce Verny. The following year, Japan's first domestically built steam warship—the ponderous 5-knot, thirty-five-man *Chiyoda* (Chiyodogata; 142 tons; three guns)—was launched. Within months, the end of the American Civil War would offer warships like none Japan had seen.

Shogunate forces staged a major show of force in May, marching through Kishu and sixteen other domains sympathetic to the Chōshū but not actively rebelling, with a reported sixty thousand troops that culminated in Kyoto, the seat of the emperor's throne. The first Chōshū expedition left matters so unresolved that a second Chōshū expedition (or Summer War) was announced by the shogun in March, and finally launched in June 1866.

Both sides renewed efforts to expand their naval forces. Iemochi called on his daimyo to accelerate their modernization, and the Confederates James Dunwoody Bulloch, John Slidell, and others quickly found themselves competing with Japanese agents for European arms. The Satsuma founded a naval academy of their own, hired foreign advisors, dispatched their own buyers to Europe, and laid down the first keel in their own shipyards. The domains of Hizen (Bizen), Tosa, and Kaga followed the Satsuma in purchasing a scattergun array of warships.[15] The Chōshū alone under Prince Mori purchased three warships from America that year—the six-gun barques *Daniel Webster* (six guns), *Lanrick* (the *Kosei*; ten guns), and *Lancefield* (the *Koshin*; four guns).

On June 7, shogunate elements opened hostilities with the naval bombardment of Suō-Ōshima, in Yamaguchi prefecture, headed by the Dutch-sourced corvette *Chōyō*, which had been delivered with a replacement Dutch marine detachment for the Tsukiji Naval Training Center in Edo.[16] If any ship embodied the complexities of the game Shogi, brought to life, it was this vessel. Almost every imperial and shogunate naval officer had trained on her. She'd served Japan's claims to the Ogasawara islands in 1862. To the shogun's embarrassment, it had been briefly captured by the Chōshū during the first shogunate expedition against them, before serving him in the Mito Rebellion and beyond under the samurai-captain Nakamuta Kuranosuke, before ending her career in a new imperial Japanese navy.[17]

While Iemochi's army was an impressive sight, burnished with further clan colors and artillery, the notable absence of the Satsuma, Tosa, Uwajima, and others meant, though dominant, it was smaller than it had been months before. Shogun Iemochi did not travel with his forces, so there was no opportunity to contrast himself with his unmartial predecessor. Instead, his commanders, Matsudaira Katamori and Osagawara Nagamichi divided their forces in what some called the four-borders war. While Iemochi's navy secured Shima Island on July 12, and they had initial success at Sekishu-guchi and Kokura-guchi, defeats at Iwami and Ozegawa to smaller rebel forces showed this wouldn't be a short, sharp campaign.

Rebel factions maintained their aggression at sea, bombarding loyal troops at Buzen and driving them back with samurai landings before the presence of French warships forced their withdrawal. By August, with new clans joining the fray, battles escalated, notably at Shijuhassaka, where Kinse Shiriaku recorded, "both sides fought with desperation, and lost so many men in killed and wounded that the field were covered with corpses."[18] When Iemochi's forces were defeated at Ono on August 16, it was clear they needed to refuse piecemeal battles with rebels featuring imported advisors, imported weaponry, and imported tactics, and consolidate their forces. While no single loss directly harmed the shogun, together they drew new forces to the rebel cause, and saw a growing number of loyal clans withholding or limiting their contributions. Resources earmarked for national priorities—like coastal fortifications—were hurriedly retasked to their flailing campaign.

By this point, rumors about Iemochi's health grew so loud, Commander Ogasawara left the front to see him personally. Messengers crossing paths with him had no further troop pledges. Instead, the shogun's urgent adoption of the three-year-old Tayasu Kamenosuke suggested that succession was a more pressing concern than command. More and more petitioners found Iemochi unable to receive them.

In the end, a solution was beyond him, and the shogun Tokugawa Iemo-chi died at Osaka castle in 1866 with wasting symptoms and a heart attack consistent with the vitamin B deficiency beriberi.

Contemporary accounts describe Iemochi as a modest, long-faced, 5-foot 1-inch, sweet-toothed, and accommodating man, who was broadly respected. Two anecdotes help us wonder what might have been if he had the health to defeat the Chōshū and time to modernize his nation. As a child, he once poured water used for Chinese ink over the head of his seventy-year-old calligraphy instructor. Far from being impetuous, though, when he realized the man had been incontinent due to his great age, a dangerous insult to his shogun, he concealed the moment from others and was careful to invite the retainer the following day. Iemochi took great interest in his navy, and its Kobe Navy Training Center. When traveling on the *Kanrin*, on encountering brutal seas, which reduced many passengers to seasickness amid calls to turn back, he calmly demonstrated confidence in her captain and future chief negotiator, Katsu Kaishū, deciding to "leave it to the gunkan bugyo (the government's naval magistrate) for issues on the sea." On hearing of his shogun's death, Kaishū lamented, "The Tokugawa shogunate is ruined because of his death," adding, "Though he was at the mercy of the period because of his youth, if he had lived a little bit longer, he might have earned his place in history as a great monarch in addition to his excellent military prowess."[19]

In a final indignity, Iemochi's directive that the three-year-old Tokugawa Iesato succeed him, "if I fall in battle or die of illness," was quietly ignored. An infant-shogun needing at least a decade of regency was too great a risk for a nation already on a war footing. Instead, Tokugawa Yoshinobu was installed as the fifteenth shogun.

Although he had been promoted as an alternative to Iemochi years before by daimyo including the Satsuma's Shimazu Nariakira, and acquitted himself honorably in the Kinmon incident, Yoshinobu's conviction had weakened to the point he privately conceded, "I have no taste for the office of Shogun." He tried to equivocate with a proposal that he head the Tokugawa house without assuming the title *shogun*, which was rejected by both sides, and which contributed to a languid 150-day period until his appointment.[20] No sooner had he spoken of personally leading an "Ouchikomi" grand attack to renew the Second Chōshū Expedition, news reached him that rebel forces had forced the loyal Kokura clan and allies to torch their own castle in a retreat to Kawara. With stores being hoarded by each clan's army, the soaring price of rice led to spreading Yonaoshi Ikki urban riots.

Yoshinobu's father, the Mito daimyo Tokugawa Nariaki (heading one of three preeminent Gosanke clans), embodied the contradictions of the age as a shogunate supporter so opposed to Western influence that he implemented his own coastal defenses. He was a traditional leader, who wanted traditional order where "[t]he samurai shows respect for his lord, the lord shows respect for the Shogun, the Shogun shows respect for the emperor." While he invested heavily in his seventh son Yoshinobu's literary and martial education, he was one of thirty-seven children Nariaki fathered, many of whom had been adopted by domain lords and families in a complicated web of influence. Tellingly, during his son's early years his belief in his son wavered. He conceded: "He could become a splendid shogun; but if things didn't go well, it could be too much for him."[21]

Yoshinobu emerged as a worldly adult who wrote about George Washington and most admired Napoleon. He had to be. His first choice in office—to either fight on with the second Chōshū expedition or negotiate a cease-fire to buy time—was arguably the most important he would ever make. He chose the latter. While he used it to trade with the Second French Empire, Russia, and England, it meant that for a second time, a major house had acted in open rebellion without paying a price. No clan who ignored his predecessor's call to arms suffered any consequences.

At best, he was a pragmatist, dismissing any suggestion he could have fought off European invasion if he'd assumed the title earlier as "total nonsense . . . even if I did become a great barbarian-quelling generalissimo, there's not a thing I can do."[22]

The second Chōshū expedition had met none of its goals, and the language of the time had shifted. Isolation from the West quietly disappeared as a goal. Instead, both sides sought to modernize fast enough to set Japan among the great powers. Yoshinobu staked his future—and Japan's—on outpacing his imperial dissenter. When he announced new policies, he did so in Western dress, and his court quickly followed. When he hosted his daimyo, he did so with Western food. New waves of Japanese agents were dispatched to Europe, which would later include his brother, who marveled at telegraphy, railways, balloons, photography, and a 50-ton steel cannon from Germany's Krupp works at the 1867 Paris Exposition.

Military liaisons were appointed to series of European governments, and Napoleon III himself convened the French military mission to Japan at the request of the shogun's emissary, Shibata Takenaka. The French foreign minister, Edouard Drouyn de Lhuys, personally signed an agreement to train the shogun's land forces. The minister of war, General Jacques Louis Randon, dispatched seventeen initial officers and men, representing infantry, cavalry, and artillery, including Captain Charles Sulpice Jules Chanoine. By January 14, 1867, they were at work, together with Léon Roches and the French Far East Squadron commander, Admiral Pierre-Gustave Roze.[23]

While the bulk of the shogun's army was still equipped with traditional weapons or early-matchlock guns, his goal was to shape the Denshutai as an elite corps that would overmatch even the latest Minié-equipped imperial forces. The new French shogunate advisor tasked with making it happen, Jules Brunet, had cut his teeth as an artillery officer in the French invasion of Mexico, leaving as a captain with the Cross of the Légion d'honneur and Knight of the Légion d'honneur. He arrived in Japan with nation-sized ambitions, an athletic figure, and walrus moustache, given to surprisingly informal photography. He quickly reported, "I must signal to the Emperor the presence of numerous American and British officers, retired or on leave, in this party [of the southern daimyo] which is hostile to French interests. The presence of Western leaders among our enemies may jeopardize my success from a political standpoint, but nobody can stop me from reporting from this campaign information Your Majesty will without a doubt find interesting."[24] He was right. While a growing number of Western experts were enticed to Japan, shogunate forces were playing catchup. Flushed with income backfilling shortages of cotton and tea stemming from the American Civil War, the Satsuma were ruthless at stealing talent and supply from under their noses. Dr. William Willis of the English legation, for example, who was approached by multiple parties, chose to work for the Satsuma, whose hospitals he then managed throughout the civil war to come.[25]

The shogun didn't neglect his control of the sea. His new French advisors expanded the Yokosuka Shipyards. England responded with the Tracey Mission founding the naval school at Tsukiji, Edo. His urgency was understandable. While some rebel clans still fired on Western merchants, others welcomed them with open purses. While he maintained Iemochi's civility at court, period accounts suggest he was a sterner match for his daimyo council. British diplomat Ernest Satow described him in increasingly positive terms as "such a gentleman."[26]

The emperor remained maddingly silent on the Chrysanthemum throne.

The fight had not gone out of the Chōshū. Not on land, and not at sea. If anything, they were more emboldened than ever, deriding Yoshinobu for his love of photography and women's company but fearing him as a "Rebirth of Ieyasu." When his offer to resign as shogun was declined by the emperor, he bounced from despair ("The bufuku is finished") to hope when the emperor praised the Aizu. The one thing he knew with conviction was that he was about to be tested, noting, "One hundred plans and one hundred arguments cannot prevail against the spirit of the times."[27]

England and France both traded with the American Confederacy but found themselves taking very different lines in Japan. The British ambassador, Harry Smith Parkes, put his opposition to France's support of the shogun on the record. His diplomats, including Sir Ernest Mason Satow, cultivated relations with the Satsuma's Saigō Takamori, who he described as having "an eye that sparkled like a big black diamond," as well as Itō Hirobumi and Inoue Kaoru of the Chōshū clan.[28]

Entering 1867, in contrast to the quick-fire succession of three shoguns, it was said Emperor Kōmei had never been ill a day in his life. The nation was therefore shocked when in January he succumbed to a rapid and violent onset of smallpox. Despite rumors of poisoning, and British diplomat Sir Ernest Satow noting "it is impossible to deny that [Emperor Kōmei's] disappearance from the political scene, leaving as his successor a boy of fifteen or sixteen [actually fourteen], was most opportune" for the rebel cause, it's likely he was simply one of millions who would do so globally.[29] Yoshinobu had only been shogun for three weeks.

Of Kōmei's five children, only his second son, Sachinomiya (Prince Sachi), born November 3, 1852, to his imperial concubine, Nakayama Yoshiko, and his sister, Princess Suma, survived infancy. Childbirth at the time wasn't just dangerous, it was symbolically unclean. As such, those in line to the throne were traditionally born in the family home, to leave the imperial palace pristine. Even isolation was no guarantee of longevity. At two years of age, his advisors were adamant he'd been so close to death, only treatment with purple snow, prayer, and diviners had saved him.

His father had lived a life so distant from his people, even the shogun had only seen him three times. Prince Sachi had been raised by his advisor Nakayama Tadayasu without ever leaving the palace. Few surviving accounts of his childhood agree. Although Kōmei was proud of the traditional waka poetry his son composed in a dedicated "Pavilion of Listening to the Snow," he also recorded he "had become unpleasant toward me and is more than I can cope with."[30] He'd been named Prince of the Blood and Heir to the Throne and formally adopted by the Empress Dowager Eishō on August 16, 1860, when he was just eight years old, and took the name Mutsuhito. It would be October 15, 1868, before he formally assumed the Chrysanthemum throne as the Meiji Tennō Emperor, and a hopefully named Ansei "peaceful government" period was declared. The Boshin Civil War (Boshin Sensō, or "War of the Year of the Dragon") was less than a year away.

Much like Europe's royal lines, his family's long-standing marriages of second cousins or closer had resulted in health challenges—he would later be identified as having mandibular prognathism's extended chin and spinal deformation.[31] It's likely a similar cause haunted the shogun's line. The new emperor Meiji was conscious that while he was versed in calligraphy and Confucian belief, he lacked the education available to his European peers, and expressed an interest in "Dutch studies" (the sciences). His formal instruction in foreign affairs only began in 1871, at the age of nineteen, which is notable for the number of actions taken in his name in the preceding years.

While a map of Japan colored by loyalty would show Yoshinobu had far stronger support among the nation's daimyo, it's telling that he became the first shogun never to enter Edo. Attempts to placate the growing Chōshū-Satsuma block with a limited transfer of power did nothing to stop reports of their rearmament.

Yoshinobu's envoys worked desperately to offset their late start on world arms markets, notably in North America, where a booming post–Civil War economy offered the surpluses of demobilization and mass production. Japan's rebels may have an army, but the shogun was keen to show only he had a national fleet. In 1866 he commissioned the wooden steam frigate *Fujiyama* (one of three vessels ordered by Iemochi before him, which had been delayed by the battles for Shimonoseki, which resulted in the other two being cancelled).[32] Later that year, the frigate *Kaiyō*, from Holland's Cornelis Gips and Sons yards at Dordrecht, which had been the largest wooden vessel ever built in the Netherlands, followed.

Imperial forces were just as driven. The fully rigged *Kaiyō* (2,632 tons; twenty-six guns) had been commissioned September 10, 1865. In 1867, the UK-built former Chinese warship *Chiangtzu* was secured by the Satsuma as the wooden-hulled, side-wheel frigate *Kasuga* (1289 tons; seven guns), which served as the shogun's personal yacht until called to war. Each of them was a generation ahead of the ships sacrificed at Shimonoseki, but none was *Stonewall*'s equal.

In August, Takamori's efforts to stage a confrontation with four daimyo, including the Tosa over the forced opening of Hyogo port by a four-nation Western fleet, was deftly and diplomatically resolved by Yoshinobu. As positive as this seemed, it convinced the Cho-Sat block that only war could achieve their aims and represented the last time words were enough for the shogun. Anti-Western violence continued sporadically. In August 1867, English consuls reported the assault on two merchants between Osaka and Jeddo while the murder of two crewmen from the HMS *Icarus* (868 tons; eleven guns) in Nagasaki saw their assailants publicly hung.[33]

All pretense of a peaceful outcome was being shed like a skin. In early November 1867, a secret order issued by the Satsuma and Chōshū in the name of Emperor Meiji commanded the "slaughtering of the traitorous subject Yoshinobu."[34] Shoguns were the flawed appointees of men. The emperor was descended from gods. Only one of them could save Japan in their eyes. It's unclear if the emperor had seen this, much less ordered it, although others in his court almost certainly had.

Only a decisive third expedition could stop the Satsuma–Chōshū insurrection before it spread. Though Yoshinobu controlled vastly more troops, more gold, more land, and East Asia's most powerful fleet, none of it had deterred the imperial rebels, and the shogun needed to make a hard-nosed calculation over which daimyo would answer a call to arms.

On November 9, 1867, Tokugawa Yoshinobu resigned his post as the fifteenth Tokugawa shogun, and formally transferred power to the fifteen-year-old Meiji emperor with a vow to "be the instrument for carrying out imperial orders."[35] The shogunate that dated back to 1603 had ended. Some called it selfless. Some called it weak.

His hope was to avoid plunging Japan into civil war, and to assume a lesser role heading the Tokugawa clan. The state's bureaucracy made a relatively smooth transition to their new titular head, though the Chōshū and Satsuma were far from sated.

The nation remained a powder keg. Rumors abounded. The traditional two-thousand-strong Aisu guard of the emperor were expelled over questions of loyalty and replaced with the Satsuma—which was no less shocking than the pope suddenly rejecting his Swiss Guard would be.[36] Two hundred Shinsengumi special police were dismissed. From this point, the Satsuma–Chōshū block would exert extraordinary control over access to the emperor.

It was one thing for Japanese forces to import advisors and weapons. It was quite another to build a domestic manufacturing capability. In truth, like Qing China before them in the second Opium War (1856–1860), the Japanese economy was actually shrinking relative to the West. Both the shogun and the emperor knew it.

The imperial court initially accepted the shogun's lesser role as part of "just government" (kōgiseitaiha), but it was a redline for the Chōshū–Satsuma block, who were concerned that a subsequent council may reinstate the Tokugawa. Takamori threatened any member of the court who opposed the dissolution of the shogun's office and the confiscation of Yoshinobu's lands. With his troops stationed outside the court, no one doubted his claim "that it would take only one short sword to settle the discussion."[37]

Matters that daimyo would have escalated to the shogun before were now being taken into their own hands. Nakaoka Shintaro, who'd helped unite former Chōshū and Satsuma enemies against the shogun, did not live long enough to see the results; he died at an assassin's hands in Kyoto in December 1867. A gang stormed the Edo yashiki of Shimazu and burned it to the ground, over allegations the Satsuma had kidnapped a princess. Survivors of the rioting fled to Shinagawa Bay where they were gathered by the Satsuma ironclad steamer, the *Shoho* (*Chōyō*), an ex-British vessel they'd refitted as a gunboat.[38]

What did honor demand?

The bushido code was a strictly codified culture that governed Japan's warrior classes from as early as the eighth century. It was quite literally the "'way of the warrior." Its model of discipline, honor, skill, sacrifice, loyalty, and courage was foundational for Japanese feudal society, though crucially, it was built on absolute loyalty to the daimyo, rather than to the emperor or shogun. It had no answer for divided clans.

While samurai were venerated in the bushido code, it was only at great cost. Some held that they would be denied a reward in an afterlife—or in other lives—due to their commitment to deadly arts. In a very literal sense, in committing to serve their daimyo at war, they were making a commitment to go through if not a Christian hell, then a conceptional hell, to serve their masters. When the samurai marched, they risked more than their lives. Fear was considered abhorrent, other than a fear of dishonor. It demanded an incredibly high price for its adherents. If a samurai lost their honor, they could only regain it with the ritual suicide, *seppuku*. To do so wasn't just redemptive, it was prestigious.

It was clear that nothing short of the Tokugawa house—and others—falling would assuage their enemies. A gathering of Yoshinobu's loyal daimyo at Osaka castle convened a war council, pledging their lives for his. On January 17, 1868, he withdrew his resignation and declared "that he would not be bound by the proclamation of the Restoration and called on the court to rescind it."[39] As if on cue, a bout of ill health prevented him marching.

The Satsuma and Chōshū immediately ordered their samurai to the capital. Yoshinobu, even then trying not to force the emperor's hand, waited until Meiji finally consented to the dissolution of the house of Tokugawa and the outer works of Edo castle, the ancestral Tokugawa seat, before unleashing his army on January 24.[40] In retaliation, the home of the Satsuma daimyo, which he didn't occupy but other anti-shogunate forces under Takamori's direction did, was torched. Like America before her, Japan was at war with itself.

Rightly so, judged Yoshinobu's council. Shogunate forces could call on three to five times more troops than the imperial rebels. His base at Osaka castle was seen as unassailable. Shogunate modernization in the north, although slower than it had been to the south with imperial forces, had accelerated with the French military mission. They commanded the most powerful fleet in Asia, with further warships contracted.

Saigō Takamori knew it. Secret preparations to spirit the emperor away to the Chūgoku mountains and launch guerrilla resistance if shogunate forces overran them were made. Yoshinobu declared that his march on the capital Edo with fifteen thousand troops would free the Meiji emperor from manipulation by his advisors. Indeed, it was reported in the West that "[t]he

Mikaido [emperor] has been seized by the Satsuma and other Daimyos."[41] Although there could be no reconciliation with the Cho-Sat block, Yoshinobu continued to hold out hope there could be with the emperor. The letters he dispatched ahead of his forces, warning him that militant clans were acting in his name, without consent, were greeted with more silence. His army flew the colors of Kuwana, Aizu, Takamatsu, Tsu, Matsuyama, and Ogaki domains, the sky-blue Shinsengumi special police, and scores of others, in multikilometer long wagon trains headed on horseback and tailed with artillery.

Prussian Dreyse needle guns and state-of-the-art French Chassepot rifles equipped the shogun's two-thousand-strong personal guard and the elite Denshūtai trained by the French military mission. Though tens of thousands more were urgently ordered, many of his troops marched with antiquated matchlock or flintlock guns (many of which predated the American black ships) or with traditional arms.[42] As reinforcements arrived from farther and farther north, the mix of traditional blades, polearms, and bows grew.

Ironically, given the accusations of collaboration with Western forces leveled against them, the shogunate ordered thousands of their best troops off to monitor the large (neutral) Western fleet docked in Osaka Bay, which would be sorely missed. On January 27, Yoshinobu's shogunate army confronted a five-thousand-strong imperial force drawn from Satsuma, Chōshū, and Tosa domains commanded by Saigō Takamori on storied ground south of Kyoto in the four-day Battle of Toba-Fushimi.

The region's soft mineral waters were famous then (as now) for their sake, beer, and plum wine. Shogunate forces advanced past the Fushimi castle built by thirty thousand men for the great unifier Toyotomi Hideyoshi onto ground their enemy had carefully selected and prepared. It was here that Tokugawa Ieyasu's final victory at the Battle of Sekigahara was made possible by his vassal Torii Mototada holding off vastly larger forces in a thirteen-day siege that ended in a mass suicide so gory that it was said when the castle was later broken down and recycled that its blood-red boards could be identified in countless new castles and templates. History was watching. History was being made.

British diplomat A. H. Mitford noted of the shogun's army, "A more extravagantly weird picture it would be difficult to imagine. There were some infantry armed with European rifles, but there were also warriors clad in the old armour of the country carrying spears, bows and arrows, curiously shaped with sword and dirk, who looked as if they had stepped out of some old pictures of the wars in the Middle Ages. Hideous masks of lacquer and iron, fringed with portentous whiskers and mustachios, crested helmets with wigs from which long streamers of horsehair floated to their waists, might strike terror into any enemy. They looked like the hobgoblins of a nightmare."[43]

While the shogun's forces held a three-to-one advantage in men, imperial forces had a far higher proportion of troops organized along Western
lines, with modern French Minié rifles supported by British-sourced howitzers and including at least one of the terrifying new fast-firing Gatling guns
that Chicago's Richard Jordan Gatling had developed in 1862 to try and end
the American Civil War sooner. Many of the rebel troops had been hardened by clashes with Western forces, and all were in well-prepared positions.
Nothing was certain. For a second time, arrangements for the emperor's
evacuation were made.

The American Civil War had seen a bloody learning curve for leaders
confronted with massed field artillery and rifle fire. It begged the question,
what role was there for elan? For esprit de corps? For heraldry and pageantry?

Imperial forces waited across the bottleneck Koeda Bridge with a nine-
hundred-strong Satsuma vanguard supported by four guns, and to the south-
east across the Bungobashi Bridge with the wind at their backs. Their main
body deployed in ranks behind them. While eighty-five hundred of the shogun's troops advanced opposite them, the intentions of the shogunate commander Takenaka Shigekata, whose greatest prewar achievement was putting
down the Tengu party as a magistrate, were unclear. Their field guns were
not deployed. Their cavalry was absent.

In a confused first action, the Kuwana samurai approached the Satsuma
ahead of supporting riflemen, who were not in firing lines and were still
loading their rifles. The Satsuma denied them the crossing and concentrated
fire methodically on one flank. Volley after volley followed. An early cannon round struck a shogunate gun carriage, unhorsing General Shigekata and
scattering troops as their mounts bolted. The ad hoc charge that followed was
a shambles, with losses exacerbated by traditional Kuwan forces' brave but
futile efforts to hold their ground in the face of heavy imperial fire. This was
repeated with heavy losses among shogunate Aizu and Shinsengumi forces
opposite the Satsuma and Chōshū at the Bungobashi Bridge. The Boshin
War had begun.

Joseph Heco's accounts suggest that the shogunate's dismal performance
was attributable to "the treacherous defection of Todo, who went over to
the Mikado's party," though most records suggest this followed much later.
More likely is that shogunate commanders had not planned contact until the
following day but felt compelled to act suddenly at 5:00 p.m. for reasons long
since lost.

Shogunate forces withdrew to reorder overnight, firing local buildings
as they went as cover. The Satsuma and Chōshū suffered 96 dead and 230
wounded. The Tokugawa sustained 285 dead and 610 wounded, but their
loss of cohesion was out of all proportion to these casualties.[44] Once again, in

an age of close-packed wooden buildings, the overnight conflagration grew so fast that the Western expat community reported a red glow on the horizon all the way from Kansai.[45]

Conscious of their piecemeal defeats to date, Yoshinobu's multiclan forces were carefully drawn up in a new order of battle anchored by lines of European-armed troops, buttressed with modern artillery and flanked with traditional troops in macabre masks, adornments, and traditional weapons.

After dark, a sizeable force from the loyalist Tominomori joined preparations for a reversal the following day. Even better, Yoshinobu's health rallied, finally enabling him to join his forces. Here was the setting for the decisive battle the first and second Chōshū expeditions had failed to deliver. Here was the chance for Yoshinobu's loyalists to live up to the great unifiers. Opposite them, heavily outnumbered imperial forces reinforced their twin bridgeheads, drew up more heavy guns, and waited.

On the morning of January 28, though, at first light, it wasn't a national leader or general who shaped events. It was a single rider and flag.

But first, in this nation indivisible from its seas, came a naval war only the former *Stonewall* could end.

WAR OF THE YEAR OF THE DRAGON

23

The 1863 Battle of Shimonoseki Strait was the first clash between modern warships in Japanese waters. On January 28, 1868, the Battle of Awa became the first major clash between Japanese steam forces at sea. With modern arms flooding through a growing number of ports, controlling them had become the key to victory on land.

Mindful of the rebel landings at Osaka in the Kinmon incident, Admiral Enomoto Takeaki's shogunate navy supported their army's march with aggressive coastal patrols. As their land forces looked to redeem their disastrous start to the battle of Toba-Fushimi, two of their warships spotted the smoke of the Satsuma's converted transport ship *Shōō* (*Shōryōmaru*; *Shoho*; *HoHo*; 461 tons; formerly the British *Lochius*).

The smaller *Kanrin* under Captain Sawa (whose studies in Holland, 1862–1867, had overlapped with his admiral's) and larger *Kaiten* (1,827 tons; twelve guns), formerly the Prussian warship *Danzig* under the sideburn-sporting Dutch-schooled Captain Kamjiro, charged the *Shōō* without hesitation, firing as they closed and recording several penetrations.

Rather than running, the *Shōō* under Akatsuka Genroku launched an improbable ram-run toward *Kaiten*, which holed her no less than twenty-eight times, before she proved fast enough to escape to the free-trade port of Hyogo.[1] The aggressive *Shōō* had made a good account of herself. When *Kaiten* passed the HMS *Rodney* (2,598 tons; ninety guns) the next day, they noted her forward yardarm had been shot clean off. Admiral Takeaki transferred his flag to the newer Amsterdam-built corvette *Kaiyō* and kept his fleet at sea, hunting.

Later that month, the shogunate *Kaiyō* had a fleeting contact with the imperial warship *Kasuga*, which was able to break off and steam away. The shogunate Vice Commander Takeaki—the highest-ranked naval official at sea—was dissatisfied with both results, war gamed them extensively, and redeployed his forces to achieve more concentrated fire. They were tested almost immediately.

Awa Bay, near Osaka in today's Tokushima prefecture on Shikoku island, had been conquered by the unifier Hideyoshi, and ruled for generations from Tokushima castle by the descendants of his victorious General Masakatsu. It was a cool region, nestled below the snowline, that even today has scarcely forty thousand citizens. In the nineteenth century, it was largely known for the Buddhist temples of the Shikoku Pilgrimage.

One hundred and sixty kilometers from the Toba battlefield, Satsuma forces were preparing for a transfer of troops to their capital Kagoshima aboard the transports *Shōō* and *Heiun*, escorted by the warship *Kasuga*. Wisely so. The shogunate navy under Enomoto Takeaki had probed south with the steam frigate *Kaiyō* and saw the opportunity to bottle them in. The imperial Commodore Genroku, brother to the future Admiral Ito, sounded general quarters, and her crew raced to their stations. With Toba-Fushimi still in the balance, the rebel transports steamed out at first light, only to find *Kaiyō*'s smoke plume closing.

South of Awaji Island, light fog limited visibility. Wildly outmatched, the Satsuma chose to separate and run. The *Heiun* escaped through the Strait of Akashi. *Kasuga* escorted the *Shōō*, still scarred from her previous encounter, south toward the Strait of Kien. Among his officers was Togo Hiehachiro, who would one day face the *Stonewall* as a captain. The sail and steam frigate shogunate *Kaiyō* made straight for the rebel pair.

With a top speed of more than 17 knots (31 kilometers per hour), the wooden-hulled paddle wheel warship *Kasuga* was the fastest warship in Japanese waters. She had served in the Taiping Rebellion in her earlier incarnation as *Keangsoo* (*Jiangsu*) in the Chinese navy, commanded by Akatsuka Genroku (who spent almost four times his approved budget to acquire her, and quit in disgust when it was initially decided to deploy her as a merchantman to work off the difference).[2]

Kaiyō fired a powder-only warning shot, signaling the imperial ships must stop. They did not. At ranges of 2,500 to 1,200 yards as they closed, *Kaiyō* launched a barrage of twenty-five shots on the Satsuma ships. *Kasugo* returned thirty-eight shots, with three hits, one from Hiehachiro's gun, without material damage. Being on the receiving end was terrifying—splinters or "shivers" as they were known in the age of sail—flew like shrapnel and gave rise to the expression "shiver me timbers." The thickening fog was the Satsuma's best hope. *Kasuga* put herself between the hunter *Kaiyō* and her second transport.

The shogunate *Banryū* and *Hazuru* then appeared, signaled by Takeaki's flags, and steaming for the cannon fire. The iron-reinforced screw-propelled schooner *Banryū* had been presented to the shogun years earlier by the British as the emperor's royal yacht. *Kasuga*'s loyalty to her transport had reached its limits. She broke off and poured on coal to race for Kagoshima. The second imperial transport, *Shōō*, would not be lucky a second time. Without her escort, there was no question of her fighting her way out. Her journey started in Aberdeen, Scotland, but she ended up being run aground at Yūzaki and destroyed in place by her crew.

All of it was closely observed by European warships, moving with absolute freedom, and in numbers, the length and breadth of the country. Japan's waters still presented dangers of their own. In the naval war to come, as many warships were lost to typhoons as direct fire. On January 7, the American Admiral Belle had been among 12 crewmen drowned crossing a bar off Osaka.[3]

Vice Commander Takeaki, a man of slight build who favored a Western-style uniform, samurai sword and oiled moustache for his portraiture, was impressed with the seamanship and spirit the imperial trio had shown, recording, "Although they are enemies, how remarkable."[4] Takeaki's rise would be more remarkable still—before the war's end an entire nation would follow him.

His family had served the shogun for generations. There was no chance he'd become anything but a samurai like his father. He excelled at the Shōheikō academy in the capital, Edo, and at sixteen he was selected to study rangaku sciences (Dutch studies). On his graduation at nineteen, he was selected for the Nagasaki Naval Training Center established the year before. In 1859, the center shifted to Tsukiji with the nation's first paddle wheel steamship, the Dutch-built *Kankō* (769 tons; four guns), Dutch Marine instructors, and a policy to screen out clans agitating against the shogun (wisely, but too late).[5]

Takeaki made such an impression while studying medicine under the impressively named Johannes Lydius Catherinus Pompe van Meerdervort that arrangements were made to send him to study maritime sciences in the Netherlands, where he quickly learned English and Dutch. This wasn't education for education's sake. It was in preparation for war and included direct supervision of at least one ironclad under construction for the shogun. His rise was relentless. On his return, he was promoted to vice commander in chief of the shogunate navy and granted the title of Izumi-no-kami.

The shogun had unearthed an extraordinary talent. A student at the Army Cadet School, Shiba Gorō, would later write, "We also combed the shops for portraits of Napoleon, Washington, Enomoto Takeaki, and other great men we admired. Of course, I refused to touch a portrait of anyone from Chōshū or Satsuma." When he was finally able to meet him in his later years, Takeaki's advice was succinct, "First, build up your physical strength. Second, be honourable and fair. Third, acquire learning. That's all."[6]

Though the shogun's navy had interdicted Satsuma reinforcements, preserving their numerical advantage, January 28, which started with such promise, ended in calamity. At first light in Toba-Fushimi, the shogunate army were confused by the banners of their enemy being pulled down—a profound dishonor on the battlefield. Out came a single rider, with a message more powerful than gunpowder.

The emperor's silence since his impossible eight-week deadline to expel the barbarians had ended. Yoshinobu—and all who followed him—were hereby declared enemies of the Chrysanthemum throne.

New imperial banners with the now familiar red sun rising on a white background—premade and preplaced—were being raised along the imperial lines. The imperial Prince Yoshiaki—a relative of the emperor and former Buddhist monk—was declared commander in chief of a new imperial army (kangun). In an instant, the shogun passed from a patriot freeing the emperor to himself being a rebel. Fighting on was treason.

When shocked shogunate leaders didn't advance, imperial forces did. Without the initiative, General Shigekata could only react, and any chance to unwind their shambolic first-day performance was lost. Despite their inferior numbers, it was the emperor's forces who controlled the field after a day's fighting. Shogunate forces retreated toward Yodo castle.

Imperial forces were relentless. January 29 opened with a Satsuma assault that had shogunate forces heavily pressed. General Shigekata held his ground. Prince Yoshiaki's banners were a sea of red and white. Months earlier, while the shogun was focused on avoiding war, this heraldry had been prepared by Ōkubo Toshimichi, Iwakura Tomomi, and others intent on winning one. Given that Meiji's edict was less than twenty-four hours old, it's plausible they did so without the emperor's consent.[7]

Riders began delivering the colors nationwide, and reassuring Western powers that all treaties with foreign forces would be honored. The overtures worked, and a series of new Western hires such as Dr. William Willis followed from ostensibly neutral powers.[8]

Retreating would dishonor Shigekata. Moving forward risked some clans not joining him. Imperial advances with concentrated riflemen were relentless. By afternoon, he was being driven back toward Nōsho. Shogunate forces finally reaching Yodo castle found their daimyo had renounced his loyalties in the face of the emperor's banners. The castle gates were closed to them. The following day brought no relief as imperial Meiji forces crossed the Kizu River in hot pursuit. Renewed efforts to form a coherent defense were shattered when the Tsu (Mie) clan, like the Yodo before them, switched sides and fired on their erstwhile comrades.

Order began breaking down. The shogunate retreat became a rout. Units became entangled. Equipment was lost and abandoned. Small units fought honorably—and futilely—to buy their forces time. The venerated commander's standard that Tokugawa Ieyasu carried to victory at Sekigahara in

1600 was left behind, forcing the shogun's loyal retainer Shinmon Tatsugorô and a small band of followers to fight their way to it and march it all the way to Edo when the retreating shogunate fleet left without them. The Gilbert & Sullivan song "Miyasama" from the musical *The Mikado* can be traced back to the victory songs the imperial forces sang marching north.

Shogun Tokugawa Yoshinobu received them at Osaka castle on January 30 and gathered his war council. Additional northern elements joined them overnight, and more were on their way. Their superiority in numbers—if not in equipment or firepower—remained. Brushing aside concerns over his health, Yoshinobu declared his intention to lead them into battle the following morning, energizing his daimyo as they returned to their commands.

Just as the Satsuma had arranged to slip the emperor away from any shogunate victory, the Aizu and Kuwana prepared to steam the shogun away to Edo on the warship *Kaiyō* if required.

At first light, imperial forces were once again the first to advance. Far from seeing blocks of French-trained riflemen interspersed with traditional samurai opposite, they saw a rearguard in place, as well as a wave of departing carts and horses on the roads behind them. Once again, Yoshinobu had found his limit.

"Handle them somehow," Yoshinobu directed his generals after his war council the night before, before seemingly to stir, "all right. If there is to be a battle, let there be no delay." Within the hour, Itakura was later afforded a more honest position, when imploring his shogun to lead his men. "Those are not my officers and men now. That is a mob."[9]

Yoshinobu slipped away overnight, and when the warship *Kaiyō* was delayed, he took refuge on the American *Iroquois* (1,032 tons; six guns), which had served the Union throughout the American Civil War instead. When the *Kaiyō* arrived the next morning, he was transferred and steamed away. Without him, the bulk of his forces began retreating along the winding banks of the Katsura and Uji Rivers. Behind them, the defense of Osaka castle was desultory. It had been built over fourteen years from 1583 by the unifier Toyotomi Hideyoshi and spanned more than a square kilometer. It had successfully held off a two-hundred-thousand-man army in 1614 and was so esteemed that the fourteenth Tokugawa shogun, Iemochi, chose it for his death. Without leadership, shogunate forces fractured. By February 2, imperial forces entered Osaka castle unopposed and torched it in a blaze so fierce that it could reportedly be seen from the emperor's palace in Kyoto, 48 kilometers away. Some clans marched north to regroup. Others repledged themselves to the emperor.

Given their chaotic entry into the battle, shogunate casualties were lighter than might have been expected. One hundred and twenty-five samurai were dead; 210 were wounded, and 160 riflemen had died, with 400 wounded.

Imperial forces lost 91 lives and had 230 wounded.[10] It was an astonishing reversal. A force representing more clans than any time since the nation's three unifiers had failed. In under three days, their opponents had been recast from rebels to the Meiji emperor's imperial army. A force one-third their size carried the field, three days running. Worse still was a wave of new clans declaring for the Meiji emperor. The next—the Tsu—followed on February 2. The Yodo followed on February 5. The military balance that had overwhelmingly favored the shogun was tilting.

The Meiji restoration—the honorable restoration—was declared; however, the war was far from over, and it would increasingly be fought at sea, in conditions for which the former *Stonewall* was perfectly suited.

Two chances shaped the conflict to come. One missed. One taken. The first was rejecting a detailed plan from Oguri Kozunosuke, deputy magistrate for the army, navy, and finance, to ambush the advancing imperial army as it entered Kokone. With the resources of clans who would later be lost to them and ground of their choosing, its chances were strong, but there was too great a leadership vacuum to act. The second was Admiral Takeaki's refusal to surrender.

The fall of the Tokugawa house meant their retainers in the fleet faced an end to their stipends. Takeaki advised the admiralty he was "requesting permission" to retain the fleet until questions on "revenue and territory are settled," which they emphatically rejected. When they traveled to Shinagawa anchorage on May 4 expecting a handover in command, they found the fleet had been put to sea.[11] On Yoshinobu's capitulation, Takeaki didn't just maintain a fleet in being, he gathered the treasure, leaders, symbols, and resources needed for a sustained campaign. When he steamed north, it was with the kernel of a new nation.

Traditional daimyo continued to pledge forces for the shogun. Thousands of fresh troops marched south to them with Western arms and uniforms, or ancestral weaponry.

The failed samurai general Takenaka Shigekata was stripped of his rank and title. Though he forewent committing *seppuku*, and initially sought refuge in the priesthood, he soon formed the Junchūtai corps to serve his shogun and fight for his honor.[12]

The battle had been lost for the now post-shogunate bufuku clans, but the war had not. They still controlled more men at arms, more land, more gold, and the strongest fleet in Asia.

Stonewall's time had almost arrived.

THE RACE TO ARMS

24

Japan's future would be won and lost at sea. Controlling the nation's ports would determine the speed at which each side could modernize.

By 1865, thirteen years after the American black ships had forced their ports open, the shogun's eight-warship navy had become the strongest in Asia. Naval arsenals from French engineer Léonce Verny were live in Yokosuka and Nagasaki, with planning underway for more. In North America, hundreds of warships had been demobilized, sold off or broken down, and the *Stonewall* continued to languish.

Like the Confederates before them, imperial forces looked to the United Kingdom. Joseph Heco recorded, "Prince of Choshiu had lately ordered several men-of-war and gun-boats from England through an English firm in Nagasaki, and that although some of these would be out directly, they would be practically useless, since the Prince had no officers who knew anything of navigation, and that he (the Prince) was consequently exceedingly anxious to have some of his people placed on an English war-ship. The Admiral's answer was that it would give him great pleasure to comply with the prince's request."[1]

The shogunate delegation to the Washington Navy Yard in 1860 had been observers. When his representatives returned to the yard prewar in May 1867, it was as customers. Row upon row of paid-up Union and Confederate warships awaited them. Coverage of their inspections circled back to the London *Times*. Ships were emblems of national pride and state. That "the Japanese deputation have come to buy ironclads" was news on both sides of the Atlantic.[2]

Hundreds of wartime vessels had been handed off to federal revenue, lighthouse, survey, postal, and other services. Some, like the hastily improvised ninety-day ships of the initial blockade period, barely lasted the war and were simply broken up. Others were permanently demilitarized for commercial service. Even so, scores remained ready for rearmament. While more than forty were ironclads, most were coastal craft poorly suited to crossing the inaptly named Pacific Ocean. With the serving U.S. Navy dominated by coastal and riverine monitor derivatives, the U.S. oceanic fleet would lag not just the European powers but even some in Latin America well into the 1890s and their renewal with the great white fleet.[3]

The Japanese delegation assigned to expanding their navy was led by Ono Tomogoro, who passed from ship to ship with little comment until reaching the former *Stonewall*; by now she had shed any vestige of her Spanish transition from Havana.[4] Nothing else came close. A contemporary photograph of the Washington Navy Yard facing the Eleventh Street bridge and Anacostia Sound captures the former *Stonewall* stripped of all rigging, moored offshore in a scattering of warships including three monitors, a Confederate torpedo boat, a double-ended gunboat, and the experimental battery *Resaca*.[5]

Money was no object. In July 1867, U.S. secretary of state William H. Seward advised the minister resident to Japan, Robert B. Van Valkenburgh, that they had agreed to her sale. "She is now being fitted for sea at the navy yard here . . . under the command of Captain George Brown . . . who has been granted the necessary leave of absence to act as an agent of the Japanese commissioners."[6] Brown was seconded from the U.S. Navy to State Department accordingly.

Prior to her refit, nothing had changed for the former *Stonewall* since the Civil War. She leaked the day she launched, and leaked the day she was struck off. Her twin rudders made her surprisingly maneuverable. Her draft was shallow enough to enter river mouths. She submerged in heavy swells and reemerged as great plumes of water were shipped across her deck. Her plaques and instruments were in a mishmash of languages. French. English. Danish. Her hull was reworked here and there as underaged wood shifted and her armor did not. Her bilge was constantly being drained by chain pumps that could move hundreds of gallons of water a minute and proved unspeakable in bad weather. Her 300-pounder's forecastle gunport faced the world through a trapdoor that made her look cyclopean. Individual shogunate clan buyers followed, like the Akita securing the former Union screw steam gunboat *Pawtuxet*, which served as the *Kaiten*.

Imperial agents were just as active in Western markets. The Chōshū acquired the schooner *Swan-bow* and the rugged English-built screw steamer *Teibo 2* (236 tons, following *Teibo 1*, which had become a template for the first Japanese-built screw gunboat, *Moisshin* [347 tons; one gun]). The Amsterdam-built brig-rigged ram-bowed *Chōgei* (*Un'yō*) with her sixty-five-strong crew and the self-named *Chōshū* (295 tons; three guns) quickly followed. Growing newspaper coverage cited lesser gunboats acquired by others.[7]

On August 5, 1867, after agreeing on an initial payment of $30,000 and total purchase price variously reported up to $400,000, new colors were raised on the former *Stonewall*, and she was reborn as the Japanese shogunate navy's warship *Kotetsu* ("iron ship").[8] When she made for the port of Shinagawa in Edo Bay, seen off with minimum ceremony by the yard's commander, William Radford, it was with a predominantly American crew.[9] After three years of demobilization and refit, the Washington Navy Yard was transitioning toward naval ordnance production behind her. She would never see America again.

With the Panama Canal not yet open, Captain Brown, a stern, heavyset man with a bulldog jawline and down-swept moustache, transited via the Strait of Magellan up to Hawaii. For the months it took to cross more than 7,000 kilometers at sea, she was seen by no one, an island unto herself. Brown was a Civil War veteran who had commanded the side-wheelers *Octorara* (829 tons; six guns) and *Indianola* (511 tons; four guns), on which he was wounded and captured when his gunboat was sunk by four Confederate warships off Palmyra Island. After a prisoner exchange, he'd fought on with the *Itasca* (691 tons; five guns) at the Battle of Mobile Bay and continued a distinguished postwar naval career that ended with him as rear admiral, before passing the baton to his two sons.[10]

Confederate navy secretary Stephen Mallory's plans for the *Sphinx* and *Cheops* in France had included a larger battery of guns than was ultimately fitted. *Stonewall* was significantly refitted in the months prior to her departure to fulfill his ambition. One of her two aft-castle 70-pounder guns was removed. Two Armstrong 6-pounder guns were added. Four further 4-pounder field guns were mounted to the port and starboard. Like the Confederate *Atlanta* before her, she also had a brutal anti-personal weapon mounted at the leading edge of the aftercastle, secured under tarpaulins.[11]

On deck, her mixed Japanese American crew struggled to communicate. Below deck, the engineers (kika-no) ran their own crews—if a team member stepped out of line it was his engineer he'd answer to. They quickly bonded over the brutal hours worked during their trials. The thought of being unpowered with her notorious seakeeping mid-Pacific was deeply disturbing. Shakedown cruises indicated her top speed had fallen below 10 knots, though clearing her copper hull and boilers of fouling suggested an upside.

Some differences applied. Her new shogunate clerks and paymasters were civilian bureaucrats rather than navy men like Richard Curtis had been. Japanese officers were poorly paid relative to their American predecessors, and so were heavily skewed to independently wealthy samurai. Confederate crews had often flouted their regulations on underage boys favored as powder monkeys. The Japanese crew were all above age.[12] With relatively few warships in Japanese service, competition for placements was fierce. Some applicants were screened on literature, math, or Dutch studies, as the sciences were known. Some were appointed on familial or clan associations. Some had never left land behind before. Captains ate alone, or with senior officers. Japanese wardroom and gunroom warrant officers and so on ate together, while the Americans tended to gather across roles for Western fare a little more. Sake was served, cold in summer, warm in winter, as rum had been for her Confederates.[13] Most officer and crew roles were analogous to those held by Americans before them, though others like graduation chief and institution commander hint at key differences.[14]

Her Japanese crewmen entertained themselves between commitments with song, dance, competitions in traditional fencing, or hosting dignitaries (with several women recording the beautiful paper chrysanthemums made for them in Japanese ports, which is an oddly imperial choice for a shogunate acquisition).

Out went Western superstitions like boarding with your right foot (as the devil favored the left), avoiding bananas (which could actually hasten the ripening of other foods), never saying "good luck," or never whistling (which could "whistle up a storm"). While a cat was likely aboard and feeding well on rats, it should never be black. Seabirds were no longer thought to carry sailors' souls but remained bad luck to kill.

In came new superstitions in their place. The number 4 was unlucky, and the numbers 7 and 8 were fortunate, which prompted a wave of relabeling. Cutting nails by night could mean missing your parents on their deathbed. Names should never be written in red (which was used for grave markers). Whistling at night wouldn't summon a storm but, instead, either snakes or snake-like thieves. A lucky cat could be any color at all.[15]

The two-month negotiation and refit proved to be a fateful delay. When the *Kotetsu* first reached Shinegawa harbor, near Edo, on January 22, no one knew it would take a year for her to determine the balance of power at sea.

Imperial agents had toured her after the shogun's contract was signed. They knew the *Niagara* and *Sacramento* had refused to face her. They knew post-shogunate forces were reorganizing to the north, and that crossing the seas to meet them would be at her mercy. They knew they needed her more. The Chōshū political instincts that had seen off the first expedition against them swung into action again.

Kobe opened as a further treaty port to serve the accelerating arms race. Merchants attacked by imperial forces years, or, in some cases, even months before, now found their safety was being guaranteed by them, and each order was larger and more lucrative than the last. Joseph Heco, who'd served briefly on the *Powhatan* before his career in journalism, noted, "Yokohama, Nagasaki, and the China ports all sent their quota of bearded foreigners on the hunt for the Almighty Dollar." In February, he accompanied Francis Groom of Glover & Co., who had already secured the warship *Union* for the Chōshū, to Osaka to help somehow finagle the shogun's newly acquired *Kotetsu* for the emperor.[16]

Heco shrewdly muddied the waters over a previous U.S. deal for three shogunate warships—of which only the warship *Fusiyam* was delivered, which had incorrectly used the terms *mikado* (as the emperor was known) and *shogun* interchangeably.

Before the United States could formally respond, the imperious opponent of black suffrage, President Andrew Johnson, was impeached over his attempted dismissal of the secretary of war, Edwin M. Stanton. In the ensuing political turmoil, and with the outbreak of the Boshin War, a series of contracts were frozen, including *Kotetsu*'s, despite $30,000 having been paid by the shogun.

Yoshinobu launched a series of carefully composed messages to the emperor, to suppliers including the U.S. Navy, and to the great European powers of the day. Despite the outbreak of war, Yoshinobu still seemed to think no irrevocable line had been crossed. Yet again, when he confined himself to the temple of Ueno Kanei-ji to demonstrate peaceful intentions, it only read as weakness to his enemies. Meiji forces were unclouded. The Chōshū–Satsuma block was growing fast. Within weeks, they were joined by new armies of the Tokaido, Tosando, and Hokurikudo under the supreme commander, Prince Taruhito.

Who was the legitimate leader of Japan? Who spoke for them? In Japan, Europe's foreign ministers gathered in the harbor at Hyōgo (present-day Kobe) to issue a declaration of recognition for the Tokugawa shogunate as the legitimate government of Japan.

Within days, representatives of the Meiji emperor were calling on these Western figures to argue the shogunate was abolished. A resignation had been received. The Tokugawa had been dispossessed. More to the point from a Western perspective, assurances were made that the so-called unequal treaties would be honored and that foreigners would be protected when they prevailed.

Even with the shogun in self-declared exile, tensions remained so high that the next flashpoint of the war only took a pair of sailors.

House Bizen had pledged to the emperor. Their neighboring Amagasaki were pledged to the shogun. On January 27, five hundred Bizen troops led by Karo Tatewaki Heki marched the old Saigōku-kaido Road to avoid the newer shogunate route designed to separate foreigners accessing the port of Hyogo. When two French sailors stepped from a building near the San-nomiya-jinja Shrine, they attempted to cross their advance. This was considered a *tomowari* insult. The Bizen artillery chief, Zenzaburo Masanobu Taki, repeatedly blocked the sailors' attempts to move through the procession. When he could not make himself understood and they persisted, he thrust his spear, whether to injure or redirect, and drew blood.

The terrified French crewmen fled to a nearby building and drew their sidearms. Taki's cry of "pistols! pistols!" was taken by some as an order to shoot. In the confusion, not only did they fire on the building sheltering the pair, but others fired on Western minister-counselors gathered to inspect their march. Whether they were shooting to kill or firing warning shots is debated. Certainly, the national flags above the customs office were holed. The English minister Harry Parkes sent emergency messages to the fleet at anchor, who responded with a body of U.S. Marines, British guards, and French sailors that occupied the settlement. The Bizen withdrew.

No one was killed, but Western forces responded with the seizure of an imperial warship at harbor. On February 8, the Meiji emperor rushed out a diplomatic announcement they had shifted from a policy of Sonnō jōi (expulsion of foreigners) to "Opening of a country to the world and amity." Michitomi Higashikuze began talks on securing diplomatic recognition. The *Stonewall* was requested. To reinforce their commitment, the Bizen invited Western observers to watch artillery chief Taki commit *seppuku* in repentance.[17] While the message was sent to an international audience, it was not published for a domestic one until July.

Compromises were building. Sir Harry Parkes, a veteran of the Chinese Opium Wars, British imperialist, and notorious martinet who'd survived three imperial attempts on his life, was an early voice calling for neutrality, despite his skepticism. "Your country speaks of opening up to foreigners in a friendly way, but to judge from the actions of the Bizen men yesterday, Japan is still full of exclusionists."[18] Within months, he would show Western opinion could switch just as quickly.

Neither side repeated the early advances of the American Civil War.

On March 6, 1868, more than a hundred French veterans of the Bombardment of Shimonoseki in 1864 from the corvette *Dupleix* (1,801 tons; ten guns) were welcomed by an official delegation to the open port of Sakai, Osaka. A series of transgressions were quickly reported to the Tosa samurai patrolling the area. Sailors had entered homes and temples without permission. Citizens were treated with disrespect. Women had been harassed. The Tosa guard captains Inokichi and Nishimura Saheiji led their efforts to de-escalate. They may have succeeded, but for a French sailor stealing the Tosa regimental flag and fleeing. He was pursued, caught, and beaten with a staff. French forces trying to free him were said to have fired on responding samurai. The Tosa's return fire was overwhelming. Eleven French sailors died. Every Western embassy closed their doors in protest.

In prior years, imperial clans had accepted no accountability for Western attacks, leaving the shogun to make amends on their behalf at vast expense. With their new open policy, the emperor's representatives were dispatched immediately. A sum of 150,000 piatres in compensation was demanded and paid. Twenty-nine samurai admitted to firing on the French; twenty chosen by lottery—including both captains—were gathered and ordered to commit *seppuku*. All complied.

With this distraction addressed, Meiji forces were once again the first to act. Three imperial army groups began advancing toward the capital, Edo. The failure of shogunate forces to consolidate saw Koshu castle, a Koyo-Chinbutai army (March 29, 1868), and a Shohotai infantry force (April 1) defeated alone. The shogunate was over. In its place, new leadership would see a new northern alliance recover the initiative on the battlefield.

While land forces would determine when victory would be achieved, only naval forces could determine who the victor would be across the Japanese home islands. Imperial forces staged a naval show of strength with six warships from six domains totaling 2,456 tons for the emperor on March 26, 1868.[19] As far as they had come in a short space of time, the remaining shogunate eight-ship navy was still the most powerful in Asia. While the international community still recognized the shogun as Japan's legitimate ruler, America continued to withhold delivery of the former Confederate flagship.

On the eve of the largest ironclad battle even seen in Japanese waters, suddenly the most important fight in Japan was the fight for the *Stonewall*.

KOTETSU'S WAR   **25**

*S*taerkodder had a fleeting part in Otto von Bismarck's wars for a unified Germany. *Stonewall* had stared down the Union navy's *Niagara* and *Sacramento* en route to the American Civil War, though all too late. It was only in Japan that she played the defining role James Dunwoody Bulloch had dreamed of. Men had lived and died on her, but she had never been fired on and never fired a shot. All that would change.

It was hardly surprising to Western observers—and suppliers—that war would reshape Japan. A unified America, Germany, and Italy had all been fought for. The Muslim Dungan revolt continued in China. The Ottoman Empire was seeing off the Macedonian Rebellion. Civil wars raged from Peru to the Kalang War in present-day Malaysia. The English fought expeditionary wars from Abyssinia to Auckland. The Middle East—a flashpoint then as now—saw the Qatari and Bahraini at war.

Messengers crisscrossed the home islands as more than three hundred clans threatened, implored, and crossed one another like a game of Shogi. Europe was edging from recognizing the shogun as the legitimate leader of Japan toward a commercially driven neutrality, selling to both sides as fast as they could buy. America sat on the thousands the shogun had already paid for the *Stonewall* and held her in port under Captain George Brown.

In January 1868, the shogun had marched on the emperor with superior forces. In February, he was reaffirmed as the legitimate ruler of Japan by the international community. On March 4, the shogun left Edo for a temple in Ueno, deciding once and for all that he could not oppose the emperor, leaving it to others to surrender. The shogun's commander in chief, Kaishu Katsu, a former captain of the warship *Kanrin*, dispatched Tesshu Yamaoka to discuss terms. He was sent back with an offer for the immediate surrender of all troops and warships and his confinement in Bizen. At age thirty-two,

Yoshinobu agreed word for word, declared himself retired, and passed the Tokugawa clan's lands to his adopted son, Tokugawa Iesato. British ambassador Ernest Satow described a fallen figure on his departure. "We took off our hats to fallen greatness. He was muffed in a black hood and wore an ordinary war-hat. What could be seen of his countenance looked worn and sad. . . . One could not but pity him, so changed as he was from the proud, handsome man of last May. Now he looked thin and worn, and his voice had a sad tone."[1] For imperial clans, it was the ultimate vindication. The shogun was merely appointed by men. The emperor was chosen by the goddess Amaterasu.

The term *bukufu* had originally referred to the household of a shogun. It now encapsulated a traditional feudal military leader with the emperor as a spiritual and cultural figure above temporal politics. Many of the nation's oldest, proudest, and most powerful clans remained loyal—if not to Yoshinobu, to the "bufuku" ideal. After Toba-Fushimi, a leadership vacuum prevented shogunate forces from counterattacking at Kokone. When Yoshinobu's acquiescence thwarted plans developed with Napoleon III's French ambassador Léon Roches to counterattack imperial forces at Odawara, the last strategic bastion before Edo, Roches resigned in indignation.

By early March, foreign nations walked back their recognition of the shogun and signed a mutually binding neutrality agreement. The Japanese would decide their ruler.

The Meiji administration's new Ministry of Military Affairs staged a commemorative naval review in Osaka Bay with six ships drawn from the Saga, Chōshū, Satsuma, Kurume, Kumamoto, and Hiroshima clans, chiefly for the larger European warships watching.[2] By March 29, an imperial Tosando-led army reached Edo almost unopposed and was preparing for an assault on the shogun's ancestral stronghold.

The *Kotetsu* had sat idle for two months, despite a clear contract for delivery to Yoshinobu's representatives. On April 2, 1868, Indiana-born lieutenant George Brown steamed the former *Stonewall* from Shinegawa harbor, near Edo, the short distance south around the headland to Yokohama Bay where it was felt she was more secure. By sheer chance, Midshipman Alfred Thayer Mahan—on board the warship *Iroquois*, which had sheltered the last shogun overnight when he fled Osaka castle—recognized her from his own time in the Washington Navy Yard.[3]

At sea, even with French advisors serving the admiralty, Vice Commander Enomoto Takeaki's leadership was absolute. On land, even on April 26, when the imperial envoys Saneyana Hashimoto and Sakimitsu Yanagiwara marched into Edo castle demanding the castle's surrender, bufuku leadership was opaque at best. Despite their humbling performance to date, the shogun's leading clans still held greater numbers and dismissed them without an answer. Imperial forces besieged the city.

In May 1868, the former shogunate bufuku forces selected the army minister, Katsu Kaishu, as an interim leader, but without a clear mandate to march out and break their envelopment, his hands were tied. Bufuku allies began to peel off. None went further than the twenty-two samurai who accompanied arms dealer John Henry Schnell all the way to San Franciso with silkworms, tea seeds, and mulberry seedlings, only for him to abandon them in 1871 when their defeated daimyo, Matsudaira Katamori, was pardoned and ended his subsidies to the men.[4]

America continued to stall on *Kotetsu*'s delivery. Both sides maintained their months-long campaigns for delivery, despite the contract and payments only the shogun could claim. Vice Commander Takeaki announced his intention to transfer his flag to her from the *Fujiyama* on delivery. Her crew, some of whom had steamed her from Washington, stood ready, but to Western eyes, it wasn't that simple as America followed the European powers into a policy of neutrality.

Many leading postwar figures like Secretary William H. Seward were content to complete her contracted delivery. Others, led by Robert Van Valkenburgh—a former five-term New York congressman, colonel at the Battle of Antietam, and acting commissioner of Indian affairs, now serving as U.S. minister to Japan—were unconvinced.[5] Valkenburgh may have had a limited grasp of Japanese politics, but he was quite clear on what the *Kotetsu* would mean if delivered. "The Tycoon [Shogun] . . . would at once command the seas; could blockade successfully Osaka, Hiogo, and Nagasaki, all now in possession of the Mikado."[6]

The shogun initially saw this simply as a delay—after all, their present flagship *Fujiyama*, crewed by the same 130-strong complement as *Kotetsu*, which had been one of three ships ordered from America in 1863, had also been delayed by a review after the Battle of Shimonoseki Strait.[7]

Imperial forces argued that releasing the *Kotetsu* to the now-rebel bufuku would be akin to France's betrayal of secretly building her in the first place. The ranking local U.S. naval officer, Rear Admiral Rowan aboard the screw steamer *Piscataqua* (2,400 tons; twenty guns) in Yedo Bay, advocated for neutrality. It was no small decision. This was a warship that was expressly designed for—and capable of—destroying the wooden-hulled ship he commanded, much less any local warships. Down came her Japanese ensign, and up went the U.S. Stars and Stripes, to forestall any rumored attempt on her by Vice Commander Takeaki.[8]

Joseph Heco, now working for the firm Glover & Company, noted the difference she could make, "it [*Stonewall*] would have a great moral effect upon all waverers as a practical recognition by a great foreign power of one or other of them as the legitimate rulers of the country. Hence the extreme anxiety of the Mikado's party to get possession of the vessel, which they fancied would bring a speedy end to the struggle."[9]

After making no further headway with the U.S. minister or British minster, Heco noted, "the Vice-Governors, Terashima and Iseki, informed me that my Minister positively and absolutely refused to deliver the *Stonewall* to any party as long as the so-called rebellion lasted."[10]

While the U.S. State Department wavered, it was the U.S. minister to Japan, Valkenburgh, with no clear mandate or authority, who unilaterally decided to nullify her contract and award her to imperial forces for the remaining funds owing. Imperial forces responded gleefully with gold within days. While total payments are disputed, Valkenburgh boasted a final delivery payment of $10,000, which was a clear profit. However grudgingly, America's naval and diplomatic leaders fell into line with the decision.

The vision of the American black ships was complete. Japan was open for business. By year's end, Congress authorized the Naval Academy at Annapolis to admit imperial Japanese candidates.[11]

Yet again, the shogun had paid for what benefited his enemies. The decision was hugely divisive. President Andrew Johnson only supported it privately. Secretary Seaward called it irregular quite publicly. A second naming ceremony inducted her as the flagship for the First Imperial Naval Squadron.

The bufuku were livid. Her contract had been broken. It was illegal. Their money had been stolen, in effect. This wasn't American neutrality; it was one nation playing kingmaker for another. None of it mattered. Captain Brown led his crew offboard and never saw her again. Takeaki had a trained crew ready to step aboard. The predominantly Chōshū crew honored to serve instead faced a crash course in how to operate this ship, longer than the Statue of Liberty was tall and by some counts heavier than the sphinx in Giza, Egypt.

Rebels had guns, but nations had fleets. *Kotetsu* was immediately pressed into a series of high-profile rededication ceremonies from port to port, every bit as much a source of national pride as the HMS *Warrior* had been for England or *La Gloire* for France. When a new U.S. consul was appointed, it was the *Kotetsu* that received him with a multigun salute.[12]

Yoshinobu was silent. The new bufuku leader, Kaishu, was powerless to stop the handover. Takeaki had other ideas. The Americans were right to have shifted her from her original pier in Yokohama Bay, and to have raised their flag. As the delay on her delivery stretched from days to weeks and months, he'd scouted her moorings extensively for opportunities to intervene.

After her induction into the Meiji emperor's navy, he reluctantly headed north without her. Captain Sahiro Nakajima, who went uncharacteristically informally as "Shiro" when off-duty, was appointed to succeed Captain Brown's command in a brief ceremony in the port of Shimizu in Surushu attended by the governor general. The five-nation ship was in exclusively Japanese hands for the first time. *Stonewall* had served slightly below strength with 130 men. In Japanese service, she hosted 150, including a complement of samurai with traditional polearms including Shitiagawa, Hijikata, and Waki.[13]

The sick bay, once home to doctors Bennett Green and James Herty, welcomed third class medical officer Torii Shunpei and second medical officer Yori Crew Yoshida Akizo. Where Richard W. Curtis once managed the ship's finances now the treasurers Sato Hiko and Harada Sabei Mizu served, and so on.[14]

One of *Kotetsu*'s engines failed the following day with Admiral Nakajima Shiro aboard, diverting first class officers Ishida Ding Zo and Yamane Bunjiro with their engineering group. Urgent works restored her pressure, but if her top speed was 12 knots leaving Bordeaux, it was certainly less for the moment. When she stopped at Miyako in present-day Kyoto, where she'd soon fight for her life, coal was so scarce that wood was substituted, slowing her further.

At Edo castle, there seemed little point delaying the inevitable. On May 3, army minister Kaishu threw open its gates, the shogun's forces laid down their weapons, and the imperial armies of the Owari and Higo domains marched in without a shot being fired. At a stroke, years of French training and armament were swept away.

The calculations for war at sea had flipped for Vice Commander Takeaki. Instead of leading with *Kotetsu*, he now faced the most powerful ship in Japanese waters. Koga Genroku, the captain of the bufuku *Kaiten*, a modest former U.S. revenue service cutter, called for an immediate surprise attack on the new imperial flagship as she steamed north. Takeaki conferenced with his captains, simulating a range of scenarios. When he was called to a war council, he left behind a daring plan to do even more.

Numerous American Civil War veterans were now active on both sides, ranging from Union corporal William Elliot Griffis all the way to Confederate general P. G. T. Beauregard, who was offered the same commission in Japanese land forces. Japan's recruitment of American veterans for the Sino-Japanese War (1894–1895) is much better documented, culminating in Henry Walton Grinnell's service as rear admiral at the Battle of Yalu River.[15] Surprisingly, in turn, hundreds of people from Asia and the subcontinent had served in the United States and returned to China (seventy-four), India (forty-nine), the Philippines (fifty-six), and Japan, from where at least two men served the North with the anglicized names Private John Williams and Private Simon Dunn.[16] Spared Genroku's proposed attacks,

Kotetsu continued north and assumed leadership of a seven-ship squadron based on the island of Hokkaidō.

The scattered bufuku land forces that had not fallen with Edo castle consolidated. Fresh new loyalist troops continued southward to reinforce them. Takamori led imperial forces northward toward them, bolstered by new daimyo pledges of his own.

When Western policy shifted to neutrality between shogun and emperor, no blow was more bitter than the withdrawal of support from Napoleon III's France, who proved no more loyal to them than he had to the Confederacy. In October 1868, when the bulk of the French shogunate mission was recalled, Jules Brunet and four of his non-commissioned officers (Fortant, Marlin, Cazeneuve, and Bouffier) resigned from the French army to fight on.[17] Brunet remained a believer. "A revolution is forcing the Military Mission to return to France. Alone I stay, alone I wish to continue, under new conditions: the results obtained by the Mission, together with the Party of the North, which is the party favorable to France in Japan. Soon a reaction will take place, and the Daimyos of the North have offered me to be its soul. I have accepted, because with the help of one thousand Japanese officers and non-commissioned officers, our students, I can direct the 50,000 men of the confederation."[18]

The weakness in the shogunate campaign had been at the top. In the field, they continued contact with imperial forces, fighting with selflessness and honor. At the Battle of Kōshū-Katsunuma, on March 29, 1868, three hundred Shinsengumi samurai, in sky-blue coats with mountain motifs embroidered on their sleeves as intricate as any Swiss guard's in Europe, stayed behind like their namesake three hundred Spartans against the Persians to buy their retreating forces time. Their chief surgeon, Ryojun Matsumoto, worked with the bloody speed and brutality any civil war veteran would understand. One hundred and eighty-seven were killed or wounded before contact was broken off, and their retreat resumed, but they inflicted such harm that imperial forces stopped to reorganize for days before renewing their advance.[19] When writers speak of this honor guard beyond this point, the sky-blue coats were largely gone, and new men stepped into their place with a patchwork of bufuku house colors.[20] The mission continued.

The Chōshū and Satsuma no longer drew a distinction between their enemies and the emperor's. When the honorable Shinsengumi commander Kondō Isami—already wounded at Toba-Fushimi—was later captured, he was summarily beheaded and publicly displayed over suspicions of involvement in the assassination of the Tosa samurai Sakamoto Ryōma (who, ironically, as an advocate for U.S.-style democracy, was in almost as much danger from imperial forces).

Yoshinobu had been reluctant to take power, poorly positioned to hold it, and incapable of fighting for it. While 260 years of shogunate power ended, the Japanese Boshin Civil War would be fought for longer without him. Daimyo continued to pledge to the bufuku cause for debt, family, or honor. Traditional leaders were horrified to see the Chrysanthemum throne exercising day-to-day rule, or worse, legitimizing the rule of others.

Japan's civil war was not over. As Carl von Clausewitz would later write in *On War*, the conflict would burn as long as the bufuku's will to fight allowed it. "Even the ultimate outcome of a war," he wrote, "is not always to be regarded as final. The defeated state often considers the outcome merely as a transitory evil, for which a remedy may still be found in political conditions at some later date."[21]

The campaign devolved into a series of localized battles. On May 24, a loose confederation of former shogunate forces encamped between Ichikawa City, Kamagaya City, and Funabashi City were confronted by fewer but better-equipped imperial forces—and were sharply defeated.[22] The retreat north resumed. Local forces resisted imperial advances in northern Kanto with French-trained Desnshu-tai special forces at Oyama castle in Shimotsuke province and in the brief capture of Utsunomiya castle, on May 11, before once again being forced to retreat. Bufuku forces were defeated again at the Battle of Ueno by imperial forces with concentrated riflemen and improved quick-firing, breech-loading cannon like the Snider and powerful 12-inch Armstrong guns from the same family as the *Kotetsu* mounted in her aftercastle.[23]

Imperial forces were increasingly frustrated at the failure to achieve a decisive victory. Every kilometer marched north put them closer to the bufuku power base and further from theirs. Cracks began to appear. The commander of the Tosando army, Saigō Takamori, was criticized for his close relationship with the bufuku leader, Katsu. The Chōshū hard-liner, Masujiro Omura, was appointed Hanji commander of the Defense Secretariat and began a purge of "soft" elements, who bristled at the insult but accepted his authority. By early July, a Sendai-led government (the Ouetsu-reppan alliance) anchored on Tohoku and Echigo regions was proclaimed, and resistance to the emperor was put on a more strategic footing. The bufuku had become the Northern Alliance.

If anything, Omura's leadership of imperial forces was even more driven. On July 4, he shattered local Shogitai forces that hadn't connected with their new allies. The southern imperial alliance demanded a northern surrender. The bufuku retreated north to fight on. By September, it was clear the northern forces lacked the strength or will to push south again, and with an international audience in mind, the emperor's forces simply proclaimed victory. A new imperial age had begun, but the war was not over and the bufuku fleet was untouched.

The former shogun was transported from Edo to exile in Sumpu aboard the iron schooner and royal yacht *Banryū* that had fought for the shogunate navy against the Satsuma at Awa. As harsh as it sounds, he was already an irrelevance. The shogun was gone. The Northern Alliance remained, now with a competing model of Western engagement, feudal authority, and a distant emperor. In a bitter irony, the war's leading casualty had been isolationism.

The proclamation of victory in Edo prompted Western powers to declare the emperor Meiji Japan's legitimate ruler, just months after they'd done the same for the shogun and seized imperial shipping in the Bizen incident. England's Harry Parkes voted with them, just three months after the latest in a string of imperial attempts on his life. The French followed, even with their advisors serving the shogun as privateers.

What the north needed was leadership. Their alliance had started as a political grouping to lobby for a pardon of the Aizu and Shonai domains. In the face of imperial advances, the assassination of the local imperial superintendent, Shuzo Sera, and skirmishing in Shiraishi-guchi, it became a military one.

Even then, not all of Japan's more than three hundred clans had pledged to either side. Intrigue, claim, and counterclaim continued. The Yonezawa domain offered a surrender that was refused by imperial forces. Meiji forces offered the Sendai and Yonezawa the Aizu's domain if they defeated them. Fourteen domains petitioned the emperor's commander, Kujo, for a pardon of the Aizu and Shonai, and when it was rejected, they carried the petition to the emperor himself. Couriers raced from port to castle to capital. Rumors flew. By May 16, twenty-five domains were cosigning requests for pardons. By August, thirty domains were part of the Northern Alliance. Some saw it as a defensive pact. Some wanted the installation of the imperial Prince Rinojinomiya Kogen as Emperor Tobu in Meiji's place. The difference now was that they were the rebels, and the weight of numbers and gold was now against them on land and, newly with the loss of the *Kotetsu*, at sea.

The northern Admiral Enomoto Takeaki continued to work toward a solution. It was clear the impasse could only be resolved by battle, and that as the civil war spread across the home islands, the battle at sea would come to the fore.

Kotetsu's time had come.

BULLETS LIKE RAIN   26

*K*otetsu changed everything. As the great powers switched their allegiance from shogun to emperor, the Northern Alliance had the stark choice to sink her, storm her, or surrender to her.

Takeaki was a man with a foot in two worlds as science graduate and samurai. When the shogunate dream ended at Toba-Fushimi, he refused to surrender. When the bufuku dream followed at Ueno, he refused to surrender. Their cause retained support in the north. All they needed in his view was space and time. Although his network reported *Kotetsu*'s every move, he resisted calls for raids south. Rebels had guns, but nations had fleets. Very much like admiral Sir John Jellicoe in World War I, who Winston Churchill recognized as "the only man on either side who could lose the war in an afternoon," Takeaki losing the fleet would mean invasion in the north and no claims to sovereignty.[1]

Until the *Kotetsu*'s arrival, his three-masted sail and steam flagship, the *Kaiyō* (2,632 tons; thirty-one guns), had been the foremost warship in Japan. At launch, she was the largest wooden-hulled ship the Danes had ever built, and she'd acquitted herself well in the Battle of Awa. Takeaki had expected nothing less, having served on her delivery cruise under Danish captain J. A. E. Dinaux.

Warships had always been symbols of state. When the Mutsu and Dewa clans announced themselves for the bufuku, they asked, "Who in the empire can resist us, being in command of such a powerful war-vessel? It will be perfectly easy for us to roam at will over the sea and lend aid to the land forces."[2] It was not.

After Yoshinobu's initial confinement to a three-meter by three-meter room overlooking the fifth shogun's mausoleum, his servitude soon saw the former shogun freed to roam the twenty-six temples of the Kaneiji complex.[3] He received no communication from the Northern Alliance and offered them none. "How could such a great tree abandon its own limbs," asked his loyal servant, Katamori, who resigned himself to fight and die for the bufuku.[4] Yoshinobu's world shrank, answering the puzzle of how he'd live out the "endless days of my life" with photography, painting, archery, and embroidery while imperial forces marched on to destroy those who'd sworn to him.

The imperial advance continued. Despite inflicting serious losses on imperial forces in early May 1868, the daimyo of Nagaoka was forced to retreat, and his castle fell on May 19. Like the wave of earthquakes and tsunami and cholera that haunted Shogun Iesada after the American black ships, there were poor omens everywhere. On May 30, Okita Soji, considered the finest swordsman in the Shinsengumi, too ill to march north, died of tuberculosis in Edo. It was said he had vowed, "I'll take up my sword to kill the enemy" from his deathbed. Staggering outside to prove it, he swung his sword at a cat, and missed. The next day he tried again and failed. His last words the next day were, "I bet that cat is here."[5]

Takeaki's fleet was a beacon for bufuku loyalists. While imperial forces had already declared a new Meiji era, until they prevailed, they risked Western powers switching their loyalties again like a game of Shogi.

Takeaki steadfastly refused all demands from the imperial naval commander to surrender. Shifting north meant leaving the warship *Fujiyama* behind. At more than 1,000 tons, she was among his most powerful, but she was laid up undergoing deep repairs alongside three lesser gunboats. The *Fujiyama* only returned to duty after the civil war. The three remaining vessels never would.[6]

Kotetsu changed the balance of power at sea. The Meiji fleet was a composite of their daimyo's acquisitions. As the leader of the imperial drive, the Chōshū were honored to crew her. A surviving order, on April 29, declares to the Chōshū, "an ironclad shall be deposited with your clan for the time being, members of crew should go down to East as soon as possible to receive the ship."[7] Before a renewed drive north was approved on June 15, 1868, the minister of war inspected the *Kotetsu* and *Kasuga* along with the former merchant ships *Teibo 1* and *Teibo 2* (236 tons; two guns, which launched as the SS *Hinda* and *Assunta*; each with sixty-five crew and undergoing their final conversion shakedowns as warships).[8]

Kotetsu looked much as she had at launch. Heavy set. Dominated by a raised forecastle with its single gunport eye. Observers were amused to see crew members walk down into the water to bathe. She leaked, as she always had. Her engineering spaces were coal dust, dark, and smoke scented. Signage and gauges were here in Japanese, there in English, and elsewhere in Dutch.

Rice had replaced biscuits in her stores, sake replaced rum, and so on, but the fundamentals of each officer's duties were unchanged.

The northern retreat continued. On August 20, Takeaki departed Shinagawa with his flagship, the steam frigate *Kaiyō* from the Dutch firm Cornelis Gips, along with the warships *Kaiten, Banryū, Chiyo,* and the steam gunboats *Kanrin, Mikaho, Shinsoku,* and *Chōgei.* With them went northern officials including the vice commander in chief of the bufuku army Matsudaira Taro, Nakajima Saburozuke, and French military advisors headed by Jules Brunet, together with more than two thousand Tokugawa warriors.[9] Their leader, Takewaki, declared, "The Meiji government is at the mercy of the powerful domains, and this is not a true restoration of the monarchy." A further three thousand Tokugawa troops bolstered their forces at Sendai.[10]

Takeaki had cherry-picked the nation's finest naval leaders. The *Banryū*'s Bankichi Matsuoka, for example, was a long-standing student of Dutch studies, was a Shinto Nenryu swordsman, graduated from the Nagasaki Naval Training Center in 1856, served on the first diplomatic mission to the United States in 1860, and had surveyed the Ogasawara Islands to fend off British claims.[11]

With their army in retreat, the northern navy didn't have the luxury of waiting out dangerous weather. Shortly after their depiction by artist Masanoshin Kosugi, typhoon conditions off Choshi resulted in the loss of the small steamer warship *Mikaho.*[12] The kamikaze winds, which had saved Japan from the Mongols, seemed bent to the emperor's will. The corvette *Kanrin,* which had been the first screw warship ordered from the West, took such severe damage in the same weather she was forced into the nearest port, where she was fired on and stormed by imperial forces from the warships *Fuji, Mutsahi,* and *Hiryu,* who put every man aboard to death.

Prince Kitashirakawa Yoshihisa assumed leadership of the Northern Alliance. With the commitments of thirty-one domains including the Sendai, Yonezawa, and Nagaoka with their Tokugawa, Aizu, Soma, and Shonai allies, northern forces commanded more than fifty thousand men at arms.[13] The campaign that followed on land was short, sharp, bloody, and decisive.

Finally consolidated, the north leveraged a series of castles to secure their positions and refocus on Western supplies. When battle was joined again, it's little surprise it was over the bustling trade port in Niigata. The northern commander, Tsugunosuke Kawai, waged a considered campaign. Though he briefly lost Nagaoka castle in early September, he went on to reclaim it along with most of the Echigo region from the imperial Yonezawa and Aizu domains in the Hokuetsu War, which was the costliest imperial forces had yet faced.[14] Having already claimed victory, imperial forces fought on.

Both sides lobbied for the loyalty of wavering clans. Assassinations were rife. Neutrality was no longer an option. Some changed their allegiances.

Some more than once. On August 21, the murder of an imperial emissary to the Sendai by a Kubota retainer was enough to send them back to the emperor's side. The Akita domain was overwhelmed by the heavily western-ized Shonai, Sendai, and Nanbu armies converging on three sides. Despite the fall of Kubota castle, the Akita retreated north to fight on. Skirmishing at Shirakawaguchi was indecisive but ended in northern retreat once again.

While imperial forces remained focused, the Northern Alliance struggled to define a purpose. Were they a defensive block to hold this new line? Were they a bastion for traditional culture? Did they have a mandate—or the re-sources—to advance south?

On November 8, a united Northern Alliance counterattack took the Sen-dai's home castle and forced their surrender. Far from being a major reversal, though, it left them divided across a larger front. While the imperial south hadn't achieved a decisive victory, like the Union forces in the American Civil War, it was increasingly clear they may not need to.

Despite their relentless success on land, Admiral Takeaki's fleet continued to deter the imperial navy. The longer it could do so, the more Western arms and supplies could flow. Against the Northern Alliance's eight warships and thirty-six auxiliaries, the emperor assembled the smaller aggregate warships of his loyalists. The Satsuma deployed nine steamships; the Chōshū, five; the Kaga, ten; and the Chikuzen, eight.

While this count excludes scores of lesser gunboats and auxiliaries, it risks overstating the Meiji's deployable forces. Most were wooden. Some were sail ships. Some were more troopship than warship. Some didn't dare face the weather conditions that cost the north the *Mikaho*, *Kanrin*, and *Shisoku*. Some were so cumbersome they would slow the fleet more than help it. Their guns were a polyglot of predominantly lighter designs. Some had crews hardened by conflict with the West, though all lacked experience in coordinated engagements.

Takeaki chose Sendai, celebrated as the city of trees and named by the great unifier Tokugawa Ieyasu himself, to consolidate his fleet on August 26. Above them loomed Sendai castle, which had been destroyed by earthquakes and rebuilt in 1616, 1648, 1668, and 1710. The Sendai knew about setbacks.

The port was in constant motion. Tenders skittered among warships, mer-chants, and warehouses. Camps and fires filled every field. Roads swarmed with carts and men. Much of their heavy equipment—notably their heavier field artillery—had been spiked and left behind. The weaponry that remained was a confused mix of the very latest and the most traditional. Adaptation was everywhere. Workshops produced a stream of improvised cannon with wooden barrels bound by iron bands and rope that could fire as few as four rounds before becoming a greater danger to their crew than their enemy.

Their marketplaces bustled. Two thousand modern French rifles, the equal of the emperor's Minié's, were purchased from the German weapons dealer Henry Schnell and in soldiers' hands the day they landed. Two of only three known Gatling guns in Japan were sourced by the daimyo of Nagaoka.[15]

In September, a Northern Alliance council chaired by Takeaki at Sendai castle selected Hijikata Toshizō as their commander in chief. Though his father had been a wealthy farmer, he'd been a traveling salesman for their family medicines for a time, teaching himself the Kenjutsu arts as a personal passion, until his resolve won him a seat in the Tennen Rishin Ryu's dojo in Hino, recognition as a sword master, and recruitment by the Shinsengumi.[16] The fervor that saw him nicknamed "Devil Vice Commander," after he reportedly drove dozens of samurai to *seppuku* over even minor infractions of honor, won him command from the wounded Kondo Isami at Toba-Fushimi, and saw their doctor Matsumo Ryojun describe him as "keen and calmly courageous, he does everything like thunder."[17]

Before their decisions could be ratified, Yonezawa city in Yamagara prefecture fell, opening their rivers to imperial forces.

Despite their long march north, imperial morale was high, and their leadership was resolute. The emperor's forces advanced slowly and methodically, deploying superior artillery to reduce each stronghold in front of them. The martial bushido code dictated that samurai serve their new leaders to the death, and so they did, with such conviction that kites were flown before them as a sign of northern contentment.[18]

It may have been noble, but by this point, more than four in five of the nation's clans opposed them. While the north had avenged the fall of Akita castle with Sendai castle's capture, it left them so sparsely resourced over October and November 1868 that they could no longer deploy as an army, and largely retreated behind its walls. Imperial forces advanced at whatever pace they chose. The Shinsengumi defeated at the Battle of Bonari Pass on October 6 were outnumbered ten to one, sending remnants north yet again, and opening their largest remaining clan, the Aizu, to imperial forces. Faced with near-certain defeat, soldiers and samurai wrote their death poems, dispatched the treasures to loved ones and allies, drank to one another, and resolved to sell their lives dearly.

The Northern Alliance's last major bastion on the main island of Honshu—the Aizu clan—had been pinned with their last five thousand supporters in Wakamatsu castle by October 1868. With their forces behind walls, supplies and communications tapered off. For imperial forces, the end seemed in sight. No terms were offered. The men before them were rebels. Their heads belonged on pikes, scattered across the emperor's cities.

The imperial siege was launched languidly. The castle was well sited in broken and hilly terrain, which meant that, while heavy artillery could be deployed on its walls, imperial forces were limited to hauling up 12-pounders and lighter guns. For days, they poured in fire to reduce the city walls, and overshot into the city beyond. The north's flags flew on, undaunted, until a first assault was launched and repulsed. And a second. And again and again in the days and weeks that followed as the return fire lessened, but the defenders' resolve held.

As more and more heavy imperial artillery was wrestled into place, conditions worsened. By October 29, the Meiji's fifty heaviest guns fired fifty rounds or more each, every day. It was said, "as the fighting intensified, the sickrooms came to have not even enough space to stand, crowded with those missing hands, with crushed legs, bodies covered in rot, groaning and crying out in pain . . . and as the bombardment of the troops of the new imperial government grew more intense, explosive rounds would burst into the sickrooms and women's rooms, pulverizing entire bodies and scattering lumps of flesh and covering all the walls in blood. The result was sights too terrible to describe" and that "bullets from enemy rifles fell like rain." Their defense was so resolute, even after their devoted young Byakkotai (White Tiger Corps) warriors mistakenly took smoke in the distance to mean their castle had fallen and committed suicide en masse, that it would take more than a month for them to finally admit defeat on November 6. Twenty-four hundred northern fighters had become casualties, not including the suicides of twenty-one members of their chief retainer's family and others. Countless civilians harmed or killed were not counted.[19]

Among the fallen was the samurai Nakano Takeko, who led her all-female Joshigun unit into imperial riflemen armed with naginata polearms and swords. She cut down five men before succumbing to her wounds, aged just twenty-one, and her head was taken by her sister Masako so it couldn't be flaunted as a trophy. Her death poem read, "I would not dare to count myself among all the famous warriors—even though I share the same brave heart." Her absolution was not isolated. Kawahara Asako, the wife of the magistrate Zenzaemon, cut her hair and decapitated her daughter and mother-in-law before seeking—and finding—a warrior's death on the battlefield. Others, such as the female Yamakawa Futaba, and gunner Yamamoto Yaeko, survived, the former becoming a noted advocate for female education.[20]

It was too much to bear. The dam broke. There would be no Emperor Tobu. Japan's engagement with the West would be dictated by the sixteen-year-old emperor Meiji. The northern coalition began to unravel, and only a subset resumed their long march north under their general and co-leader Otori Keisuke.[21]

The bufuku story would continue, and an entire republic was yet to rise and fall, but for Meiji Japan, the future started now. Four years before, imperial forces were dying in battle with Western navies, and the shogun seemed unassailable. They now committed themselves to the new world order imposed by the black ships.

The 1868 "Charter Oath of Five Principles," developed by Sakamoto Ryôma, outlined the emperor's vision for Japan:

- Item. We shall determine all matters of state by public discussion, after assemblies have been convoked far and wide.
- Item. We shall unite the hearts and minds of people high and low, the better to pursue with vigour the rule of the realm.
- Item. We are duty bound to ensure that all people, nobility, military and commoners too, may fulfil their aspirations and not yield to despair.
- Item. We shall break through the shackles of former evil practices and base our actions on the principles of international law.
- Item. We shall seek knowledge throughout the world and thus invigorate the foundations of this imperial nation.[22]

The oath was pronounced in the Hall of Ceremonies in the imperial palace at Kyoto, witnessed by a procession of nobles and officials from the imperial clans. Salt water and rice purified it. The Head of the Office of Shinto Worship sang over it. The emperor's opening prayer invoked the gods of heaven and earth. Cloth offerings were made on sacred wood. No shogun was present, but 767 signatures, many gathered well after the event, and some after the Boshin War itself, symbolically ratified it. They became so defining that in the chaos after Japan's defeat in World War II, they were cited by Emperor Hirohito to legitimize changes imposed on their constitution.

Even then, the bufuku story was not over. The southern navy's reticence to advance, even with the dominant *Kotetsu*, left Japan's northernmost ports open. On October 12, Takeaki's fleet steamed 535 kilometers from Sendai to Hokkaidō, reinforced with two newly arrived gunboats from allied clans.

The Shinsengumi's commander, Toshizō, and the northern army's vice commander in chief, Taro, converged on the semitropical city of Esashi, where it was said, "Even Edo is not as busy as Esashi in May," when its seas were said to turn white with herring for their fishermen. Takeaki dispatched his flagship *Kaiyō* under Captain Nishikawa and the *Shinsoku* to escort their merchant fleet. Once again, the kamikaze winds, which had saved Japan from Korean invasion, did not favor him. On November 14, the *Kaiyō*, one of the most advanced ships in Japanese waters, purpose-built in the Netherlands under the supervision of Masao and Noriyoshi, and victor in the Battle of Awa, struck a concealed rock and began to founder in a terrifying storm. Her captain flung her desperately at the coast to ground her, only for her to sink so close to shore, she settled in less than 10 meters of water (where she would be discovered by the submarine *Yomiuri-Gō* in 1968 and partially excavated[23]). Displacing almost twice as much as the *Kotetsu*, and with a full complement of eighteen 6-inch, eight 30-pounder, and assorted lesser guns, she was a bitter loss. Any confrontation between them would have showcased what might have been if the *Niagara* had faced off with the *Stonewall*.

Given the choice of safe harbor or steaming to their rescue, the smaller schooner-rigged *Shinsoku* bravely labored out toward her, before she too struggled to stay bow-on to the sea; flooding killed her engines, and she was lost with many of their best and brightest. The waters in which the Boshin War were fought are some of the most challenging in the world. The *Kanrin*—disabled by the imperial navy in the bufuku's initial run north—would later be raised and sink very near this same point in 1871.

The balance of Takeaki's fleet rejoined their army at Esashi. Among his warships and auxiliaries steamed a polyglot force of one thousand former bufuku troops under Ōtori Keisuke, twelve surviving Shinsengumi troops under Toshizō now funded by the Aizu, and the Yugekitai under Katsutaro Hitomi. With them went the four French advisors Léonard Fortant, Émile Marlin, Léon Bouffier, and Garde, who'd marched overland to Sendai.[24] Thirty-one houses had formed the Northern Alliance. Just eighteen remained.

With them went wealth and supplies enough to institute a new state, much as the Kuomintang did when fleeing to Taiwan from victorious Chinese communist forces in 1949.

The remaining northern forces were a patchwork of French-patterned riflemen, hybrid and traditional elements. Some were like brothers. Some knew little about the men around them. Toshizō, vice commissioner of the army, for example, was suspicious that Admiral Takeaki might seek his own terms of surrender. Takeaki was under no illusions that the odds were stacked against them, especially with the *Kotetsu* heading the Meiji fleet, but he had a samurai's conviction. If he made peace with his enemy, he stated, he would never be able to look General Toshizō in the face when they "would meet underground" in their afterlife.

On October 26, Edo—the former seat of the shogun—was renamed Tokyo. The ensuing Meiji period would continue unbroken until shortly before World War I.

The Northern Alliance remnants couldn't simply land at Hakodate, which was controlled by the imperial Matsumae clan. Instead, they executed the largest seaborne invasion staged by Japanese troops since their second invasion of Korea in 1597 and waged a lightning campaign that culminated in the bloody seizure of the Goryōkaku fortress on October 26. A series of expeditions were staged from this new hub to consolidate power, including Toshizō storming the castle of Matsumae with eight hundred troops after an extensive offshore bombardment from the *Kaiten* and Captain Bankichi's *Banryū*, which mirrored the Union fleet's support against forts Jackson and St. Philip in the assault on New Orleans six years before.

Although Japan's second-largest island, Hokkaidō is the most sparsely populated of its prefectures even today and represented perhaps one in twenty of Japan's population of 30 million at the time. It was not technically part of Japan, and home to more native Ainu than it was to "Wajin" Japanese immigrants, who'd brutally put down an indigenous Ainu rebellion in 1456 and had only widened their technological lead over them since. Land tensions on the island had escalated after the discovery of alluvial gold in 1617 when immigration exploded as it had for previous gold towns like Ballarat or Bathurst in England's Australian colony. A rough equilibrium in trading local agriculture for imported metal, cloth, and sake broke down in a second failed rebellion in 1669 over the harm that gold mining runoff was causing to native rivers and their salmon. One thing they could agree on was the ruthless persecution of Christians, with 106 being publicly executed the year before. While the Tokugawa shogunate offered some concessions to the native Ainu in 1798 to ward off further rebellion, Japan had looked to the imperial Matsumae clan to guard against Russian expansionism or native rebellion ever since.[25]

Retreat was no longer an option for the Northern Alliance. There was simply nowhere else to go. It had been their navy that had rallied them since Toba-Fushimi, and it was their navy they looked to now. What some had seen as Takeaki's reticence to fight was now recognized as a calculation. Despite their defeats on land—often with isolated and piecemeal forces—their consolidated northern fleet had deterred any intervention to their supply or relocation. Takeaki held his warships together for mutual strength, patrolling from a single port. Like the Confederacy, they were still gambling on international recognition that was impossible to imagine without a fleet.

While commander in chief Toshizō remained, it was the now Admiral Takeaki who formally reconstituted the Northern Alliance as the new nation of Ezo, on December 25. By this point, both sides dressed in Western-style clothes, and their music, diet, and bureaucracy had undergone irreversible changes. Whoever prevailed, the battle for a traditional way of life was over.

While first proclaiming themselves the Hakodate Seicho, the Ezo quickly embraced a republican mantle after its use by the British legation secretary Francis Adams as Japan's first (and last) republican government.[26] The former shogunate forces shed any remaining declarations against international engagement. Instead, the new Ezo republic modeled itself on the United States, which had taken their money, withheld the *Kotetsu*, and awarded her to the emperor. Takeaki was voted president by an overwhelming majority in the first such elections Japan had even seen. French leader Jules Brunet became de facto foreign minister.

Imperial access to Western markets remained vastly superior—the Ezo would soon find themselves opposed by American Spencer repeating rifles and 1863 pattern Smith & Wesson No. 2 pistols among the Satsuma. The emperor's flag flew over a new army of dark uniforms with a growing number of British or French officers. Only those who would recognize clan variations in headgear (tall for the Satsuma, flat for the Chōshū, or red, black, and white faux bear hair helmets for the Tosa, like small-scale echoes of the British Foot Guards) would recognize the clan identities beneath.[27] They were their daimyo's men, but they were the emperor's army.

As the Confederacy had found, there weren't just sharks in the water. There were few warships built anywhere in Europe during the American Civil War not linked at some point—right or wrong—with the American South. With so much money at stake, both sides of the Boshin War also had to contend with charlatans and frauds. At one point, Joseph Heco attests an "American adventurer had come to Choshiu and bought the steamer *Lancefield* (which had been sunk by the *Wyoming* in 1863) for $30,000 and paid for her by a promissory note." No money was ever paid, and the ship passed through unknown hands until it resurfaced in the Philippines as the *Yung Haian* in 1868.[28] Rumors that imperial forces paid for ghost ships that were never delivered or others so wildly misrepresented they couldn't serve are unsubstantiated. The Ezo lacked the funds to try.

Ikunosuke Arai assumed Takeaki's former role of admiral, while interior ministries were divided along clan lines. Like the Confederacy did, Brunet launched a series of diplomatic missions to Western powers to secure recognition for this new nation, almost the size of Ireland. The American Confederacy had thought they would be acknowledged by Europe because "cotton was king." The Ezo had nothing to offer but idealism.

Even so, initial signs were promising. A joint British-French delegation from the warships *Satellite* and *Venus* conceded, "We maintain neutrality about this domestic issue. We do not approve any privileges as a 'warring group.' We approve it [the Ezo republic] as Authorities De Facto." The new Ezo president was delighted, "This is a useful description. We can take it in any way."[29] In time, though, its ambiguity was stripped away. The money to be made in Japan was being made with the emperor. No nation recognized them.

Francis Ottwell Adams, aboard the *Satellite*, noted, "The [Ezo] fleet was in a very sorry condition" and disparaged "the streets full of soldiers . . . who seemed as if they had picked up their motley costumes here and there in the slop shops of Yokohama."

Takeaki was a realist about his chances of outright military victory. He sent missives to the emperor's court affirming his loyalty, committing himself to building a stronger Japan, and reframing their northern territory as a new buffer against Russian aggression. "The farmers and merchants," he wrote, "are unmolested, and live without fear, going their own way, and sympathising with us; so that already we have been able to bring some land into cultivation. We pray that this portion of the Empire may be conferred upon our late lord, Tokugawa Kamenosuke; and in that case, we shall repay your beneficence by our faithful guardianship of the northern gate."[30]

Any claim to the office of shogun or Chrysanthemum throne was renounced. Tokyo was recognized as the nation's capital. Those dreams were over. This was now simply about self-determination.

The offer wasn't as fanciful as it first appeared. Russia's Sakhalin Island was just 42 kilometers away across the Sōya Strait. Russia had expanded to the Pacific as early as 1639, and the 1860 treaty of Chinese Peking granted them a long stretch of additional coastline they immediately buttressed with the Vladivostok naval base. Any ambitions further south needed a year-round ice-free port. In 1861, they attempted to seize the Japanese subtropical island of Tsushima, situated so close to the Korean mainland that one could see the mountains of Busan on a clear day, with a fleet under Vice Admiral Ivan Likhachev. With the *Kotetsu* then six years away, there was no way for Japan to oppose them. Instead, it was the British, under Vice Admiral John Hope, that forced their withdrawal.[31]

In practice, any real Ezo claim to their former seat of power was a fantasy. The emperor didn't need the recognition of a shogunate office that no longer existed. The proposal was rejected by the Imperial Governing Council.[32] While the emperor Meiji's involvement remains opaque, it's clear that what Chōshū and Satsuma hard-liners wanted, they got.

Former shogunate titles, lands, and rice entitlements were already being distributed as rewards. Castles from Edo to Aizu-Wakamatsu would soon follow.

In their place, the Ezo republic set about preparing its defenses along the southern peninsula of Hakodate and, above all, the new fortress of Goryokaku at its heart. Roads and docks were hurriedly expanded. Walls were raised. Fields were ploughed and sown. Homes worthy of daimyo were requisitioned or crafted. Warehouses filled and multiplied. Their fleet escorted wave after wave of transports scuttling the 20-kilometer-wide Tsugaru Strait between the main island of Honshu and Hokkaidō. Merchants named their price for every weapon they could supply.

French advisor Eugène Collache was greeted by the Tsugaru daimyō at Aomori after escaping arrest warrants to the south, and tasked with organizing land defenses across the island's volcanic mountain chain. Ezo troops were reorganized in four brigades headed by the French non-commissioned officers Fortant, Marlin, Cazeneuve, and Bouffier. Artillery was reconstituted under Hiroemon Seki, with a wave of new appointments. Engineering would be headed by Shinnosuke Kosuge, mechanics under Ichinosuke Miyashige, hospital services under Ryoun Takamatsu, and French translators under Masachika Tajima. Collache's colleague, Henri Nicol, was assigned to naval support. Overall command was assumed by commander in chief Otori Keisuke and seconded by French captain Jules Brunet, whose diplomatic options had been exhausted. Each brigade was then divided into eight smaller units.[33] Riflemen lined up with riflemen, in European-style uniforms. Bowmen lined up with bowmen and swordsmen with swordsmen in traditional garb the great unifiers would instantly recognize.

Other independent units were furiously recruiting and refitting. Though their devotion had seen them almost disappear, the Shinsengumi were represented by a samurai vice commissioner in the new administration.[34]

The equation for the Ezo republic was simple.

If the imperial forces could stage a successful sea invasion, they would prevail. If the navy of the Ezo republic could defeat the Meiji fleet, they could continue as a state, much as Taiwan would for the defeated Kuomintang remnants of the Chinese civil war.

By January 1869, in the second year of Emperor Meiji's forty-four-year reign, imperial forces had massed more than sixteen thousand troops across the Tsugaru Strait. The *Kotetsu*—which hadn't fired a shot in anger since arrival in Japanese waters in January the previous year—was the key to all of it. So decisive was she that the Ezo republic's President Takeaki didn't even plan on sinking her. His solution was simple, elegant, and decisive.

He would steal her.

STEALING *KOTETSU* 27

Every warship fit to serve was in place.
Hurried final refits were completed, which for *Kotetsu* included heavy iron mounts off-center on the aftercastle for a new weapon draped under tarpaulins. Engineers on both sides repaired what they could, and patched what they must. At the war's outset, Vice Commander Takeaki's shogunate fleet was the most powerful in Asia. With the *Kaiyō* and *Shinsoku* lost to storm damage, the *Kanrin* seized with the loss of all hands, and the *Kotetsu* being awarded to the emperor, its supremacy was now in question.

The incoming Ezo admiral Ikunosuke was an Edo-born son of a Tokugawan vassal too low on the social ladder to have ever seen the shogun or emperor, but talented enough that he was sponsored to study swordsmanship from age twelve, at a shogunate academy from age fourteen, in gunnery from age eighteen, and finally in Dutch studies (sciences) from age twenty. Like Takeaki before him, he was quickly identified as a rising star. By 1862, he was running the Naval Training Academy. In 1864, he was reposted to the shogunate's Kōbusho military academy, and lastly he was promoted to study French-style infantry tactics in Yokohama in 1865. As well as serving as admiral, he was Ezo's naval minister, and next to Takeaki, arguably their foremost talent.[1]

Kotetsu wasn't just a major disruptor because of her ram. Her 5-inch armor was specifically rated for the weight of guns the Ezo republic fleet mounted. Her foregun, commanded by a second-class officer and crewed by Nakamura Iwataro, among others, was the heaviest single piece in Japanese waters.[2] Though the Ezo fleet matched the emperor's in firepower, every one of her warships was wooden hulled.

Kotetsu's delivery to imperial forces was a heartbreaking reversal for the Ezo. On March 9, 1869, her 150 officers and men led the Meiji fleet out of

Tokyo under the emperor's rising sun banner. By March 20, they reached Miyako Bay on the main island's northeast coast. Unlike the typhoon-strength storm the bufuku had retreated through, the weather was calm. A bitter winter was behind them. The days were getting longer and warmer.

Kotetsu spent five days in Miyako Bay with craftsmen swarming over her, almost certainly for recurrent leaks that had been the bane of the Confederate lead carpenter, Joseph Mather, and now haunted the dedicated wooden Takumi (craft) chief.[3] Word of it quickly reached Ezo's leaders.

Takeaki had studied the latest naval theory in Europe and worked alongside Dutch and French talent for years. Wherever he went, his treasured Dutch texts and code books went with him. Ikunosuke was a modern thinker. Lessons from the Crimean War were war gamed and debated at length. While their samurai instinct was to strike, their discipline held, the fleet remained consolidated, and no tactical raiding was indulged.

Ikunosuke knew what an ironclad and explosive shells meant for his wooden hulls, no matter how much more firepower they mounted, and had no intention of simply forming up his fleet and waiting. The Ezo intended to change the contest entirely. When he gathered his captains, he calmly waited out their suggestions to deploy here or attack there and laid out a plan led not by the gun, but by the sword. The poetry of it was beautiful. *Kotetsu* had been acquired by the shogun but diverted to the emperor. Takeaki and Ikunosuke intended to right this wrong with their forefathers' weapons.

By April 20, the emperor's fleet—confident the Ezo didn't plan a strike south to Tokyo, then in the middle of cherry-blossom season—was still sheltering in Miyako harbor in the lee of Cape Hiisaki. It was exactly what the Ezo wanted.

Takeaki's plan was for three Ezo warships led by the Prussian-built *Kaiten* to steam into Miyako Bay at dawn, flying American colors to sow confusion. Each would embark an elite boarding force of samurai. These included the reconstituted Shinsengumi under Toshizō (to whom the French advisor paid the compliment that if he was in Europe he'd be a general) and the former French navy military advisor, Henri Nicol, who knew the *Kotetsu* indirectly from having been raised in Bordeaux not far from the yards that built her. The *Banryū* and *Takao*, under Captain Kenzo Ogasawara, would draw alongside *Kotetsu* at anchor and storm aboard her.[4] *Kaiten* would deploy her heavy broadside to keep any responding imperial ships at a distance, or in a best-case scenario, strike them down with cold boilers, trapped at anchor. The remainder of the Ezo fleet would deploy as a distant screen to engage individual Meiji pursuers.

With *Kotetsu* in their rightful hands, the emperor's army would be checked by the 20-kilometer-wide Tsugaru Strait that connected the Sea of

Japan to the Pacific Ocean east-west and divided the Ezo on Hokkaido from imperial forces on Honshu, north-south.

Thirty-seven years before Japan announced herself with the shock defeat of Russia at Tsushima, Japan had no material naval tradition in Western eyes. Contemporary writers such as Bayard Taylor had sneered when the warship *Banryū* was gifted to "the Mikado," stating that "they were so unfit for such a gift" that it was offered "with as much propriety as if we should present a wife to the Pope."[5] That was about to change.

Much of the detailed planning for a coordinated approach and a very specific sequence of troop landings was prepared by the French advisor, Eugène Collache. He remained a believer and committed to serving aboard the *Takao* with the revered Shinbokutai samurai.[6]

One element he could not account for was the weather.

May 6 was expected to deliver the last of the year's spring weather, with perhaps a one in three chance of raining. Instead, fierce storms closed in, and worsened steadily overnight. The three Ezo warship crews endured a difficult night and did well to embark hundreds of troops in the predawn dark of May 7 without injury. In fighting trim, there was little space and no shelter for them. Some withdrew into their thoughts, but others were quickly prostrate and seasick. Low cloud seemed to scatter the noise of their engines, making it hard for the three vessels to orientate themselves. Rain squalls cut down the visibility of flag signals and stole their smoke.

Waiting for better weather risked *Kotetsu* and the Meiji fleet disappearing, or worse, meeting them in a dynamic ad hoc engagement on their terms. The most they could hope for was that dangerous weather would pin their enemy at anchor and conceal their approach. Ikunosuke was resolute. They'd launch regardless.

Almost immediately, the Ezo plan went awry.

The fifteen-year-old *Takao* had originally been built for coastal service as a U.S. revenue cutter. In mounting seas, with torrents of water sweeping below from her decks, she quickly experienced engine trouble and slowed to as little as 3 knots an hour. Surprise meant everything, so the *Banryū* (376 tons; six guns), carrying former French navy quartermaster Joseph Clateau, signaled for her to follow and disappeared ahead into rain and fog. *Kaiten* was unaware.

Miyako Bay is a triangular-shaped stabbing 10 kilometers in from the Pacific Ocean, 4 kilometers wide at its mouth and narrowing as it goes. Most of it is between 20 and 40 meters deep and full of prized fisheries, shellfish, and seaweed where the Hei-gawa River and the north-flowing warm-water Kuroshio and Oyashio currents converge.

Once again, it appeared the Sun Goddess had been cruel. As *Kaiten* entered the bay with the breaking dawn and closed on *Kotetsu* at anchor, *Banryū* and *Takao* were nowhere to be seen.

The stakes were too high for any hesitation—there may never be another chance to take her. Ikunosuke's ship, the former Prussian side-wheeler *Danzig*, had been the pride of Prussia on launch, gleaming with Berlin copper, Danzig timbers, and English iron, and she had been the lead warship in the Battle of Tres Forcas in 1856 against Riffian pirates. Napoleon III himself had inspected her, and her subsequent refits by the English firm Dorset & Blythe were lavishly funded and extensive.[7]

Koga, her captain, recorded, "Success or failure depends upon the will of Heaven. The brave man's dearest wish is, when the occasion arises, to die doing his duty to the utmost. Now that we have come to this pass, why should we hesitate?" The crew gripped one another's hands for a moment and tied a strip of white cloth across their shoulders to better identify themselves. Grenades and swords were readied.[8]

On she came. The battle of Miyako Bay began.

Kotetsu was unmistakable—the only other ship afloat that looked like her, the SMS *Prinz Adalbert*, was almost 9,000 kilometers away, laid up in Prussia's Geestemünde naval depot for interminable works to her hull and armor. *Kaiten*'s 153-strong crew steamed directly for her, heartened to see they had achieved complete surprise.

The new imperial flagship was not configured for battle. It's not clear if Captain Sahiro Nakajima was aboard—there's every chance he was ashore, leaving her in the hands of first-class officers Ishida Ding Zo or Yamane Bunjiro. Her boilers, while lit, weren't at full pressure. Her davit boats were up, limiting her crew's visibility, and ready to be reduced to deadly splinters. Her upper spars and sail rigging were in place, where they could be shot away and foul her screws or rudder. So many of her crew were ashore; few could be seen on deck.

Flying the American flag on *Kaiten* bought the Ezo ship precious time as her target's gun crews waited for an order to fire. The missing *Banryū* and *Takao* had been chosen as assault ships as their screw-propulsion meant they could draw alongside their target and disembark their waiting swordsmen in an overwhelming wave. Because *Kaiten*'s immense side paddle wheels prevented her drawing alongside, she was forced to come in head-on, channeling her boarding parties down a single narrow axis. Admiral Ikunosuke had intended that she hold off the imperial response with her ten 68-pounder cannonades and traversing Armstrong cannon. Their heavy throw-weight was perfect—range would not be an issue when her targets would come to her. Instead, here she was, boilers straining, coming in like a missile. As the gap between them dropped to a kilometer, down came the American Stars and Stripes flag and up went the new red star, white circle, and deep blue background of the Ezo republic.

She might be alone, but she had caught the Meiji's fleet at anchor, fires stoked, boats lowered, and shorthanded. Shocked imperial sailors ran to the rails, shouting "the rebels have come," "fire," and "weigh anchor" over one another.[9]

It was little wonder she hadn't been recognized at first—either the storm that had left *Banryū* and *Takao* behind her had knocked down two of her three masts, or they had been removed to imitate an American ship. She only had eyes for one target. Finally, just a little luck went their way, and a break in the weather smoothed the waters and flashed patches of brilliant blue sky. Imperial captain Hiehachiro on board the *Kasuga* later commended the success of their dawn timing and the heroism of the men who pursued the attack alone.[10]

Kaiten's first attempt on the *Kotetsu* glanced off with a deep scream of metal, their crews just yards apart for a moment, shouting orders and hurling taunts. Her second run struck home, digging her bow into *Kotetsu*'s forward port side and preventing most of the Meiji fleet from firing for fear of hitting their own. *Kotetsu* might as well have been alone.

It was a precarious bridgehead. The Ezo flagship was at least 9 feet higher than *Kotetsu*, which was conceived to oppose low-slung Union monitor iron-clads. Where *Banryū* and *Takao* had broader bows and open flanks to disgorge men in a wave, the *Kaiten* tapered to a sharper point and was hemmed in by paddle wheels vastly taller than any man aboard. As a result, the Ezo could only advance one or two at a time, negating their greater numbers and silhou-etting them to the defenders looking down the length of her deck.

Meiji forces around the bay scrambled to respond, laying on coal, run-ning powder, bleeding smoke into the fog, and hurriedly launching tenders and litters for their crews. Runners scrambled from armories and magazines.

Kaiten's gunners fired a broadside of solid rounds, point blank. Her miss-ing sister ships had been carefully loaded out with grapeshot, but, expecting to screen *Kotetsu* from the emperor's fleet, she'd been prepared for ship-to-ship fire instead. Her forwardmost 56-pounder was more telling, scything down the length of *Kotetsu*'s deck. As many as three hundred men rose from a crouch with swords in hand, rather than rifles, and pressed forward.

French-cut uniforms stood side by side with traditional robes, armor, and lacquered war masks. *Kotetsu*'s forward 300-pounder was facing past the *Kaiten* uselessly. Her rear castle guns didn't traverse like a turret—her crews would have to physically wrestle her to a new firing port before they could return fire. With so many of the Meiji fleet's heavier guns either unready, or checked by the ships being locked together, small arms and lighter guns began to pepper the *Kaiten*'s outward-facing flank, slowly at first, but picking up their tempo.

The Ezo samurai leader Gengo had been pressing Admiral Ikunosuke for this opportunity for months. "Let's attack aggressively rather than waiting for the enemy," he called, convinced that, "[e]ven my ship is enough to defeat the enemy."[11]

The first of the Shinsengumi flung themselves down a drop described between 9 and 13 feet and struggled for their footing. Their bannermen stood proud in the melee, flying the white flag with the red "Makoto" character, and the mountain motif now absent from most uniforms. The imperial samurai Shitiagawa, Hijikata, and Waki rushed to meet them with pikes, but they were driven back and then forced from the gunwales altogether by a final 56-pounder blast down *Kotestsu*'s length.[12] This was the moment.

A growing number of Ezo samurai made the drop from one ship to another, including Nomura Risaburo, and the first defenders of the *Kotetsu* were quickly cut down. As her crewmen fled toward the aftercastle, they opened a path down her decks that the reloading Ezo gun crews could not exploit.

The *Kaiten*'s Captain Koga directed battle unflinchingly from his exposed bridge as men began to fall to small arms fire around him. It was brave, but there was an inevitability to him taking a first shot in his left leg and a second to his right arm. He clung to a stanchion and held his post, dividing his attention between gun crews and his assault party, right to the moment when a third shot to his head took him instantly.[13]

Admiral Ikunosuke assumed direct command. When the ship's quartermaster was shot down in front of him, he took a station at the wheel, screaming to be heard over the roar of cannon, man, and machine. Imperial fire was growing.

The shogunate daimyo of Nagaoka had sourced two of only three known Gatling guns in Japan. Now, the strange mounts on *Kotetsu*'s aftercastle's bulwark rail were revealed to be supporting the third. When Ezo swordsmen began to move forward in numbers, their leaders proudly first, they were mercilessly cut down. Hand-cranking the Gatling gun's six rotating barrels pulled brass-cased rounds from a 12 o'clock position above, fired them as they rotated past 4 o'clock and ejected a stream of hot shells to 9 o'clock on its left. Different operators ranged from 300 to 500 rounds a minute or more, and the only thing that would stop it firing was to run out of ammunition. Each round left the barrel with a supersonic crack at 426 meters per second, as loud as 165 decibels, and so powerful that it was enough to instantly and permanently damage hearing, vibrate the gunner's vision, and even make it hard to swallow.[14]★

On a deck less than 33 feet wide, it unleashed carnage.

Nicol was shot twice. Waves of samurai followed. Heedless of the danger, admiral and naval minister Ikunosuke appointed an acting captain and ran forward to urge his men on from the exposed bow.[16] On they came, regardless of the slaughter, sworn to serve, and down they went, torn limb from limb.

By now, the Meiji fleet was unleashing waves of fire into the stationary *Kaiten*, firing with greater accuracy as they repositioned themselves from anchor. Shellfire shredded the rigging clinging to her remaining mast and splayed her superstructure open, shivering her timbers and killing as they went.

The Ezo's Shinsengumi continued to drop into the Gatling gun's slaughter until Admiral Ikunosuke, just yards away, could bear it no more. He stepped forward at *Kaiten*'s bow to block more swordsmen from following and rushed back to the helm screaming an order that *Kaiten* reverse. The remaining officers compelled their men back, and dropped to their haunches below the *Kaiten* side bulwarks for shelter. To the *Kotetsu*, it was like they disappeared.

For anxious moments, their bowsprint sail was so entangled with the shrouds and ratlines of the *Kotetsu*'s main mast she couldn't sheer off. When she did, she did so as hard and fast as she could with the whole Meiji fleet converging on them.[17] At a stroke, every swordsman was rendered useless. This was a sailor's fight now. Her gun crews fired desperately on converging imperial ships, port and starboard.

She turned in a wide arc and made full speed from Miyako Bay with devils of smoke bleeding from her shot-pierced funnel. Up came the powder monkeys, feeding the guns. Down went the wounded, screaming as they were manhandled down ladderways to the tight space that Bennett W. Green had formerly run for the Confederacy. Coal was fed into her as fast as her firemen could shovel, with new pairs stepping in regularly in the hellishly hot space. The break in the weather closed, returning the world to driving rain and shades of gray. Regardless, men scurried across the precarious mast ways and wrestled what little sail they could into place. Most of their remaining rigging were so thoroughly holed that they had to be cut away and dragged overboard instead, where they floated like a trail of breadcrumbs for the Meiji fleet to follow.

Less than thirty minutes had passed.

★So-called coffee grinder guns had preceded it—and even had been ordered by Abraham Lincoln for the American Civil War—before Gatling had solved their overheating problems. Without the relentless opposition of the luddite Union chief of ordnance, Colonel John W. Ripley, there's every chance it could have fulfilled Gatling's wish to shorten the war.[15]

Kotetsu was a scene of carnage. Medical officers Yori and Yoshida Akizo, serving under third-class medical officer Torii Shunpei in what had been the Confederate Bennett Green's domain, had a butcher's bill to pay, daubed in blood, and did what they could to stabilize the wounded. Shimosawa would later recount that "blood covered the deck. Corpses were piled high, and pieces of human flesh were scattered about."[18] Sixteen bodies were later recorded on *Kotetsu*'s deck, though scores more had fallen overboard, had been pushed off to clear their gunports, or had fallen on the *Kaiten*. More than fifty other Ezo were dead or wounded on *Kaiten*.[19] Eight ships and dozens of guns had struck her hundreds of times without a decisive blow to her magazine or boilers. Ikunosuke survived it all, miraculously untouched.

It was unforgettable to all who saw it. Writing sixty years later, an imperial Japanese admiral who fought on the day as a third-class officer on the *Kasuga*, declared of the fallen Ezo samurai Kōga Genroku, "Although he is an enemy, he is also a hero." *Kaiten* survivor Taro Ando recognized it as the end of an era, writing, "such fighting was resorted to in Nelson's time; but nowadays with navies so highly developed, such fighting never takes place and this fight at Miyako has probably never since had a parallel."[20] It never would.

It was only then, with *Kaiten* streaming away at full speed, that the Ezo's *Takao* labored into Miyako Bay. She passed the retreating side-wheeler *Kaiten* closely enough to see the extent of the damage done to her, and for Ikunosuke to signal her French captain Eugène Collache to retreat. While she made a cumbersome 180-degree turn, the two ships lost sight of each other again in the fog, and *Takao*'s machinery failed her again.

Gunfire was mounting from unseen ships ahead, leaving Collache with an impossible choice. It had taken more than an hour to get her back underway after her first machinery failure. Now she'd have to face the converging Meiji fleet, floating dead in the water. The plan had been for *Banryū* to land the lion's share of their boarding parties. He had just forty seamen on deck.

The Ezo still had the larger fleet. He opted to preserve the lives of his officers and crew, steering for the coast and grounding her at Same-Minat. There was no chance to preserve the powder and shot their fleet needed, or to heave her guns overboard. The 350-ton iron-braced former U.S. Revenue Marine's schooner *Ashuelot*, which had seen off a seven-hundred-man Fenian Brotherhood attack in New Brunswick after the Civil War prior to her acquisition by the Akita clan, had run her race. A fire party set about torching her as the Confederacy had been forced to time and again for the *Virginia*, *Arkansas*, *Fredericksburg*, *Louisiana*, *Richmond*, and so many others. Few made it back to Ezo lines. Collache survived an attempted overland trek back, which ended in a Tokyo jail. His war was over, too.

The *Kotetsu*, now under full steam, and the *Yoshun* (530 tons; six guns), another former U.S. warship first launched as the *Sagamore*, led the imperial pursuit for 14 kilometers until they came across the burning *Takao* off Raga, just minutes after the last crewman had reached shore.[21]

Kaiten outsteamed her pursuers to Hokkaidō. On the Ezo's *Banryū*, Captain Bankichi, convinced the larger and faster *Kotetsu* would run him down if she was found in the fog, instructed his helmsmen to ram any enemy on sight and readied his boarding parties. He later recounted, "I washed my face, changed into a new shirt, and joked, today is a good day to die."[22] For the first time, the winds favored the Ezo, with a sudden shift helping fill his spread of sail, so he could rejoin *Kaiten* and disembark hundreds of swordsmen horrified at their inaction. The Battle of Miyako Bay and its high-stakes gamble to steal the *Kotetsu* had failed.

Three imperial ships were damaged, including the *Kotetsu*, whose armor had held against 68-pound guns with a 2,700-meter range, firing 31 kilograms shot at more than 481 meters per second from under 10 yards away. Damage parties under their twin Takumi chief craftsmen and captain of forges began repairs at once, sending regular updates to first-class officers Ishida Ding Zo and Yamane Bunjiro. Their twin treasurers, Sato Hiko and Harada Sabei Mizu, though never dealing with the astonishing sums in gold and cash Paymaster Curtis had handled for the *Stonewall*, ensured immediate payment.

The European powers were there for it all. Diplomats. Spies. Merchants. Arms dealers. Advisors. HMS *Pearl* (2,187 tons; twenty-one guns) and the French warship *Coëtlogon* (1,930 tons) had been in range through it all. Imperial precautions against another raid were immediate. Sailors who'd enjoyed more settled nights onshore were ordered to remain onboard. Several ships were kept under pressure at all times, greatly increasing their coal consumption. Further picket boats, lookouts, and riflemen were posted.

The Ezo's *Kaiten* and *Banryū*, along with their screening ship *Chiyoda* under Captain Hirosaku Morimoto, rejoined the balance of their fleet at Hakodate. While Ezo spies shadowed the Meiji fleet, their heightened readiness was quickly reported, and no further opportunities to storm her were identified.

After the battle of Miyako Bay, *Kotetsu*'s remaining aft Armstrong 70-pounder was replaced with two smaller cannons, either because their barrels had showed signs of burning out or, more likely, as the result of battle damage.

The Ezo shifted their focus closer to home. Hakodate had been the first Japanese city opened to trade in 1854 after the American black ships. Streets that once carefully segregated foreigners and citizens now heaved with commerce without such distinctions. As a long-term base of operations for the Matsumae magistrate's office, it was a capable bureaucratic center. The confluence of the warm waters of the Sea of Japan and the cold waters of the Pacific Ocean made it a fisherman's paradise. The resulting sea fogs—pooling with the smoke of their fleet, factories, and the signature red-brick warehouses scattered across the city's nineteen "saka" hills—sometimes left the 334-meter-high Mount Hakodate floating like a storybook castle to crews at sea.[23]

Behind them, the imperial consolidation of power in the main island of Honshu was complete. No further reinforcements would reach the Ezo. The Meiji fleet steamed north to rendezvous with their combined army at Aomori unopposed.

No further raids south were attempted. *Kotetsu* was now screened by gunships at all times, and manned twenty-four hours a day among the second-class officers Takino Toranosuke, Harakenzo, Yamagata Shaotaro, Yamagata Penjiro, Shinagawa Shikata, Waki Ujihei, Ikuta Ichitaro, and Yamada Kenjiro. Gunners like Nakamura Iwataro slept aboard. Takeaki needed a fleet-in-being to achieve his aims. Ikunosuke kept his naval forces concentrated accordingly.

Across the dividing Tsugaru Straits, the imperial Chōshū and Satsuma pressed for an immediate confrontation at sea. Captain Hiehachiro of the *Kasuga* joined them, but cooler heads prevailed as a transport fleet was methodically assembled. It had taken the winter for former bufuku forces to roll up Hokkaidō to found Ezo. On the verge of summer, imperial Meiji forces followed in their footsteps.

The imperial invasion force had been building for months. Even now, with more than three hundred clans behind the emperor and the remnants of just eighteen before them, the Cho-Sat block had an outsize role. More than a thousand vessels had been gathered from the ironclad *Kotetsu* to the smallest tenders and fishing boats to cross the Tsugaru Strait. Time was on their side. There would be no need to press through the type of near typhoon that had cost the Ezo the warships *Kaiyō* and *Shinsoku*.

Only once thousands of tons of coal and hundreds of barrels of powder had been manhandled into position was the Meiji fleet ready to force the crossing. *Kotetsu*'s casualties at Miyako Bya had been backfilled among the Chōshū. Her superstructure showed signs of repair, and she smelled of smoke, cut wood, and paint. In early April 1869, their final push began.

Uncertain of the Ezo fleet's deployment, Meiji forces started tentatively, with a Chōshū squadron escorting transports with two thousand troops through the Aomori gulf to Otobe. When no contact with Ikunosuke's Ezo navy was made, *Kotetsu* and *Kasuga* split off at Hiradate harbor and steamed on 40 kilometers before returning with news the strait was clear. The warships *Teiu* and *Yoshun* escorted a second column of five thousand troops northward without a shot being fired.

After their reduction with heavy broadsides, landing parties quickly overcame the Ezo's limited shore fortifications. Not unlike the Japanese island forces in the Pacific during World War II, the Ezo had chosen not to divide their forces trying to be strong everywhere and concentrated their forces inland instead. Thirteen hundred further imperial troops forming a third column of advance were landed unopposed by four imperial ships, including two transports and *Kotetsu* herself on the southwest coast.

The first imperial wave drove north with only a limited baggage train, while a second gathered behind them. First to fall for the Ezo was Matsumaya castle, under the guns of the Meiji fleet. When the Ezo magazines thinned and their artillery fire began to taper out, a direct assault with everything the Meiji army had was ordered. With little imperial artillery in place, fighting quickly degenerated in brutal close quarters. Resistance was spirited but brief, and remnant Ezo forces faced a difficult retreat along a coastal road under the *Kasuga*'s guns. The island's strongest redoubt and deep-water harbor was further north. The Ezo fleet waited.

Imperial reinforcements followed faster and faster as it became clear the strait was not going to be contested. The Meiji forces rolled back the Ezo's gains with two columns of advance until only the sea fort Benten Daiba and the immense Goryokaku complex remained. Imperial probes forward at sea went unanswered. At night, they carefully screened *Kotetsu*.

As imperial forces closed, Ezo escalated counterattacks from prepared ground. In mid-April, 230 Ezo troops under Tohizo were engaged by 600 attackers at Futamata attempting to complete an encirclement just north of their last strongholds. In sixteen hours of fierce fighting, Meiji forces poured more than thirty-five thousand rounds into their positions, inflicting only a single casualty, before being repulsed. The Ezo held them off a second day and, that night, slipped from their lines, swords in hand, and caused such terror that their imperial attackers abandoned the effort altogether. Tohizo celebrated with his men on the sake found in imperial stores.[24] The Ezo scouted extensively, and harried the emperor's army, without finding isolated elements they could destroy. Lookouts and ambush points were contested and abandoned one by one.

President Takeaki gathered his ministers and laid out their options. Their fate if they surrendered was unknown. Their fate if they fought on was not. For the clans that had sworn themselves, first to a shogun and then to a president, there was only one honorable path. They would not give the emperor their flag. His army would have to take it. Nothing held their last French advisors but loyalty. They opted to fight on with them.

The last Ezo strongholds were not the hurried works of a retreating army—they were purpose built at great expense to allow the Matsumae clan to hold out for months in the event of either Russian aggression or native Ainu rebellion.

The Ezo's capital, Goryokaku, was the nation's first modern star-shaped fort, laid out in the style of Vauban's work for France's King Louis XIV by architect Takeda Ayasaburo and completed barely two years prior after seven years of labor. The beautiful multistory swept-roofed towers of traditional Japanese castles were notably absent. Instead, low-set 5.5-meter walls were as thick as 29 meters in places and steeply angled to deflect incoming shots. Her inner works sprawled below their height across more than 62 acres. Its 5-points enabled denser concentrations of cannon and eliminated the blind spots of squared-off predecessors. Expansive 29-meter-wide moats stood off aggressors. Its wells ran deep, and its close-packed red-brick blockhouses were scaled for long sieges.

Any approach on their capital from the sea would have to go through Hakodate Bay. And to do that, it would have to go through Benton Daiba, the smaller and closer of the two remaining Ezo strongholds. Its roughly rectangular shape overlooked the bay on a shallow spur of land edging into the water that, auspiciously, was previously used for a shrine to the goddess of fortune, Benten herself.

It had been sixteen months since the shogun surrendered. It was time it all ended. Commander Masuda Toranosuke's imperial strategy was to draw out and destroy the Ezo navy, reduce the isolated Benton Daiba, and besiege Goryokaku.

With *Kotetsu*, Admiral Ikunosuke would have gone on the offensive long before the Tsugaru Strait was crossed. Without her, he elected to deploy his fleet at anchor with carefully interlocked fire zones with shore-based guns centered on Benten Daiba. *Kotetsu* may have been dominant, and her 5.5-inch armor unrivaled; however, her men could bleed like any other, and any penetration of her boiler or magazine could be as catastrophic as a single shot from the victorious *Wyoming* had been to the Chōshū's *Koshin* at Shimono-seki. There was hope. If they could prevail at sea, it would take years for the emperor's forces to develop or acquire a renewed fleet. While the Sat-Cho block would never waver, all they needed was a material block of other clans prepared to do nothing.

Hakodate was a beautiful, generous bay, wide enough that the Ezo fleet could form a staggered semicircle facing its mouth but narrow enough that the emperor's fleet would have to approach as a column.

For the emperor's fleet, there was no choice.

The emperor's army couldn't advance with the Ezo fleet screening their approaches. Here, finally, there could be no retreat for rebel forces that had fought on longer after the shogun's resignation than before it.

There was only one way in and out, and *Kotetsu* would take it head on.

MY SPIRIT GUARDS MY LORD IN THE EAST
28

T he *Stonewall* had been too late to turn the tide of the American Civil War. The *Stærkodder* served the Prussian-Danish War without impact. Here, finally, was an opportunity for the five-nation ship to make her mark.

The Ezo fleet displaced 3,030 tons, more than half of it accounted for by the *Kaiten*, and boasted twenty-nine heavy guns. The Meiji fleet displaced 3,931 tons, more than one-third of it *Kotetsu*'s, with the same twenty-nine heavy guns. Only the Ezo would fight with the cover of the purpose-built harbor fortress Benten Daiba.

Both sides framed the coming battle as a defining one for modern Japan. The Satsuma general, Takamori, who'd led the shogun's army until switching to serve the Cho-Sat Rebellion in the emperor's name, had been unwavering since Toba-Fushimi. "We are fighting for the Emperor. We must all do our best for His Majesty." Though President Takeaki had offered to serve the emperor, and no longer had any claim beyond Ezo or to the office of shogun, he rallied his troops with a wider Japanese identity, declaring, "We have risen to protect the Imperial Court and defend the Empire. This is a rebellion against traitorous vassals."[1] Any talk of resisting the West was long gone.

When the Meiji fleet came for the Ezo, *Kotetsu* led them, front and center. Behind her steamed the English-built *Kasuga* (1,289 tons; six guns), which had served as the flagship of the Lay-Osborn Flotilla during the Chinese Taiping Rebellion before being acquired by the Satsuma. Next came the corvette *Chōyō* (591 tons; twelve guns), a veteran of the Mito Rebellion, which had launched in the Netherlands in 1856 as one of two ships ordered immediately after the American black ship humiliation. After her came the sloop *Hōshō* (326 tons; two guns), which had been launched in Scotland in 1868 and acquired by the Chōshū. To either flank steamed the lesser gunboats *Mos-*

hun (305 tons; two guns) with her sixty-five crewmen, launched in 1867 for the Saga, and the diminutive gunboat *Teibo 2* (125 tons; two guns), launched in 1867 and also acquired by the Chōshū.

It was almost the whole naval strength of the emperor. Only the laid-up 1,000-ton, thirteen-gun frigate *Fujiyama*, launched in 1863 in the United States; the *Kanrin*, which they captured after storm damage eight months prior; and the twin 1867-built Chōshū gunboats *Teibo 1* (125 tons; two guns) and *Shinsoku* under the command of Masuda Toranosuke could not be made ready in time.

Against them, the Ezo were led by the flagship *Kaiten* (1,920 tons; ten guns)—a side-wheeler launched in 1851 for the Prussian navy, captured while in service to the daimyo Satake of Akita—that still sported hard wood plugs where she'd been holed in the close-fought attempt to seize *Kotetsu*. Neither of her lost masts had been replaced. Of their remaining squadron, she alone would have the scale and firepower to take on the Meiji flagship.

Of the eight ships Takeaki had led from disaster at Toba-Fishimi, five remained, of which two were so marginal that they would play no material part in what was to come. As a result, Ikunouke avoided a meeting engagement at sea and, instead, reached back to Lord Nelson's classic adage that a ship's a fool to fight a fort. Carefully staggered about the bay so their fire could be concentrated was the lushly appointed paddle frigate *Banryū* (370 tons; six guns), launched in 1856 in England for the shogun as a gift from Queen Victoria; and the third-class gunboat *Chiyodogata* (140 tons; three guns), Japan's first modern domestically built warship, which had been taken from the shogun by the emperor in May 1868 and reclaimed by the Ezo in October 1868.

Admiral Ikunosuke was as pragmatic as Takeaki before him. Units could be risked in time of war, but he would not demand outright sacrifice. The *Hōō* (600 tons; ten guns) had been launched in 1849 as a pioneering Western-style sail frigate with a beautiful red lacquer varnish, copper hull, and distinctive black-banded sails, but despite her ten guns, her inability to move under steam and thin hull made her so vulnerable that she was stripped of her powder and quietly moored by Benton Daiba. The transports *Oe* and *Ho-o* were ordered to shelter at Muroran.[2] The paddle steamer *Chōgei*, which launched in 1856, was also de-gunned and moored close in, where she was largely overlooked; she was last noted forlornly transporting wounded rebels to an unknown fate in Tokyo.[3]

Time and again it seemed like the goddess Amaterasu favored the emperor's fleet who flew her symbol, the sun. The Ezo could only rue the ships they did not command. *Kotetsu* first and foremost. The Dutch-built corvette *Kanrin*, Japan's first steam-driven screw ship, had been seized by the emperor's forces. Japan's treacherous seas had claimed the Dutch-built

Kaiyō, U.S.-built *Shinsoku*, and *Kaiten 2* (Takao). No counterfactual for this final clash can be complete without considering their collective weight of fire. Tonnage is a crude basis for comparison, but if each of these ships still served, the Ezo fleet would have been more than three times larger than the emperor's, with more than double the firepower. None of the missing ships had been defeated by imperial forces.

Miyako Bay, where the *Kaiten* had stormed the *Kotetsu*, ended in a long, narrow channel that would have been perfect for funneling the emperor's fleet in, one by one. Hakodate Bay was not.

Hakodate had been chosen to be the first trade port conceded in 1854 for her isolation, so soon after the black ships that one of Matthew C. Perry's black ship sailors was buried there. Its open-bowl shape was neatly centered on the Kameda Peninsula and anchored at one end by shipyards. It meant the Ezo fleet could track imperial actions from the overlooking Mount Hakodate, signal her fleet by semaphore flags, and concentrate ship-based and shore-based fire on specific pre-ranged points. The bowl's width, though, ensured the Meiji fleet could move together and divide their fire. The imperial navy anchored outside the bay mouth in mild weather and waited.

Arai Ikunosuke and Bankichi Matsuoka, operating from the *Banryū*, kept their fleet under pressure and battle ready, fed by a stream of litters, night and day. Their sails were either furled or removed entirely. Davit boats were pulled down. Small arms were clustered at the base of masts. Overnight watches kept men within an arm's reach of every gun. Final code signals were checked and rechecked to keep ship and shore connected.

On May 4, the Meiji fleet launched its first assault.

Imperial commander Masuda Toranosuke led his squadron into the bay line-abreast in a shallow approach mid-morning that saw them test Ezo defenses with long-range fire for more than an hour before they withdrew in good order. While the Ezo recorded impacts, none were consequential. The imperial *Kasuga* reported towlines of unknown purpose spanning the harbor and sent out three ships that were unable to cut them overnight but managed to do so the following day. Too slight to be barrier boom nets, they were either incomplete or for an unknown purpose. The Ezo held their first positions overnight at the farthest point Fort Benten could support.

A second venture the following day saw Toranosuke's fleet close to within 1,200 yards of Admiral Ikunosuke's warships, before starting a gentle banking turn that took them within 600 yards, so each ship could cycle through a full broadside. The sheer volume of fire, together with the thick, dark smoke of each ship funnel and the lighter smoke of their cannon fire pooling languidly in the humid air, made it harder and harder for gun captains to sight their fall of shot and adjust.

Toward noon, the Ezo fleet broke anchor and retreated to their second positions mid-bay where the Benten fort could support them more closely. With the advantage of having pre-sighted their guns, each captain noted repeated impacts on their imperial targets without result. The Meiji fleet advanced in response.

An Ezo captain recorded, "When the latter followed the fugitives with yells, the shot from the battery fell right in amongst them, destroying the bridge and battery of the Chōyō and penetrating her side."[4] The imperial corvette withdrew with a recorded forty shots fired in return.[5] Though *Kotetsu* added her battery to imperial fire, she had no opportunity to make a ram run. As she turned—surprisingly tightly with her twin rudders—their squadron order began to break down, and each ship found others interfering with their gunnery. The intensity of Ezo fire suggested good supply, and no material damage was observed. Imperial captains conferred by signal flag and withdrew. The Chōshū had steamed unflinchingly into even certain defeat against European navies for years. The delay was brief.

That afternoon, the Meiji fleet surged in again in careful order to keep their channels of fire open and were driven off again, damaged but whole. After two days of preparations and re-coaling, they surged a third time. With both sides prepared, the exchanges were even heavier. Two imperial ships took damage, including the *Kasuga*. This time the Ezo's *Kaiten* was damaged in return, including a powerful penetration with the *Kotetsu*'s forecastle 300-pounder by gunners including Nakamura Iwataro. The emperor's fleet retreated again, and Ezo carpenters led their crews in emergency bracing and repairs, while tenders ferried out further coal, shot, and powder, and returned with their wounded and dead.

On May 6, the Meiji fleet played to their strength. Their next assault was coordinated with a drive on land that divided the shore fort's attention. Toranosuke ordered the *Kotetsu* forward alone, steaming gently in a brazen line right down the harbor's centerline, focused on her powerful forecastle gun rather than her ram.

Heedless of the fire bursting against her armor, she anchored herself in place and traded shots with the fortress, absorbing as many as twenty rounds in the four or five minutes it could take to reload her single 300-pound foregun. The former Confederate ram held her post for more than an hour, burning through Ezo resources. By early afternoon, the volume of fire directed against her from Fort Benten was slackening, and she held on, convinced she could survive by simply waiting them out. As disturbing as her perseverance was for the defending Ezo gunners, it was hellish for her crew, who were deafened by fire and bloodied by splintering, even where their iron held. Even screams couldn't be heard in the tight forecastle, where men worked by experience and gesture alone. The ram's cyclopean forward gun fired less and less, hitting nothing as men, concussed and insensate, began being helped down to the surgery bay of medical officers Shunpei and Akizo. Splinters from their masts rained down.

Kotetsu's 5 inches of armor—backed by up to 2 feet of hardwood—was the margin between victory and defeat. Any other ship in the emperor's colors would have been shattered in minutes. In the Ezo forts, gun masters were starting to make tough choices as their powder monkeys raced up soot-stained and barefoot with less and less black powder, forcing them to either wait for other guns to fire in a slowing cycle or continuing with less and less power. *Kotetsu*'s first officers Ding Zo and Bunjiro spotted a growing number of shots falling short. Though not engaged, lesser imperial ships moved across the harbor, observing.

On land, with relatively modest field artillery deployed against them after their forced marches, and eager to conserve their powder, Ezo forces rallied out and came so close to overrunning the Meiji camp at Nanaeshima that imperial troops retreated to Oiwake. When their withdrawal on land enabled the volume of fire on *Kotetsu* to ramp again, Captain Nakajima finally found his limit and withdrew. The fields around the Benten fort were clear for the moment.

Ezo troops harried carefully prepared imperial defensive positions over-night that precluded raiding in force. In Fort Benten, gun masters debated realigning cannon from land to sea and back. Logistics leaders listened to conflicting demands and made their choices for the day ahead. Troops worked overnight with civilian volunteers, patching the penetrations of fort walls and warship hulls, falling asleep where they could, exhausted. Imperial forces at sea were confident enough to rest their men and serve hot food. A long night passed.

The imperial ships that stood off through *Kotetsu*'s long defiance the day before hadn't missed the slackening return fire after four days of fighting. Toranosuke judged it time to press for a final victory.

In predawn darkness, *Kotetsu*'s Chōshū crew ate a light meal and completed repairs where their hot-rolled French iron armor had been struck without penetration, but with minor spalling to the hardwood reinforcement. Gun crew assignments were fixed for men like Nakamura Iwataro and *Kotetsu*'s cyclopean forward gun, so they'd fight face-on to the enemy with the same few who'd had their bell rung with scores of hits the day before.

They knew what they faced, as surely as Raphael Semmes's officers had with the death of the Confederate raider *Alabama*, "Smoke stung their eyes until, red and watered, they could hardly see. Each roar of a gun assaulted the ears until they were temporarily deaf. It was nearly impossible to breathe as particles of gunpowder, smoke, dust, and fumes from the ship's stack choked their lungs nearly shut. Snaking lines wrenched arms and legs; deadly splinters flew with each shot the enemy landed; shrapnel was always flying about, and the noise and the pounding literally rattled their brains inside their skulls."[6]

Each fleet's gunners reopened their gunports in the hull bulwarks and removed tampion plugs from their batteries. Gun carriages were carefully checked. A worm was used to clear the bore. A wet swab followed to clear any remaining residue that risked a premature detonation. Their first powder was prepositioned. Vent holes were checked. Loaders stepped in with powder, wad, and shot for their rammers to pack in. Bedding was taken down and stowed. Kitchen fires were extinguished. Loose items were tied down, lest they become missiles of their own.

Shortly after dawn, *Kotetsu* announced herself with a plume of smoke, and repeated her brazen approach, slow, steady, and proud, right down the centerline of the bay. Her masts were bare of sail. Her davit boats, gone. The imperial sun flag flew bow, mast, and stern. *Kaiten* opened up first with her 68-pounder cannon, and as she closed, with her supporting cannonades. *Banryū* joined her from the next anchor point, firing and reloading her 12-pound battery as fast as she could. Next came *Chiyoda*'s Armstrong gun and 6-pound smoothbores as the former Confederate ram closed. Finally, Benten Daiba's guns joined their chorus, firing solid shot with full powder from their heavier battery. This was it. Whatever their supply situation, the Ezo held nothing back; a contemporary account declared they "kept up such an incessant fire as caused the sea to rock."[7]

Ezo gun captains cheered each hit on *Kotetsu*, exhorting their men to fire faster. No warship at the battles of Shimonoseki, Awa, or Miyako Bay had survived anything even close to it. Behind her, the Meiji squadron eased forward to open fire at longer ranges with batteries of their own.

The Ezo storm continued until "[a] shot from the Kisuga [*Kasuga*] hit the Banriu [*Banryū*] in her engines, while those of the iron-clad [*Kotetsu*] killed several tens of men in the fort. The 'rebel' [Ezo] fire slackened suddenly, but the fleet judged it expedient to retire, as the evening was closing in."[8] First blood on land and sea was Ezo's, but the wooden *Banryū* had been in the thick of it, and her casualties were mounting.

When *Kotetsu* withdrew, the Meiji squadron followed.

The emperor's fleet then switched their tactics, surging next at night. Given the limited accuracy in fighting during daylight to this point, they had less to fear from the Hakodate forts, though the defenders, of course, had less to fear in return. Imperial fire thundered in unison, then beat a staccato as each ship completed their broadsides one by one and made their way out of the bay's mouth and silence returned. The Ezo gunboat *Chiyoda*, impeccably disciplined to this point, even under fire from an ironclad ram ship more than four times her size, chose this moment to break anchor. No orders to do so were given, and it proved too dark for her to see the signal flags desperately calling her back.

Ikunosuke watched in horror as she disappeared into the ink of night. On board, Captain Morimoto appeared to lose his bearings. They were still within the nearer half of the bowl-shaped bay when *Chiyoda* struck a concealed shoal and stuck fast. Even at full steam, her screw couldn't shift her forward or back. Her only defense was the darkness—being caught fast alone and out of reach of her fleet's guns could only mean death for her thirty-nine crew in the morning. Every effort to dislodge her failed. Coal and stores were ordered overboard to try and lighten her. Morimoto's last act was to heave her lighter guns and shot after them, without result. All seemed lost. Her captain reluctantly ordered his crew to stove in her machinery, break the touchhole of her remaining gun, and abandon ship, all completely ignoring the state of the tides.

She was a forlorn sight on the morning of May 8, alone in the bay as the incoming tides shifted her bit by bit to float free and ease gently out to sea. The Meiji fleet stood off, fearing a fireship or a trap, until the *Kotetsu* closed cautiously, identified there wasn't a soul aboard, and dispatched a tender to take her helm.[9] The Ezo order of battle was down a heavy Armstrong cannon and four smoothbores. Down came the Ezo flag and up went the emperor's rising sun, to no further effect in the Battle of Hakodate and only ignoble imperial service as a whaler until 1911. Onshore, Benton Daiba fort shifted her last heavy guns to sea, in some cases leaving land-facing battery points with only improvised iron-banded wooden guns almost as dangerous to her crews as the enemy. On his return, shamefaced, the *Chiyoda*'s Captain Morimoto was field demoted to able seaman and chose to serve on. One of his officers, Ichikawam, committed suicide out of contrition in his place.[10]

As many as fifteen thousand Meiji troops had now rolled up the Hokkaidō's Oshima Peninsula to them. Each day saw new field artillery in place, some so close now the twin Ezo holdouts stood like islands. Behind them, the imperial flotilla was ferrying across a multiclan force almost as large again.

On May 10 came the final battle that *Kotetsu* had been summoned for. Imperial troopships, transports, and escorts could never be safe with Admiral Ikunosuke aboard the *Kaiten*. The defending fleet's destruction was required.

The Ezo rotated the little powder and shot remaining between their ships and Benten Daiba. *Banryū* had been penetrated so much she could no longer steam and was converted to a floating battery under the harbor fort's guns. Her boilers cooled. Part of her coal was scuttled to others.

President Takeaki had to be persuaded not to take to sea with his men. Ikunosuke remained stoic. Together they had dreamed of what the *Kotetsu* could do, and together they'd come agonizingly close to seizing her back. Instead, their hopes now rested on the 1,890 ton, thirteen-gun *Kaiten*. Their magazines were almost empty. *Chiyoda* was in his enemy's hands, and *Banryū* looked like she'd never move again, but they were samurai. They had fought because that still meant something that an imperial soldier in a British uniform with a French gun and foreign masters could never understand. The choice to fight on was no choice at all.

On the Meiji fleet came, in such a tight line that only partial broadsides were possible for fear of friendly fire. Caution was thrown to the wind. They'd seen the worst the Ezo could throw at them. Confidence was high.

The Ezo held nothing back, firing with full charges, and the *Chiyoda's* crew parceled out across their decks to stand in for their wounded. Smoke grew so thick as they fired and fired at shortening ranges that ships were reduced to ghostly outlines, and gun captains stared down their barrels and fired on the last targets seen. Every ship was an island. Reload, fire. Step up where men were blasted down. Reload, fire.

It had been the *Kaiten* that had nearly stolen *Kotetsu* back. It was the *Kaiten* that was the last warship in any shape to steam out. They could have stayed anchored near the *Banryū's* ruin under shore guns, but their powder was almost gone, and if ramming or boarding was the only way left to sink her enemy, then ramming or boarding it would be. She set a course to pass the smaller imperial *Chōyō* and raised all the pressure she could, while the gunship poured more than forty shots into her in passing.[11]

Kaiten charged *Kotetsu*, Asia's heaviest ram, a supreme irony, as at least four crewmen desperately worked her twin rudders to veer her away. A local account recorded, "The Kuaiteii [*Kaiten*] was the only vessel which they were able to oppose to the fleet, and a 300-pounder shot which the iron-clad immediately discharged killed several tens of 'rebel' troops, and smashed the eccentric, an important part of her machinery, thus rendering her also unable to move."[12]

The Meiji fleet parted around *Kaiten*, struggling to stay clear of one another and checking each other's fire. When *Kaiten* managed a piercing shot into *Kasuga* with significant casualties among her 137 crew, the emperor's fleet withdrew once again.[13] *Kaiten's* crew managed to ground her on a shoal at the harbor's edge. She'd been pierced from bow to stern. Scores of sailors were dead and dying. Her rigging was shot to pieces, draping down like hands reaching for her crew. Her last remaining mast leaned drunkenly. Her twin funnels had been compromised, leaving her working spaces a smoky nightmare. The side wheels looming over her deck, which had made coming alongside the *Kotetsu* with her samurai boarders so problematic, had their hardwood sheathing shot away, with great holes rent in places there was no coming back from. Like the *Banryū* before her, her crew bled off her boiler pressure, shuttered her works one by one, and came on deck to man the guns or take up small arms. Blades appeared. To a man, they resolved to fight on.

That the Ezo were surrounded was academic. Nothing and no one was coming from the home islands to help. Still, if imperial forces thought it was over, they were keen to prove them wrong. Takeaki's troops sallied out from their twin strongholds with more than three hundred men in heavy rain overnight, once again overrunning a forward camp, imparting serious casualties, and returning with all the supplies they could carry. There wasn't a magazine in their capital left with more than a few barrels of powder. When the *Stonewall* first crossed the Atlantic, she'd had more than 150 in her magazine alone. Their larders were thinning rapidly.

The Ezo shifted their remaining ships closer to one another and to shore, so *Kotetsu* couldn't make a ram run with any confidence that she could then extricate herself. *Banryū* and *Kaiten* gave no sign they'd ever move again. Their wounded were dragged to the ship's surgeon or on litters to Benten Daiba. Death poems and letters had long since been written. Now came the last conversations, and the decision on who to leave them with. Final rigging was cut away. Carpenters worked through the night patching bulwarks and hull piercings where they could. Engineers—knowing the Meiji had come at night—effected what repairs they could while keeping their boilers under pressure. On came more coal, load after load, for a 50-degree fireroom, to burn above 1,000 degrees.

The next morning—Naval Battle of Hakodate's last—the gunboats *Chōyō* and *Teibo* led the imperial Meiji fleet into Hakodate harbor with the *Kasuga* and *Hōshō* behind.

Kotestsu ignored the Ezo fleet and steamed into the bay independently with insolent slowness, to anchor directly under the guns of Benten Daiba. In the days before, she'd been struck so hard and so often that the shots were hard to tell apart. Little came her way now, and much of that was fired with so little charge that there was almost no sign of it ever having happened. Still, imperial captains reported sighting new guns being hauled into place along the Ezo's coastal walls.

The Ezo general, Keisuke Otori, recorded, "the warship *Kotetsu* approached the coast off Kameda village and fired. . . . Her 70 pound shells fell within the fortifications and burst with terrific effect. They struck the roofs and banks, broke pillars or split stones and caused great injuries, so that we were unable to continue to fight any longer."[14]

Kotetsu signaled her squadron to close in.

As they did so, the Ezo's *Banryū*—which was so heavily damaged that *Kotetsu* had taken her to be abandoned—sprang to life. Furious work overnight had restored some limited steam pressure. Under Commander Matsuoka Hankichi, she cast off and made for the incoming *Kasuga* that had advanced ahead of her line of ships, which sheered away just in time to avoid collision. The *Chōyō* alone fired more than forty shots at her in the attempt. The *Banryū* had just passed by the imperial *Kasuga*, so close two men could speak or throw a parcel from one to another, when her gunner Nagakiira achieved a catastrophic penetration of the imperial *Chōyō*'s powder magazine from more than 1,200 yards away. The resulting explosion was so loud it was said to echo for 10 ri (~40 kilometers) and so violent that the 600-ton, 49-meter-long steam imperial corvette sank in under two minutes with the loss of eighty-six lives.[15] Captain Kuranosuke, standing prominently on her bridge, was among the few who survived.

The *Banryū* fired on any ship that tried to rescue the scattered imperial survivors in the water, holding off the Meiji fleet until *Kotetsu* was ordered to break her remorseless onshore fire and position herself like an iron wall between the Ezo warship and their men. While she took further shipborne fire as a result, it was becoming clear that the *Banryū* was firing with partial charges. *Kotetsu*'s aftercastle guns—lighter than the Armstrongs she'd left Bordeaux with—were muscled from firing port to port until they faced her, so close that almost every shot was observed to be penetrating, and casualties quickly mounted. *Banryū* turned back toward the Benten Daiba fort and struggled away with what little power remained. Her guns were silent; her shot expended; her powder gone. When they kissed the shore just seaward of the habor fort, she'd been holed so extensively there was almost no machinery left to destroy. Hankichi's crew heaved her guns overboard, set her on fire, and abandoned ship. With her went English fittings and furnishings quite literally hand wrought to be fit for a king. While she would later be raised and serve as the SS *Emperor* in China and as the Imperial Japanese Navy's *Raiden*, her war was over. Most of her crew sought shelter in Benten Daiba fortress and watched her burn. Some slipped through the Meiji army's outer pickets at great risk to reach Goryokaku.

Kotetsu steamed forward to oppose Benten Daiba once again. Within an hour, gunfire from the remaining Ezo warships spluttered and died out.

Kasuga reported having fired 170 times and being struck in eighteen different places.[16] As sunset approached, *Kotetsu* weighed anchor and eased out of the bay to take up a new station facing outward to the sea, near the European warships who'd observed the whole action. Her work was done. Toranosuke's fleet followed, knowing they'd have total freedom of action from this point.

The naval battle of Hakodate Bay was over.

President Takeaki had lost 1,300 dead, 1,300 captured, and 400 wounded. Two steam screw warships had been lost. *Chiyoda* had floated into Meiji hands.

Imperial forces lost 770 casualties; one steam ship sunk (and later raised), and the Dutch-sourced corvette *Chōyō* succumbed to a spectacular detonation.[17]

The following morning the last Ezo vessels, their powder expended and their guns silent, were seized. The crew of the bufuku corvette *Kanrin* had been summarily executed when captured by the Meiji warships *Fuji*, *Mutsahi*, and *Hiryu* after storm damage. The remaining Ezo sailors were taken into custody instead.

Kotetsu had proved every bit as overwhelming as Confederates John Slidell and James Dunwoody Bulloch had hoped she could be in the American Civil War. This was the end of the line for their stalwart French advisors, who slipped away to the French frigate *Coetlogon*, which had entered the harbor without incident.

Takeaki was a samurai long before he'd been sent to study in the Netherlands and emerged as admiral and president. Although he dispatched runners with his remaining treasures, including all but two of the Dutch journals he'd carried everywhere since studying abroad, he stayed to fight as the last pickets at Yunokawa in the east, Akagawa in the northeast, and Nanaye Beach on the south were swept away.[18]

The Shinsengumi's commander, Toshizō, wrote his death poem that evening and entrusted his fifteen-year-old page, Ichimura Tetsunosuke, with a lock of his hair, photos, two swords, and a letter addressed to his family's lands in the south, knowing the act of delivering them would save the boy, despite his protests. His words survived. "Though my body may decay on the island of Ezo, My spirit guards my lord in the east."[19] The Satsuma and Chōshū who had fought without quarter for so long, accepted a second day of inaction. An imperial messenger seeking Ezo's surrender returned empty handed, with due decorum, the next day.

With the bay lost, the Ezo general and Shinsengumi's commander, Toshizō, ordered the retreat of his final forces outside the capital's walls. True to character, he was the last man to turn and leave, and nearest the enemy. Doing so on horseback, he took a bullet to the back that he only acknowledged when every man was safely behind their walls, and he finally found the warrior's death that eluded him in the Gatling-gun carnage storming the *Kotetsu*. It was a bitter blow. Swordsman Kojima Shikanosuke described him as "a beautiful man. He has read many books, has a General's bearing, and is naturally good at military strategy." Samurai Ishii Yujiro recorded, "When the chief died, the Shinsengumi in the battery grieved like babies that have lost their mother. Ah, such sorrow."[20] He was thirty-four.

By day, the Ezo watched Meiji forces manhandle artillery closer and closer. By night, they watched their campfires glow, frustrated that there would be no more raiding.

The Meiji fleet steamed in so close they crossed the first line taken by the Ezo's semicircle of warships at the battle's early stages. Benten Daiba sheltered the crews of the lost *Kaiten* and *Banryū* as, one by one, their remaining guns spluttered and died out. The extra guns previously reported by the fleet were exposed as desperate ad hoc designs with painted wooden barrels coiled in rope and banded in iron, firing nothing but stone like the world's largest shotgun. The gun crews held on station, exposed, proud, and purposeless. The powder monkeys stopped. The surgeons' work continued.

Goryōkaku fortress remained, but the Ezo soil between them and their fortress capital was now a sea of Meiji color and movement. *Kotetsu* remained at the head of the bay, facing international waters. Her work was done. Behind her, the Meiji fleet fired broadside after broadside, systematically reducing Benten Daiba, which could only offer small arms fire in return. Most rounds were absorbed by the walls, but at first occasionally, then more and more often, channels were found to the defenders inside. The trapped Ezo could hear each gun like a note, with nothing to do but clench their teeth and hold on. For the sea fort, it must have seemed like their attackers' shot and powder were unlimited. On land, further field artillery was brought to bear, though with markedly less results, and it must have seemed almost unlimited resources would be required to level a fort designed to stop the Russian Empire. Inside, morale held.

On May 12, the Ezo's defeat seemed such an inevitability that imperial forces ceased fire and sent up an officer named Nagayama to offer terms that President Takeaki promptly declined. The refusal of the Ezo to acknowledge certain defeat was infuriating. The Cho-Sat block lobbied for massacre and scorched earth. President Takeaki used the lull to disclose his refusal to surrender and commend his troops. When he offered to open the gates to let his men chose their own fate, just a handful marched out to the dubious mercy of the Aizu or besieging forces.

The surrender of the president's Shinsengumi honor guard might have been unthinkable under Toshizō; however, the fact remained that they'd fired the last of their artillery shot and powder, and even rifle fire was being carefully metered. Logistics had proved an Achilles' heel. They'd retreated north with only what they could carry, and the fort's stores were never filled with more than a fraction of what they could hold. Their water was limited, with several wells fouled by debris and rubble.

After two days of deliberations, Benten Daiba commanders Kazue Soma and Nagai Naomune were selected as those who would dishonor themselves with surrender. On May 15, the Ezo flag came down on the smaller of the two last rebel bastions. Benten Daiba was lost. The port was the emperor's.

With the star fort capital more than 4,500 meters inland, the Meiji fleet's guns were finally silenced. After eleven days of intense fleet action, some imperial gun-captain inspections revealed cannon so compromised by their rate of fire that they could only be stripped out and replaced.

Imperial forces slackened their fire on the Ezo capital and waited out the afternoon for their colors to come down. On they flew. With no signs of surrender from the daunting Vauban-style star fort Goryokaku, a full assault was staged early the following day.

Imperial artillery, now thoroughly emplaced and sighted, fired with almost total impunity. The Ezo could be seen shifting on the walls but largely conserved their powder for the assault that must follow. Guns alone couldn't carry the fort. At some point, it would take blood.

When Meiji forces finally opened a breach in the capital's walls large enough for a man to pass through, it was Ezo general Nakajima Saburoske who stepped up to hold it and the imperial samurai Taruzawa who charged forward to exploit it. Seven times, they closed on one another and seven times they separated again, until both fell where they stood, each with ten wounds or more. It was a display so extraordinary that others ceased fighting to witness it, and a spontaneous lull ensued.

As few as eight hundred troops in fighting order remained in Goryokaku. Imperial artillery fire resumed at dawn the next day, concentrating on the hastily assembled wood and rubble barrier that filled their previous breach in the wall. With an equally committed opponent, Meiji forces had no intention of resolving the matter with one-on-one combat, sword in hand. They wanted an opening an army could march through with rifle and bayonet.

The fort had been designed to hold on until the shogun could gather his daimyo and respond. Here, no one was coming, and the Ezo could only watch under fire as a whole imperial army under Kuroda Kiyotaka joined Meiji forces and set about deploying artillery of their own.[21] By day, the air was full of shells. By night, stars and fires.

President Takeaki could ask no more of those serving him, but honor dictated that he could not simply surrender. Commander in chief Otori Keisuke counseled that living on and serving the emperor could be honorable. "If it's dying you want you can do it anytime."[22] Instead, a middle path was chosen.

Takeaki sent a messenger out with the final volumes of the Dutch *Complete Digest of the Maritime Laws of All Nations*, which he'd carried reverently in all the years since his study there as a twenty-six-year-old.

No surrender accompanied them, but the gesture was instantly understood, and the imperial reply was gracious. "We thank you for presenting us with two volumes the likes of which are not to be found in Japan, out of regret 'that they should become the property of the crows.' Your generous feeling lays us under a great obligation."[23]

Would a less worldly president have fought to the last man? Japan's history is filled with deadly last stands. Surrender meant the end of a democratic republican ideal, but peace for Japan. The war was over. Ezo samurai retained their swords. Food and water were delivered. Working parties set about clearing streets and wells without interference.

The Ezo republic outlived its fleet, briefly.

Though dates are contested, it was as late as June 24 when Ryoun Takamatsu recorded his commander Soma presenting a letter of obedience to the emperor and leading the last elements of the Benten Daiba garrison out.[24]

President Enomoto Takeaki followed three days later on the sole condition that he alone would be held accountable for what the Meiji considered rebellion and was immediately placed under arrest. There were many calls for his head or for *seppuku*, but the samurai general and future prime minister Kuroda Kiyotaka held that his defeat was honorable and spared him and his men. Instead, they were transported to the Tatsunokuchi Tadasu Interrogation Office in Tokyo with Ezo loyalists including the Banryū's Captain Matsuoka and General Kazue.[25]

Less those specifically named, orders in the emperor's name directed every man to return to their domain. The Ezo's last serviceable warship, *Hōō*, was seized by imperial forces while attempting a 140-kilometer flight up the coast toward the port city of Muroran with 305 colonists who promptly went into custody.

It is a constant challenge to identify what the emperor knew or did—and when—throughout the Boshin War. In this temperate response to the Ezo's final surrender, we see a likely decision from him to stare down the ruthlessness of the Chōshū-Satsuma block at the heart of imperial forces. Whatever the case, Emperor Meiji was confident enough to let his forces disperse from the field with no central imperial army in place. Hundreds of commandeered civilian vessels were tasked with recrossing the Tsugaru strait, then released. Hakodate's fishermen returned to the sea.

Though the Meiji era had been declared the year before, the emperor's power was now complete. No clan stepped into this military vacuum, despite several daimyo (including the Kishū clan) being able to raise a force of twenty thousand troops or more, which was larger than the army Shogun Yoshinobu had ordered to march on the emperor at the war's outset.[26]

The Goryokaku fortress itself remained, so redoubtable and well sited it served until the close of World War II. It can still be visited today, alternatively colored with thousands of cherry trees and autumn-red leaves.

On September 20, the island was given her present name, Hokkaidō, and was subsumed into Meiji Japan with scant regard for the indigenous Ainu.

The imperial Matsumae clan were not reinstated. Instead, federally appointed Kuroda Kiyotaka led Japan's efforts to intensify the island's development; after soft initial results, he resorted to recruiting the American Horace Capron, a former commissioner of agriculture for Ulysses S. Grant's post–Civil War administration. American William S. Clark later succeeded Capron, and Clark's own parting words from the role were, "Boys, be ambitious!" In less than a decade, the population administered by the newly appointed Date clan exploded from less than fifty-eight thousand to almost a quarter of a million citizens, validating President Takeaki's vision for it.[27]

The balance of power of the sea had shifted forever. As Royal Navy admiral Sir John Hay put it, "The man who goes into action in a wooden vessel is a fool, and the man who sends him there is a villain."[28] The shogun's story was over. The bufuku's story was over. The Ezo's story was over.

The ironclad ram ship *Kotetsu*'s was not.

THE IMPERIAL PACIFIC   29

The Ezo republic was dissolved on June 27. Less than fourteen years after the American black ships, a shogunate lineage dating back to 720 CE was broken forever.

More than 120,000 troops had fought. Estimates of those killed directly run to more than 8,200.[1] By the standard of nineteenth-century warfare, relatively few civilians had been lost. Fishing fleets and farms went largely unchanged, in all but the most contested prefectures. No blockade was launched. In that regard, the Boshin War was far more like the professional Danish-Prussian clashes where the *Stærkodder* had served than the nation-at-arms clash she'd served as the *Stonewall*.

Kotetsu remained the most powerful ship in Asia. U.S. Navy officials had been skeptical of the *Stonewall* in their first Cuban inspections after her surrender, but in light of her performance, a U.S. diplomat in Tokyo reported that the Japanese navy "has been rapidly increased into quite a large and serviceable one, while our own is in fact unrepresented here with anything that could for the moment live in conflict with the *Stonewall*."[2]

The great irony of the campaign was that each step toward modernization was a step away from the traditions they claimed to be fighting for. Imperial forces who started the war to usurp a shogun who hadn't expelled the barbarians, finished it with unprecedented Western influence over how they ate, drank, worked, and played.

The result was a new policy of relentless engagement. Waves of new advisors followed, among them British admirals Sir Edward Hobart Seymour and Sir George Rooke Hopkins and the leading French naval architect M. Bertin to reshape their navy.[3] Foreign investment spiked. Western merchants blossomed. More ports opened. Publishing flourished. Schools expanded. More,

more, more. The faster they could modernize, the faster they could reset the unequal treaties blamed on the shogun.

America reveled in her role opening Japan's ports. Commodore Matthew Perry's ship's flag flew proudly at the U.S. Naval Academy until 1945, when it was flown to wave at the Japanese surrender ceremony aboard the USS *Mississippi* at the conclusion of World War II.[4]

Imperial forces recognized the debt they owed *Kotetsu*. The forward gunner, "Nakamura Iwataro, warrior class of Kagoshima Prefecture," and four other crewmen of the *Kotetsu*, *Chōyō*, and *Hōshō* were singled out by the War Ministry's Yori Sen on September 13, 1869, for a "Hakodate Battle Merit" to receive special allocations of rice and Vice Mitsui Bank Securities that would previously have been reserved for samurai alone.[5]

The emperor shifted his seat from Kyoto to Tokyo in late 1868. Japan's three hundred domains were streamlined into fifty prefectures with governors appointed by the emperor. The samurai class was abolished. Some successfully transitioned into administrative or bureaucratic roles. Many fell into poverty and despair. In 1876, their traditional rice stipend trailed off into a lesser cash rate, bonds, and, finally, to nothing at all, and their right to bear swords was revoked.[6]

At war's end, many Japanese citizens had never laid eyes on a Westerner. In a short space of time, most did. The Chōshū, Satsuma, and Tosa clans were rewarded with key government roles in a *genro* Meiji oligarchy that lasted for decades.

The Yasukuni shrine (originally Tōkyō Shōkonsha, the "shrine to summon the souls") was instituted in June 1869 to commemorate their war's dead, much as the United States had with Arlington cemetery on land once owned by the South's General Robert E. Lee. Today, though it honors more than 2.5 million fallen soldiers, the presence of convicted World War II war criminals makes it controversial.

With the fighting over, there was finally a place for moderate voices. The last samurai, Saigō Takamori, who had been instrumental in forming the Cho-Sat block while commanding the shogunate expedition sent to punish the Chōshū, was not alone in calling for clemency. British envoy Harry Parkes, who had forgiven at least three imperial attempts on his life, argued "that severity towards Keiki [Yoshinobu] or his supporters, especially in the way of personal punishment, would injure the reputation of the new government in the opinion of European Powers."[7]

Interclan reparations were demanded. Wealth and land were transferred. Loyalty was rewarded. Disloyalty was punished. All of it was in the emperor's name, but from the start, there was uncertainty on how figurative or literal this may be. Shogunate domains throughout the Tohoku and Echigo regions were reduced so aggressively that many fell into bankruptcy. Some were allocated such marginal land that their forces starved or drifted apart, taking storied names like Tonami with them.[8]

The shogunate Sendai's clan's maximum assessed domain value was capped at 280,000 goku, with any holding above this cutoff summarily seized. Two retainers were executed. Two were forced to commit *seppuku*. The Aizu were capped at 30,000 and had a retainer executed. On and on it went across the Northern Alliance: the Morioka (130,000; one execution), Yonezawa (140,0000), Shonai (120,000), Yamagata (140,000; one execution), Nihonmatsu (50,000), Tanagura (50,000), Echigo-Nagaoka (28,000), and Jozai (10,000; one execution). And so on and so on, each clan having seizures, jailing, and representative executions in place of their daimyo's.[9] Some killings were reverential and discreet. Others left heads on pikes.

Imperial forces called it mercy.

The emperor was held in such high esteem that when he declared all clans' military resources would be nationalized in exchange for the assumption of debts in 1871 (after almost all bufuku daimyo had been released), he had only a token eight-thousand-man vanguard drawn from Satsuma, Chōshū, and Tosa in Tokyo. Not a single daimyo opposed the measure.

More change followed, hard and fast. The four classes of shogunate society were abandoned. The last traces of Confucian philosophy were swept away. The feudal system was abolished in 1871. At least six years of compulsory education became universal for boys and girls in 1872, expounding their moral duty to the emperor, country, and family alongside mathematics and reading. The thirst for knowledge was deeply ingrained. The "Civilization Ball Song" was sung in schoolyards across the nation in time with a rubber ball bounced ten times for the ten Western desirables—gas lamps, steam engines, horse carriages, cameras, telegrams, lightning-conductors, newspapers, schools, letter-post, and steamships.[10]

Meiji Japan hired advisors from around the world. Students were sent out in turn, much as Takeaki had been a generation before, who affirmed, "Knowledge shall be sought all over the world, and thereby the foundations of imperial rule shall be strengthened." In 1871, this was formalized as the one-hundred-delegate, eighteen-month Iwakura Mission to Europe and the United States to blueprint Japan's future.[11]

Surviving leaders from both sides of the naval war were held in high esteem, and many rose to great heights in the Meiji era. Captain Kuranosuke, who survived the cataclysmic sinking of the *Chōyō*, became chief of the Imperial Japanese Navy General Staff in 1892 and commandant of the Naval Staff College before being awarded the title viscount under the kazoku peerage system.[12] The Ezo Tarozaemon, captain of the *Kaiyō*, served in the Army-

Navy Ministry and founded new gunpowder factories of unprecedented national scale.[13]★

Honor was their currency. Without it, there was obscurity at best. General Shigekata, whose mismanagement of the battle of Toba-Fushimi robbed the shogun of his last best hope for quick victory, fought prominently in the Battle of Ueno, and when separated from their forces, he fought a guerrilla campaign northward until he rejoined Takeaki's fleet in Sendai. While the Ezo president could not find a place for him in his army, he appointed him as judge advocate general. Shigekata repaid him by slipping away on a foreign vessel from Hakodate before the city's final fall. He was pardoned for having served the shogun in 1873 but, after a brief period in public service, could only find work with his brother's company. He died in 1891, largely unremembered, at the age of sixty-three.[15]

Others struggled to reconcile their personal codes with the transformation underway. The last Ezo Shinsengumi commander, Kazue, for example, was demoted from general to a fifteenth-rank attendant after his surrender and, despite attempts to found a small carpentry school, was embroiled in assassinations and transportation before ending his life by *seppuku*.[16]

The *Kotetsu* had been named, quite literally, as the iron ship to showcase that Japan had entered a new world. As new ironclads joined the fleet, on December 7, 1872, she was renamed for the seventh and final time as the Imperial Japanese Navy warship (IJN) *Azuma* (East) to reflect the dawn of Japan's new age.[17]

President Takeaki was pardoned in 1872 by the same General Kiyotaka who'd accepted his surrender at Goryokaku and was named as secretary-general of the Hokkaidō Development Commission. In 1874, he was appointed vice admiral in the Imperial Japanese Navy (IJN). The following year, he concluded the Treaty of Saint Petersburg with Russia that exchanged the Sakhalin and Kuril Islands. In 1880, he became naval minister over Satsuma protests. To abrogate their dissent, he was appointed ambassador to China and served variously as minister of education, foreign affairs, agriculture, commerce, and communications, for which he is regarded as a transformational figure. His ascent to the peerage was confirmed in 1887 and culminated in his appointment to the Imperial Privy Council.

In an era when the Chōshū and Satsuma dominated public office, his influence was extraordinary. He founded what became the Tokyo University of Agriculture and oversaw a growing émigré population in Latin America and

---

★His former command, the *Kaiyō*, was rediscovered by a submarine a century later, partially raised and recreated with a replica vessel in 1990 that remains viewable at Esashi. Japan's first steamship, the Dutch-gifted *Kankō*, was also recreated by the Verolme Shipyards in 1987 as an attraction for the Huis Ten Bosch theme park in Sasebo, Nagasaki.[14]

the Pacific. He remained deeply principled throughout. In 1887, he resigned his offices in protest at the Ashio Copper Mines incident, which polluted the Tone and Watarase Rivers and caused an ecological disaster for the farmers of the Northern Kantō plain, bitterly disappointed that he was alone in responding. He remained a man with a foot in two worlds. In 1895, he purchased a stone that had once been used in a pickle-press when it was identified by geologists as being a Shirahagi meteorite. Decades after the dissolution of his samurai heritage, he commissioned master swordsman Okayoshi Kunimune to fashion it into five Ryuseito swords ("comet swords") rippling with black waves, one of which was presented to the then crown prince and future emperor Taisho, and three of which can be seen today in the Toyama Science Museum in Toyama City, Tokyo University of Agriculture, and Ryugu Shrine in Otaru.[18] He lived to see Japan's crushing defeat of Russia in Port Arthur as a sixty-nine-year-old in retirement, before his death in 1908 and internment in the temple of Kissho-ji, Bunkyo-ku in Tokyo.[19]

Once stripped of his titles, land, and authority, the last shogun, Tokugawa Yoshinobu, exchanged house arrest for a comfortable retirement indulging in falconry, hunting, painting, photography, and archery in Shizuoka. He showed no remorse for the followers who had died for the shogunate. In 1875, when informed his loyal retainer Shinmon Tatsugorô—who had fought for and won back shogun Ieyasu's centuries-old standard at Osaka castle after his defeat at Toba-Fushimi—had died, it was said his expression barely flickered. Though he might have been an able administrator in other circumstances, was modest, and held little personal ambition, his father's observation had been prophetic. "He could become a splendid shogun; but if things didn't go well, it could be too much for him."[20]

His march on the emperor started from a position of greater strength. There is a case that when daimyo began throwing in with the Meiji, further resistance would only have wrought more destruction, and his decision to abdicate all claims was noble. This is a generous argument. If he had simply left a clear successor before fleeing Toba-Fushimi overnight, then Oguri Kozunosuke's bold plans to strike with their army at Kokone and navy at Suruga Bay remains a great what-if in Japanese history. In a 1904 interview with Ōkuma Shigenobu, he harbored no doubts about his choices. "I decided to restore the political power to the Emperor, thus putting an end to our feudalism. . . . This I did in obedience to the spirit of the secret injunctions I had received from my father, and which were due to the profound foresight of our ancestor Ieyasu. . . . The whole nation had to stand like one man and make clear wherein the real sovereign power lay; an enlightened form of government must be adopted. The Shogunate could never meet these requirements, and it was now worse than useless. . . . But at that very moment I failed to control my own vassals, and they consequently gave trouble to the new authorities. Thus, conscious of my great fault towards the Emperor and our ancestor, I gave up worldly affairs and now lead a secluded life of penitence."[21]

Perhaps the tragedy isn't that he didn't continue the fight for the bufuku, but that he started to at all.

The three-year-old declared heir by the second-to-last shogun Ieyasu proved a wholly more capable figure. After a disrupted early childhood, he was sheltered in Alaska from 1872 (freshly sold from Russia to America); raised by the widow of the thirteenth shogun, Iesada; and studied in Britain for five years. His loyalty to the emperor saw him declared a prince on his return. In 1903, he began a thirty-year term as president of the House of Peers, during which he represented Japan at the post–World War I Washington Conference and served as president of the Japanese Red Cross. He died quietly in 1940, during World War II, at the age of seventy-six.[22]

Emperor Meiji was still just seventeen years old on his final victory and would rule until 1912. The rallying cry of "revere the emperor, expel the barbarians" gave way to the feverish modernization of "rich country, strong army." Even before the Ezo republic was erased, billboards begun going up forbidding violence against the foreigners they needed to make it happen. This was reinforced when the semidivine emperor received the quite mortal Alfred, Duke of Edinburgh, in Tokyo, "as his equal in point of blood."[23]

Meiji's charter oath, while far short of Ezo's Western democratic model, committed to public assemblies and opportunities for common people to grow strong and rich as Japan grew strong and rich; additionally, the oath repudiated "evil customs of the past," in a coded reference to their antiforeigner conviction, and enlightenment "to strengthen the foundations of imperial rule."[24]

The emperor forgave France her support for the shogun, and he received a second military mission in 1874 and a third in 1884, supplemented by French naval engineer Louis-Émile Bertin from 1886.

The Japanese navy was a source of national pride. With economic growth quickly outpacing the Boshin Civil War's cost, a new Naval Department was raised in 1873 with a bold seventy-ship fleet goal. While the Yokahama shipyards had progressed to laying down new 900- and 1,450-ton designs, when Director General Okuma and Governor-General Saigō in Nagasaki called for immediate action against aggressive Taiwanese pirates, it was the renamed *Azuma* and her newer companion *Ryōshō* that were called on to solve "the Taiwan situation."[25] Unsurprisingly, given their wild overmatch, when they steamed toward Xiamen on April 26, 1874, no one and nothing dared challenge them.[26]

The great losers of the age were the samurai class, who held no special place in a Western-pattern military, and whose claims to hereditary prestige and courtly patronage were quickly forgotten. In 1873, conscription was introduced. The samurai cause flared briefly as the 1874 Saga Rebellion in Hizen under former justice minister Etō Shinpei. While it started with protests against the overbearing home minister's Tosa delegate, Takatoshi Iwamura (who was so divisive that he managed to convert his traveling companion, the former Akita governor Shima Yoshitake, to the rebel cause when they traveled together), it showed that while the samurai felt disenfranchised, their daimyo did not.[27]

While individual samurai and ronin rallied to them, no whole prefectures did. Shinpei lost a skirmish with imperial forces on February 22 and a battle on February 27. Both leaders proclaimed their conviction to fight but fled, ostensibly to lobby the Satsuma or Tozu to join them, with Shinpei being pursued by the police force he'd help found. When captured on April 12, they were hung with eleven followers after a token one-day trial. Shinpei's head was left on public display and became the subject of a thriving market in souvenir photos. While these images were later banned, they continued to hang in the reception room of the Home Ministry in Ōkubo for years. The imperial navy was limited to transporting marines, bombarding towns including Imari, and capturing a ship intended for Shinpei's escape. The IJN's *Azuma* remained unopposed.

The first of Japan's three shogun great unifiers had said, "Let us have intercourse with foreign lands, let us learn their drills and tactics, then when we have made our nation united as one family, we shall be able to go abroad, and give lands in foreign countries to those who have distinguished themselves in battle."[28] The imperial embrace of westernization wasn't for its intrinsic value; it was for the extrinsic value of expansion.

In 1875, Japan used an incident of shore fire at the Chōshū-built gunboat *Un'yō* (249 tons; two guns) at Ganghwa Island, which had been a previous flashpoint with the French in 1866 and Americans in 1871, to force Korean ports open to trade with an "unequal treaty" of their own.

Japan's days of acquiring used warships were largely over. While her domestic shipbuilding progressed, she looked to England for a new generation of warships led by the steam-and-sail corvettes *Kiei* and *Kongo* and their first barque-rigged second-class battleship. When the *Fuso* joined them in 1878 with an armored belt up to 9 inches thick and the latest 6.6- and 9.4-inch Krupps rifles, Japan was ready to act. The *Azuma* was deployed to Korean waters at the height of the confrontation and kept the navy of the Korean Kingdom of Joseon so thoroughly bottled up that not a single shot was fired in anger.

At home, a series of violent "shizoku uprisings" flared across Japan. The Shinpūren Rebellion in October 1876 saw two hundred samurai slaughter three hundred troops in their barracks before retribution saw almost all killed or committing *seppuku*. Other clashes with samurai were recorded in Akizuki, Kyūshū, and western Honshu.[29] Worse was to come.

Samurai dissent culminated in the Satsuma Rebellion. Saigō Takamori, who had sworn to the Satsuma's imperial cause while leading the shogun's army, had wisely counseled clemency for the Ezo's forces at the end of the Boshin War. His retirement to hunt, fish, and enjoy hot springs was brief. In 1869, he was made a Satsuma counselor. In 1871, he watched their military be transferred to the emperor's command with equanimity, and in April, he was appointed to organize the new imperial army. In July, the Meiji emperor summoned his daimyo to announce the dissolution of domains. Takamori's clan lord, Hisamitsu, was the only one to publicly rail against it, shooting off fireworks for an entire day to express his outrage before retiring to foster Shigakko martial and Confucian private schools that could never hold back the tide of change.

Takamori had become a beacon for samurai who feared that the price for Western militarization was Western values. Both the shogun and emperor had chosen him as a battlefield leader. It was not these new massed ranks of riflemen who had built their country. It was the samurai now at risk of disappearing. Petitioner after petitioner seeking his intervention was turned away. In the end, the decision to act was made for him.

When government forces marched in to transfer military stores from the Satsuma capital Kagoshima to Kyoto, locals protested fiercely. Takamori was absent. More than a thousand samurai first drove off the naval parties assigned to the task, then opened the armories themselves and began distributing arms. Word quickly spread. By the time Takamori returned, rumors that he was the insurrection's leader had already seen him declared a traitor with a bounty on his head.

On February 7, 1877, he announced his intention to go the capital to question the imperial government. When the Mito and shogun had done so in 1864 and 1868, it was called rebellion. So it was again.

Eight long years of dishonor and penury were enough. Samurai took up a new cry of their own for "new government, high morality." An imperial fleet built around the victorious ram *Azuma* and *Ryōshō* precluded any sea-born movement on Tokyo. When they advanced by land instead, it was as an irregular force, and the lack of artillery and provisions meant they bogged down in a bloody fifty-five-day siege of Kumamoto castle just 175 kilometers away. While their numbers grew from twelve thousand to more than twenty thousand, despite as many as fifty-three hundred casualties, once again it was with a scattering of the very newest and very oldest weapons. Little attempt was made to link with other clans or reach out to the new peasant soldiery. It was an army larger than that which initially invaded Ezo, but the delay gave imperial forces time to respond with more than forty thousand troops.

Takamori wrote to the emperor on the eve of the resulting Battle of Tabaruzaka in March 1877, proclaiming this was not a rebellion and requesting an audience that was immediately denied. With uncontested sea control, further imperial forces were landed behind him, escorted by the *Azuma*. He retreated to Hitoyoshi in response. After several weeks of resupply, an imperial offensive—depicted with huge artistic license in the 2003 Tom Cruise film *The Last Samurai*—scattered many of his followers and pushed the rump of his forces to Miyazaki. The imperial navy staged further landings at Ōita and Saik to pincer him, north and south. Each setback saw more samurai killed, and more samurai putting down their arms. By the time they fought at Mount Enodake, just thirty-five hundred remained.

The Satsuma were not the only clan guided by the past. The Aizu, for one, who had fought and lost for the shogun, now served the emperor and could have their revenge. "Samurai of Satsuma, see with your own bodies, are the swords of the Aizu sharp or dull."[30] When asked if they could still prevail, the last samurai offered only a stoic "chance to die for principle."[31]

Six hundred rebels escaped. Far more died in battle or committed *seppuku*.[32] The Satsuma Rebellion's last stand clustered around Mount Shiroyama's caves was an epoch for Japan; 372 samurai remained, and 30,000 imperial troops besieged them. No chances were taken. After two weeks of preparation, a withering three-hour imperial artillery barrage was followed by a dawn assault.

On September 24, 1877, in a frantic scramble through the surrounding hills, Takamori succumbed to bullet wounds in the leg and stomach, with as few as forty samurai surviving him. It's thought that Ichimura Tetsunosuke—who Commissioner-General Toshizō had ordered to escape the last battles of Ezo with his death poem—died with him.[33] His follower, Beppu Shinsuke, determined that his head must not be displayed on a pike, decapitated him and claimed he had earned a true samurai's death by *seppuku*.[34] Takamori was gone, and the samurai era with him.

It was a tragic turn, but once again, we see the distinction between the Chōshū and Satsuma samurai who lost the peace, and their clan leaders who won it. Takamori never renounced the emperor. He fought and died in an imperial uniform. 6,959 war dead were enshrined at the Yasukuni Shrine that Emperor Meiji renamed Yasukuni Jinja (Pacifying the Nation) two years later.[35] He remained such a revered figure that the Meiji emperor pardoned him posthumously in 1889.

For the most part, Japanese citizens parted ways around the conflict. Perhaps typical is Souha Hatono, a surgeon pressed to serve Satsuma forces, who only agreed on the condition he treat imperial forces equally. Post-rebellion charges that he aided the enemy were dismissed in less than three days. He no longer saw himself as imperial or traditional. He was simply Japanese.[36]

Henri Nicol, the French advisor who fought in the Battle of Miyako, returned to France on November 29, 1868, with Eugène Collache on the Swiss-chartered ship, the *Sophie-Hélène*. Found guilty of treason for deserting the French navy's *Minerva* in Yokohama harbor to serve the bufuku, Nicol only received a token sentence. His luck ran out as a draftee in the Franco-Prussian War of 1871, dying aged just twenty-four.[37] Collache, who'd participated in the attack on *Kotetsu*, detailed it all for the world in the 1874 book, *Une aventure au Japon*.

The French captain and second in command of Ezo forces, Jules Brunet, escaped the final Ezo siege at Goryokaku on the French warship *Coëtlogon* along with the brigade commanders Léonard Fortant, Émile Marlin, Léon Bouffier, and Léon Cazeneuve. The five advisors had won the bufuku samurais' respect as being "very brave" men who "showed great performance in the military advance to Matsumae." When they left, they left with Takeaki's consent and thanks.[38] They steamed to Yokohama, where Brunet was taken into custody and transferred to Saigōn by the *Dupleix* to steam home. Though the imperial Meiji government requested their extradition, they were popularly acclaimed at home, and the French government declined. After less than six months detention, Brunet joined the French army and served in the Franco-Prussian War (1870–1871) before being taken prisoner. Postwar, he served as military attaché to Rome and rose to the rank of general.[39] The former admiral and president, Takeaki, never forgot his service, and secured him Japanese medals in 1881 and 1885, membership in the Order of the Rising Sun, and, ultimately in 1895, the Order of the Sacred Treasure, though all were awarded in Paris, and he never saw Japan again. He rose steadily through the ranks of the French navy to chief of staff before his death in 1911.[40]

The Ezo republic admiral and naval minister Arai Ikunosuke, who'd fought for the *Kotetsu* at Miyako Bay before she shattered their remaining fleet in Hakodate, spent his time in prison post war compiling a new English–Japanese dictionary. After his death sentence was commuted, he had a varied career in land reclamation and education before his talents were recognized with leadership of the Central Meteorological Agency. Ikunosuke brought Japan the metric system, founded the Hokkaidō University, and instituted standard time before dying of diabetes in 1909, aged seventy-four.[41]

The lessons that the new imperial Japanese navy had learned went on to change the world. The Greenwich Naval College–educated Togo Heihachiro, who served as third-class gunnery officer on the *Kasuga* in the Battle of Miyako Bay for the *Kotetsu*, went on to a storied career studying in London, circumnavigating the world, skirmishing with Korean and Chinese elements, and sinking a British merchant ship laden with Chinese troops in the 1894–1895 Sino-Japanese War, before being tasked with defeating Russia at sea. He was remembered in England from his time aboard the HMS *Victory* as "unusually quiet, but inside he was like a lion."[42] In 1905, when Russia's Baltic fleet completed its arduous 33,000-kilometer transit to Port Arthur in Manchuria in the Russo-Japanese War, he met them in the Tsushima Strait with a brilliant deployment that saw his capital ships "crossing the T" of the Russian line so he could fire full broadsides, and they could only file enfilade ahead. His fleet destroyed or captured twenty-two warships, ending the war and sending shockwaves around the world. Russia lost 5,000 lives and 6,000 prisoners. Japan lost just 117 dead.[43] No Asian nation had ever bested a European naval power before. When the Japanese court needed a tutor for the future World War II emperor Hirohito, it was Heihachiro they chose.

Shinsengumi general Hijikata Toshizō, killed in the last days of the Ezo republic, was commemorated with a monument in Takahata Kudo Temple in Hino in 1888, though his actual grave is lost. He had demanded *seppuku* from dozens of samurai, but embodied the same sacrifice, recording, "I am not going to battle to win. With the Tokugawa government about to collapse, it would be a disgrace if no one is willing to go down with it. That is why I must go. I will fight the best battle of my life to die for the country."[44] More than a hundred years later, a bronze statue was raised with him resolute, sword in hand, fist clenched, ready to face the honorable fallen in the underground, as he had written to his president.[45]

The *Kotetsu*'s Captain Nakajima was promoted to navy lieutenant commander, reassigned to the newly acquired warship *Ryōshō* in 1871 and rose to a naval rank equivalent to an army colonel before exiting the military for a public career. He and his wife Shigeko had no children. The lessons he learned keeping the troubled *Kotetsu* in the fight he applied to his career in the public service, where he served as head of shipbuilding and production rights (1881) for the Ministry of Engineering, associate commissioner of the Maintenance and Repair Bureau (1882), and minor secretary of the Ministry of Engineering (1888), before his ascent to the senate in 1889. That same year he died from stomach cancer, aged just fifty-four, at home in Hongo, every bit as esteemed as his predecessor, Captain Thomas Jefferson Page.[46]

A cabinet system of government was adopted in 1885. In 1889, a new Japanese constitution based on Prussia's constitutional monarchy was adopted by four-time prime minister Hirobumi. This was not the Ezo's Western democratic dream, with even the limited elections of the Diet body restricted to as little as 1 percent of the population, and a long period of decline would continue for the native Ainu.[47] The emperor was pronounced "sacred and inviolable" and above all executive, legislative, or judicial power.

Emperor Meiji is considered a sponsor of these changes more than an author. His personal conviction and role is contested. If he is credited with modernization, though, then equally, he is responsible for Japan's seizure of islands including Taiwan, the invasion of Korea, and the exploitative Treaty of Shimonoseki that closed the first Sino-Japanese War (1894–1895). His regime's urgency is perhaps understandable. Expansion was not an abstract goal—it was playing out all around them. The United States purchased Alaska from Russia in 1867; added Midway, American Samoa, and Wake Island in quick succession; and followed with Hawaii and the former Spanish territories of the Philippines, Puerto Rico, and Guam in 1898.[48]

This duality—modernist but exploitative—was characterized throughout the *genrō* statesmen like the Chōshū samurai Itō Hirobumi, who was as ardently for a modern civil service as he was for war with China. He last served as resident-general in Korea from 1906 to his assassination in 1909, which Meiji Japan used shamelessly as a pretext to invade.[49] Korea was annexed outright in 1910.

Nineteenth-century Japan might be ascendant in Asia, but she wasn't ready to rival western European powers. When the special rights that imperial Japan imposed on China's Liaotung peninsula interfered with Western possessions, including Vietnam, Laos, and Cambodia (for France) or Hong Kong and (later) the Yangtze valley (for England), she was forced to give them up and watch as Russia exploited the peninsula instead.

Emperor Meiji's removal from the public eye was not absolute. He completed six "Grand Circuits" between 1872 and 1885, opening schools and bridges, meeting notables, and staging a limited series of tightly choreographed public appearances thereafter when at war.

The Meiji era would continue until 1912. While it was cloaked in the language of democracy, particularly in the emperor's engagement with foreigners, his regime's power was absolute. The parliament he formed had little authority. If anything, it became something of an extended oligarchy, with his rule backed directly by a *genro* of the daimyo rewarded in a further restructure into seventy-two prefectures.

Meiji married Ichijō Haruko, the daughter of a court official three years his senior, to whom he granted the new title, "Empress Consort Shōken"; well versed in the arts, ceremony, and music, she maintained a higher profile than any of her predecessors. While the emperor had no children with the empress consort, he fathered fifteen children with the court's ladies-in-waiting, including his successor, Haru-no-Miya Yoshihito, who was decreed emperor Taishō on Meji's death. Not unusually for the time, and despite every advantage of the court, just four of his children reached adulthood, including princesses Kane-no-miya Fusako and Yasu-no-miya Toshiko who lived through Japan's highs and lows in the twentieth century.

The flip side of modernization was the loss of tradition. Meiji survived an assassination attempt as late as 1910 in the socialist anarchist "high treason incident." Its stated goal was taking power back for the people, and it ended with the execution of conspirators including Shūsui Kōtoku.[50]

The emperor born as Mutsuhito may have worn Western clothes and eaten Western-style food, but he saw himself as part of an unbroken tradition around the Chrysanthemum throne. He composed tens of thousands of traditional Gyosai poems in perhaps the one constant from his childhood isolation to his ascent and rule. Consanguineous marriages among the upper classes were the same issue for Japanese royalty as they were for their European counterparts. Accounts of his personal health differ, but many suggest congenital difficulties, albeit far less pronounced than those of the late Tokugawa shogun Iesada. In his later years, diabetes saw doctors swear him off sake; this only led to him discovering a love of red wine, which quickly became a gift of choice at court.

His peaceful death of renal failure on July 30, 1912, was a shock, as word of his ill health had been tightly contained until ten days before. For many, it felt like the passing of greatness. For all their progress in the forty-three years since the Boshin War had ended, storm clouds were building over Europe, and the world seemed like a divided and uncertain place. The change was hard for some. His contemporary, Tokutomi Roka, wrote, "I felt as if the name of Meiji would continue forever. . . . When Meiji became Taishô, I felt as if my life had been broken off."[51]

The *New York Times* declared, "the contrast between that which preceded the funeral car and that which followed it was striking indeed. Before it went old Japan; after it came new Japan."[52]

Perhaps Meiji's most beautiful tribute is the Forest Shrine of Meiji Jingu, raised in barren land outside Tokyo with more than one hundred thousand seeds from across the nation.[53] Given his focus on Japan's military strength, just as fitting would be the declaration of Japan as a "big-five power" in the post–World War I Treaty of Versailles alongside France, Italy, the United Kingdom, and the United States.

Through it all, the *Azuma*'s service continued.

PASSING THE TORCH   30

The five-nation ship witnessed the world transform.

A united Germany had defeated France, seized Alsace Lorraine in 1871, and sowed the seeds for World War I. Italy was unified. Austria had been expelled from the German sphere of influence, shorn of her Italian territories and limped into the twentieth century with the Austro-Hungarian Empire. A reduced Denmark prospered. Mexico was free from French control. America was united and prospering. Japan was unified under the Meiji emperor and planning a fleet that would shatter Russia's and win a (brief) Pacific empire.

It is easy to see the Meiji victory in the Boshin War and Japan's subsequent modernization as inevitable, given the Western arms race that underpinned it. The alignment of the nation's daimyo had been in flux throughout, though, and the likelihood of additional clans either withdrawing from the conflict or reinstating support for the shogun under other circumstances cannot be discounted.

The Meiji flagship had served five flags under seven names—*Sphinx, Stærkodder, Olinde, Stonewall, Nuetsra Salud del Carmen, Kōtetsu,* and *Azuma*—but her journey was far from over. Having shaped Japanese history, she was about to do so for China and Formosa (present-day Taiwan). Prussia was selected as a template for the army. An imperial decree in 1870 established the British Royal Navy as the template for their fleet.[1]

With the Ezo republic's defeat, *Kotetsu* was docked for repairs until August 1870, continuing a lifelong battle with leaks that had already seen her Prussian sister ship, the SMS *Prinz Adalbert*, relegated to static roles in port. She then resumed leadership of the imperial flotilla, based in the port of Yokohama, to control the Tokai coast.[2]

Fortunes had been made supplying these conflicts. When Japan sought new warships, she quickly found sellers. In came the corvette *Tsukuba*, built in 1853 in Burma as the HMS *Malacca* (1,947 tons; ten guns) with the newly commissioned Scottish-built gunboats *Un'yō* and *Wun Yo* and the sloop *Nisshim* (1,490 tons; seven guns), which was ordered by the Hizen clan but diverted to the emperor.[3] The armored *Ryōshō* followed in 1870, built by Thomas Blake Glover for the Kumamoto Daimyo (2,530 tons; ten guns; naval ram), which assumed *Azuma*'s flagship status until it was passed to the IJN *Fusō* in 1878 in turn. This emperor's favorite is best known for her doctor establishing that the wasting disease beriberi that plagued Asian fleets the way scurvy had in Europe (and potentially claimed Shogun Iemochi) was the result of a vitamin B deficiency that could be readily addressed with diet.[4]

On November 15, 1871, *Kotetsu* was reclassed as a third-class warship, and would later be reclassified again as a coastal defense battleship, defined not by her service or merit, but by the size of her battery and crew.[5] The brief window of the ram ship was closing.

While the *Azuma* (aside from the unfortunate merchant cleaved in half in her transit from Cuba to Washington) never completed the ram run she was designed for, the Confederacy's designers were vindicated by the 1866 Seven-Week War between Italy and Austria. The battle of Lissa, which was the largest naval clash seen until the Russo-Japanese War in the twentieth century, saw twelve Italian ironclads face seven from the Austro-Hungarian fleet. The Italians focused on their greater broadside and fired more than 1,450 rounds. Austrian rear admiral Wilhelm von Tegethoff, a veteran of the Crimean War and Battle of Heligoland against the Danes, painted his ships black and declared, "When we get into the fight, you must ram away at anything you see painted grey."[6] Tegethoff's flagship, SMS *Erzherzog*, promptly rammed the American-built *Red'Italia* so squarely and deeply that she took 450 lives down with her, in a victory so pronounced that Italian admiral Carlo Pellion di Persano was court-martialed. Ramming worked. Two years after winning her independence, French mediation added Venetia to Italy's borders.

Rapid advances in guns and gunnery ensured no major ram ships followed. The mighty Confederate Laird rams that America had threatened to go to war with England over were quickly downclassed. The HMS *Scorpion* was reduced to the static defense of Bermuda for three decades before a second life as a merchant.[7] HMS *Wyvern* did as little in Hong Kong.

Early postwar calls for a grand Japanese fleet were curtailed by rebellion and internal investment priorities, leading to a temporary "Rikushu Kaiju" ("Army first, Navy second") policy, which split the fleet into two squadrons focused on coastal defense. When the Ministry of the Navy was founded in 1872, it commanded fourteen warships and three transports of just 13,832 tons displacement, which wasn't just smaller than any European peer, it was less than that of Qing China.[8] *Azuma*'s armament was updated to 9-inch Armstrong muzzle-loading rifles in December 1871, with four further 6.5-inch Parrot guns expanding her battery and keeping her in step with the newer IJN *Ryōshō* as the nation's two principal warships.

She remained an instrument of state under her new captain, Hayashi.[9] In the Mudan incident of December 1871, a Japanese ship from Okinawa foundered on the southern horn of Taiwan (then a Chinese protectorate). Fifty-four surviving crew members were beheaded by the native Paiwan people; twelve survivors were rescued by Han Chinese. While they were returned home at Chinese expense, the Qing court refused Japanese claims for compensation on the grounds the indigenous Taiwanese were not under their control. After diplomatic overtures failed, and at the urging of American military advisor Charles Le Gendre and legal advisor Gustave Emile Boisson-ade, a punitive Japanese fleet was dispatched in 1874, which marked the first international deployment of the Imperial Japanese Army. Two further advisors steamed with them—the American Civil War veterans James Wasson (Union army), and Douglas Cassel (Union navy). A series of ensuing skirmishes, which included natives firing on tender boats of the warship *Nisshin* and culminated in the Battle of Stone Gate, cost Japan seven soldiers. The loss of more than 550 to malaria saw their expedition abandoned. Among them was the younger brother of Confederate John Slidell, who'd joined the expedition as an observer. His transit to Europe had instigated the Trent flashpoint with England, and he was instrumental in the *Azuma*'s creation.[10] Their departure was screened by the IJN *Azuma*, against any possible Qing intervention.

China's navy, though larger, had nothing that could withstand the *Azuma* or *Ryōshō*. In an English-brokered deal Sir Harry Parkes described as showing "China's willingness to pay to be invaded," China offered Japan 18.7 tons of silver as compensation. England received further warship orders from Japan. China incurred a bitter debt, as well as a punitive expedition of their own against the Botans that cost them another 250 lives. The Botan, in echoes of the Chōshū, conceded nothing. Though small, the expedition was a first step for an increasingly outward-looking and expansionist imperial Japanese worldview. *Azuma* patrolled so actively in this period that, by January 1873, she had to undergo further refits.[11]

The *Azuma* remained a potent symbol of state. In 1874, she was selected to escort the imperial household's representative Ariyuki to meetings with the Chinese Qing dynasty in a none-too-subtle reminder that, while China's fleet had more hulls, only Japan had a nation-defining flagship.

Later that year, on the outbreak of the Saga Rebellion, *Azuma* was ordered to escort the gunboat *Un'yo* "to suppress rebels in Kyushu," Japan's third-largest island, which would prove to be her final act of aggression.[12] With the warships of the Hizen, Saga, and others having long since been nationalized, the emperor's fleet could act with impunity.

By late 1874, as *Azuma* patrolled the China Sea with the warship *Ryōshō*, a British spy in Japan claimed that Chinese sailors would desert rather than go to sea when *Azuma* was in their waters.[13] Her last such tour concluded with the *Azuma* taking up station as a moored guardship in Nagasaki, watching over the port and a flotilla of lesser warships.

In 1875, Japan forced Korea to open her ports, just as America forced hers. She proved just as adept at gunboat diplomacy, ordering *Azuma* on a high-profile circuit of the Korean coastline in emphasis. They were difficult waters for a ship that, after a decade of service, still leaked and plunged her bow so deeply in heavy seas that Confederate sources reported she disappeared like a ghost. Chief engineer W. P. Brooks's exceptional work in her Confederate service continued to pay off—there are no further records of the troubles with water distillers, boilers, and other systems he addressed while crossing the Atlantic.

In 1876, Japan imposed a "renegotiated" Ganghwa Treaty upon Korea that forced her merchants to accept payment in Japanese script and exempted her trade from any tariffs, amoug other concessions. Once again, *Azuma* prowled their waters to reinforce the point.[14]

She returned to service as a guardship once again until the 1877 Satsuma Rebellion. The imperial navy's capital ships sought out opportunities for shore bombardment and screened two waves of seaborne invasions behind the last samurais' forces that were so extensive that more than one thousand private craft of all descriptions were mobilized. Eight years after the fall of Ezo, there was still no regional navy that could challenge her. *Azuma* was held as a strategic asset deploying from the Seto Island Sea to check any Chinese or Korean opportunism.

In 1879, Japan annexed the entire Ryukyu archipelago over desperate protests the Chinese lodged with the American general-turned-president Ulysses S. Grant, who was on an Asian tour at the time but had no interest in intervening.

Azuma's greatest enemy through these postwar years remained the sea. She suffered serious damage in a typhoon in January 1874 that required such extensive repairs to her steam pumps and leaks at the flat bottom of her hull that Director General Okuma referred to them as "salvage" and Consul Shinagawa employed an English consultant on behalf of the Ministry of the Navy for her return shakedown cruise.[15]

On August 19, 1877, *Azuma* was hit by a typhoon described as being worse still. Minor works helped her limp back to the Yokosuka Naval Arsenal. Major works were required. Her Prussian sister ship had been stricken at this point, with nothing more to offer a unified German navy. Once again, whole sections of armor had to be lifted and major machinery had to be disassembled to assess and replace structural beams.[16] Lesser ships had been struck off the register for less, but she remained a unique deterrent. When she returned to sea, Captain Hayashi recorded a "submarine plunge" and significant flooding in the first heavy weather she confronted.[17]

It was only in 1883, with the launch of an eight-year, thirty-two-ship fleet plan that Japan's vision began to outgrow *Azuma*. By the 1894 Sino-Japanese War, she had commissioned thirty-one principal warships and twenty-four torpedo boats.[18] Taiwan was first invaded by the French in the Sino-French War, and then by the Japanese in 1894–1895, as part of what the Chinese now refer to as their century of humiliation.

These clashes with China were the first where the IJN *Azuma* was not deployed among their first-line combatants. China's leading ships were not just five times the displacement of the five-nation ship and twice as thickly armored, but crucially as targets of a ram ship, they were faster. While China had acquired the 7,400-ton German-sourced *Ting-Yuen* and *Chen-Yuen* with 12-inch guns (one of which was captained by an American, the U.S. Naval Academy graduate Commander Philo N. McGiffin), Japan's victory, including a decisive torpedo boat strike at Weihaiwei in weather so extreme that men died of exposure on deck, was so overwhelming that China's Admiral Ting committed suicide.[19]

The IJN *Azuma*'s fighting days were over. Like the ram ships *Prinz Adalbert*, HMS *Wyvern*, and HMS *Scorpion* before her, *Azuma* was de-gunned and relegated to service in port as a training and depot vessel. She served last of all as an accommodation ship and was recorded by an American traveler some years later as "peacefully rusting away."[20] The *Azuma* was finally decommissioned on January 28, 1888.

By December 12 of that year, contracts to begin stripping her fittings and breaking her down were signed. Though U.S. naval records indicate a possible second sale to a fishing fleet operator in 1891, it was not completed; in 1895 records instead show her iron plates were repurposed in electric generator armature shafts for the Asakusa Thermal Power Station of Tokyo, fragments of which survive in the Yokohama Electric Power History Museum; she is finally projecting power in a more poetic sense.[21]

The name Azuma lived on. Her successor, the new armored cruiser namesake *Azuma* (3,800 tons; twenty-four guns) was also French built, though in St. Nazaire rather than Bordeaux. After being commissioned in

1889, she served with distinction in the Russo-Japanese War, taking damage in the battles of Ulsan and the Russian cataclysm at Tsushim (where Russia falsely claimed she'd been sunk) and served all the way to World War II.[22]

The five-nation ship had ushered in a new era for Japan. By the end of Emperor Meiji's reign, Japan had transformed from a traditional, feudal, and isolationist nation to one of the eight largest economies in the world. Her control of Asia's oceans was absolute.

Her ambitions, if anything, were growing. As early as 1869, American observers of Japan's new imperial state—and its postwar navy—"perhaps entertained a conceit that they were strong enough to defy our government."[23] It was President Theodore Roosevelt who helped broker the peace treaty between Japan and Russia after their humiliation in Port Arthur in 1905; Roosevelt was the nephew of James Dunwoody Bulloch, whose European excursion had created the *Stonewall* in the first place.

Japan's tumultuous twentieth-century history was defined by an expanding imperial worldview, and the knowledge of how much difference a few thousand tons of wood and iron and a few hundred men could make.

A WORLD OF IRON

31

T he age of sail had given way to an age of steam. Wood had yielded to iron. Guns had swept away blades. Much of the modern map of Europe and Asia had been settled within a remarkably small space of time. It's tempting to see all of this as inevitable, but it was an outcome many had scarified everything to achieve.

Few ships embody this change better than the ironclad ram ship known variously as the *Sphinx*, *Stærkodder*, *Olinde*, CSN *Stonewall*, *Nuetsra Salud del Carmen*, *Kotetsu*, and the IJN *Azuma*.

It can be argued that the *Stonewall* could have extended the American Civil War, but she certainly could not have ended it, even under the most favorable circumstances. While U.S. naval figures like Rear Admiral S. W. Godon and the *Monadnock*'s Captain William Ronckendorff were somewhat dismissive of her in Havana, given her impervious performance against the combined Ezo fleet and Benten Daiba fortress, it is probable she would have overcome the *Niagara* and *Sacramento* at the start of her service. The Union's low-slung and cumbersome coastal monitor classes had serious disadvantages against the Confederate ram, and if they'd almost certainly have had the advantage of numbers when facing her, *Stonewall* would always have had the option to retreat to open seas where they couldn't follow. U.S. diplomatic dispatches from Japan, based on her performance in battle, conceded that the Japanese navy "has been rapidly increased into quite a large and serviceable one, while our own is in fact unrepresented here with anything that could for the moment live in conflict with the *Stonewall*."[1]

The stakes for the five-nation ship in Japan were considerably higher.

Before we consider *Kotetsu*, any counterfactual of the Boshin War must start with Shogun Iemochi's first Chōshū expedition. Given that their rebellious leaders were already executed by the time his army reached their gates, and that Iemochi was at death's door, could more have been done? The shogun's acceptance of their internal resolution was, in retrospect, clearly not enough. The mixed battlefield results of the second Chōshū expedition make this the first and last moment when his office controlled overwhelming force.

Outside of the naval equation, there are several possible turning points in the failed shogunate march to Edo at the outset of the Boshin War. A decision not to leave thousands of troops—including many with their most modern equipment—idle opposite the English fleet at Osaka alone could have sent history down a very different path. Why shogunate commander Takenaka Shigekata moved thousands of troops before rebel forces with unloaded rifles, artillery in tow, and the cavalry elsewhere in the opening stages of the battle of Toba-Fushimi will never be known. What would have happened if Shogun Tokugawa Yoshinobu had led his army as he had pledged January 31 at Osaka castle, instead of slipping away overnight on the American warship *Iroquois*? The hypotheticals are as many and varied as they are for Alexander Kerensky in Russia or the Marquis de Lafayette in France.

If shogunate forces had won Toba-Fushimi, an emperor in flight would have been vastly weakened. The fear of it was real enough that plans to smuggle out the emperor and revert to guerrilla warfare were in place. It was only after the shogun's flight that daimyo for the Tzu and Todo swung their allegiance to imperial Meiji forces, and others followed. The Chōshū and Satsuma had rivals and enemies of their own. Here, we should remember the Buzen clan at the second Battle of Simonoseki putting it in writing that they'd only pretend to fire at Western warships so they would not be forced into a second confrontation with imperial clans. Even if Shogun Yoshinobu didn't have it in him to oppose the emperor when his rising-sun flags were raised, his flight without a successor cost his forces any chance of a sharp victory with Kozunosuke's plan to ambush imperial forces under the guns of the fleet in Suruga Bay.

The equation at sea is far simpler.

If Robert Van Valkenburgh hadn't summarily awarded the *Kotetsu* to the emperor, the balance of Japanese naval forces would be wildly different. From there, the possibilities quickly compound. With local superiority, there would be no need for the risky storm run north that cost Takeaki's navy the warships *Kaiyō* and *Shinsoku*, and there may have been time to reinstate the abandoned 1,000-ton warship *Fujiyama*, for example. Takeaki's performance at the Battle of Awa shows he would likely have patrolled aggressively and sought a decisive clash at sea. The Chōshū's sacrifices to vastly superior forces at the twin battles of Shimonoseki suggest they would have played straight into his hands.

Dominance at sea did not mean dominance on land, however. There was no possibility of a bufuku blockade of imperial forces, even with

Kotetsu. A 626-ship Union fleet had only intercepted a minority of the Confederacy's runners in the American Civil War. Western warships—and merchants—would have had their run of Japanese ports. Once it had begun, there is little *Kotetsu* could have done to reverse the imperial march north from Toba-Fushimi to the shogun's surrender. No coastal interdiction could offset Minié rifles in the hands of troops facing bufuku matchlocks or samurai with polearms.

Almost certainly, if Admiral Takeaki had surrendered the shogunate fleet, the Boshin War would have ended with the shogun's surrender, and the samurai rebellions, which would likely have followed, would have remained minor and regional.

If we move forward to consider the final imperial landings on the Ezo's Hakodate Island, there was no scenario in which *Kotetsu* could prevent the fall of the fledgling Edo republic or her Western, democratic, and republican ideals once enough imperial boots were on the ground. The Shinsengumi and allied daimyo of the Northern Alliance fought with honor, but they fought with a material shortfall in artillery and logistics so severe that their last shots from the formidable Goryōkaku fortress were likely from a half-charge, wooden cannon with stone shot.

Every Ezo scenario for naval victory plays out in the 20-kilometer-wide Tsugaru Strait between Honshu and Hakodate, and they all depend upon Valkenburgh or the Battle of Miyako Bay. When the bufuku *Kaiten* charged the imperial *Kotetsu*, the disparate heights of their decks and the Ezo warship's side-mounted paddle wheels meant she could only land her troops one or two at a time along a single axis. If the warships *Takao* and *Banryū* had stormed the Meiji flagship from either side instead, the battle's outcome may have been very different. Hundreds of troops could then have deployed along a broader run of the deck, faster. This takes nothing away from the valor of party commander Kōga Gengo and the Shinsengumi who followed him from the *Kaiten* into a storm of lead. Rather, it reflects that the decisive Gatling gun's role could not apply in almost any other circumstances.

It's not automatic that the Ezo capturing the deck would mean controlling the ship, but without the heavy watertight compartments of future designs to stop them, an assault on the partially crewed vessel would likely only have failed if her machinery could be sabotaged in time. The arms lockers Sergeant John Prior had once owned for the Confederacy were below decks, under lock and key, and ill-suited to a surprise boarding. Resistance from crewmen with personal blades and tools could only be short and bloody against attacking samurai. It follows that the Ezo could have controlled *Kotetsu* and fought with her. Their crews had had her documentation for more than a year and included men who'd crossed the Pacific on her. Suddenly the equation at sea would have been profoundly altered. After the final naval battle in Hakodate Bay, at least twelve to eighteen months would pass before major new warships were delivered by European shipyards. Local production took longer still.

Kotetsu matched her opponents for speed, could withstand even their heaviest shot, and with her twin rudders, exceeded most for maneuverability. In a protracted campaign, the risk of her sortieing out would mean either no imperial landing on Ezo would proceed, or any landing would have happened much later, incurred significant losses, been smaller, been more widely dispersed, and carried less artillery and stores.

Ezo was viable in isolation. In the shadow of imperial Japan, she would need time, though, and lots of it to have any chance. Her industrial shortfall versus imperial Japan's home islands was significantly larger than the Confederacy's had been against the Union, but she had a quarter of the nation's farmable land, alluvial gold, and, after its discovery in 1890, so much coal that it was still being mined in the twenty-first century. The Uraga Dock Company that Takeaki founded became one of the world's foremost shipbuilders by World War I, launching more than a thousand vessels, military and civilian, and continuing production until 2003.[2]

The Confederacy had been wrong to think that cotton was king, and that they would be recognized by Europe's powers. Ezo was wrong to think they would either.

England's Harry Parkes had helped shift England's recognition for Japan's legitimate ruler from the shogun to the emperor when it suited her commercial interests despite at least three imperial attempts on his life. The French advisors who served Ezo had resigned from the French army or gone AWOL to do so. While France was lenient upon their return, there is no indication Napoleon III was ever tempted to recognize Ezo. Instead, his next military advisors for a newly imperial Japan were scarcely two years off.

It was America's black ships that opened Japan to trade. America had already played kingmaker with *Kotetsu*'s delivery. There were plenty of monarchies she was happy to engage with and numerous democratic governments they were happy to ignore. While America intervened shamelessly in post–civil war Mexico, dealing with Japan most profitably meant dealing with imperial forces. There could be no recognition from the United States.

Recognition from the Russian czar was Ezo's strongest hope—potentially in exchange for recognizing their claims to additional Japanese islands. The nearest Russian territory was only 42 kilometers away. Russia had maintained a Pacific fleet since 1731 and had landed parties of up to twenty soldiers on Hakodate soil, who in September 1806 looted and torched a Matsumae trading post and, in April 1807, repeated the effort, going as far as kidnapping a Matsumae official at Iturup.[3]

They had a pretext for conflict if they wished. The 1855 Russo-Japanese Treaty of Shimoda left the status of the Sakhalin islands unresolved (which Enomoto Takeaki, working for the Meiji administration, resolved in 1875). They had the strength to intervene. Russia had previously deployed a whole fleet from the Baltic to the Pacific under Admiral A. A. Popov in 1860, and her navy was expanding. By 1870, she'd laid down the 10,406-ton, 10-gun, two-torpedo warship *Petr Velikiy* that only England or France could oppose, and which, if operating with the *Kotetsu*, could almost guarantee the island's sovereignty. The imperial Japanese invasion of the Ezo home island was on the smaller scale of the Danish-Prussian wars. Russia was a nation accustomed to mobilizing and had recruited more than 888,000 men for the Crimean War thirteen years prior. In 1874, the Japanese Ministry of Military Affairs noted, "They [Russia] are also pressing upon the borders of Japan, China, and Korea. If they expand their territory to the Sea of Japan, gain a good port, and build up a navy there, it will become impossible to restrain their greed, and they will do immense harm to Asia and Europe. This should be Japan's greatest concern, and we must take steps to prevent this from happening."[4]

If the Russian bear had moved south in force, she could guarantee any land divided with Ezo. Even then, Russia's support of the American North in the American Civil War argues against any support of insurrection. Certainly, a democratic republican model had no interest for them. Russian recognition of Ezo was possible but, once again, unlikely.

Without a European sponsor, it's hard to argue that an imperial Japanese regime that invaded Taiwan and Korea would not forcibly reabsorb Ezo. It was not certain Ezo would survive with *Kotetsu*, but it was certain she could not survive without her. A warship conceived in America and built in France, which served Denmark and surrendered to the Spanish, had shaped the naval outcome of the Boshin War.

The Meiji restoration was an extraordinary period of modernization. Centuries of samurai tradition gave way to a modern conscript army. Traditional dress, art, and culture, while not lost, had to find space for their Western equivalents. The national diet took on much of its modern character with polished rice, tea, fruit and sugar, and soy sauce, alongside a growing range of Western staples. In came steam, foundries, railways, telegraphs, and more.

The world had changed since the five-nation ship had been laid down in 1864. Denmark had fallen to her twentieth-century profile. A Prussian-led Germany was only two years away. France's loss of Alsace-Lorraine, likewise. Italy, America, and Japan had become recognizable to us today. China had not, and her years of humiliation would only worsen with her defeat in the first modern Sino-Japanese War (1894–1895).[5]

The *Kaiten*'s survivor, Taro Ando, was right, writing of the assault on *Kotetsu*, when he recorded, "this fight at Miyako has probably never since had a parallel."[6] As the ascendancy in warship design passed from armor back to firepower, warships entered an arms race that would lead to the disruptive HMS *Dreadnought* in 1906. Rams and monitor classes disappeared. Sail was romanticized but dropped. Torpedoes and mines grew more deadly and far ranging. Coal gave way to oil. The war beneath the seas, once started, could never end. Steel armor hardened and thickened. Engagement distances grew. New sensors sought out the enemy. The era of boarding and repelling with flesh and blood was over.

Any earlier in history, and the ship that became *Azuma* would survive only in paintings full of pomp and artistic license. Navies were a symbol of their nation. Their victories were glorious, as with J. M. W. Turner's depiction of Horatio Nelson's victory at Trafalgar. Their defeats were tragedies. Their end, lamentable. Turner's painting *The Fighting Temeraire Tugged to Her Last Berth to Be Broken Up* (1839), recording the Trafalgar veteran's obsolescence, has been described as the most melancholy painting ever captured of a nonhuman subject. The burgeoning field of photography gave us an unprecedented view of the American Civil War. Numerous images of the five-nation ship survive, heavy, low, and menacing. They take her from the abstract to the real. Here were the rigging lines men scaled in all weather. Here was the cyclopean forecastle that absorbed everything the Ezo fleet could throw at it, and above all, here was the ram for which she had been built, that her Japanese sailors had walked down to bathe.

She was born in Stephen Mallory's sketches of a disruptive new class of ironclad warship longer than the White House, shallow enough for the Mississippi River, and large enough to cross an ocean, based on the insight that armor was in ascendancy and the act of ramming would be their principal means of destroying an opponent. It took 130 men or more to make it happen, but thousands more had funded her, built her, concealed her, and directed her in war.

She showcased the Confederacy's remarkable ability to fashion a fleet from near scratch. She helped position Japan for empire and, ultimately, a redefining war with the nation that provided her. Countless other Civil War projects had never left their sketchbooks or yards. For a few years, almost every warship built was rumored to be Confederate. It had taken an extraordinary chain of men to bring Confederate naval secretary Mallory's sketches to life: Every rebel cutout who passed plans and information for "teak." Every man, like paymaster Richard W. Curtis, who dealt in cash and gold with remarkably little oversight but great integrity, handling millions of dollars in transactions for which there were few records. Still, there was a host of others: John Dunwoody Bulloch, with his tireless network operating from their Little White House in the United Kingdom. Napoleon III and his opportunist's eye for commerce. Lucien Arman with his political connections and yards. G. P. Schönheyder's meticulous supervision of the five-nation ship's construction for the Danish navy, which saw her fulfil her potential as her sister ship, the *Cheops* (*Prinz Adalbert*), never did. It needed Thomas J. Page's willingness to fight Union lawyers and captains of larger vessels like the *Niagara* and *Sacramento* with equal vigor; his faith in a vessel that leaked nowhere more heavily than in his own cabin, making every order into open seas a test of character; and his honorable shepherding of the vessel into Spanish hands.

The five-nation ship needed the Washington yardmen who sustained her as the Union monitors, rebel gunboats, and battery ships around her were sold, repurposed, and broken up, and who refitted her when the contract with the shogun was signed.

Men had died on her in transit. Scores more had died in a boarding so bloody, with one foot in the past and one in the future, that it was a clash of Gatling gun and samurai sword. Hundreds had served on her, anxious as she porpoised into heavy sea that she would ever rise again, fighting the leaks she had from her first day to her last, overcoming their first seasickness leaving the lee of the British isles, gaining their sea legs on her, moving smoothly through her corkscrewing motion, performing mechanical feats in the deafening dark, bearing the basic food when the gimballed stoves were lit and worse when they were not, and pressing on through isolation, mail that would never catch up to them, infestation, and poor hygiene. Her lifeblood was the "black watch" crews below decks, laboring mightily in temperatures above 50 degrees, and engineers like William P. Brooks who left us his steam logs and knew every pipe, every valve, and every gauge like the back of his hand and saw to it she responded to every order.

Stonewall was the sum of the soldiers like Sergeant John Prior, sworn to maintain her discipline, to make warriors of her sailors against those who sought her for themselves. She lived and breathed by the grace of long-lost trades. Sail men, rope men, caulk men, and so on. Every one of them consumed the newspapers that reached them when they could, some only weeks old, to devour rebel victories at Kernstown, the Crater, Deep Bottom, and a hundred other places largely forgotten, who knew their only reward for effort would be to face a six-hundred-ship Union fleet alone.

We must remember the Japanese crewmen who marched aboard in their place as Commander George Brown finally departed with his American crew, far from home. The shogunate Japanese who transited the Pacific in her but never set foot on her again. Those new Chōshū officers and men who entered her hot, dark, heavy world, with its baffling labels and nameplates in Dutch and English, steaming relentlessly through the seas that took warships like the *Kaiyō* with cleaner lines and stronger seakeeping to the bottom.

What greater measure of devotion can there be than imperial samurai Shitiagawa, Hijikata, and Waki charging the *Kaiten* in the Battle of Miyako Bay, down the barrel of the 56-pounder that cleared the deck, or samurai like Nomura Risaburo who dropped single-file into a Gatling-gun hellscape for a cause their shogun had already abandoned.

Just as remarkable were those men—especially in her forecastle with Nakamura Iwataro and others—who steamed into the final Battle of Hakodate Bay, time and again, knowing they weren't just the fools to fight a fort but that they'd face a whole fleet as bait, soaking all the shot and powder from the magazines that they could, battered and concussed, knowing that all it took was one shot to pierce their magazine or boiler for it to all end in steam and fire and darkness.

Like no ship before or since, the five-nation ship bridged the transition from wood to iron, sail to steam, and from ram to gun. She served kings and emperors, loyalists and rebels, under seven names for five nations. She witnessed the formation of Denmark, Germany, Italy, Austria, America, Japan, and Korea that we know today. She fought with gunpowder and blade.

Her five flags had been lowered for the last time, but she had reshaped her world, and set us on a course to ours.

THOSE WHO SERVED
Officers and Crew of the Five-Nation Ship

32

Naval warfare is often romanticized. Ships are anthropomorphized, characterized as feminine, heralded for their beauty, and said to engage one another. But it was men who built them, men who sailed them, and men who fought and died on them. Unfortunately, the ship's logs and muster rolls of the *Stonewall* have not survived, though correspondence from the time, contemporary accounts, and the steam logs of William P. Brooks have. While far from complete, and with a lamentable bias to officers over the crew, a partial list of those who served aboard her in the Confederate and Meiji navy follows.[1]

STONEWALL

Officers

Barron, Samuel, Jr.
Born in Virginia. Appointed from Virginia. Acting master, September 14, 1861. Lieutenant for the war, February 26, 1863. First lieutenant, Provisional Navy, June 2, 1864, to rank from January 6, 1864. Served on CSS *Jamestown*, 1861–1862 ; participated in Battle of Hampton Roads March 8–9, 1862, and Battle of Drewrys Bluff, Virginia, May 15, 1862. On CSS *Beaufort* and commanding CSS *Roanoke*, James River Squadron, 1862–1863. Service abroad, 1863–1865; C S cruiser *Florida*, 1864; CSS *Stonewall*, 1865. Acting master.

Borchert, George A.
Born in Georgia. Appointed from Georgia. Formerly midshipman, U.S. Navy. Midshipman, July 25, 1861. Acting master, August 22, 1861. Acting lieutenant, September 24, 1861. Second lieutenant, February 8, 1862. First

lieutenant, January 7, 1864, to rank from October 2, 1862. First lieutenant, Provisional Navy, June 2, 1864, to rank from January 6, 1864. Served on CSS *Florida* (Selma), 1861–1862. CS steamers *Baltic* and *Morgan*, Mobile Squadron, 1862–1863. Abroad, 1863–1865; on CSS *Rappahannock*, Calais, France. Ordered to CSS *Stonewall*, January 10, 1865.

Boynton, William
Appointed from Alabama. Paymaster's clerk. Served on CSS *Stonewall*, 1865. Paymaster's clerk.

Brooks, William P.
Born in Louisiana. Appointed from Louisiana. Second assistant engineer, May 11, 1861. First assistant engineer, August 15, 1863. First assistant engineer, Provisional Navy, June 2, 1864. Served on CSS *Sumter*, 1861–1862; CSS *Alabama*, 1862–1864; participated in engagement with USS *Kearsarge* off Cherbourg, France, June 19, 1864. CSS *Stonewall*, 1865. Chief engineer.

Carter, Robert Randolph
Born in Virginia. Appointed from Virginia. Formerly lieutenant, U.S. Navy. Original entry into U.S. Navy, June 10, 1861. First lieutenant, October 23, 1862, to rank from October 2, 1862. First lieutenant, Provisional Navy, June 2, 1864, to rank from January 6, 1864. Served on Richmond station, 1861–1863; CSS *Teaser*, 1861; CSS *Richmond*, 1862–1863. Special service abroad, 1863–1864; commanding blockade-runner *Coquette*, 1864. Wilmington station, 1864. CSS *Stonewall*, 1865. First officer. Executive officer.

Closh, J. C.
Appointed from Texas. Second assistant engineer, January 24, 1865. Served on CSS *Stonewall*, 1865. Assistant engineer.

Curtis, Richard W.
Paymaster. Enlisted March 1863. Formerly of Georgia. CSS *Stonewall*, 1865.

Dukehart, John M.
Appointed from Maryland. Acting boatswain, boatswain, January 6, 1865. Abroad, 1864–1865; serving on CSS *Stonewall*, 1865. Boatswain.

Green, Bennett W.
Born in Virginia. Appointed from Virginia. Formerly assistant surgeon—U.S. Navy. Assistant surgeon, May 23, 1861. Passed assistant surgeon, October 25,

1862. Passed assistant surgeon, Provisional Navy, June 2, 1864. Army service at Culpeper Court House, Virginia, 1861. CSS *Pamlico*, New Orleans station, 1861–1862. Jackson station, 1862. Naval Hospital, Richmond, 1862–1863. Service abroad, 1863–1865; CSS *Stonewall*, 1865. Surgeon.

Herty, James W.
Born in Georgia. Appointed from Georgia. Formerly assistant surgeon, U.S. Navy. Assistant surgeon, February 1862. Passed assistant surgeon, October 25, 1862. Passed assistant surgeon, Provisional Navy, June 2, 1864. Prisoner at Hampton Roads, November 26, 1861; exchanged February 24, 1862. Special service, Richmond station, 1862. CSS *Richmond*, James River Squadron, 1862–1863. CSS *Rappahannock*, Calais, France, 1863–1864. CSS *Stonewall*, 1865. Assistant surgeon.

Jackson, William Hutcheson
Born in Virginia. Appointed from Virginia. Third assistant engineer, June 5, 1861. Second assistant engineer, August 27, 1862. Resigned June 26, 1863. Acting second assistant engineer, July 3, 1864. Resigned August 4, 1864. Served on U.S. steamers *McRae* and *Jackson*, New Orleans station, 1861–1862. CSS *Arkansas*, 1862. Richmond station, 1862. U.S. cruiser *Florida*, 1862–1863. CSS *Chicora*, Charleston station, 1863. Service abroad, 1863–1864. Ordered to CSS *Rappahannock*, Calais, France, 1864. CSS *Stonewall*, 1865. Assistant engineer.

King, J. B.
Born in Virginia. Appointed from Virginia. Acting master's mate, July 11, 1864. Gunner, January 24, 1865. Served on U.S. cruiser *Florida*, 1864. Ordered to the CSS *Rappahannock*, Calais, France, December 1864. CSS *Stonewall*, 1865. Gunner.

Klosh, J. C.
Assistant engineer.

Mather, Joseph
Appointed from Maryland. Carpenter (no date). Served on CSS *Stonewall*, 1865.

Newton, Virginius
Born in Virginia. Appointed from North Carolina. Acting midshipman, September 30, 1861. Midshipman, Provisional Navy, June 2, 1864. Served on

CSRS *United States*, 1861. Gosport Navy Yard, 1861. CSS *Beaufort*; participated in the battles of Elizabeth City, North Carolina, February 8, 1862, and Hampton Roads, Virginia, March 8–9, 1862; commended by commanding officer. CSS *Qaines*, Mobile Squadron, 1862–1863. Service abroad, 1863–1865; CSS *Rappahannock*, Calais, France, 1864; ordered to CSS *Stonewall*, 1864; reported at Havana, Cuba, 1865.

Page, Thomas Jefferson

Born in Virginia. Appointed from Virginia. Formerly commander, U.S. Navy. Served in Virginia navy. Commander, CSN, June 10, 1861; commander, October 23, 1862, to rank from March 26, 1861. Captain, Provisional Navy, June 2, 1864, to rank from May 13, 1863. Commanding Gloucester Point battery, York River, 1861–1862. Chaffins Bluff, Virginia, 1862–1863. Service abroad, 1863–1865. CSS *Stonewall*, 1864–1865; commanding when she was surrendered to Spanish authorities at Havana, May 19, 1865.

Prior, John M.

Sergeant of Marines. Prior of the Confederate States Marine Corps, formerly of the CSS *Rappahannock*.

Read, Edmund Gaines

Born in Virginia. Appointed from Virginia. Formerly midshipman, U.S. Navy. Acting midshipman, June 11, 1861. Acting master, September 24, 1861. Lieutenant for the war, February 8, 1862. Second lieutenant, February 8, 1862. First lieutenant, January 7, 1864, to rank from August 24, 1863. First lieutenant, Provisional Navy, June 2, 1864, to rank from January 6, 1864. Served on CSS *Patrick Henry*, 1861. Evansport batteries, 1861–1862. CSS *Patrick Henry*, 1862. CSS *Mississippi*. New Orleans station, 1862. Jackson station, 1862. CSS *Baltic*, Mobile Squadron, 1862–1863. Service abroad, 1863–1864. CSS *Stonewall*, 1865.

Savage, William H.

Appointed from Maryland. Acting master's mate (no date). Service abroad, 1864–1865; CSS *Stonewall*, 1865. Master's mate.

Shyrock, George S.

Born in Kentucky. Appointed from Kentucky. Formerly lieutenant, U.S. Navy. First lieutenant, August 15, 1861. First lieutenant, October 23, 1862, to rank from October 2, 1862. First lieutenant, Provisional Navy, June 2, 1864, to rank from January 6, 1864. Commanding CSS *Segar* and on CSS

Mobile, New Orleans station, 1861–1862. CSS *Louisiana*; escaped at the surrender of forts Jackson and St. Philip, April 28, 1862. Jackson station, 1862. Richmond station, 1862. CSS *Palmetto State*, Charleston station, 1862–1863; participated in attack upon federal blockading squadron off Charleston, South Carolina, January 31, 1863. Service abroad, 1863–1865; CSS *Stonewall*, 1865.

Wilkinson, William W.
Born in South Carolina. Appointed from South Carolina. Resigned as acting midshipman, U.S. Navy, December 22, 1860. Acting midshipman, June 15, 1861. Midshipman, Provisional Navy, June 2, 1864. Served on CSS *Huntress*, 1861–1862. CSS *Louisiana*, New Orleans station, 1862. Drewrys Bluff, Virginia, 1862–1863. Service abroad, 1863–1865; CSS *Stonewall*, 1865. Master.

Crew

Baptiste, John
Muster: July 1, 1865—*Macedonian*
October 24, 1865—*Stonewall*
Ships: *Hartford, Macedonian, Shenandoah, Stonewall*

Christian, John
Place of Birth: New Kent Co., Virginia
Muster: March 31, 1864—*Mystic*
October 24, 1865—*Stonewall*
Ships: *Macedonian, Mystic, Stonewall*

Dean, Joseph
Place of Birth: Richmond, Virginia
Muster: September 30, 1864—*Mystic*
October 24, 1865—*Stonewall*
Ships: *Dacotah, Macedonian, Mystic, Shenandoah, Stonewall*

DeBaron, Manuel A.
Muster: May 4, 1863—*Kensington*
October 24, 1865—*Stonewall*
Ships: *Kensington, Macedonian, Stonewall, Swatara*

H. G.
First-class fireman
Ships include: *Stonewall*

Mayne, Joseph N.
Place of Birth: Cartagena, New Granada
Muster: September 30, 1863—*Fuchsia*
October 24, 1865—*Stonewall*
Ships: *Don, Ella, Fuchsia, Stonewall*

Redmond, Isaac J.
Place of Birth: Virginia
Muster: October 1, 1864—*King Philip*
October 24, 1865—*Stonewall*
Ships: *King Philip, Stonewall*

Robinson, Iveson
Place of Birth: King William Co., Virginia
Muster: May 23, 1864—*Mackinaw*
October 24, 1865—*Stonewall*
December 31, 1865—*Winnipec*
Ships: *Mackinaw, Mohican, Stonewall, Winnipec*

Sheehan, Jeremiah
Muster: October 24, 1865—*Stonewall*
Ship: *Stonewall*

Smith, Robert
Place of Birth: Maryland
Muster: March 31, 1864—*Baltimore*
October 24, 1865—*Stonewall*
Ships: *Baltimore, King Philip, Stonewall*

KOTETSU PERSONNEL, 1868

Officers[2]

Admiral Sahiro Nakajima (Shiro Nakajima)
First Class Officer Ishida Ding Zo
First Class Officer Yamane Bunjiro
Second Class Officer Takino Toranosuke
Second Class Officer Harakenzo
Second Class Officer Yamagata Shaotaro
Second Class Officer Yamagata Penjiro

Second Class Officer Shinagawa Shikata
Second Class Officer Waki Ujihei
Second Class Officer Ikuta Ichitaro
Second Class Officer Yamada Kenjiro
Second Class Medical Officer Yori Crew Yoshida Akizo
Third Class Officer Kenkichi Hijikata
Third Class Medical Officer Torii Shunpei
Treasurer Sato Hiko
Treasurer Harada Sabei Mizu
Graduation Chief Fujita Katsuzo
Institution Commander Akisaku Tsukahara

(Incomplete) Crew

4 Men
3 Gunners
Unspecified artillery crewman—Nakamura Iwataro
1 Deputy Chief Mizusaki
1 Wooden Takumi Chief
4 Squad Commanders
1 Sailor Chief
1 Takumi Chief
1 Captain of Forges

NOTES

CHAPTER 1: THE SCOTTISH MONSTER

1. Thomas E. Sebrell, "Battlefields & Beyond: London, UK," HistoryNet, May 10, 2011, accessed November 7, 2022, https://www.historynet.com/battlefieldsbeyond-london-uk/.

2. Tom Huntington, "From Dixie to the Land of the Rising Sun," HistoryNet, October 27, 2016, https://www.historynet.com/from-dixie-to-the-land-of-the-rising-sun/.

3. "U.S. Navy Personnel Strength, 1775 to Present," Naval History and Heritage Command, https://www.history.navy.mil/research/library/online-reading-room/title-list-alphabetically/u/usn-personnel-strength.html.

4. William P. Roberts, "James Dunwoody Bulloch and the Confederate Navy," *North Carolina Historical Review* 24, no. 3 (July 1947): 315–66.

5. "Stephen Mallory to C. G. Memminger, June 8, 1863," in Letters Received by Confederate Treasury Secretary, National Archives and Records Administration, Record Group 365, Roll 35, 402.

6. Lowell E. Gallaway and Richard K. Vedder, "Emigration from the United Kingdom to the United States: 1860–1913," *Journal of Economic History* 31, no. 4 (December 1971): 885–97.

7. Thomas E. Sebrell II, "The American Civil War in Britain," Essential Civil War Curriculum, https://www.essentialcivilwarcurriculum.com/the-american-civil-war-in-britain.html.

8. "Scots and the American Civil War: So Whose Side Were We On?," *Scotsman*, April 11, 2011, https://www.scotsman.com/arts-and-culture/scots-and-american-civil-war-so-whose-side-were-we-1679768.

9. Susan Morrison, "American Civil War: How Clyde Shipbuilders Helped Confederate Forces Run the Union Blockade," *Scotsman*, September 9, 2023, https://www.scotsman.com/news/opinion/columnists/american-civil-war-how-clyde-shipbuilders-helped-confederate-forces-run-the-union-blockade-susan-morrison-4285571/; Chris Jones, "Sailing Down the Clyde: 'Doon the Watter,'" Glasgow History, July 18, 2010, https://www.glasgowhistory.com/sailing-down-the-clyde-doon-the-watter.html.

10. Warren F. Spencer, *The Confederate Navy in Europe* (Tuscaloosa: University of Alabama Press, 1983), https://archive.org/details/confederatenavyi0000spen/page/n9/mode/2up; Jönköping N. Sweden, "Visingsö Oak Forest," Atlas Obscura, https://www.atlasobscura.com/places/visingso-oak-forest.

11. Mike Coppock, "How the South's European Spymaster Built a Formidable Fleet That Challenged the Union Naval Power," HistoryNet, July 1, 2021, https://www.historynet .com/how-the-souths-European-spymaster-built-a-formidable-fleet-that-challenged-union -naval-power/.

12. "James and George Thomson to Messrs. W. S. Lindsay & Co., July 14, 1862 (George Thomson)," in CBF Private Letter Book, no. 3, UCS 1/11/1, Glasgow University Archives; Douglas H. Maynard, "The Confederacy's Super 'Alabama,'" *Civil War History* 5 (March 1959): 80–95; Frank Merli, *Great Britain and the Confederate Navy, 1861–1865* (Bloomington: Indiana University Press, 2004), 120–26.

13. James Dunwoody Bulloch, *The Secret Service of the Confederate States in Europe; or, How the Confederate Cruisers Were Equipped* (New York: Putnam, 1884), https://archive.org/details /secretserviceofc02bulluoft/page/36/mode/2up?q=coal; and "Bulloch to Capt. T. J. Page, February 14, 1865," in *Official Records of the Union and Confederate Navies in the War of the Rebellion* (hereafter ORN), series 1, vol. 3, *Operations of the Cruisers—Union, April 1, 1864, to December 30, 1865* (Washington, DC: Government Printing Office, 1896), 737–39; "Jackson to Frederick W. Seward, Asst. Secy. of State, March 1, 1865," in *ORN*, series 1, 3:737–39.

14. Eric Nielsen, "Danish Warship Procurement in the Early Steamship Age 1824–1862," Danish Military History, December 2013, https://milhist.dk/1922/.

15. Philip Van Doren Stern, *The Confederate Navy: A Pictorial History* (New York: Da Capo, 1992).

16. Johnny E. Balsved, "Armored Frigate DANMARK (1864–1900)," Danish Naval History, https://www.navalhistory.dk/English/TheShips/D/Danmark%281864%29.htm.

CHAPTER 2: BORROWING AN ARMY

1. "Civil War Diplomacy—Confederate Agents in Washington and Europe," American Foreign Relations, https://www.americanforeignrelations.com/A-D/Civil-War-Diplomacy -Confederate-agents-in-washington-and-Europe.html.

2. Louis Martin Sears, *John Slidell* (Durham, NC: Duke University Press, 1925); "Slidell, John," in *Biographical Directory of the United States Congress*, https://bioguide.congress.gov /search/bio/S000487.

3. William Seale, "The Other White House," Whitehouse Historical Association, https:// www.whitehousehistory.org/the-other-white-house.

4. "Selected Manpower Statistics—Fiscal Year 1997," table 2-11, Department of Defense, 2024, http://alternatewars.com/BBOW/Stats/DOD_SelectedStats_FY97.pdf.

5. John C Widerman, *Naval Warfare: Courage and Combat on the Water* (New York: Metro Books, 1997); "First Voyage of the United States Steamship *Niagara*; April 24th–May 13th, 1857," History of the Atlantic Cable & Undersea Communications, https://atlantic-cable .com/Cableships/Niagara/index.htm.

6. Benjamin T. Arrington, "Industry and Economy during the Civil War," National Parks Service, https://www.nps.gov/articles/industry-and-economy-during-the-civil-war.htm.

7. Micheal Clodfelter, *Warfare and Armed Conflicts: A Statistical Encyclopedia of Casualty and Other Figures, 1492–2015*, 4th ed. (Jefferson, NC: McFarland, 2017).

8. "The Naval War of the Civil War," History of the Net, August 18, 2022, https://www .historyonthenet.com/civil-war-the-naval-war.

9. Robert F. Reilly, "Medical and Surgical Care during the American Civil War, 1861– 1865," National Library of Medicine and National Institutes of Health, https://www.ncbi .nlm.nih.gov/pmc/articles/PMC4790547/.

10. Vermont Humanities, "The Union Suffers Horrific Defeat at Fredericksburg," Civil War Book of Days, December 7, 2012, https://civilwarbookofdays.org/2012/12/07/union -suffers-horrific-defeat-at-fredericksburg/.

11. "War Watchers at Bull Run during America's Civil War," HistoryNet, June 12, 2006, https://www.historynet.com/war-watchers-at-bull-run-during-americas-civil-war/.

12. Ship statistics unless otherwise noted: "Dictionary of American Naval Fighting Ships— Index," Naval History and Heritage Command, https://www.history.navy.mil/research /histories/ship-histories/danfs.html; and Naval Encyclopedia (website), accessed September 10, 2024, https://naval-encyclopedia.com/industrial-era/confederate-navy-1861–65.php.

13. Thomas E. Nank, "Ready for War? The Union Navy in 1861," American Battle-field Trust, August 23, 2021, https://www.battlefields.org/learn/articles/ready-war-union -navy-1861.

14. "Value of CSA Currency from 1861 to 1865," CSA Currency, http://uncon.atweb pages.com/cs/csacur/csavcw.htm.

15. Independence Hall Association, "33b. Strengths and Weaknesses: North vs. South," U.S. History, https://www.ushistory.org/us/33b.asp.

16. "Letter to Horace Greeley, Washington, August 22, 1862," Abraham Lincoln Online, https://www.abrahamlincolnonline.org/lincoln/speeches/greeley.htm.

17. Jennifer L. Weber, "American Civil War: United States History," in Encyclopedia Britannica Online, last updated July 30, 2022, https://www.britannica.com/event/American -Civil-War.

18. "10 Facts: Civil War Navies," American Battlefield Trust, https://www.battlefields .org/learn/articles/10-facts-civil-war-navies.

CHAPTER 3: THE HOPES OF A WHOLE PEOPLE

1. Gary McQuarrie and Neil P. Chatelain, "Confederate Shipyards," Civil War Navy Magazine, https://civilwarnavy.com/confederate-shipyards/, citing William N. Still Jr., Confederate Shipbuilding (Athens: University of Georgia Press, 1996); and William N. Still Jr., ed., The Confederate Navy: The Ships, Men and Organization, 1861–65 (London: Conway Maritime Press, 1997).

2. John V. Quarstein, "Proving the Power of Iron over Wood," Naval History Magazine 26, no. 2 (April 2012), https://www.usni.org/magazines/naval-history-magazine/2012/april /proving-power-iron-over-wood.

3. Spencer C. Tucker, "Confederate Naval Ordnance," in "Special Commemorative Naval Issue: CSS Alabama, 1864–1989," ed. Frank J. Merli, special issue, Journal of Confederate History 4 (1989).

4. Thomas E. Nank, "Ready for War? The Union Navy in 1861," American Battle-field Trust, August 23, 2021, https://www.battlefields.org/learn/articles/ready-war-union -navy-1861.

5. "Evolution of the Confederate States Navy," American Civil War High Command, https://americancivilwarhighcommand.com/navies/evolution-of-the-confederate-states -navy/.

6. Nank, "Ready for War?"

7. "Early Ironclads: Europe and America I," Weapons and Warfare, October 13, 2019, https://weaponsandwarfare.com/2019/10/14/early-ironclads-europe-and-america-i/.

8. "American Civil War: CSS Virginia," ThoughtCo, https://www.thoughtco.com/css -virginia-2360566.

9. Raimondo Luraghi, *A History of the Confederate Navy* (Annapolis, MD: U.S. Naval Institute Press, 1996).

10. "Early Ironclads: Europe and America I."

11. John V. Quarstein, "The First Ironclad Emerges: Battle of the Head of Passes," Mariners Museum and Park, July 9, 2020, https://blog.marinersmuseum.org/2020/07/the-first-ironclad-emerges-battle-of-the-head-of-passes/.

12. Larrie D. Ferreiro, "The Wrong Ship at the Right Time: The Technology of USS *Monitor* and Its Impact on Naval Warfare," *International Journal of Naval History*, May 13, 2021.

13. "Ericsson Battery—Interesting Statement from the Inventor," *Chicago Tribune*, March 17, 1862, 4; "USS *Monitor* Contract Specifications," and "Ericsson to Joseph Smith, October 2, 1861," in NARA RG 45, entry 502 AD, box 51, folder 10, National Archives and Records Administration.

14. "A Brief Naval Chronology of the Civil War (1861–65)," Naval History and Heritage Command, https://www.history.navy.mil/content/history/nhhc/research/library/online-reading-room/title-list-alphabetically/n/navy-civil-war-chronology.html.

15. Jennifer L. Weber, "American Civil War: United States History," in *Encyclopedia Britannica Online*, last updated July 30, 2022, https://www.britannica.com/event/American-Civil-War; Douglas Southall Freeman, *R. E. Lee: A Biography*, vol. 2 (New York: Scribner, 1934).

16. Quarstein, "Proving the Power of Iron over Wood."

17. Dwight Hughes, "Recruiting the Crew: Iron Men for Iron Ships," Emerging Civil War, June 3, 2021, https://emergingcivilwar.com/2021/06/03/recruiting-the-crew-iron-men-for-iron-ships/.

18. Hughes, "Recruiting the Crew."

19. Catesby ap Roger Jones, "Services of the Virginia," in *Southern Historical Society Papers*, vol. 11, *January–December 1904*, ed. John William Jones, Robert Alonzo Brock, and James Power Smith (Richmond, VA: Southern Historical Society; Virginia Historical Society, 1876–1959), 66–67.

20. William Norris, "The Story of the Confederate States Ship *Virginia* (Once *Merrimac*): Her Victory over the *Monitor*," in *Southern Historical Society Papers*, vol. 42, *September 1917*, ed. John William Jones, Robert Alonzo Brock, and James Power Smith (Richmond, VA: Southern Historical Society; Virginia Historical Society, 1876–1959), 206.

21. Donald L. Canney, *The Old Steam Navy: The Ironclads, 1842–1885*, vol. 2 (Annapolis, MD: U.S. Naval Institute Press, 1993).

22. "USS *Monitor*: John Ericsson," National Ocean Service, https://monitor.noaa.gov/150th/ericsson.html.

23. "USS *Monitor*: John Ericsson."

24. "USS *Monitor*: John Ericsson."

25. Ferreiro, "The Wrong Ship at the Right Time."

26. Olav Thulesius, *The Man Who Made the Monitor: A Biography of John Ericsson, Naval Engineer* (Jefferson, NC: McFarland, 2007).

27. Stephen C. Thompson, "The Design and Construction of USS *Monitor*," *Warship International* 27, no. 3 (1990).

28. Thulesius, *The Man Who Made the Monitor*.

29. "Hampton Roads, *Monitor* vs. *Merrimack*," American Battlefield Trust, https://www.battlefields.org/learn/civil-war/battles/hampton-roads.

CHAPTER 4: THE BATTLE OF HAMPTON ROADS

1. "The Sortie of the CSS *Virginia* Saturday 8 March 1862," Mine Creek Battlefield, last updated April 28, 2023, https://www.minecreek.info/fort-monroe/the-sortie-of-the-css -virginia-saturday-8-march-1862.html.

2. John V. Quarstein, "Proving the Power of Iron over Wood," *Naval History Magazine* 26, no. 2 (April 2012), https://www.usni.org/magazines/naval-history-magazine/2012/april /proving-power-iron-over-wood.

3. "Strange and Interesting Civil War Facts," American Civil War Story, http://www .americancivilwarstory.com/strange-and-interesting-civil-war-facts.html.

4. "War Watchers at Bull Run during America's Civil War," HistoryNet, June 12, 2006, https://www.historynet.com/war-watchers-at-bull-run-during-americas-civil-war/.

5. "The Sortie of the CSS *Virginia* Saturday 8 March 1862."

6. U.S. Naval War Records Office, *Official Records of the Union and Confederate Navies in the War of the Rebellion*, series 1, vol. 7, *North Atlantic Blockading Squadron—March 8, 1862 to September 4, 1862* (Washington, DC: Government Printing Office, 1898), 44.

7. William C. David, *Duel of the First Ironclads* (Essex, CT: Stackpole Books, 1994), 72.

8. Royce Lee Smith, "Union and Confederate Secretaries of the Navy: A Comparative Study of the Secretaries during the Civil War" (master's thesis, University of Illinois, 1983); Dwight Hughes, "The Most Frightened Man and the Ironclads," Emerging Civil War, March 9, 2022, https://emergingcivilwar.com/2022/03/09/the-most-frightened-man-and -the-ironclads/; Albert L. Demaree, "Our Navy's Worst Headache: The *Merrimack*," *U.S. Naval Institute Proceedings* 88, no. 3/709 (March 1962), https://www.usni.org/magazines /proceedings/1962/march/our-navys-worst-headache-merrimack; Quarstein, "Proving the Power of Iron over Wood."

9. Keith Milton, "The *Monitor* and the *Merrimack*: The Battle of Hampton Roads," Warfare History Network, Summer 2012, https://warfarehistorynetwork.com/article/the -monitor-the-merrimack-the-battle-of-hampton-roads/.

10. Benjamin Brimelow, "The First Battle between Ironclad Warships Was a Dud, but It Changed Naval Warfare Forever," *Business Insider*, March 10, 2021, https://www.business insider.com/monitor-virginia-first-battle-of-ironclad-ships-changed-naval-warfare-2021-3.

11. "There Isn't Even Danger Enough to Give Us Any Glory," National Museum of Civil War Medicine, May 19, 2021, https://www.civilwarmed.org/navy-marine-casualties/.

12. Peter C. Luebke, "African Americans in the U.S. Navy during the Civil War," Naval History and Heritage Command, https://www.history.navy.mil/content/history/nhhc /browse-by-topic/wars-conflicts-and-operations/civil-war/general-studies-civil-war/african -americans-in-the-u-s--navy-during-the-civil-war.html.

13. Robert J. Schneller, "'A State of War Is a Most Unfavorable Period for Experiments': John Dahlgren and U.S. Naval Ordnance Innovation during the American Civil War," *International Journal of Naval History* 2, no. 3 (December 2003).

14. "Buchanan to Mallory, March 27, 1862," in *ORN*, series 1, 7:46.

15. "Hampton Roads: *Monitor* vs. *Merrimack*," American Battlefield Trust, https://www .battlefields.org/learn/civil-war/battles/hampton-roads; John V. Quarstein, *The Monitor Boys: The Crew of the Union's First Ironclad* (Charleston, SC: History Press, 2011), 181.

16. Demaree, "Our Navy's Worst Headache."

17. Demaree, "Our Navy's Worst Headache."

18. John Taylor Wood, "First Fight of Iron-Clads," in *Battles and Leaders of the Civil War*, ed. Robert U. Johnson and Clarence C. Buel (New York: Thomas Yoseloff, 1956), 1:709.

19. "From the Richmond, Va., *Times*, April 15 and 22, 1894, 'What It Accomplished during the War. As read by Mr. Virginius Newton in the Company of General R. E. Lee,'" in *Southern Historical Society Papers*, vol. 22, *January–December*, ed. John William Jones, Robert Alonzo Brock, and James Power Smith (Richmond, VA: Southern Historical Society; Virginia Historical Society, 1894).

20. Jones, Brock, and Smith, *Southern Historical Society Papers*, vol. 22.

21. Jones, Brock, and Smith, *Southern Historical Society Papers*, vol. 22.

22. "The *Monitor* Is No More," National Marine Sanctuaries, https://monitor.noaa.gov/150th/sinking.html.

23. "USS *Monitor*," Monitor National Marine Sanctuary, https://monitor.noaa.gov/shipwrecks/uss_monitor.html.

24. "Hampton Roads: *Monitor* vs. *Merrimack*," American Battlefield Trust, https://www.battlefields.org/learn/civil-war/battles/hampton-roads.

25. "The Naval War of the Civil War," History of the Net, August 18, 2022, https://www.historyonthenet.com/civil-war-the-naval-war.

26. Brent Swancer, "Curious Mystery Monsters of the American Civil War," Mysterious Universe, February 2016, https://mysteriousuniverse.org/2016/02/curious-mystery-monsters-of-the-american-civil-war/.

27. "Evolution of the Confederate States Navy," American Civil War High Command, https://americancivilwarhighcommand.com/navies/evolution-of-the-confederate-states-navy/.

28. R. Thomas Campbell, *Confederate Ironclads at War* (Jefferson, NC: McFarland, 2017).

29. Larrie D. Ferreiro, "The Wrong Ship at the Right Time: The Technology of USS *Monitor* and Its Impact on Naval Warfare," *International Journal of Naval History*, May 13, 2021.

30. "American Civil War Ironclads," Weapons and Warfare, May 17, 2020, https://weaponsandwarfare.com/2020/05/17/american-civil-war-ironclads/.

31. "Union and USN Monitors," Weapons and Warfare, April 8, 2017, https://weaponsandwarfare.com/2017/04/08/union-and-usn-monitors/.

32. Sean Vanatta and Dan Du, "Civil War Industry and Manufacturing," in *New Georgia Encyclopedia*, last modified August 24, 2020, https://www.georgiaencyclopedia.org/articles/history-archaeology/civil-war-industry-and-manufacturing/.

33. George E. Turner, *Victory Rode the Rails: The Strategic Place of the Railroads in the Civil War* (Indianapolis and New York: Bobbs-Merrill, 1953).

CHAPTER 5: THE WRONG SHIPS

1. Stephen R. Mallory Papers, Mss. 75 M29, William & Mary Libraries, https://scrcguides.libraries.wm.edu/repositories/2/resources/4808.

2. Phill Greenwalt, "The Stephen Mallory You May Not Have Known," Emerging Civil War, February 4, 2021, https://emergingcivilwar.com/2021/02/04/the-stephen-mallory-you-may-not-have-known/.

3. James M. McPherson, *War on the Waters: The Union and Confederate Navies* (Chapel Hill: University of North Carolina Press, 2012).

4. Lt. J. G. Michael and B. H. Sobelman, "The Long Blue Line: 'The Last Full Measure of Devotion'—the Life and Death of Revenue Cutter Capt. Thomas Dungan," United States Coast Guard, April 1, 2022, https://www.mycg.uscg.mil/News/Article/2974187/the-long-blue-line-the-last-full-measure-of-devotionthe-life-and-death-of-reven/.

5. "A Ship's a Fool to Fight a Fort," Navy Matters, July 7, 2016, https://navy-matters
.blogspot.com/2016/07/a-ships-fool-to-fight-fort.html.

6. Larrie D. Ferreiro, "The Wrong Ship at the Right Time: The Technology of USS
Monitor and Its Impact on Naval Warfare," *International Journal of Naval History*, May 13, 2021.

7. "The Sea Battle of Sinop Was Fought 30 November 1853," Boris Yeltsin Presidential
Library, https://www.prlib.ru/en/history/619768.

8. Raimondo Luraghi, *A History of the Confederate Navy* (Annapolis, MD: U.S. Naval
Institute Press, 1996).

9. "FS *La Gloire* (1860)," Military Factory, https://www.militaryfactory.com/ships/detail
.php?ship_id=La-Gloire.

10. "Why HMS *Warrior* Was the Most Cutting Edge Warship of Its Day," History Hit,
April 29, 2022, https://www.facebook.com/watch/?v=842886857088462; "What Was It
Like to Serve in HMS *Warrior*," History Hit, May 16, 2022, https://www.facebook.com
/watch/?v=5087211997981169.

11. "Early Ironclads: Europe and America I," Weapons and Warfare, October 13, 2019,
https://weaponsandwarfare.com/2019/10/14/early-ironclads-europe-and-america-i/; "The
Battle of Lissa: The Trafalgar of Ironclads," in *Naval Encyclopedia*, January 2, 2019, https://
naval-encyclopedia.com/industrial-era/the-battle-of-lissa-1866.php.

12. Lawrence Sondhaus, *Naval Warfare 1815–1914* (New York: Routledge, 2001).

13. "Stephen Mallory to C. G. Memminger, June 8, 1863," in Letters Received by Confederate Treasury Secretary, National Archives and Records Administration, Record Group
365, Roll 35, 402.

14. "Civil War Diplomacy—Confederate Agents in Washington and Europe," American
Foreign Relations, https://www.americanforeignrelations.com/A-D/Civil-War-Diplomacy
-Confederate-agents-in-washington-and-Europe.html.

15. "Liverpool's Abercromby Square and the Confederacy during the U.S. Civil War,"
Lowcountry Digital History Initiative, https://ldhi.library.cofc.edu/exhibits/show/liverpools
-abercromby-square/abercromby-southern-club/embassy-confederacy.

16. David W. Shaw, *Sea Wolf of the Confederacy: The Daring Civil War Raids of Naval Lt.
Charles W. Read* (Dobbs Ferry, NY: Sheridan House, 2005).

17. Captain C. W. Read, "Reminiscences of the Confederate States Navy," Civil War
Talk, September 18, 2011, https://civilwartalk.com/threads/reminiscences-of-the-confederate
-states-navy.26950/.

18. Will Pearson and Erik Sass, *The Mental Floss History of the United States: The (Almost)
Complete and (Entirely) Entertaining Story of America* (New York: HarperCollins, 2010).

19. "The Confederate Navy (CSS)," in *Naval Encyclopedia*, February 4, 2018, https://naval
-encyclopedia.com/industrial-era/confederate-navy-1861-65.php.

20. Gary McQuarrie and Neil P. Chatelain, "Confederate Shipyards," *Civil War Navy
Magazine*, https://civilwarnavy.com/confederate-shipyards/, citing William N. Still Jr., *Con-
federate Shipbuilding* (Athens: University of Georgia Press, 1996) and William N. Still Jr., ed.,
The Confederate Navy: The Ships, Men and Organization, 1861–65 (London: Conway Maritime
Press, 1997).

21. Mark K. Christ, "CSS *Pontchartrain*," in *Encyclopedia of Arkansas*, last updated March 28,
2022, https://encyclopediaofarkansas.net/entries/css-pontchartrain-5914/.

22. John W Wallis, The Confederate STETS Navy Sidewheel Ironclads," Civil War
Talk, February 2016, https://civilwartalk.com/threads/the-confederate-navys-side-wheel
-ironclads.122237/.

23. Still, *Confederate Shipbuilding*.

24. John V. Quarstein, "Proving the Power of Iron over Wood," *Naval History Magazine* 26, no. 2 (April 2012), https://www.usni.org/magazines/naval-history-magazine/2012/april /proving-power-iron-over-wood.

25. "Evolution of the Confederate States Navy," American Civil War High Command, https://americancivilwarhighcommand.com/navies/evolution-of-the-confederate-states -navy/.

26. Adam C. Edmonds, "Confederate Wooden Gunboat Construction: Logistical Nightmare" (PhD diss., East Carolina University, May 2011).

27. John V. Quarstein, "The First Ironclad Emerges: Battle of the Head of Passes," Mariners Museum and Park, July 9, 2020, https://blog.marinersmuseum.org/2020/07/the-first -ironclad-emerges-battle-of-the-head-of-passes/.

28. "From the Richmond, Va., *Times*, April 15 and 22, 1894, 'What It Accomplished during the War. As read by Mr. Virginius Newton in the Company of General R. E. Lee,'" in *Southern Historical Society Papers*, vol. 22, *January–December*, ed John William Jones, Robert Alonzo Brock, and James Power Smith (Richmond, VA: Southern Historical Society; Virginia Historical Society, 1894).

29. Luke Spencer, "How a Champagne-Laden Steamship Ended up in a Kansas Cornfield," Atlas Obscura, July 20, 2016, https://www.atlasobscura.com/articles/how-a-champagneladen -steamship-ended-up-in-a-kansas-cornfield#:~:text=It%20was%20here%20in%201856,but%20 in%20a%20corn%20field. And let me say, for anyone actually venturing down into these notes, if you haven't looked at Atlas Obscura, you'll love it when you do. Dean Klinkenberg, "Mississippi River Geology," Mississippi Valley Traveler, March 5, 2011, https://web.archive.org /web/20181230081157/https://mississippivalleytraveler.com/mississippi-river-geology/.

30. Naval History and Heritage Command, Confederate States Navy, *Diagram of the Rebel Ram Atlanta Now on Exhibition, Foot of Washington Street, for the Benefit of the Union Volunteer Refreshment Saloon.* (Washington, DC: Navy Department Library Rare Book Collection, n.d.).

31. "CSS *Tennessee* 1863," Rebellion Research, July 25, 2021, https://www.rebellionre search.com/css-tennessee-1863.

32. William N. Still, *Iron Afloat: The Story of the Confederate Armorclads* (Columbia: University of South Carolina Press, 1988), 45; J. Thomas Scharf, *History of the Confederate States Navy: From Its Organization to the Surrender of the Last Vessel* (New York: Rogers & Sherwood, 1887), 266.

33. "10 Facts: Civil War Navies," American Battlefield Trust, https://www.battlefields .org/learn/articles/10-facts-civil-war-navies; "Diary of Stephen R. Mallory," May 15, 1862, in *Stephen R. Mallory Diary and Reminiscences*, vol. 1, #2229, Southern Historical Collection, Wilson Library, University of North Carolina at Chapel Hill.

CHAPTER 6: RAIDERS AND RUNNERS

1. Maurice Rigby, "'Dixie Traitor'—the Life and Times of Clarence Randolph Yonge, C.S.N.," *Crossfire* 48 (December 26, 2011), https://www.acwrt.org.uk/post/dixie-traitor-the -life-and-times-of-clarence-randolph-yonge-c-s-n.

2. Rigby, "'Dixie Traitor.'"

3. "Young to W. H. Seward, April 20, 1864," in *Despatches from U.S. Consuls in Belfast*, National Archives Microfilm Publication T368, roll 4.

4. U.S. Naval War Records Office, *Official Records of the Union and Confederate Navies in the War of the Rebellion* (hereafter *ORN*), series 1, vol. 3, *Operations of the Cruisers—Union, April 1, 1864, to December 30, 1865* (Washington, DC: Government Printing Office, 1896), 453–500.

5. Rigby, "'Dixie Traitor.'"

6. "Wm. Atherton and Roundell Palmer to Earl Russell, July 29, 1862," in *The Case of Great Britain*, 1:445–46, cited in. G. W. Bill, *Catalogue of the Papers of Roundell Palmer (1812–1895), First Earl of Selborne* (London: Lambeth Palace Library, 1967), 56.

7. Craig Symonds, "*Kearsarge* and *Alabama*: The Civil War's Classic Ship-to-Ship Duel," American Battlefield Trust, https://www.battlefields.org/learn/articles/kearsarge-and-alabama.

8. "Civil War Naval Events from 1861 to 1865," Civil War Timeline, https://www.civilwartimeline.net/military-naval-actions.php.

9. "Most Successful U-Boat Commanders: Men That Sank over 100,000 Tons during World War One," U-Boat, https://www.uboat.net/wwi/men/commanders/most_successful.html.

10. Confederate States Commercial Agency, "List of Papers, London, July 4, 1864," in *ORN*, series 2, 3:1152–1204.

11. Frank Howard, "Early Ship Guns. Part I, Built-up Breech-Loaders," *Mariner's Mirror* 72 (1986): 439–53.

12. "Naval Guns," Encylcopedia.com, https://www.encyclopedia.com/history/encyclopedias-almanacs-transcripts-and-maps/naval-guns.

13. William C. Davis, *Duel between the First Ironclads* (New York: Doubleday, 1975).

14. John Mcintosh Kell, "Cruise and Combats of the *Alabama*," American Battlefield Trust, https://www.battlefields.org/learn/primary-sources/cruise-and-combats-alabama.

15. "Civil War Scholar Expands on Confederate Ship's 'Noble Death,'" Virginian Plot, February 10, 1997, https://scholar.lib.vt.edu/VA-news/VA-Pilot/issues/1997/vp970210/02100049.htm.

16. Symonds, "*Kearsarge* and *Alabama*."

17. Confederate States Commercial Agency, "List of Papers, London, July 4, 1864."

18. "Liverpool's Abercromby Square and the Confederacy during the U.S. Civil War," Lowcountry Digital History Initiative, https://ldhi.library.cofc.edu/exhibits/show/liverpools-abercromby-square/abercromby-southern-club/embassy-confederacy.

19. Kevin J. Foster, "The Diplomats Who Sank a Fleet: The Confederacy's Undelivered European Fleet and the Union Consular Service," *Prologue Magazine* 33, no. 3 (Fall 2001), https://www.archives.gov/publications/prologue/2001/fall/confederate-fleet; "Vessel nos. 294 & 295, *Scorpion* & *Wyvern*," in Laird Brothers, *Estimate Book* no. 2, 67–74, and *Contract Book* no. 2, 217, 246, 287, 288, 297 (Birkenhead, England: Cammel-Laird Archives).

20. Mike Coppock, "How the South's European Spymaster Built a Formidable Fleet That Challenged the Union Naval Power," HistoryNet, January 7, 2021, https://www.historynet.com/how-the-souths-European-spymaster-built-a-formidable-fleet-that-challenged-union-naval-power/.

21. William W. Wade, "The Man Who Stopped the Rams," *American Heritage* 14, no. 3 (April 1963), https://www.americanheritage.com/man-who-stopped-rams.

22. William J. Cooper, *Jefferson Davis, American* (New York: Knopf Doubleday, 2000).

23. U.S. Naval War Records Office, *ORN*, series 2, vol. 2, *Navy Department Correspondence, 1861–1865, with Agents Abroad* (Washington, DC: Government Printing Office, 1921), 11 (1861 Contents).

24. James M. McPherson, *War on the Waters: The Union and Confederate Navies, 1861–65* (Chapel Hill: University of North Carolina Press, 2012), 222–23.

25. Frank Lawrence Owsley Jr., *King Cotton Diplomacy* (Vancouver: University of British Columbia Press, 2008), 250–90; Stephen R. Wise, *Lifeline of the Confederacy: Blockade Running during the Civil War* (Columbia: University of South Carolina Press, 1988), 221.

26. Thomas E. Nank, "Ready for War? The Union Navy in 1861," American Battlefield Trust, August 23, 2021, https://www.battlefields.org/learn/articles/ready-war-union-navy-1861.

CHAPTER 7: THE EUROPEAN SOLUTION

1. David Howath, *A Brief History of British Sea Power: How Britain Became Sovereign of the Seas* (London: Robinson, 1974).

2. James McPherson, *Battle Cry of Freedom: The Civil War Era* (Oxford, UK: Oxford University Press, 1988), https://archive.org/details/battlecryoffreed0000unse/page/n5/mode/2up.

3. "Bakumatsu & Meiji Era Ships," in *Naval Encyclopedia*, https://naval-encyclopedia.com/industrial-era/bakumatsu-meiji-era-ships.ph2.

4. U.S. Naval War Records Office, *Official Records of the Union and Confederate Navies in War of the Rebellion* (hereafter *ORN*), series 2, vol. 2, *Navy Department Correspondence, 1861–1865, with Agents Abroad* (Washington, DC: Government Printing Office, 1921), 11 (1861 Contents).

5. "1863 Russian Involvement in the US Civil War," Stolen History, December 2020, https://stolenhistory.org/articles/1863-russian-involvement-in-the-us-civil-war.168/#:~:text=1%20Alexander%20Newsky%20%28flagship%29%20-%20was%20a%20screw,-%20was%20a%20screw%20clipper%20mounting%207%20cannons; Oleg Yegorov, "What Role Did Russia Play in the U.S. Civil War?," Russia Beyond, August 16, 2017, https://www.rbth.com/politics_and_society/2017/08/16/what-role-did-russia-play-in-the-us-civil-war_823252.

6. "John Slidell: Biography," FAMPeople, https://fampeople.com/cat-john-slidell.

7. "Trent Affair," History Network, September 11, 2009, https://www.history.com/topics/american-civil-war/trent-affair.

8. "Britain, the Blue, and the Gray," Key Military, June 2022; https://www.keymilitary.com/article/britain-blue-and-gray.

9. "Ericsson Battery—Interesting Statement from the Inventor," *Chicago Tribune*, March 17, 1862, 4; "USS *Monitor* Contract Specifications," and "Ericsson to Joseph Smith, October 2, 1861," in NARA RG 45, entry 502 AD, box 51, folder 10, National Archives and Records Administration.

10. Thomas Sheppard, "Matthew C. Perry's Forgotten Successor," *Naval History Magazine* 36, no. 2 (April 2022), https://www.usni.org/magazines/naval-history-magazine/2022/april/matthew-c-perrys-forgotten-successor.

11. U.S. Naval War Records Office, *ORN*, series 2, 2:11 (1861 Contents).

12. U.S. Naval War Records Office, *ORN*, series 2, 2:11 (1861 Contents).

13. "John Slidell," A Continent Divided: The US—Mexico War, https://library.uta.edu/usmexicowar/item?bio_id=18; Joseph Tregel Jr., "The Political Apprenticeship of John Slidell," *Journal of Southern History* 26, no. 1 (February 1960): 57–70; and "John Slidell," Smithsonian Institution, https://americanart.si.edu/artwork/john-slidell-20139.

14. Frank Merli, *Great Britain and the Confederate Navy* (Indianapolis: Indiana University Press, 2005), 127–33.

15. "Deposition of Richard Spendiff, laborer, Sheerness, enclosure within F. H. Morse to W. H. Seward, Dec. 11 1863 (No. 127)," and "Samuel H. Chase to F. H. Morse, Dec. 18, 1863 (No. 130)," in *Despatches from U.S. Consuls in London*, National Archives Microfilm Publication T168, roll 32; Warren F. Spencer, *The Confederate Navy in Europe* (Tuscaloosa: University of Alabama Press, 1983), 134–41; and Merli, *Great Britain and the Confederate Navy*, 218–26.

16. "The Virginian Plot: Civil War Scholar Expands on Confederate Ship's 'Noble Death,'" February 10, 1997, https://scholar.lib.vt.edu/VA-news/VA-Pilot/issues/1997/vp970 210/02100049.htm.

17. "James & George Thomson to Messrs. W. S. Lindsay & Co., July 14, 1862, (George Thomson)," in CBF Private Letter Book, no. 3, UCS 1/11/1, Glasgow University Archives; Douglas H. Maynard, "The Confederacy's Super 'Alabama,'" *Civil War History* 5 (March 1959): 80–95; and Merli, *Great Britain and the Confederate Navy*, 120–26, 49.

18. "*Alexandra*," Naval History and Heritage Command, https://www.history.navy.mil /research/histories/ship-histories/confederate_ships/alexandra.html.

19. Jack Greene and Alessandro Massignani, *Ironclads at War: The Origin and Development of the Armored Battleship* (New York: Hachette Books, 1998).

20. "A Brief Naval Chronology of the Civil War (1861–65)," Naval History and Heritage Command, https://www.history.navy.mil/content/history/nhhc/research/library/online -reading-room/title-list-alphabetically/n/navy-civil-war-chronology.html.

21. James Dunwoody Bulloch, *The Secret Service of the Confederate States in Europe; or, How the Confederate Cruisers Were Equipped* (New York: Putnam, 1884), https://archive.org/details /secretserviceofc02bulluoft/page/36/mode/2up?q=coal; and "Bulloch to Capt. T. J. Page, February 14, 1865," in *Official Records of the Union and Confederate Navies in the War of the Rebellion*, series 1, vol. 3, *Operations of the Cruisers—Union, April 1, 1864, to December 30, 1865* (Washington, DC: Government Printing Office, 1896), 737–39; "Jackson to Frederick W. Seward, Asst. Secy. of State, March 1, 1865," in *ONR*, series 1, 3:737–39.

22. Chris Eger, "Guns of the (Confederate), 1863," Guns.com, February 2013, https:// www.guns.com/news/2013/02/23/guns-of-the-confederate-grunt-1863.

23. John Grady, "Forbes and Aspinwall Go to War," *New York Times*, July 26, 2013, https://archive.nytimes.com/opinionator.blogs.nytimes.com/2013/07/26/forbes-and-aspin wall-go-to-war/.

24. "Scots and the American Civil War: So Whose Side Were We On?," *Scotsman*, April 11, 2011, https://www.scotsman.com/arts-and-culture/scots-and-american-civil-war-so -whose-side-were-we-1679768; David Keys, "Historians Reveal Secrets of UK Gun-Running Which Lengthened the American Civil War by Two Years," *Independent*, June 24, 2014.

25. Susan Morrison, "American Civil War: How Clyde Shipbuilders Helped Confederate Forces Run the Union Blockade," *Scotsman*, September 9, 2023, https://www.scotsman.com /news/opinion/columnists/american-civil-war-how-clyde-shipbuilders-helped-confederate -forces-run-the-union-blockade-susan-morrison-4285571/; Chris Jones, "Sailing Down the Clyde: 'Doon the Watter,'" Glasgow History, July 17, 2010, https://www.glasgowhistory .com/sailing-down-the-clyde-doon-the-watter.html.

26. "Charles F. Adams to Earl Russell, October 23, 1863," in *The Alabama Arbitration*, by Thomas Willing Balch (N.p.: Allen, Lane & Scott, 1900), 15–21.

27. "Wm. Atherton and Roundell Palmer to Earl Russell, July 29, 1862," in *The Case of Great Britain* (repr., n.p.: Anatiposi Verlag, 2023), 1:445–46.

28. *The Case of Great Britain* (repr., n.p.: Anatiposi Verlag, 2023), 2:185–86; "Wm. Atherton and Roundell Palmer to Earl Russell, July 29, 1862," 1:445–46.

29. "John Young to W. H. Seward, August 20, 1862," in *Despatches from U.S. Consuls in Belfast, Ireland, 1796–1906*, National Archives Microfilm Publication T368, roll 4, RG 59, NACP.

30. Kevin J. Foster, "The Diplomats Who Sank a Fleet; The Confederacy's Undelivered European Fleet and the Union Consular Service," *Prologue Magazine* 33, no. 3 (Fall 2001);

"Vessel nos. 294 & 295, *Scorpion & Wyvern*," in Laird Brothers, *Estimate Book* no. 2, 67–74, and *Contract Book* no. 2, 217, 246, 287, 288, 297 (Birkenhead, England: Cammel-Laird Archives).

31. Donald L. Canney, *The Old Steam Navy: The Ironclads, 1842–1885*, vol. 2 (Annapolis, MD: Naval Institute Press, 1993).

32. Thomas E. Nank, "Naval Operations in Charleston Harbor," American Battlefield Trust, https://www.battlefields.org/learn/articles/naval-operations-charleston-harbor.

33. "American Civil War: The War in 1863," in *Encyclopedia Britannica Online*, https://www.britannica.com/event/American-Civil-War/The-Southern-home-front; Jennifer L. Weber, "American Civil War: United States History," in *Encyclopedia Britannica Online*, last updated July 30, 2022, https://www.britannica.com/event/American-Civil-War.

CHAPTER 8: THE LAIRD RAMS

1. Thomas E. Sebrell II, "The American Civil War in Britain," Essential Civil War Curriculum, https://www.essentialcivilwarcurriculum.com/the-american-civil-war-in-britain.html.

2. "American Civil War: The War in 1863," in *Encyclopedia Britannica Online*, https://www.britannica.com/event/American-Civil-War/The-Southern-home-front.

3. "States during the Civil War," "Confederate States in 1863," in *Civil War Encyclopedia*, vol. 3 (New York: Appleton, 1868); "The American Annual Cyclopaedia and Register of Important Events of the Year, 1861–1865," in *Civil War Encyclopedia*, vol. 5 (New York: Appleton, 1868).

4. "S. R. Mallory, Secretary of the Navy, to Captain James D. Bulloch and Lieutenant North," in *Official Records of the Union and Confederate Navies in the War of the Rebellion*, series 2, vol. 2, *Navy Department Correspondence, 1861–1865, with Agents Abroad* (Washington, DC: Government Printing Office, 1921).

5. Vermont Humanities, "The Union Suffers Horrific Defeat at Fredericksburg," Civil War Book of Days, December 7, 2012, https://civilwarbookofdays.org/2012/12/07/union-suffers-horrific-defeat-at-fredericksburg/.

6. J. Thomas Scharf, *History of the Confederate States Navy: From Its Organization to the Surrender of the Last Vessel* (New York: Rogers & Sherwood, 1887).

7. Mike Coppock, "How the South's European Spymaster Built a Formidable Fleet That Challenged the Union Naval Power," HistoryNet, January 7, 2021, https://www.historynet.com/how-the-souths-European-spymaster-built-a-formidable-fleet-that-challenged-union-naval-power/.

8. "Dudley to W. H. Seward, October 4, 1862," in *Despatches from U.S. Consuls in Liverpool*, M141, roll, 22, NACP; "F. H. Morse to W. H. Seward, September 4, 1863 (No. 94)," in *Despatches from U.S. Consuls in London, England, 1790–1906*, National Archives Microfilm Publication T168, roll 32, RG 59, NACP.

9. "Dudley to W. H. Seward, October 3, 1863," in *Despatches from U.S. Consuls in Liverpool*, M141, roll 25, NACP.

10. Kevin J. Foster, "The Diplomats Who Sank a Fleet: The Confederacy's Undelivered European Fleet and the Union Consular Service," *Prologue Magazine* 33, no. 3 (Fall 2001); "Vessel nos. 294 & 295, *Scorpion & Wyvern*," in Laird Brothers, *Estimate Book* no. 2, 67–74, and *Contract Book* no. 2, 217, 246, 287, 288, 297 (Birkenhead, England: Cammel-Laird Archives).

11. Maurice Rigby, "'Dixie Traitor'—the Life and Times of Clarence Randolph Yonge, C.S.N.," *Crossfire* 48 (December 26, 2011), https://www.acwrt.org.uk/post/dixie-traitor-the-life-and-times-of-clarence-randolph-yonge-c-s-n.

12. James Dunwoody Bulloch, *The Secret Service of the Confederate States in Europe; or, How the Confederate Cruisers Were Equipped* (New York: Putnam, 1884), https://archive.org/details /secretserviceofc02bulluoft/page/36/mode/2up?q=coal; and "Bulloch to Capt. T. J. Page, February 14, 1865," in *Official Records of the Union and Confederate Navies in the War of the Rebellion*, series 1, vol. 3, *Operations of the Cruisers—Union, April 1, 1864, to December 30, 1865* (Washington, DC: Government Printing Office, 1896), 737–39; "Jackson to Frederick W. Seward, Asst. Secy. of State, March 1, 1865," in *ORN*, series 1, 3:737–39.

13. Bulloch, *The Secret Service of the Confederate States in Europe*, 12.

14. Bulloch, *The Secret Service of the Confederate States in Europe*, 12.

15. "Hampton Roads: *Monitor* vs. *Merrimack*," American Battlefield Trust, https://www .battlefields.org/learn/civil-war/battles/hampton-roads.

16. "The Civil War Sailor's Life," Civil War Home, http://www.civilwarhome.com /sailorlife.html.

CHAPTER 9: AN EMPEROR, A SPY, AND A POLITICIAN

1. "American Civil War Trail 1, Liverpool, England (A)," GPSMyCity, https://www .gpsmycity.com/audio/american-civil-war-trail-1-1516.html.

2. Thomas E. Sebrell, "Battlefields & Beyond: London, UK," HistoryNet, October 11, 2011, https://www.historynet.com/battlefieldsbeyond-london-uk/.

3. U.S. Naval War Records Office, *Official Records of the Union and Confederate Navies in the War of the Rebellion* (hereafter *ORN*), series 2, vol. 2, *Navy Department Correspondence, 1861–1865, with Agents Abroad* (Washington, DC: Government Printing Office, 1921), 11 (1861 Contents).

4. Kevin J. Foster, "The Diplomats Who Sank a Fleet: The Confederacy's Undelivered European Fleet and the Union Consular Service," *Prologue Magazine* 33, no. 3 (Fall 2001); "Vessel nos. 294 & 295, *Scorpion & Wyvern*," in Laird Brothers, *Estimate Book* no. 2, 67–74, and *Contract Book* no. 2, 217, 246, 287, 288, 297 (Birkenhead, England: Cammel-Laird Archives).

5. Heinrich Gustav Euler, "Napoleon III: Emperor of France," in *Encyclopedia Britannica Online*, https://www.britannica.com/biography/Napoleon-III-emperor-of-France/Domes tic-policy-as-emperor.

6. Euler, "Napoleon III."

7. Will Pearson and Erik Sass, *The Mental Floss History of the United States: The (Almost) Complete and (Entirely) Entertaining Story of America* (New York: HarperCollins, 2010); Miss Cellania, "The Confederacy's Plan to Conquer Latin America," Neatorama, https://www .neatorama.com/2011/01/06/the-confederacys-plan-to-conquer-latin-america/.

8. Raimondo Luraghi, *A History of the Confederate Navy* (Annapolis, MD: U.S. Naval Institute Press, 1996).

9. Mike Coppock, "How the South's European Spymaster Built a Formidable Fleet That Challenged the Union Naval Power," HistoryNet, January 7, 2021, https://www.historynet .com/how-the-souths-European-spymaster-built-a-formidable-fleet-that-challenged-union -naval-power/.

10. U.S. Naval War Records Office, *ORN*, series 2, 2:11 (1861 Contents).

11. Robert Taylor, "Richard William Curtis CSN," Immigrant Ships, https://immigrant ships.net/v15/pdf/curtis.pdf.

12. James Dunwoody Bulloch, *The Secret Service of the Confederate States in Europe; or, How the Confederate Cruisers Were Equipped* (New York: Putnam, 1884), https://archive.org/details

/secretserviceofc02bulluoft/page/36/mode/2up?q=coal; "Bulloch to Capt. T. J. Page, February 14, 1865," in *Official Records of the Union and Confederate Navies in the War of the Rebellion*, series 1, vol. 3, *Operations of the Cruisers—Union, April 1, 1864, to December 30, 1865* (Washington, DC: Government Printing Office, 1896), 737–39; "Jackson to Frederick W. Seward, Asst. Secy. of State, March 1, 1865," in *ORN*, series 1, 3:737–39.

13. Mike Coppock, "How the South's European Spymaster Built a Formidable Fleet That Challenged the Union Naval Power," HistoryNet, January 7, 2021, https://www.historynet .com/how-the-souths-European-spymaster-built-a-formidable-fleet-that-challenged-union -naval-power/.

14. "From Rebel to Samurai—the Epic Career of the Confederate Ironclad CSS *Stonewall*—Part 2," Dawlish Chronicles, https://dawlishchronicles.com/2019/12/06/the-rebel -ironclad-css-stonewall-part-2/; Bulloch, *The Secret Service of the Confederate States in Europe*.

15. "*Cheops*," Naval History and Heritage Command, https://www.history.navy.mil/con tent/history/nhhc/research/histories/ship-histories/confederate_ships/cheops.html.

16. David Keys, "Historians Reveal Secrets of UK Gun-Running Which Lengthened the American Civil War by Two Years," *Independent*, June 24, 2014.

17. "Liverpool's Abercromby Square and the Confederacy during the U.S. Civil War," Lowcountry Digital History Initiative, https://ldhi.library.cofc.edu/exhibits/show/liverpools -abercromby-square/abercromby-southern-club/embassy-confederacy.

18. "Liverpool's Abercromby Square and the Confederacy during the U.S. Civil War."

19. Chris Eger, "Guns of the (Confederate), 1863," Guns.com, February 2013, https:// www.guns.com/news/2013/02/23/guns-of-the-confederate-grunt-1863.

CHAPTER 10: PAPER WARSHIPS

1. Captain Vincent-Bréchignac de Balincourt, "The French Navy of Yesterday: Ironclad Frigates, Part IV," *F.P.D.S. Newsletter* 3, no. 4 (1975): 26–30.

2. Warren F. Spencer, *The Confederate Navy in Europe* (Tuscaloosa: University of Alabama Press, 1983), 287; and Jönköping N. Sweden, "Visingsö Oak Forest," Atlas Obscura, https:// www.atlasobscura.com/places/visingso-oak-forest.

3. "The Very Short Career of CSS *Stonewall*," in *Naval Encyclopedia*, https://naval-ency clopedia.com/industrial-era/1870-fleets/japan/kotetsu.php.

4. William B. Cushing, "The Destruction of the 'Albemarle,'" in *Battles and Leaders of the Civil War*, ed. Robert U. Johnson and Clarence C. Buel (New York: Thomas Yoseloff, 1956), 4:641, 4:634–40.

5. "Armstrong Gun," Military History, https://military-history.fandom.com/wiki/Arm strong_Gun.

6. "Ironclads and the Steel Navy," Weapons and Warfare, January 5, 2019, https://weap onsandwarfare.com/2019/01/05/ironclads-and-the-steel-navy/.

7. "The Bessemer Steel Process," ThoughtCo, https://www.thoughtco.com/bessemer -steel-process-definition-1773300.

8. "Stonewall Jackson (Ram)," Naval History and Heritage Command, https://www .history.navy.mil/content/history/nhhc/research/histories/ship-histories/confederate_ships /stonewall-jackson-ram.html; Aidan Dodson, *The Kaiser's Battlefleet: German Capital Ships 1871–1918* (Barnsley: Seaforth, 2016).

9. Dan Snow, "The Tragedy of HMS *Captain*," History Hit, February 15, 2023, https:// www.historyhit.com/the-tragedy-of-hms-captain/.

10. James Phinney Baxter, *The Introduction of the Ironclad Warship* (Cambridge, MA: Harvard University Press, 1946).

11. John W. Wallis, "The Confederate States Navy Sidewheel Ironclads," Civil War Talk, February 2016, https://civilwartalk.com/threads/the-confederate-navys-side-wheel -ironclads.122237/.

12. J. R. Potts, "Naval Warfare: CSS *Stonewall* (FS Sphynx)," Military Factory, https:// www.militaryfactory.com/ships/detail.php?ship_id=Sphynx-Stærkodder-Stonewall-Kotetsu -Ironclad.

13. "Horsepower," Energy Education, https://energyeducation.ca/encyclopedia/Horse power.

14. "The Very Short Career of CSS *Stonewall*."

15. "Boiler Explosion," Chemcom Europe, https://www.chemEurope.com/en/encyclo pedia/Boiler_explosion.html.

16. "Life at Sea," Penobscot Bay History, Penobscot Marine Museum, https://www.penob scotmarinemuseum.org/pbho-1/life-at-sea/crew; "The Civil War Sailor's Life," Civil War Home, http://www.civilwarhome.com/sailorlife.html.

17. John Fletcher Owen, *Treatise on the Construction and Manufacture of Ordnance in the British Service* (London: Her Majesty's Stationery Office, 1877).

18. Howard J. Fuller, *Clad in Iron: The American Civil War and the Challenge of British Naval Power* (London: Bloomsbury Academic, 2008).

19. Clarence Stewart Peterson, *Admiral John A. Dahlgren: Father of United States Naval Ordnance* (New York: Hobson Book Press, 1945).

20. Peterson, *Admiral John A. Dahlgren.*

21. "Armstrong: The Great Gunmaker," Victorian Forts and Artillery, https://victorian forts.co.uk/armstrong.htm.

22. "New Experiments with the Armstrong Gun," *New York Times*, July 23, 1862, 2.

23. Nicholas Rodger, *The Command of the Ocean: A Naval History of Britain 1649–1815* (New York: Penguin, 2004), 420.

24. Erich Gröner, *German Warships: 1815–1945*, vol. 1, *Major Surface Vessels* (Annapolis, MD: U.S. Naval Institute Press, 1990).

25. "DANFS: USS *Vesuvius* (1888)," Naval History and Heritage Command, https:// www.history.navy.mil/research/histories/ship-histories/danfs/v/vesuvius-iii.html; "*Vesuvius III* (Dynamite Gun Cruiser)," Naval History and Heritage Command, https://www.history .navy.mil/research/histories/ship-histories/danfs/v/vesuvius-iii.html.

26. "Evolution of the Confederate States Navy," American Civil War High Command, https://americancivilwarhighcommand.com/navies/evolution-of-the-confederate-states -navy/.

CHAPTER 11: A SECOND FLAG

1. Roger Price, *The French Second Empire: An Anatomy of Political Power* (Cambridge: Cambridge University Press, 2004), https://books.google.com.au/books?id=l0LMNRvWaLIC&pg =PA407&redir_esc=y#v=onepage&q&f=false.

2. "USS *Monitor*," *Wikipedia*, https://en.wikipedia.org/wiki/USS_Monitor.

3. Navy Department, *Dictionary of American Naval Fighting Ships* (Washington, DC: Office of the Chief of Naval Operations, 1963), 2:26, 2:202; "The Pirate 'Olinda,'" *Pacific Commercial Advertiser* (Honolulu, HI), May 27, 1865.

4. U.S. Naval War Records Office, *Official Records of the Union and Confederate Navies in the War of the Rebellion*, series 2, vol. 2, *Navy Department Correspondence, 1861–1865, with Agents Abroad* (Washington, DC: Government Printing Office, 1921), 11 (1861 Contents).

5. John William Jones, Robert Alonzo Brock, and James Power Smith, eds., *Southern Historical Society Papers* (Richmond, VA: Southern Historical Society; Virginia Historical Society, June 1879), 7:263, cited in Robert Long, "The CSS *Stonewall*—Ironclad Ship of War," Cape Fear Civil War Round Table, https://cfcwrt.org/The%20CSS%20Stonewall%20-%20 Ironclad%20Ship%20of%20War.pdf; Lee Kennett, "The Strange Career of the *Stonewall*," *U.S. Naval Institute Proceedings* 94, no. 2/780 (February 1968), https://www.usni.org/magazines /proceedings/1968/february/strange-career-stonewall.

6. James Dunwoody Bulloch, *The Secret Service of the Confederate States in Europe; or, How the Confederate Cruisers Were Equipped* (New York: Putnam, 1884), https://archive.org/details /secretserviceofc02bulluoft/page/36/mode/2up?q=coal; and "Bulloch to Capt. T. J. Page, February 14, 1865," in *Official Records of the Union and Confederate Navies in the War of the Rebellion* (hereafter *CRN*), series 1, vol. 3, *Operations of the Cruisers—Union, April 1, 1864, to December 30, 1865* (Washington, DC: Government Printing Office, 1896), 737–39; "Jackson to Frederick W. Seward, Asst. Secy. of State, March 1, 1865," in *ORN*, series 1, 3:737–39.

7. Bulloch, *The Secret Service of the Confederate States in Europe*.

8. "Edwin C. Eastman to W. H. Seward, September 27, 1864," Queenstown Consular Dispatches, in *ORN*, vol. 21, https://www.archives.gov/research/alic/reference/military /civil-war-navies-records.html#ser1; *ORN*, series 2, 2:627–28, 2:688–89, 2:790–91, 2:749.

9. Susan Morrison, "American Civil War: How Clyde Shipbuilders Helped Confederate Forces Run the Union Blockade," *Scotsman*, September 9, 2023, https://www.scotsman.com /news/opinion/columnists/american-civil-war-how-clyde-shipbuilders-helped-confederate -forces-run-the-union-blockade-susan-morrison-4285571/; Chris Jones, "Sailing Down the Clyde: 'Doon the Watter," Glasgow History, July 17, 2010, https://www.glasgowhistory .com/sailing-down-the-clyde-doon-the-watter.html.

10. Jones, Brock, and Smith, *Southern Historical Society Papers*, 7:263, cited in Long, "The CSS *Stonewall*"; Captain Thomas J. Page, CSN, "The Career of the Confederate Cruiser *Stonewall*," Internet Archive, https://archive.org/details/sim_southern-historical-so ciety-papers_1900_28_contents; https://archive.org/details/sim_southern-historical-society -papers_1879-05_7_5/page/210/mode/2up.

11. "Sir Frederick W. A. Bruce to the Earl of Clarendon, December 9, 1865," in *The Case of Great Britain* (repr., n.p.: Anatiposi Verlag, 2023), 2:819; Frank Merli, "A Missing Chapter in American Civil War Diplomacy: The Confederacy's Chinese Fleet, 1861–1867," in *Global Crossroads and the American Seas*, ed. Clark G. Reynolds (Missoula, MT: Pictorial Histories, 1988), 181–96.

12. Warren F. Spencer, *The Confederate Navy in Europe* (Tuscaloosa: University of Alabama Press, 1983).

13. Joseph R. Mitchell and David Stebenne, *New City upon a Hill: A History of Columbia, Maryland* (Cheltenham, UK: History Press, 2007), 23.

14. "Helicopter Denied: Inside the Confederacy's Weird Airplane Idea," National Interest, February 13, 2021, https://nationalinterest.org/blog/reboot/helicopter-denied-inside -confederacy%E2%80%99s-weird-airplane-idea-178249.

15. Lonnie R. Speer, "John Gilleland Developed a Revolutionary Double-Barreled Cannon Meant to Sweep Union Infantry off the Field," *American's Civil War*, September 1997, 26, 28.

16. "10 Strange Civil War Weapons," Listverse, May 2, 2013https://listverse.com/2013/05/02/10-strange-civil-war-weapons/.

17. "Civil War Naval Events from 1861 to 1865," Civil War Timeline, https://www.civilwartimeline.net/military-naval-actions.php.

18. "Balloons in the Civil War: Head-Tilting History," American Battlefield Trust, March 12, 2019, updated April 13, 2021, https://www.battlefields.org/learn/head-tilting-history/balloons-civil-war#:~:text=%20Balloons%20in%20the%20Civil%20War%20%201,Congress.%20Balloons%20aren%27t%20known%20for%20their...%20More%20.

19. Robert F. Reilly, "Medical and Surgical Care during the American Civil War, 1861–1865," National Library of Medicine and National Institutes of Health, https://www.ncbi.nlm.nih.gov/pmc/articles/PMC4790547/.

20. Edwyn Gray, *Nineteenth-Century Torpedoes and Their Inventors* (Annapolis, MD: US Naval Institute Press, 2004); Benson Lossing, *The Pictorial Field-Book of the War of 1812* (New York: Harper, 1868), 240–43, 693.

CHAPTER 12: FROM PRESIDENT TO KING

1. "Schleswig-Holstein Question," in *Encyclopedia Britannica Online*, https://www.britannica.com/event/Schleswig-Holstein-question.

2. "German-Danish War: European History," in *Encyclopedia Britannica Online*, https://www.britannica.com/event/German-Danish-War.

3. Jan Schlürmann, "The Schleswig-Holstein Rebellion," Danish Military History, https://web.archive.org/web/20120320024806/http://www.milhist.dk/trearskrigen/outbreak/outbreak_uk.htm.

4. "2nd Schleswig War (1864): Triumph at Sea—but Total Defeat on Land," Danish Naval History, https://www.navalhistory.dk/English/History/1848_1864/TheNavy1864.htm.

5. Roger Chesneau and Eugene M. Kolesnik, eds., *Conway's All the World's Fighting Ships, 1860–1905* (New York: Mayflower Books, 1979).

6. Robert Steen Steensen, "Vore Panserskibe" [Our Armoured Vessels] (Copenhagen: Marinehistorisk Selskab, 1968), 178–95.

7. "1st Schleswig War (1848–50): The War Where the Navy Again Became the Leading Light—and the Ray of Comfort—for Denmark," Danish Naval History, https://www.navalhistory.dk/English/History/1848_1864/TheWars1848_50.htm#:~:text=1st%20Schleswig%20war%20%281848%20%E2%80%93%2050%29%3A%20The%20War,total%20blockade%20of%20the%20north%20German%20coastal%20harbors.

8. "2nd Schleswig War (1864)."

9. *Tidsskrift for Søvæsen* (1939), 192; cited in "The Armoured Ram *Stærkodder*," Dansk Militaeerhistorie, 2013, https://milhist.dk/the-armoured-ram-Stærkodder/.

10. Saxo Grammaticus, *The Nine Books of the Danish History of Saxo Grammaticus*, trans. Oliver Elton (1894; repr., n.p.: Leopold Classic Library, 2016).

11. *Tidsskrift for Søvæsen*, 192.

12. "War in the North Sea, 1864—the Battle of Heligoland," Dawlish Chronicles, https://dawlishchronicles.com/.

13. *Tidsskrift for Søvæsen*, 192.

14. "2nd Schleswig War (1864)."

15. "Civil War Diplomacy—Confederate Agents in Washington and Europe," American Foreign Relations, https://www.americanforeignrelations.com/A-D/Civil-War-Diplomacy-Confederate-agents-in-washington-and-europe.html.

16. Hayden Chakra, "German Unification—the Danish Prussian War of 1864," About History, September 2021, https://about-history.com/german-unification-the-danish-prussian-war-of-1864/.

17. *Tidsskrift for Søvæsen*, 192.

18. John W. Wallis, "The Confederate States Navy Sidewheel Ironclads," February 2016, Civil War Talk, https://civilwartalk.com/threads/the-confederate-navys-side-wheel-ironclads.122237/.

19. Christopher Klein, "The Final Confederate Surrender, 150 Years Ago," History Network, June 11, 2015, updated January 9, 2018, https://www.history.com/news/the-final-confederate-surrender-150-years-ago.

20. *Tidsskrift for Søvæsen*, 192.

21. *Tidsskrift for Søvæsen*, 192.

22. *Tidsskrift for Søvæsen*, 192.

23. *Tidsskrift for Søvæsen*, 192; and Warren F. Spencer, *The Confederate Navy in Europe* (Tuscaloosa: University of Alabama Press, 1923).

24. *Tidsskrift for Søvæsen*, 192.

25. Bo Bramsen, *The House of Glücksburg: The Father-in-Law of Europe and His Descendants* (in Danish), 2nd ed. (Copenhagen: Forlaget Forum, 1992).

26. "Otto Von Bizmark," A–Z Quotes, https://www.azquotes.com/author/1426-Otto_von_Bismarck.

CHAPTER 13: *CHEOPS*

1. "Stonewall Jackson (Ram)," Naval History and Heritage Command, https://www.history.navy.mil/content/history/nhhc/research/histories/ship-histories/confederate_ships/stonewall-jackson-ram.html; Aidan Dodson, *The Kaiser's Battlefleet: German Capital Ships 1871–1918* (Barnsley: Seaforth, 2016).

2. Erich Gröner, *German Warships: 1815–1945*, vol. 1, *Major Surface Vessels* (Annapolis, MD: U.S. Naval Institute Press, 1990); "C.S.S. *Stonewall*," 290 Foundation, https://sites.google.com/site/290foundation/history/c-s-s-stonewall.

3. H. M. Hozier, *The Seven Weeks' War: The Austro-Prussian Conflict of 1866* (London: Macmillan, 1867).

4. Lawrence Sondhaus, *Preparing for Weltpolitik: German Sea Power before the Tirpitz Era* (Annapolis, MD: U.S. Naval Institute Press, 1997), 83–84; cited in "SMS *Prinz Adalbert*," Wikipedia, https://en.wikipedia.org/wiki/SMS_Prinz_Adalbert_(1865); Dodson, *The Kaiser's Battlefleet*.

5. "1st Schleswig War (1848–50): The War Where the Navy Again Became the Leading Light—and the Ray of Comfort—for Denmark," Danish Naval History, https://www.navalhistory.dk/English/History/1848_1864/TheWars1848_50.htm#:~:text=1st%20Schleswig%20war%20%281848%20%E2%80%93%2050%29%3A%20The%20War,total%20blockade%20of%20the%20north%20German%20coastal%20harbors.

6. Sondhaus, *Preparing for Weltpolitik*, 83–84; cited in "SMS *Prinz Adalbert*"; Dodson, *The Kaiser's Battlefleet*.

7. Dodson, *The Kaiser's Battlefleet*.

CHAPTER 14: OF THE AMPHIBIAN KIND

1. "Black Soldiers in the U.S. Military during the Civil War," US National Archives, https://www.archives.gov/education/lessons/blacks-civil-war.

2. Will Pearson and Erik Sass, *The Mental Floss History of the United States: The (Almost) Complete and (Entirely) Entertaining Story of America* (New York: HarperCollins, 2010).

3. "Civil War Timeline," National Park Service; National Military Park Pennsylvania, https://www.nps.gov/gett/learn/historyculture/civil-war-timeline.htm.

4. Neil P. Chatelain, "A Series of International Incidents: The Transatlantic Odyssey of the Confederate Ironclad *Stonewall*," *Traversea* 5, no. 1 (2015).

5. John Bigelow, *France and the Confederate Navy, 1862–1868* (New York: Harper, 1888), 60; John R. Thompson, "Extracts from the Diary of John R. Thompson," *Lippincott's Monthly Magazine* 42 (1888): 701.

6. John William Jones, Robert Alonzo Brock, and James Power Smith, eds., *Southern Historical Society Papers* (Richmond, VA: Southern Historical Society; Virginia Historical Society, June 1879), 7:263, cited in Robert Long, "The CSS *Stonewall*—Ironclad Ship of War," Cape Fear Civil War Round Table, https://cfcwrt.org/The%20CSS%20Stonewall%20-%20 Ironclad%20Ship%20of%20War.pdf; Captain Thomas J. Page, CSN, "The Career of the Confederate Cruiser *Stonewall*," Internet Archive, https://archive.org/details/sim_southern -historical-society-papers_1900_28_contents; https://archive.org/details/sim_southern-histor ical-society-papers_1879-05_7_5/page/210/mode/2up.

7. Page, "The Career of the Confederate Cruiser *Stonewall*."

8. "States during the Civil War," "Confederate States in 1863," and "The American Annual Cyclopaedia and Register of Important Events of the Year, 1861–1865," in *Civil War Encyclopedia*, vols. 3 and 5 (New York: Appleton, 1868).

9. George C. Rable, *The Confederate Republic: A Revolution against Politics* (Chapel Hill: University of North Carolina Press, 1994).

10. Bigelow, *France and the Confederate Navy*, 60; Thompson, "Extracts from the Diary of John R. Thompson," 701.

11. "Scots and the American Civil War: So Whose Side Were We On?," *Scotsman*, April 11, 2011, https://www.scotsman.com/arts-and-culture/scots-and-american-civil-war-so-whose -side-were-we-1679768.

12. Jim Murphy, *The Boys' War: Confederate and Union Soldiers Talk about the Civil War* (New York: Clarion, 1990).

13. *Nautical Research Journal* 26–27 (1948–1996); "Confederate States Navy Officers M1860 Cutlass," Land and Sea Collection, https://landandseacollection.com/id1172.html.

14. "Evolution of the Confederate States Navy," American Civil War High Command, https://americancivilwarhighcommand.com/navies/evolution-of-the-confederate-states -navy/.

15. Robert Taylor, "Richard William Curtis CSN," Immigrant Ships, https://immigrant ships.net/v15/pdf/curtis.pdf.

16. William B. Gould IV, *Diary of a Contraband: The Civil War Passage of a Black Sailor* (Stanford, CA: Stanford University Press, 2002).

17. "Liverpool and the American Civil War," Liverpool Museums, https://www.liverpool museums.org.uk/american-civil-war/liverpool-and-american-civil-war.

18. CPI Inflation Calculator (website), https://www.in2013dollars.com/us/inflation /1860?amount=12; Edward Young, "Special Report on Immigration," "Factory Labour," "Cotton Mills," and "Special Report on Labor" (Washington, DC: Government Printing Office, 1871). For "Special Report on Immigration," see HathiTrust, https://babel.hathitrust .org/cgi/pt?id=nyp.33433007982816&seq=244.

19. Warren F. Spencer, *The Confederate Navy in Europe* (Tuscaloosa: University of Alabama Press, 1983).

20. "Officers Table: Register of Officers of the Confederate States Navy 1861–1865," compiled and revised by the U.S. Office of Naval Records and Library of the United States Navy Department, from all available data (Washington, DC: Government Printing Office, 1931), https://civilwarnavy.com/wp-content/uploads/2020/04/Register-of-Officers-of-the -Confederate-Sates-Navy.pdf.

21. "Samuel Barron," in *The American Cyclopaedia*, ed. George Ripley and Charles A. Dana, vol. 10 (New York: Appleton, 1873); Naval Academy Register, Nimitz Library, Trireme Special Collections and Archives; "George A. Borchert," U.S. Naval Academy Virtual Memorial Hall, https://usnamemorialhall.org/index.php/GEORGE_A._BORCHERT.

22. "Life at Sea," Penobscot Bay History; Penobscot Marine Museum, https://www.pe nobscotmarinemuseum.org/pbho-1/life-at-sea/crew.

23. "Confederate Military History—1899—Volume 12.djvu/116," Wikisource, https:// en.wikisource.org/wiki/Index:Confederate_Military_History_-_1899_-_Volume_12.djvu; "The Confederate Cruisers," Patriot Files, Library of Congress Veterans History Project, https://web.archive.org/web/20150601050711/http://www.patriotfiles.com/index.php?name =Sections&req=viewarticle&artid=7594&page=1.

24. Navy Department, *Dictionary of American Naval Fighting Ships*, vol. 2 (Washington, DC: Office of the Chief of Naval Operations, 1963), 26.

25. "HMS *Warrior* 1860," HMS Warrior Preservation Trust, 2015, http://www.hms warrior.org/history/armament#:~:text=The%20Admiralty%20opted%20for%20these%20 relatively%20untried%20breech,50%20seconds.%20One%20innovation%20was%20the%20 barrel%27s%20rifling.

26. W. Modell, "Hazards of New Drugs: The Scientific Approach Is Necessary for the Safest and Most Effective Use of New Drugs," National Library of Medicine, PubMed, https:// pubmed.ncbi.nlm.nih.gov/17757905/#:~:text=Oliver%20Wendell%20Holmes%20(14)%20 said,it%20would%20be%20even%20worse; Robert F. Reilly, "Medical and Surgical Care during the American Civil War, 1861–1865," National Library of Medicine and National Institutes of Health, https://www.ncbi.nlm.nih.gov/pmc/articles/PMC4790547/.

27. Jack L. Dickinson, comp., "Marshall Digital Scholar: C.S.S. *Alabama*: An Illustrated History," part 2, "Officers and Crew," Marshall University, Library Special Collections, October 10, 2017, https://mds.marshall.edu/cgi/viewcontent.cgi?article=1001&context=css_al. Gary McQuarrie and Neil P. Chatelain, "Confederate Shipyards," *Civil War Navy Magazine*, https://civilwarnavy.com/confederate-shipyards/, citing William N. Still Jr., *Confederate Shipbuilding* (Athens: University of Georgia Press, 1996) and William N. Still Jr., ed., *The Confederate Navy: The Ships, Men and Organization, 1861–65* (London: Conway Maritime Press, 1997). William Param Brooks, *Personal Steam Logs of W. P. Brooks, 1st Assistant Engineer C.S.N.*, digitized from the collection of the Virginia Museum of History & Culture; Virginia Historical Society.

28. "Letter to Robert Bontine Cunninghame Graham," quoted in *Joseph Conrad: A Biography*, by Jeffrey Meyers (New York: Scribner, 1991), 166.

29. Naval History and Heritage Command, *Living Conditions in the 19th-Century U.S. Navy* (Washington, DC: Navy Department, March 17, 1869, repr., November 2017).

30. Martha M. Boltz, "Physician's Deadly Plan to Sicken Yankees Foiled," *Washington Times*, December 31, 2005; Edward Steers, *Blood on the Moon: The Assassination of Abraham Lincoln* (Lexington: University Press of Kentucky, 2005).

31. Mitch Williamson, "The Frigate I," Weapons and Warfare, June 2, 2020, https:// weaponsandwarfare.com/2020/06/02/the-frigate-i/.

32. John Nevins, "Black Americans in the Confederate Navy and Marine Corps," Civil War, https://www.navyandmarine.org/ondeck/1862blackCSN.htm.

33. "Civil War Timeline."

34. *Journals and Papers of the Virginia State Convention* (Virginia State Convention, 1861), 3:117.

35. Ray Davidson, "Tucker's Confederate Marine Brigade," *Early County News*, February 10, 2010, https://www.earlycountynews.com/articles/tuckers-confederate-marine-brigade/; "A Brief Naval Chronology of the Civil War (1861–65)," Naval History and Heritage Command, https://www.history.navy.mil/content/history/nhhc/research/library/online-reading-room/title-list-alphabetically/n/navy-civil-war-chronology.html.

36. "The Civil War Sailor's Life," Civil War Home, http://www.civilwarhome.com/sailorlife.html.

37. "The Confederate Navy," Mine Creek Battlefield, February 25, 2022, https://www.minecreek.info/shoulder-straps/the-confederate-navy.html.

38. Mike Coppock, "How the South's European Spymaster Built a Formidable Fleet That Challenged the Union Naval Power," HistoryNet, January 7, 2021, https://www.historynet.com/how-the-souths-European-spymaster-built-a-formidable-fleet-that-challenged-union-naval-power/.

CHAPTER 15: FOR THAT IS MUSIC

1. "Page, Thomas Jefferson," Worldcat, https://www.worldcat.org/search?q=au%3APage%2C+Thomas+Jefferson%2C&qt=hot_author; "Lived Exciting Life; Thomas J. Page Who Recently Passed Away," Civil War Talk, https://civilwartalk.com/threads/page-thomas-jefferson.180765/.

2. "The Confederate Navy (CSS)," in *Naval Encyclopedia*, https://naval-encyclopedia.com/industrial-era/confederate-navy-1861-65.php.

3. "Captain Thomas Jefferson Page," in *Southern Historical Society Papers*, vol. 27, ed. John William Jones, Robert Alonzo Brock, and James Power Smith (Richmond, VA: Southern Historical Society; Virginia Historical Society, 1899), 219.

4. Captain C. W. Read, "Reminiscences of the Confederate States Navy," Civil War Talk, September 18, 2011, https://civilwartalk.com/threads/reminiscences-of-the-confederate-states-navy.26950/.

5. U.S. Naval War Records Office, *Official Records of the Union and Confederate Navies in the War of the Rebellion*, series 2, vol. 1 (Washington, DC: Government Printing Office, 1894), https://babel.hathitrust.org/cgi/pt?id=coo.31924051367062&view=1up&seq=421&q1=page.

6. "The Civil War, Regulations for the Navy of the Confederate States, 1862," Navy and Marine Organization, https://www.navyandmarine.org/ondeck/1862CSN_Regulations.htm.

7. John William Jones, Robert Alonzo Brock, and James Power Smith, eds., *Southern Historical Society Papers* (Richmond VA: Southern Historical Society; Virginia Historical Society, June 1878), 7:263; Captain Thomas J. Page, CSN, "The Career of the Confederate Cruiser *Stonewall*," Internet Archive, https://archive.org/details/sim_southern-historical-society-papers_1900_28_contents; https://archive.org/details/sim_southern-historical-society-papers_1879-05_7_5/page/210/mode/2up.

8. Page, "The Career of the Confederate Cruiser *Stonewall*."

9. "*Water Witch I* (Str)," Naval History and Heritage Command, October 21, 2015, https://www.history.navy.mil/content/history/nhhc/research/histories/ship-histories/danfs/w/water-witch-i.html.

10. Mark Corriston, "The Paraguay Expedition," Emporia State University, December 1983, accessed January 5, 2020, https://dspacep01.emporia.edu/handle/123456789/2051?show=full.

11. Thomas O. Flickema, "The Settlement of the Paraguayan-American Controversy of 1859: A Reappraisal," *The Americas* 25, no. 1 (July 1968): 59–69.

12. Gene Allen Smith and Larry Bartlett, "'A Most Unprovoked, Unwarranted and Dastardly Attack': James Buchanan, Paraguay, and the *Water Witch* Incident of 1855," *Northern Mariner / Le Marin du Nord* 19, no. 3 (2009).

13. Thomas Jefferson Page, *La Plata, the Argentine Confederation and Paraguay: Narrative of the Exploration of the Tributaries of the River La Plata during the years 1853, '54, '55, and '56 under the Orders of the United States Government* (New York: Harper, 1859).

14. Joel Haas, "185—America's War with Paraguay," War with Paraguay, June 28, 2021, https://warwithparaguay.blogspot.com/2021/06/1858-americas-war-with-paraguay.html.

15. Smith and Bartlett, "'A Most Unprovoked, Unwarranted and Dastardly Attack.'"

16. *The Ruin of the Democratic Party: Reports of the Covode and Other Committees* (Washington, DC: Republican Congressional Committee, 1860), Internet Archive, accessed December 28, 2019, https://archive.org/details/ruinofdemocratic01repu.

17. Mike Coppock, "How the South's European Spymaster Built a Formidable Fleet That Challenged the Union Naval Power," HistoryNet, January 7, 2021, https://www.historynet.com/how-the-souths-European-spymaster-built-a-formidable-fleet-that-challenged-union-naval-power/.

18. Neil P. Chatelain, "A Series of International Incidents: The Transatlantic Odyssey of the Confederate Ironclad *Stonewall*," *Traversea* 5, no. 1 (2015).

19. Frank Lawrence Owsley Jr., *The C.S.S. Florida: Her Building and Operations* (Tuscaloosa: University of Alabama Press, 1987).

20. *Sacramento Daily Union* 39, no. 6032, July 30, 1870, UCR Center for Bibliographical Studies and Research, California Digital Newspaper Collection.

21. Lawrence Sondhaus, *Naval Warfare 1815–1914* (New York: Routledge, 2001).

22. Harrie Webster, "Personal Experiences on a Monitor at the Battle of Mobile Bay," California Commandery, Military Order of the Loyal Legion of the United States War Papers, no. 14 (1894), 12.

23. Raimondo Luraghi, *A History of the Confederate Navy* (Annapolis, MD: Naval Institute Press, 1996).

24. "Letter to Horace Greeley, Washington, August 22, 1862," Abraham Lincoln Online, https://www.abrahamlincolnonline.org/lincoln/speeches/greeley.htm.

25. "A Brief Naval Chronology of the Civil War (1861–65)," Naval History and Heritage Command, https://www.history.navy.mil/content/history/nhhc/research/library/online-reading-room/title-list-alphabetically/n/navy-civil-war-chronology.html.

26. Mike Coppock, "The Unsinkable CSS *Stonewall*," *Sea Classics* 43, no. 6 (June 2010): 42–45, 58.

27. Chatelain, "A Series of International Incidents."

28. Lee Kennett, "The Strange Career of the Stonewall," *US Naval Institute Proceedings* 94, no. 2/780 (February 1968), https://www.usni.org/magazines/proceedings/1968/february/strange-career-stonewall.

29. James Dunwoody Bulloch, *The Secret Service of the Confederate States in Europe; or, How the Confederate Cruisers Were Equipped* (New York: Putnam, 1884), https://archive.org/details/secretserviceofc02bulluoft/page/36/mode/2up?q=coal; "Bulloch to Capt. T. J. Page, February 14, 1865," in *Official Records of the Union and Confederate Navies in the War of the Rebellion*

(hereafter *ORN*), series 2, vol. 2, *Operations of the Cruisers* (Washington, DC: Government Printing Office, 1896), 737–39; "Jackson to Frederick W. Seward, Asst. Secy. of State, March 1, 1865," in *ORN*, series 1, 3:737–39; Bulloch to Baron, 9 January 1865, Whittle Papers, folder II, no 36. Davidson to Bulloch, 6th February 1865, ORN, 1, 3 732–33.

30. Warren F. Spencer, *The Confederate Navy in Europe* (Tuscaloosa: University of Alabama Press, 1983); J. Thomas Scharf, *History of the Confederate States Navy: From Its Organization to the Surrender of the Last Vessel* (New York: Rogers & Sherwood, 1887).

31. Michael Martin, "What Led to Stonewall Jackson's Unusual Quirks?," Abbeville Institute Press, October 26, 2023, https://www.abbevilleinstitute.org/what-led-to-stonewall -jacksons-unusual-quirks/.

32. Kenneth Hall, *Stonewall Jackson and Religious Faith in Military Command* (Jefferson, NC: McFarland, 2005); "Stonewall Jackson," AZQuotes, https://www.azquotes.com /author/7283-Stonewall_Jackson; "Life at Sea," Penobscot Bay History; Penobscot Marine Museum, https://www.penobscotmarinemuseum.org/pbho-1/life-at-sea/crew,

33. Hall, *Stonewall Jackson and Religious Faith in Military Command*; and "Stonewall Jackson," AZQuotes, https://www.azquotes.com/author/7283-Stonewall_Jackson.

34. "Civil War Timeline," National Park Service; National Military Park Pennsylvania, https://www.nps.gov/gett/learn/historyculture/civil-war-timeline.htm.

35. "From the Richmond, Va., *Times*, April 15 and 22, 1894, 'What It Accomplished during the War. As read by Mr. Virginius Newton in the Company of General R. E. Lee," in *Southern Historical Society Papers*, vol. 22, *January–December*, ed. John William Jones, Robert Alonzo Brock, and James Power Smith (Richmond, VA: Southern Historical Society; Virginia Historical Society, 1894).

36. "What It Accomplished during the War."

37. Jones, Brock, and Smith, *Southern Historical Society Papers*, 7:263.

38. Navy Department, *Dictionary of American Naval Fighting Ships* (Washington, DC: Office of the Chief of Naval Operations, Naval History Division, 1959), https://www.history.navy .mil/research/histories/ship-histories/danfs.html; "Confederate Navy, 1861–65," in *Naval Encyclopedia*, https://naval-encyclopedia.com/industrial-era/confederate-navy-1861-65.php.

39. Tony Gibbons, *The Complete Encyclopedia of Battleships and Battlecruisers: A Technical Directory of All the World's Capital Ships from 1860 to the Present Day* (Ladysmith, BC: Salamander Books, 1983).

40. Sondhaus, *Naval Warfare 1815–1914*.

41. Navy Department, *Dictionary of American Naval Fighting Ships* (Washington, DC: Office of the Chief of Naval Operations, 1963), 2:26, 2:202; "The Pirate *Olinda*," *Pacific Commercial Advertiser* (Honolulu, HI), May 27, 1865.

42. "Reconstructing the Story of Humanity's Past," Ancient Origins, updated January 2, 2022, https://www.researchgate.net/publication/352296896_Ancient_OriginsR_Recon structing_The_Story_of_Humanity's_Past_Petroglyphic_Features_of_Portable_Rock_Art; "The American Civil War and the Battle of Shiloh's Glowing Wounds Mystery," Ancient Origins, https://www.ancient-origins.net/history-important-events/battle-of-shiloh-0016253.

43. Timothy B. Smith, "'Lick 'em to-morrow, though': First Day at the Battle of Shiloh," HistoryNet, January 2017, https://www.historynet.com/lick-em-to-morrow-though -first-day-at-the-battle-of-shiloh/.

44. Ulysses S. Grant, "Struck by a Bullet—Precipitate Retreat of the Confederates— Intrenchments at Shiloh—General Buell—General Johnston—Remarks on Shiloh," in *The Personal Memoirs of Ulysses S. Grant*, ed. John F. Marszalek (Cambridge, MA: Harvard University Press, 2017), 241–52, https://www.jstor.org/stable/j.ctvgd319.

45. Coppock, "How the South's European Spymaster Built a Formidable Fleet."

46. "The Civil War Sailor's Life," Civil War Home, http://www.civilwarhome.com/sailorlife.html.

47. Edward Stokes Miller, *Civil War Sea Battles* (New York: Combined Books, 1995).

48. "Barron's Instruction to Page, 17th December, 1864," in *ORN*, series 1, 3:719–20; "Bulloch's Letter to Barron, 1st February, 1865," Whittle Papers, folder 2, no. 38, cited 286.

49. Jones, Brock, and Smith, *Southern Historical Society Papers*, vol. 7.

50. Jones, Brock, and Smith, *Southern Historical Society Papers*, vol. 7.

51. Coppock, "The Unsinkable CSS *Stonewall*," 42–45, 58.

52. James M. McPherson, *Battle Cry of Freedom* (New York: Oxford University Press, 1988); Miles Brucker, "Historical Facts about the American Civil War," Factinate, https://www.factinate.com/things/56-facts-civil-war/.

53. James M. McPherson, "America's 'Wicked War,'" *New York Review of Book,*, February 7, 2013, citing Amy S. Greenberg, *A Wicked War: Polk, Clay, Lincoln, and the 1846 US Invasion of Mexico* (New York: Knopf, 2012).

54. "Washington, DC, during the Civil War," American Battlefield Trust, June 17, 2020, updated February 21, 2024, https://www.battlefields.org/learn/articles/washington-dc-during-civil-war.

55. "Barron's Instruction to Page, 17th December, 1864," in *ORN*, series 1, 3:719–20; "Bulloch's Letter to Barron, 1st February, 1865."

56. "*The Dallas Herald*, 1849–1873," Chronicling America (Library of Congress), https://www.loc.gov/item/sn84022278/.

57. "10–16th February," in *ORN*, series 1, 3:735–41; "9th February through 19th March 1865," Whittle Papers, folder 2, no. 38, cited 286.

58. Jones, Brock, and Smith, *Southern Historical Society Papers*, vol. 7.

59. Jones, Brock, and Smith, *Southern Historical Society Papers*, vol. 7.

60. Page, "The Career of the Confederate Cruiser *Stonewall*."

61. Page, "The Career of the Confederate Cruiser *Stonewall*."

62. Jones, Brock, and Smith, *Southern Historical Society Papers*, vol. 7.

63. Andrew Lambert, *The Alabama Affair: The British Shipyards and the American Civil War* (London: Constable, 1989).

64. Lambert, *The Alabama Affair: The British Shipyards and the American Civil War.*

65. Jones, Brock, and Smith, *Southern Historical Society Papers*, vol. 7.

66. Bulloch, *The Secret Service of the Confederate States in Europe*; Tom H. Wells, *The Confederate Navy: A Study in Organization* (Tuscaloosa: University of Alabama Press, 1971), 136; Raimondo Luraghi, *A History of the Confederate Navy* (Annapolis, MD: U.S. Naval Institute Press, 1996).

67. Alfred Roman, *The Military Operations of General Beauregard in the War between the States, 1861 to 1865: Including a Brief Personal Sketch and a Narrative of His Services in the War with Mexico, 1846–8* (New York: Harper, 1884), https://archive.org/details/militaryoperati04roma goog/mode/2up?q=india.

68. William B. Gould IV, *Diary of a Contraband: The Civil War Passage of a Black Sailor* (Stanford, CA: Stanford University Press, 2002).

69. Jones, Brock, and Smith, *Southern Historical Society Papers*, vol. 7.

CHAPTER 16: THE HUNT BEGINS

1. John C Widerman, *Naval Warfare: Courage and Combat on the Water* (New York: Metro Books, 1997); "First Voyage of the United States Steamship *Niagara*, April 24th–May 13th, 1857," History of the Atlantic Cable & Undersea Communications, https://atlantic-cable .com/Cableships/Niagara/index.htm.

2. John Bigelow, *France and the Confederate Navy, 1862–1868* (New York: Harper, 1888), 59.

3. "Letter from Horatio J. Perry to William Seward, February 7, 1865," in *Official Records of the Union and Confederate Navies in the War of the Rebellion* (hereafter *ORN*), series 1, vol 3, *Operations of the Cruisers—Union, April 1, 1864, to December 30, 1865* (Washington, DC: Government Printing Office, 1896), 416.

4. John Bigelow, *Retrospections of an Active Life* (New York, Doubleday, Page, 1909–1913), 452.

5. William B. Gould IV, *Diary of a Contraband: The Civil War Passage of a Black Sailor* (Stanford, CA: Stanford University Press, 2002).

6. Widerman, *Naval Warfare*; "First Voyage of the United States Steamship Niagara; April 24th–May 13th, 1857."

7. Lee Kennett, "The Strange Career of the *Stonewall*," *U.S. Naval Institute Proceedings* 94, no. 2/780 (February 1968): 79–81.

8. James H. Marsh, "HMS *Shannon* versus USS *Chesapeake*, War of 1812," in *The Canadian Encyclopedia*, October 30, 2014, https://www.thecanadianencyclopedia.ca/en/article /hms-shannon-versus-uss-chesapeake-war-of-1812.

9. "Scots and the American Civil War: So Whose Side Were We On?," *Scotsman*, April 11, 2011, https://www.scotsman.com/arts-and-culture/scots-and-american-civil-war-so -whose-side-were-we-1679768.

10. John William Jones, Robert Alonzo Brock, and James Power Smith, eds., *Southern Historical Society Papers* (Richmond, VA: Southern Historical Society; Virginia Historical Society, June 1879), 7:263. Captain Thomas J. Page, CSN, "The Career of the Confederate Cruiser *Stonewall*," Internet Archive, https://archive.org/details/sim_southern-historical-so ciety-papers_1900_28_contents; https://archive.org/details/sim_southern-historical-society -papers_1879-05_7_5/page/210/mode/2up.

11. Jones, Brock, and Smith, *Southern Historical Society Papers*, vol. 7.

12. Jones, Brock, and Smith, *Southern Historical Society Papers*, vol. 7.

13. U.S. Naval War Records Office, *ORN*, series 2, vol. 1 (Washington, DC: Government Printing Office, 1894), https://babel.hathitrust.org/cgi/pt?id=coo.31924051367062&view =1up&seq=421&q1=page.

14. Horatio J. Perry, *Memorial of Horatio J. Perry* (Boston: Little, Brown, 1886).

15. "Letter from Vice Consul Wilding to Horatio J. Perry, February 7, 1865," in *ORN*, series 2, vol. 1 (Washington, DC: Government Printing Office, 1894).

16. Jones, Brock, and Smith, *Southern Historical Society Papers*, vol. 7.

17. R. S. Crenshaw, "Autobiographic Sketch of Thomas Jefferson Page," *U.S. Naval Institute Proceedings*, October 1923, 1682.

18. Jones, Brock, and Smith, *Southern Historical Society Papers*, vol. 7.

19. "William Benjamin Gould Diary, 1865," MHS Online, https://www.masshist.org /database/viewer.php?item_id=681&img_step=1&pid=3&nodesc=1&br=1&mode=transcript #page1; Gould, *Diary of a Contraband*.

20. "William Benjamin Gould Diary, 1865."

21. "William Benjamin Gould Diary, 1865"; Gould, *Diary of a Contraband*.

22. William Param Brooks, *Personal Steam Logs of W. P. Brooks, 1st Assistant Engineer C.S.N.*, digitized from the collection of the Virginia Museum of History & Culture, Virginia Historical Society.

23. Crenshaw, "Autobiographic Sketch of Thomas Jefferson Page," 1682.

24. Jones, Brock, and Smith, *Southern Historical Society Papers*, vol. 7.

25. Crenshaw, "Autobiographic Sketch of Thomas Jefferson Page," 1682.

26. Crenshaw, "Autobiographic Sketch of Thomas Jefferson Page," 1682.

27. "Dictionary of American Naval Fighting Ships," Naval History and Heritage Command, https://www.history.navy.mil/research/histories/ship-histories/danfs.html; https://naval-encyclopedia.com/industrial-era/confederate-navy-1861-65.php.

28. Crenshaw, "Autobiographic Sketch of Thomas Jefferson Page," 1682.

29. "Page to Bulloch, March 25th, 1865," in Jones, Brock, and Smith, *Southern Historical Society Papers*, 7:742; 7:785.

30. Gould, *Diary of a Contraband*.

31. Page, "The Career of the Confederate Cruiser *Stonewall*.

32. Page, "The Career of the Confederate Cruiser *Stonewall*.

33. Page, "The Career of the Confederate Cruiser *Stonewall*.

34. Jones, Brock, and Smith, *Southern Historical Society Papers*, vol. 7.

35. Jones, Brock, and Smith, *Southern Historical Society Papers*, vol. 7.

36. Neil P. Chatelain, "When Portugal Bombarded a U.S. Warship to Protect a Confederate Ironclad!," Emerging Civil War, January 17, 2024, https://emergingcivilwar.com/2024/01/17/when-portugal-bombarded-a-u-s-warship-to-protect-a-confederate-ironclad/.

37. "William Benjamin Gould Diary, 1865."

38. Page, "The Career of the Confederate Cruiser *Stonewall*.

39. Jones, Brock, and Smith, *Southern Historical Society Papers*, vol. 7.

40. Crenshaw, "Autobiographic Sketch of Thomas Jefferson Page," 1682.

41. "Thomas Craven Court-Martial Document, November 7, 1865," U.S. Naval War College Archives, file—box 4, folder 20

42. "Thomas Craven Court-Martial Document, November 7, 1865."

43. "Thomas Craven Court-Martial Document, November 7, 1865."

44. "Craven, Thomas Tingey," in *Appleton's Cyclopædia of American Biography*, ed. J. G. Wilson and J. Fiske (New York: Appleton, 1900).

45. Perry, *Memorial of Horatio J. Perry*.

CHAPTER 17: IF THE THING IS PRESSED

1. William Param Brooks, *Personal Steam Logs of W. P. Brooks, 1st Assistant Engineer C.S.N.*, digitized from the collection of the Virginia Museum of History & Culture; Virginia Historical Society.

2. "Young to W. H. Seward, Apr. 20, 1864," in *Despatches from U.S. Consuls in Belfast, 1796–1906*, National Archives Microfilm Publication T368, roll 4.

3. Stephen R. Wise, *Lifeline of the Confederacy: Blockade Running during the Civil War* (Columbia: University of South Carolina Press, 1988), 218–19; Amanda Foreman, *A World on Fire: An Epic History of Two Nations Divided* (London: Penguin, 2011), 764–65, 787.

4. Lee Kennett, "The Strange Career of the *Stonewall*," *U.S. Naval Institute Proceedings* 94, no. 2/780 (February 1968); https://www.usni.org/magazines/proceedings/1968/february/strange-career-stonewall.

5. Neil P. Chatelain, "A Series of International Incidents: The Transatlantic Odyssey of the Confederate Ironclad *Stonewall*," *Traversea* 5, no. 1 (2015).

6. Captain Thomas J. Page, CSN, "The Career of the Confederate Cruiser *Stonewall*," Internet Archive, https://archive.org/details/sim_southern-historical-society-papers_1900_28 _contents; https://archive.org/details/sim_southern-historical-society-papers_1879-05_7_5 /page/210/mode/2up.

7. John William Jones, Robert Alonzo Brock, and James Power Smith, eds., *Southern Historical Society Papers* (Richmond, VA: Southern Historical Society; Virginia Historical Society, June 1879), 7:263; Page, "The Career of the Confederate Cruiser *Stonewall*."

8. "Confederate States Army Casualties: Lists and Narrative Reports, 1861–1865," Microfilm Publication M836, 7 rolls, ARC ID: 653994, Records of the Adjutant and Inspector General's Department, War Department Collection of Confederate Records, Record Group 109, National Archives, Washington, DC.

9. James M. Merrill, *From the Fresh-Water Navy: 1861–1864: The Letters of Acting Master's Mate Henry R. Browne and Acting Ensign Symmes E. Browne*, ed. John D. Milligan (Annapolis, MD: U.S. Naval Institute Press, 1970), https://academic.oup.com/jah/article-abstract/58/4 /1020/760705?redirectedFrom=fulltext.

10. "'There Isn't Even Danger Enough to Give Us Any Glory': U.S. Navy and Marine Casualties in the Civil War, Part 1," National Museum of Civil War Medicine, May 19, 2021, https://www.civilwarmed.org/navy-marine-casualties/.

11. Jim Murphy, *The Boys' War: Confederate and Union Soldiers Talk about the Civil War* (New York: Clarion, 1990).

12. Naval History and Heritage Command, *Living Conditions in the 19th-Century U.S. Navy* (Washington, DC: Navy Department, March 17, 1869, repr., November 2017).

13. *Nautical Research Journal* 26–27 (1980).

14. J. Thomas Scharf, *History of the Confederate States Navy: From Its Organization to the Surrender of Its Last Vessel* (New York: Rogers & Sherwood, 1887), https://www.civilwarphilatel icsociety.org/wp-content/uploads/2019/07/Res-Book-Hist-CSA-Navy.pdf209.

15. Mike Coppock, "How the South's European Spymaster Built a Formidable Fleet That Challenged the Union Naval Power," HistoryNet, January 7, 2021, https://www.historynet .com/how-the-souths-European-spymaster-built-a-formidable-fleet-that-challenged-union -naval-power/.

16. Scharf, *History of the Confederate States Navy*.

17. "9th February through 19th March 1865," in *Official Records of the Union and Confederate Navies in the War of the Rebellion* (hereafter *ORN*), series 1, vol. 3, *Operations of the Cruisers— Union, April 1, 1864, to December 30, 1865* (Washington, DC: Government Printing Office, 1896), 735–41.

18. "Thomas E. Sebrell II: Britain's Involvement in the US Civil War," History News Network, October 28, 2010, https://www.historynewsnetwork.org/article/thomas-e-sebrell -ii-britains-involvement-in-the-us.

19. "Confederate States of America. Navy. Emma Henry. ca. 1862–5/11/1865; Other Names: Department of the Navy. Wasp (Sidewheel steamer). 6/13/1865–1876," National Archives Catalog, https://catalog.archives.gov/id/10589081.

20. Navy Department, *Dictionary of American Naval Fighting Ships* (Washington, DC: Office of the Chief of Naval Operations, 1963), 2:26.

21. Lawrence Sondhaus, *Naval Warfare 1815–1914* (New York: Routledge, 2001).

22. "The Daybook: Civil War Navy Special Edition-Technology," Hampton Roads Naval Museum, https://www.history.navy.mil/content/dam/nhhc/browse-by-topic/War%20 and%20Conflict/civil-war/cwsetech.pdf.

23. Wise, *Lifeline of the Confederacy*, 218–19.

24. "William Benjamin Gould Diary, 1865," MHS Online, https://www.masshist.org /database/viewer.php?item_id=681&img_step=1&pid=3&nodesc=1&br=1&mode=transcript #page1; William B. Gould IV, *Diary of a Contraband: The Civil War Passage of a Black Sailor* (Stanford, CA: Stanford University Press, 2002).

25. Brooks, *Personal Steam Logs*.

26. Texas State Historical Association, "A Digital Gateway to Texan History," *Southwestern Historical Quarterly*, July 2013, https://web.archive.org/web/20131224084205/http://www .tshaonline.org/shqonline/apager.php?vol=021.

27. "Sailor's Creek," American Battlefield Trust, https://www.battlefields.org/learn/civil -war/battles/sailors-creek; "Abraham Lincoln," A–Z Quotes, https://www.azquotes.com /author/8880-Abraham_Lincoln.

28. "10 Facts: Sailor's Creek, April 6th, 1865," American Battlefield Trust, https://www .battlefields.org/learn/articles/10-facts-sailors-creek.

29. "A Brief Naval Chronology of the Civil War (1861–65)," Naval History and Heritage Command, https://www.history.navy.mil/content/history/nhhc/research/library/online -reading-room/title-list-alphabetically/n/navy-civil-war-chronology.html.

30. Paul Martin, "Lincoln's Missing Bodyguard: What Happened to Officer John Parker, the Man Who Chose the Wrong Night to Leave His Post at Ford's Theatre?," *Smithsonian Magazine*, April 7, 2010, https://www.smithsonianmag.com/history/lincolns-missing-body guard-12932069/.

31. Martin, "Lincoln's Missing Bodyguard."

32. Wilfred Knight, *Red Fox: Stand Watie's Civil War Years* (Glendale, CA: Clark, 1988).

33. Page, "The Career of the Confederate Cruiser *Stonewall*."

34. Page, "The Career of the Confederate Cruiser *Stonewall*."

35. Page, "The Career of the Confederate Cruiser *Stonewall*."

36. William Watson, *The Adventures of a Blockade Runner* (London: Unwin, 1892).

37. "William Ronckendorff Papers," Archivegrid, New York Public Library, https:// archives.nypl.org/mss/2617.

38. "The War Is Over: But Not for the Navy," Hampton Roads Naval Museum, May 7, 2015, http://civilwarnavy150.blogspot.com/2015/05/the-war-is-over-but-not-for-navy.html.

39. Page, "The Career of the Confederate Cruiser *Stonewall*."

40. Jones, Brock, and Smith, *Southern Historical Society Papers*, vol. 7.

41. Jones, Brock, and Smith, *Southern Historical Society Papers*, vol. 7.

42. Jones, Brock, and Smith, *Southern Historical Society Papers*, vol. 7.

43. James Dunwoody Bulloch, *The Secret Service of the Confederate States in Europe; or, How the Confederate Cruisers Were Equipped* (New York: Putnam, 1884), https://archive.org/details /secretserviceofc02bulluoft/page/36/mode/2up?q=coal; "Bulloch to Capt. T. J. Page, February 14, 1865," in *ORN*, series 1, 3:737–39; "Jackson to Frederick W. Seward, Asst. Secy. of State, March 1, 1865."

44. Jones, Brock, and Smith, *Southern Historical Society Papers*, vol. 7.

45. Bulloch, *The Secret Service of the Confederate States in Europe*.

46. "The *Stonewall*," *Bradford Reporter* (Towanda, PA), June 1, 1865.

47. "William Ronckendorff Papers."

48. Philip Van Doren Stern, *The Confederate Navy: The Ships, Men and Organization, 1861–65* (New York: Doubleday, 1962).

49. "Camp Sumter / Andersonville Prison," National Parks Service, https://www.nps.gov/ande/learn/historyculture/camp_sumter.htm.

CHAPTER 18: AFTERMATH

1. "Civil War Casualties: The Cost of War: Killed, Wounded, Captured, and Missing," American Battlefield Trust, https://www.battlefields.org/learn/articles/civil-war-casualties.

2. Steve Wiegand, "Life in the South after the Civil War," Dummies, March 2016, https://www.dummies.com/article/academics-the-arts/history/american/life-in-the-south-after-the-civil-war-151521/; and "Sharecropping," in *Gale Encyclopedia of U.S. Economic History*, ed. Thomas Carson and Mary Bonk (Farmington Hills, MI: Gale, 2000), 2:912–13.

3. "Historical Facts about the American Civil War," Factinate, https://www.factinate.com/things/56-facts-civil-war/.

4. "Ku Klux Klan Hate Organization, United States," in *Encyclopedia Britannica Online*, August 2022, https://www.britannica.com/topic/Ku-Klux-Klan.

5. Richard H. Pildes, "Democracy, Anti-Democracy, and the Canon," *Constitutional Commentary* 17, no. 2 (2000): 12, 27.

6. James Dunwoody Bulloch, *The Secret Service of the Confederate States in Europe; or, How the Confederate Cruisers Were Equipped* (New York: Putnam, 1884), https://archive.org/details/secretserviceofc02bulluoft/page/36/mode/2up?q=coal; and "Bulloch to Capt. T. J. Page, February 14, 1865," in *Official Records of the Union and Confederate Navies in the War of the Rebellion* (hereafter cited as *ORN*), series 1, vol. 3, *Operations of the Cruisers—Union, April 1, 1864, to December 30, 1865* (Washington, DC: Government Printing Office, 1896), 737–739; "Jackson to Frederick W. Seward, Asst. Secy. of State, March 1, 1865."

7. "A Brief Naval Chronology of the Civil War (1861–65)," Naval History and Heritage Command, https://www.history.navy.mil/content/history/nhhc/research/library/online-reading-room/title-list-alphabetically/n/navy-civil-war-chronology.html.

8. Alan M. Tigay, "The Deepest South," *American Heritage* 49, no. 2 (April 1998): 84–95.

9. Andrew F. Rolle, *The Lost Cause: The Confederate Exodus to Mexico* (Norman: University of Oklahoma Press, 1965).

10. "The Royal Navy's Size throughout History," Historic UK, https://www.historic-uk.com/Blog/British-Navy-Size-Over-Time/.

11. James M. McPherson, *War on the Waters: The Union and Confederate Navies, 1861–65* (Chapel Hill: University of North Carolina Press, 2012), 222–23.

12. 3 Cour d'Appel de Paris, 3–5; John Bigelow, *France and the Confederate Navy, 1862–1868* (New York: Harper, 1888), 91.

13. "W. H. Seward to Adams, no. 421, December 8, 1862," in *Southern Historical Society Papers*, vol. 1, ed. John William Jones, Robert Alonzo Brock, and James Power Smith (Richmond, VA: Southern Historical Society; Virginia Historical Society, 1876).

14. Thomas Sheppard, "Matthew C. Perry's Forgotten Successor," *Naval History Magazine* 36, no. 2 (April 2022), https://www.usni.org/magazines/naval-history-magazine/2022/april/matthew-c-perrys-forgotten-successor.

15. David Keys, "Historians Reveal Secrets of UK Gun-Running Which Lengthened the American Civil War by Two Years," *Independent*, June 24, 2014.

16. Glyndon G. Van Deusen, *William Henry Seward: Lincoln's Secretary of State, The Negotiator of the Alaska Purchase* (Oxford: Oxford University Press, 1967), 497–505; Doris W. Dashew,

"The Story of an Illusion: The Plan to Trade the Alabama Claims for Canada," *Civil War History* 15 (December 1969): 332–48; Frank W. Hackett, *The Geneva Award Acts* (1882), v.

17. Taru Spiegel, "Under Six Flags: The Curious Career of the CSS *Stonewall*," *Library of Congress Blogs*, June 14, 2019, https://blogs.loc.gov/international-collections/2019/06/under -six-flags-the-curious-career-of-the-css-stonewall/.

18. Maurice Rigby, "An English Romance: William Param Brooks, Confederate States Navy," *Crossfire* 54 (August 1997), https://www.acwrt.org.uk/post/an-english-romance -william-param-brooks-confederate-states-navy.

19. Register of Officers of the Confederate States Navy, *Officers of the Confederate States Navy*. (Washington, DC: Government Printing Office, 1898); "Samuel Barron," in *The American Cyclopaedia*, vol. 10, ed. George Ripley and Charles A. Dana (New York: Appleton, 1873); "George A. Borchert," Naval Academy Register, https://usnamemorialhall.org/index .php/GEORGE_A._BORCHERT.

20. "Samuel Barron" and "George A. Borchert," in Ripley and Dana, *American Cyclopaedia*.

21. Robert Taylor, QSM, "Richard William Curtis CS Navy," *Bugle* 28 (November/December 2010), http://www.acwrtq.net/uploads/The%20Bugle%2028.pdf.

22. "Richard William Curtis," Friends of Toowong Cemetery, https://www.fotc.au /research/richard-william-curtis/.

23. Charles Lee Lewis, *Matthew Fontaine Maury: The Pathfinder of the Seas* (Annapolis, MD: U.S. Naval Institute, 1927).

24. Terry Hulsey, "Confederates in Mexico," Abbeville Institute, July 24, 2018, https:// www.abbevilleinstitute.org/confederates-in-mexico/.

25. "Maximilian," in *Encyclopedia Britannica*, February 2019, https://www.britannica.com /biography/Maximilian-archduke-of-Austria-and-emperor-of-Mexico.

26. William B. Gould IV, *Diary of a Contraband: The Civil War Passage of a Black Sailor* (Stanford, CA: Stanford University Press, 2002); Lee D. Bacon, "Civil War and Later Navy Personnel Records at the National Archives, 1861–1924," *Prologue Magazine* 27, no. 2 (Summer 1995), https://www.archives.gov/publications/prologue/1995/summer/navy -records-1861-1924.html.

27. "Stephen Mallory," National Parks Service, https://www.nps.gov/people/stephen -mallory.htm.

28. John Ericsson, in a letter flagging the sales of his caloric engine (1860), Abe Books, https://www.abebooks.com/John-Ericsson-inventor-USS-Monitor-discusses/30136872673 /bd.

29. Olav Thulesius, *The Man Who Made the Monitor: A Biography of John Ericsson, Naval Engineer* (Jefferson, NC: McFarland, 2007).

30. "Union and USN Monitors," Weapons and Warfare, https://weaponsandwarfare .com/2017/04/08/union-and-usn-monitors/.

31. "John Ericsson," USS *Monitor*, https://monitor.noaa.gov/150th/ericsson.html.

32. "Page, Thomas Jefferson," Worldcat, https://www.worldcat.org/search?q=au%3APage %2C+Thomas+Jefferson%2C&qt=hot_author.

33. "Thomas Jefferson Page," Find a Grave, https://www.findagrave.com/memorial/160 861974/thomas-jefferson_page.

34. Heinrich Gustav Euler, "Napoleon III: Emperor of France," in *Encyclopedia Britannica Online*, https://www.britannica.com/biography/Napoleon-III-emperor-of-France/Domes tic-policy-as-emperor.

35. Walter E. Wilson and Gary L. McKay, *James D. Bulloch; Secret Agent and Mastermind of the Confederate Navy* (Jefferson, NC: McFarland, 2012).

36. Beckles Wilson, *John Slidell and the Confederates in Paris: 1862–65* (Minton: Balch, 1932), https://archive.org/details/johnslidell0000unse/page/n7/mode/2up.

37. C. de Saint Hubert, "Builders, Engine Builders, and Designers of Armored Vessels Built in France 1855–1940," *F.P.D.S. Newsletter* 14, no. 3 (1986): 2–8.

38. Avi Selk, "Why Jefferson Davis Was Loathed in the Confederacy He Led," *Washington Post*, December 8, 2018, https://www.washingtonpost.com/history/2018/12/08/why-jeffer son-davis-was-loathed-confederacy-he-led/; "Jefferson Davis's Scots Host Was a Remarkable Character in His Own Right," *Herald Scotland*, September 6, 2012.

39. William Param Brooks, *Personal Steam Logs of W. P. Brooks, 1st Assistant Engineer C.S.N.*, digitized from the collection of the Virginia Museum of History & Culture, Virginia Historical Society.

40. Navy Department, *Dictionary of American Naval Fighting Ships* (Washington, DC: Office of the Chief of Naval Operations, 1963), 2:26, 2:202; "The Pirate *Olinda*," *Pacific Commercial Advertiser* (Honolulu, HI), May 27, 1865.

41. "Confederate Military History—1899—Volume 12.djvu/116," Patriot Files, http://www.patriotfiles.com/index.php?name=Sections&req=viewarticle&artid=7594&page=1395.

42. "Gideon Welles Papers, 1777–1911," Manuscript Division, Library of Congress, https://hdl.loc.gov/loc.mss/eadmss.ms003053.

43. "Bureau of the Public Debt: The 19th Century," Bureau of the Public Debt, https://web.archive.org/web/20141009002141/http://www.publicdebt.treas.gov/history/1800.htm.

44. "Could the South Have Won the Civil War?," History on the Net, Salem Media, January 28, 2023, https://www.historyonthenet.com/could-the-south-have-won-the-civil-war.

45. "Robert E. Lee," "Philip Alexander Bruce," and "Chapter X, Siege of Petersburg and Appomattox," Lee Family Digital Archive, https://leefamilyarchive.org/reference/books/.

46. "S. R. Mallory, Secretary of the Navy, to Captain James D. Bulloch and Lieutenant North," in *Official Records of the Union and Confederate Navies in the War of the Rebellion*, series 2, vol. 2, *Navy Department Correspondence, 1861–1865, with Agents Abroad* (Washington, DC: Government Printing Office, 1921).

47. Albert L. Demaree, "Our Navy's Worst Headache: The *Merrimack*," *U.S. Naval Institute Proceedings* 88, no. 3/709 (March 1962), https://www.usni.org/magazines/proceedings/1962/march/our-navys-worst-headache-merrimack.

48. Roger Chesneau and Eugene M. Kolesnik, eds., *Conway's All the World's Fighting Ships, 1860–1905* (New York: Mayflower Books, 1979).

49. "American Civil War Ironclads," Weapons and Warfare, May 17, 2020, https://weap onsandwarfare.com/2020/05/17/american-civil-war-ironclads/.

50. "*Huáscar*," in *Naval Encyclopedia*, https://naval-encyclopedia.com/industrial-era/chile/huascar-1865.php.

51. McPherson, *War on the Waters*, 84–85.

52. J. Thomas Scharf, *History of the Confederate States Navy: From Its Organization to the Surrender of the Last Vessel* (New York: Rogers & Sherwood, 1887).

53. "A Brief Naval Chronology of the Civil War (1861–65)."

54. James Dunwoody Bulloch, *The Secret Service of the Confederate States in Europe; or, How the Confederate Cruisers Were Equipped* (New York: Putnam, 1884), https://archive.org/details/secretserviceofc02bulluoft/page/36/mode/2up?q=coal; and "Bulloch to Capt. T. J. Page,

February 14, 1865," in *ORN*, series 1, 3:737–39; "Jackson to Frederick W. Seward, Asst. Secy. of State, March 1, 1865."

55. Citing U.S. Steamer Sacramento Watch, Quarter & Station Bills, 1866–1917 (bulk 1866–1867), MS 72 held by Special Collections & Archives, Nimitz Library at the United States Naval Academy.

56. Arnold A. Putnam, "The Building of Numbers 294 & 295: The Laird Rams," in *Warship 1999–2000*, ed. Antony Preston (London: Conway Maritime Press, 1999).

CHAPTER 19: WAR-TORN MAPS

1. Kallie Szczepanski, "Overview of the Tokugawa Shogunate of Japan," ThoughtCo, updated June 21, 2019, https://www.thoughtco.com/tokugawa-shoguns-of-japan-195578.

2. Jonathan Clements, *A Brief History of Japan: Samurai, Shogun and Zen: The Extraordinary Story of the Land of the Rising Sun* (Rutland, VT: Tuttle, 2017).

3. Arimichi Ebisawa, "Oda Nobunaga," in *Encyclopedia Britannica*, last updated May 7, 2024, https://www.britannica.com/biography/Oda-Nobunaga.

4. Stephen R. Turnbull, *Samurai Invasion: Japan's Korean War, 1592–98* (New York: Cassell, 2002), https://books.google.com.au/books?id=ABJ-QgAACAAJ&redir_esc=y.

5. Luís Fróis, *Historia de Japan* (in Portuguese) (Lisbon: Biblioteca Nacional Portugal, 1976), https://books.google.com.au/books?id=kMZXav_pL7YC&redir_esc=y.

6. Mark Cartwright, "Oda Nobunaga," World History, June 2019, https://www.worldhistory.org/Oda_Nobunaga/.

7. "Oda Nobunaga," Samurai Archives, archived from the original on June 6, 2017, accessed April 16, 2013, https://samurai-archives.com/wiki/Oda_Nobunaga.

8. "Admiral Yi Sun-shin—Military Hero and God of War," Antique Alive, https://www.antiquealive.com/Blogs/Admiral_Yi_Sun_Shin.html and 1; John Richard Hale, *Famous Sea Fights from Salamis to Tsu-Shima* (Boston: Little, Brown, 1911).

9. Mark Cartwright, "The Japanese Invasion of Korea, 1592–8 CE," in *World History Encyclopedia*, https://www.worldhistory.org/article/1398/the-japanese-invasion-of-korea-1592-8-ce/.

10. Kallie Szczepanski, "The Boshin War of 1868 to 1869," ThoughtCo, updated October 31, 2019, https://www.thoughtco.com/the-boshin-war-in-japan-195568.

11. Stephen R. Turnbull, *The Samurai: A Military History* (New York: Routledge, 1996), 260.

12. "Admiral Yi Sun-shin—Military Hero and God of War"; Hale, *Famous Sea Fights from Salamis to Tsu-Shima*.

13. Tadachika Kuwata, "Toyotomi Hideyoshi," in *Encyclopedia Britannica Online*, https://www.britannica.com/biography/Toyotomi-Hideyoshi.

14. Conrad D. Tolman, "Tokugawa Ieyasu: Shogun of Japan," *Encyclopedia Britannica Online*, https://www.britannica.com/biography/Tokugawa-Ieyasu.

15. A. L. Sadler, *The Maker of Modern Japan: The Life of Tokugawa Ieyasu* (London: Allen and Unwin, 1937; repr., Rutland, VT: Tuttle, 1978).

16. Anthony Bryant, *Sekigahara 1600: The Final Struggle for Power*, Osprey Campaign Series 40 (Oxford: Osprey, 1995).

CHAPTER 20: BLACK SHIPS AND BARBARIANS

1. Andrew Gordon, *A Modern History of Japan: From Tokugawa Times to the Present* (New York: Oxford University Press, 2014).

2. Mark Cartwright, "Oda Nobunaga," World History, June 2019, https://www.world history.org/Oda_Nobunaga/.

3. A. L. Sadler, *The Maker of Modern Japan: The Life of Tokugawa Ieyasu* (London: Allen and Unwin, 1937; repr., Rutland, VT: Tuttle, 1978), 164.

4. Anthony Bryant, *Sekigahara 1600: The Final Struggle for Power*, Osprey Campaign Series 40 (Oxford: Osprey, 1995).

5. Sadler, *The Maker of Modern Japan*, 164.

6. "Japanese Warship *San Buena Ventura*," Primidi, https://www.primidi.com/japanese _warship_san_buena_ventura.

7. Hiromi Rogers, *Anjin—the Life and Times of Samurai William Adams, 1564–1620* (Amsterdam: Amsterdam University Press, 2016), 121.

8. Stephen R. Turnbull, *The Samurai: A Military History* (New York: Routledge, 1996), 260.

9. Naoko Sajima and Kyochi Tachikawa, *Japanese Sea Power: A Maritime Nation's Struggle for Identity*, Foundations of International Thinking on Sea Power 2 (Canberra: Sea Power Centre, Royal Australian Navy, 2009).

10. Noell Wilson, "Tokugawa Defense Redux: Organizational Failure in the Phaeton Incident of 1808," *Journal of Japanese Studies* 36, no. 1 (2009): 1–32, https://www.doi.org /10.1353/jjs.0.0131.

11. Sadler, *The Maker of Modern Japan*.

12. "Bakumatsu & Meiji Era Ships," in *Naval Encyclopedia*, https://naval-encyclopedia .com/industrial-era/bakumatsu-meiji-era-ships.ph2.

13. Navy Department, *Dictionary of American Naval Fighting Ships* (Washington, DC: Office of the Chief of Naval Operations, 1963), 2:26.

14. Kenneth E. Shewmaker, "Forging the 'Great Chain': Daniel Webster and the Origins of American Foreign Policy toward East Asia and the Pacific, 1841–1852," *Proceedings of the American Philosophical Society* 129 (September 1985): 225–59.

15. Hsuan L. Hsu, "Personality, Race, and Geopolitics in Joseph Heco's *Narrative of a Japanese*," *Biography* 29, no. 2 (Spring 2006).

16. W. G. Beasley, *The Japanese Experience: A Short History of Japan* (Oakland: University of California Press, 1999); Warrick L. Barrett, "Charles Lennox Richardson," Find a Grave, https://www.findagrave.com/memorial/9682763/charles-lennox-richardson.

17. "Sakamoto Ryoma and Nakaoka Shintaro: Very Different, Yet Very Similar," Samurai Revolution, October 4, 2015, http://www.samurai-revolution.com/sakamoto-ryoma-and -nakaoka-shintaro-very-different-yet-very-similar/.

18. Ken Yamaguchi, *Kinsé shiriaku: A History of Japan, from the First Visit of Commodore Perry in 1853 to the Capture of Hakodate by the Mikado's Forces in 1869*, trans. Ernest Mason Satow (Yokohama: Wetmore, 1876).

19. "The Treaty of Kanagawa," National Archives, March 7, 2017, https://www.archives .gov/exhibits/featured-documents/treaty-of-kanagawa.

20. National Institute of Information and Communications Technology (NICT), trans., "Tokugawa Iesada," Japanese Wiki, https://www.japanesewiki.com/person/Iesada%20 TOKUGAWA.html.

21. National Institute of Information and Communications Technology (NICT), trans., "Tokugawa Iesada," citing "Ansei Kiji" by Chiso Naito.

22. "The United States and the Opening of Japan, 1853," Office of the Historian, https:// history.state.gov/milestones/1830-1860/opening-to-japan.

23. John Denney, *Respect and Consideration: Britain in Japan 1853–1868 and Beyond* (Leicester: Radiance Press, 2011); Mako Taniguchi, *Kiri-sute Gomen* (Tokyo: Yamakawa Shuppansha, 2005).

24. "Bakumatsu & Meiji Era Ships."

25. Ō-Edo Rekishi Hyakka, "Great Earthquakes of Ansei" (Ansei Daijishin), in *Historical Encyclopedia of Great Edo* (Tokyo: Yamakawa Shuppansha, 1989), 253.

26. "Under Six Flags: The Intriguing Saga of the CSS *Stonewall*, the Confederate Ironclad That Helped Forge an Empire," From Small Causes Great Events, August 25, 2020, https://fromsmallcausesgreatevents.org//2020/08/25/under-six-flags-the-intriguing-saga-of-the-css-stonewall-the-confederate-ironclad-that-helped-forge-an-empire/.

27. Jonathan Clements, *A Brief History of Japan: Samurai, Shogun and Zen: The Extraordinary Story of the Land of the Rising Sun* (Rutland, VT: Tuttle, 2017); Conrad Totman, *The Collapse of the Tokugawa Bakufu, 1862–1868* (Honolulu: University of Hawai'i Press, 1980).

28. National Institute of Information and Communications Technology (NICT), trans., "Tokugawa Iemochi: The Life and Times of the 14th Shogun," Tokugawa Memorial Foundation, 2007, https://www.japanesewiki.com/person/Iemochi%20TOKUGAWA.html.

29. National Institute of Information and Communications Technology (NICT), trans., "Tokugawa Iemochi," Japanese Wiki, https://www.japanesewiki.com/history/Saccho%20Domei%20(Satsuma-Choshu%20Alliance).html.

30. "Gossip about the Strangers," *New York Times*, May 17, 1860; Dallas Finn, "Guests of the Nation: The Japanese Delegation to the Buchanan White House," *White House History* 12 (Winter 2003): 24–25.

31. F. W. Seal, "Oda Nobunaga," Samurai Archives, https://web.archive.org/web/20170606234308/http://www.samurai-archives.com/nobunaga.html#2.

32. M. G. Haynes, "Samurai Invasion: Japan's 1609 Conquest of Ryukyu," HistoryNet, August 13, 2022, https://www.historynet.com/japan-invasion-of-ryukyu/.

33. William McOmie, *The Opening of Japan, 1853–1855* (Folkestone, UK: Global Oriental, 2006), 138.

34. Navy Department, *Dictionary of American Naval Fighting Ships* (Washington, DC: Office of the Chief of Naval Operations, 1963), 2:26.

35. A. J. Watts, "Japan," in *Conway's All the World's Fighting Ships 1860–1905*, ed. Roger Chesneau and Eugene M. Kolesnik (New York: Mayflower Books, 1979), 216–39.

36. Kōichi Hagiwara, *Illustrated Life of Saigō Takamori and Okubo Toshimichi* (in Japanese) (Tokyo: Kawade Shobō Shinsya, 2004), 34.

37. Jorge Álvarez, "Saigō Takamori: The True Story of the Last Samurai," *LBV Magazine* (English ed.), January 3, 2021, https://www.labrujulaverde.com/en/2021/01/Saigō-takamori-the-true-story-of-the-last-samurai/.

38. Samuel J. Cox, "H-063-3: The Battle of Shimonoseki Strait, Japan, 1863," Naval History and Heritage Command, July 2021, https://www.history.navy.mil/about-us/leadership/director/directors-corner/h-grams/h-gram-063/h-063-3.html.

39. John Bishop, *The Last Shogun: The Life of Tokugawa Iemochi* (Tokyo: Aozora, 2010).

40. Elijah Palmer, "Unexpected Enemies in the Civil War: The Japanese (Part One)," Hampton Roads Naval Museum, October 26, 2015, https://hamptonroadsnavalmuseum.blogspot.com/2015/10/unexpected-enemies-in-civil-war.html.

CHAPTER 21: THE BATTLE OF SHIMONOSEKI STRAIT

1. Bayard Taylor, "Preface Map," in *Japan: In Our Day* (New York: Scribner, Armstrong, 1872).

2. Elijah Palmer, "Unexpected Enemies in the Civil War: The Japanese (Part One)," Hampton Roads Naval Museum, October 26, 2015, https://hamptonroadsnavalmuseum .blogspot.com/2015/10/unexpected-enemies-in-civil-war.html.

3. George Alexander Ballard, *The Influence of the Sea on the Political History of Japan* (Boston: Dutton, 1921).

4. Edward J. Marolda, "The Washington Navy Yard: An Illustrated History," Naval Historical Center, August 22, 2019, https://www.history.navy.mil/content/dam/nhhc/research /publications/Publication-PDF/WashingtonNavyYard.pdf.

5. Ballard, *The Influence of the Sea on the Political History of Japan*.

6. Samuel J. Cox, "H-063-3: The Battle of Shimonoseki Strait, Japan, 1863," Naval History and Heritage Command, July 2021, https://www.history.navy.mil/about-us/leadership /director/directors-corner/h-grams/h-gram-063/h-063-3.html.

7. Lieutenant Commander Thomas J. Cutler, "Lest We Forget: The Forgotten Battle of Shimonoseki Straits," *U.S. Naval Institute Proceedings* 145, no. 1 (January 2019): 391; Jon Guttman, "Showdown at Shimonoseki Strait," HistoryNet, August 1, 2017, https://www .historynet.com/showdown-shimonoseki-strait/.

8. David Howath, *A Brief History of British Sea Power: How Britain Became Sovereign of the Seas* (London: Robinson, 1974).

9. William Loney, RN, citing "1863–1864 Anglo-Japanese Hostilities," *The Times*, 1864, https://archive.org/details/illustratedlondov42lond/page/n3/mode/2up?q=1863; W. Laird Clowes, *The Royal Navy: A History from Earliest Times to the Present*, vol. 1 (London: Sampson, Low, Marston, 1897), https://web.archive.org/web/20120306090243/http://www.pdavis .nl/Japan.htm.

10. W. G. Beasley, *The Japanese Experience: A Short History of Japan* (Oakland: University of California Press, 1999); Warrick L. Barrett, "Charles Lennox Richardson," Find a Grave, https://www.findagrave.com/memorial/9682763/charles-lennox-richardson.

11. Sidney DeVere Brown, "Nagasaki in the Meiji Restoration: Chōshū Loyalists and British Arms Merchants," University of Wisconsin, accessed January 25, 2009, https://www .uwosh.edu/faculty_staff/earns/meiji.html.

12. "Mito Rebellion," Japan Reference, September 19, 2012, https://jref.com/articles /mito-rebellion.178/.

13. National Institute of Information and Communications Technology (NICT), trans., "Bakumatsu," Japanese Wiki, https://www.japanesewiki.com/history/Bakumatsu.html.

14. Nihon Rekishi-gakkai, ed., *Meiji Ishin Jinmei Jiten* (Tokyo: Yoshikawa Kobunkan, 1981), n.p.

15. A. L. Sadler, *The Maker of Modern Japan: The Life of Tokugawa Ieyasu* (London: Allen and Unwin, 1937; repr., Rutland, VT: Tuttle, 1978), 164.

16. "Kinmon Incident," Infogalactic, https://infogalactic.com/info/Kinmon_Incident.

17. "Kyoto History Facts and Timeline," World Guides, http://www.world-guides.com /asia/japan/kansai/kyoto/kyoto_history.html.

18. Loney, citing "1863–1864 Anglo-Japanese Hostilities."

CHAPTER 22: THE SECOND BATTLE OF SHIMONOSEKI STRAIT

1. Samuel J. Cox, "H-063-3: The Battle of Shimonoseki Strait, Japan, 1863," Naval History and Heritage Command, July 2021, https://www.history.navy.mil/about-us/leadership/director/directors-corner/h-grams/h-gram-063/h-063-3.html.

2. Joseph Heco, *The Narrative of a Japanese: What He Has Seen and the People He Has Met in the Course of the Last Forty Years*, vol. 1 (San Francisco, CA: American-Japanese Publishing Association, 1895), https://archive.org/details/narrativeofjapan02hecoiala/mode/2up?q=stonewall.

3. Heco, *The Narrative of a Japanese*.

4. "H-Gram 062: "Battles That You've Never Heard Of, Part 1," Naval History and Heritage Command, June 11, 2021, https://www.history.navy.mil/content/history/nhhc/about-us/leadership/director/directors-corner/h-grams/h-gram-062.html.

5. Edward J. Reed, *Our Ironclad Ships, Their Qualities, Performance and Cost* (London: John Murray, 1869), 138–39; "W. L. Clowes on the Anglo-Japanese Hostilities of 1863–1864," Victorian Royal Navy, https://www.pdavis.nl/Japan.htm.

6. Yukio Hiyama, "How Japan Honors Its War Dead: The Coexistence of Complementary Systems," Nippon, August 21, 2013, accessed December 26, 2013, https://www.nippon.com/en/in-depth/a02402/?cx_recs_click=true.

7. W. Laird Clowes, *The Royal Navy: A History from Earliest Times to the Present*, vol. 1 (London: Sampson, Low, Marston, 1897), https://web.archive.org/web/20120306090243/http://www.pdavis.nl/Japan.htm494.

8. Jonathan Clements, *A Brief History of Japan: Samurai, Shogun and Zen: The Extraordinary Story of the Land of the Rising Sun* (Rutland, VT: Tuttle, 2017).

9. Conrad Totman, *The Collapse of the Tokugawa Bakufu, 1862–1868* (Honolulu: University of Hawai'i Press, 1980).

10. "Saigō Takamori, the 'Last Samurai,'" Samurai World, 2018, https://samurai-world.com/Saigō-takamori-the-last-samurai/.

11. National Institute of Information and Communications Technology (NICT), trans., "Tokugawa Iemochi: The Life and Times of the 14th Shogun," Tokugawa Memorial Foundation, 2007, https://www.japanesewiki.com/person/Iemochi%20TOKUGAWA.html.

12. National Institute of Information and Communications Technology (NICT), trans., "Choshu Conquest," Japanese Wiki, https://www.japanesewiki.com/history/Choshu%20Conquest.html.

13. "Imperial Japanese Navy Deck Officers: Captain Kuranosuke," Archive Today, https://archive.md/20121204191935/http://homepage2.nifty.com/nishidah/e/px00.htm.

14. National Institute of Information and Communications Technology (NICT), trans., "Tokugawa Iemochi," Japanese Wiki, https://www.japanesewiki.com/history/Saccho%20Domei%20(Satsuma-Choshu%20Alliance).html.

15. J. Charles Schencking, *Making Waves: Politics, Propaganda, and the Emergence of the Imperial Japanese Navy, 1868–1922* (Stanford, CA: Stanford University Press, 2005).

16. David Evans and Mark R. Peattie, *Kaigun: Strategy, Tactics, and Technology in the Imperial Japanese Navy, 1887–1941* (Annapolis, MD: U.S. Naval Institute Press, 1997); "The United States and the Opening of Japan, 1853," Office of the Historian, https://history.state.gov/milestones/1830-1860/opening-to-japan.

17. "The Bakumatsu (Part 7): Choshu Expeditions," Exploring History, June 24, 2016, citing David Murray, *Japan* (New York: Putnam, 1896), https://exploringhist.blogspot.com/2016/06/the-bakumatsu-part7.html.

18. Murray, *Japan*.

19. Ryōtarō Shiba, *The Last Shogun: The Life of Tokugawa Yoshinobu* (New York: Kodansha International, 2004), https://archive.org/details/lastshogunlifeof0000shib/page/76/mode/2up?q=Iemochi.

20. Margaret Mehl, "A Long Retirement: Tokugawa Yoshinobu, the Last Shogun," June 16, 2018, https://margaretmehl.com/a-long-retirement-tokugawa-yoshinobu-the-last-shogun-2/. Mehl is citing Ernest Satow, *A Diplomat in Japan* (1869) (Tokyo and London: Stone Bridge Press, 2007), 299; and Yoshinobu, quoted in Ôkuma Shigénobu and Marcus Bourne Huish, *Fifty Years of New Japan* (London: Smith, Elder, 1909), 1:67, 1:69, https://wellcomecollection.org/works/ek6pjaj4.

21. Mehl, "A Long Retirement."

22. Mehl, "A Long Retirement."

23. "French Military Mission to Japan (1867–68)," Infogalactic, https://infogalactic.com/info/French_military_mission_to_Japan_(1867%E2%80%9368).

24. Christian Polak, *Soie et lumière: L'âge d'or des échanges Franco-Japonais* (Tokyo, Hachette Fujingaho, 2002).

25. John Denney, *Respect and Consideration: Britain in Japan 1853–1868 and Beyond* (Leicester: Radiance Press, 2011); and Mako Taniguchi, *Kiri-sute Gomen* (Tokyo: Yamakawa Shuppansha, 2005).

26. Satow, *A Diplomat in Japan*, 299.

27. Hiroaki Sato, *Tokugawa Yoshinobu: From Shogun to Retired Shogun* (Oakland: University of California Press, 2003.

28. Satow, *A Diplomat in Japan*.

29. Donald Keene, *Emperor of Japan: Meiji and His World, 1852–1912* (New York: Columbia University Press, 2005), 165–66.

30. Margaret Mehl, "Emperor Meiji (1): Monarch for a New Era," April 17, 2019, https://margaretmehl.com/emperor-meiji-1-monarch-for-a-new-era/.

31. "Emperor Meiji Biography (Emperor of Japan [1867–1912])," TheFamousPeople, https://www.thefamouspeople.com/profiles/emperor-meiji-34089.php.

32. Clowes, *The Royal Navy*.

33. "Boshin War," in *New World Encyclopedia*, https://www.newworldencyclopedia.org/entry/Boshin_War.

34. Romulus Hillsborough, *Shinsengumi: The Shogun's Last Samurai Corps* (Rutland, VT: Tuttle, 2005).

35. Andrew Marshall, "What Was the Boshin War?," Bootcamp and Military Fitness Institute, January 20, 2022, https://bootcampmilitaryfitnessinstitute.com/2022/01/20/what-was-the-boshin-war-1868-1869/.

36. Hillsborough, *Shinsengumi*.

37. Robert Morton, *The Japan Society: A. B. Mitford and the Birth of Japan as a Modern State: Letters Home* (Tokyo: Renaissance Books, 2017).

38. Kōichi Hagiwara, *Illustrated Life of Saigō Takamori and Okubo Toshimichi* (in Japanese) (Tokyo: Kawade Shobō Shinsya, 2004), 34.

39. Marshall, "What Was the Boshin War?"

40. Marius B. Jansen, *The Making of Modern Japan* (Cambridge, MA: Harvard University Press, 2000).

41. "Japan," *Sydney Morning Herald* (NSW, 1842–1954), March 23, 1868, 3, https://trove.nla.gov.au/newspaper/article/13157790?searchTerm=BOSHIN%20WAR.

42. "The Battle of Toba—Fushimi," Samurai World, 2017, https://samuraiwr.com/battles/the-battle-of-toba-fushimi.

43. Morton, *The Japan Society*.

44. "Battle of Fushimi Toba," Japan Experience, December 24, 2012, https://www.ja pan-experience.com/plan-your-trip/to-know/japanese-history/fushimi-toba#:~:text=It%20 was%20here%20in%20the%20winter%20of%201868,Fushimi-Toba%20%28also%20 known%20as%20the%20Battle%20of%20Toba-Fushimi%29.

45. Totman, *Collapse of the Tokugawa Bakufu*.

CHAPTER 23: WAR OF THE YEAR OF THE DRAGON

1. "A Maritime Nation's Struggle for Identity," Foundations of International Thinking on Sea Power no. 2 (Sea Power Centre, Royal Australian Navy); Hiroyuki Kanazawa, *The Rise and Fall of the Shogunate Navy: Japan Naval Construction at the End of the Tokugawa Shogunate* (Tokyo: Keio University Press, 2017).

2. Izumi Haraguchi, "The Influence of the Civil War in the US on the Meiji Restoration in Japan," *South Pacific Study* 16, no. 1 (1995): [1].

3. "Japan," *Sydney Morning Herald* (NSW, 1842–1954), March 23, 1868, 3, https://trove .nla.gov.au/newspaper/article/13157790?searchTerm=BOSHIN%20WAR.

4. J. Charles Schencking, *Making Waves: Politics, Propaganda, and the Emergence of the Imperial Japanese Navy, 1868–1922* (Stanford, CA: Stanford University Press, 2005), 11.

5. "Bakumatsu & Meiji Era Ships," in *Naval Encyclopedia*, https://naval-encyclopedia .com/industrial-era/bakumatsu-meiji-era-ships.ph2.

6. "Biographies: Enomoto Takeaki," Japan Reference, March 1, 2012, updated July 22, 2017, https://jref.com/articles/enomoto-takeaki.104/.

7. Donald Keene, *Emperor of Japan: Meiji and His World, 1852–1912* (New York: Columbia University Press, 2005), 165–66.

8. John Denney, *Respect and Consideration: Britain in Japan 1853–1868 and Beyond* (Leicester: Radiance Press, 2011); Mako Taniguchi, *Kiri-sute Gomen* (Tokyo: Yamakawa Shuppansha, 2005).

9. Ryōtarō Shiba, *The Last Shogun: The Life of Tokugawa Yoshinobu* (New York: Kodansha International, 2004), https://archive.org/details/lastshogunlifeof0000shib/page/76/mode /2up?q=Iemochi.

10. "The Battle of Toba—Fushimi," Samurai World, 2017, https://samurai-wr.com/the -battle-of-toba-fushimi/.

11. "Van Valkenburgh, Robert Bruce, 1821–1888," Biographical Directory of the United States Congress, https://bioguide.congress.gov/search/bio/V000061; Lieutenant (J. G.) Hyman Kublin, "Admiral Enomoto and the Imperial Restoration," U.S. Naval Institute, April 1953, https://www.usni.org/magazines/proceedings/1953/april/admiral-enomoto-and-im perial-restoration.

12. Nihon Rekishi-gakkai, ed., *Meiji Ishin Jinmei Jiten* (Tokyo: Yoshikawa Kobunkan, 1981).

CHAPTER 24: THE RACE TO ARMS

1. Joseph Heco, *The Narrative of a Japanese: What He Has Seen and the People He Has Met in the Course of the Last Forty Years*, vol. 1 (San Francisco, CA: American-Japanese Publishing Association, 1895), https://archive.org/details/narrativeofjapan02hecoiala/mode/2up?q=stonewall.

2. William R. Hawkins, "The Emperor's Confederate Ironclad," *Naval History* 18, no. 6 (December 2004): 57–60.

3. Lawrence Sondhaus, *Naval Warfare 1815–1914* (New York: Routledge, 2001).

4. "The Very Short Career of CSS *Stonewall*," in *Naval Encyclopedia*, https://naval-ency clopedia.com/industrial-era/1870-fleets/japan/kotetsu.php.

5. "CSS *Stonewall* (1865)—: At Washington, DC, 1865–67," Naval Historical Center, Department for the Navy, https://www.ibiblio.org/hyperwar/OnlineLibrary/photos/sh-us -cs/csa-sh/csash-sz/stonew-c.htm.

6. Thomas T. Wiatt, *The* Stonewall*: The True Story of a Ship without a Port* (Brisbane, Australia: Limelight, 2021); Lewis R. Hamersly, "Captain George Brown (1878)," in *The Records of Living Officers of the U.S. Navy and Marine Corps, 1878 (Compiled from Official Sources)* (Philadelphia, PA: Lippincott, 1878), 128.

7. Hansgeorg Jentschura, Dieter Jung, and Peter Mickel, *Warships of the Imperial Japanese Navy, 1869–1945*, trans. Antony Preston and J. D. Brown (London: Arms and Armour, 1976).

8. Tom Huntington, "From Dixie to the Land of the Rising Sun," HustoryNet, October 27, 2016, https://www.historynet.com/from-dixie-to-the-land-of-the-rising-sun/.

9. "Under Six Flags: The Intriguing Saga of the CSS *Stonewall*, the Confederate Ironclad That Helped Forge an Empire," From Small Causes Great Events, August 25, 2020, https:// fromsmallcausesgreatevents.org//2020/08/25/under-six-flags-the-intriguing-saga-of-the-css -stonewall-the-confederate-ironclad-that-helped-forge-an-empire/.

10. Wiatt, *The* Stonewall*: The True Story of a Ship without a Port*.

11. "The Very Short Career of CSS *Stonewall*."

12. Lee Kennett, "The Strange Career of the *Stonewall*," *U.S. Naval Institute Proceedings* 94, no. 2/780 (February 1968), https://www.usni.org/magazines/proceedings/1968/february /strange-career-stonewall.

13. A. C. Yu, "Japanese-English Bilingual Corpus of *Wikipedia*'s Kyoto Articles," trans. National Institute of Information and Communications Technology (NICT), Japanese Wiki, https://www.japanese-wiki-corpus.org/history/The%20Boshin%20War.html.

14. "Title: Item Ministry of Military and Naval Affairs Documents Extract Warship *Kotetsu* Crewing Personnel Number Investigation," Japan Center for Asian Historical Records; National Archives of Japan, reference code C09090003900.

15. "Snakes, Combs, and Spiders: 10 Eerie Japanese Superstitions for the Curious," Live Japan: Perfect Guide, April 9, 2018, https://livejapan.com/en/article-a0001290/.

16. Heco, *The Narrative of a Japanese*.

17. "Kobe Incident," in A. C. Yu, "Japanese-English Bilingual Corpus of *Wikipedia*'s Kyoto Articles."

18. Ian C. Ruxton, "The Kobe Incident: An Investigation of the Incident and Its Place in Meiji History" (Sir Harry Parkes speaking to Ito Shunsuke, January 12), *Journal of Comparative Cultural Studies* 25 (1994): 91–117.

19. National Institute of Information and Communications Technology (NICT), trans., "Choshu Conquest," Japanese Wiki, https://www.japanesewiki.com/history/Choshu%20 Conquest.html; J. Charles Schencking, *Making Waves: Politics, Propaganda, and the Emergence of the Imperial Japanese Navy, 1868–1922* (Stanford, CA: Stanford University Press, 2005).

CHAPTER 25: *KOTETSU'S* WAR

1. Ernest Satow, *A Diplomat in Japan* (1869) (Tokyo and London: Stone Bridge Press, 2007).

2. National Institute of Information and Communications Technology (NICT), trans., "Choshu Conquest," Japanese Wiki, https://www.japanesewiki.com/history/Choshu%20 Conquest.html.

3. "Alfred Thayer Mahan," Naval History and Heritage Command, January 30, 2020, https://www.history.navy.mil/content/history/nhhc/research/library/research-guides/z -files/zb-files/zb-files-m/mahan-alfred.html.

4. "Lecture Note: The True Story of the Last Samurai Who Were the First to Colonize America—Filmmaker Brian T. Maeda—Jan 19, 2010," Cultural News, n.d., accessed February 27, 2015, https://www.culturalnews.com/?p=1142.

5. "Van Valkenburgh, Robert Bruce, 1821–1888," Biographical Directory of the United States Congress, https://bioguide.congress.gov/search/bio/V000061; Lieutenant (J. G.) Hyman Kublin, "Admiral Enomoto and the Imperial Restoration," U.S. Naval Institute, April 1953, https://www.usni.org/magazines/proceedings/1953/april/admiral-enomoto-and-im perial-restoration; "Robert B. Van Valkenburgh," Historical Society of Prattsburgh, September 2010, http://historyofprattsburgh.com/2010/09/robert-b-van-valkenburgh/.

6. Kublin, "Admiral Enomoto and the Imperial Restoration."

7. Roger Chesneau and Eugene M. Kolesnik, eds., *Conway's All the World's Fighting Ships, 1860–1905* (New York: Mayflower Books, 1979).

8. Romulus Hillsborough, *Shinsengumi: The Shogun's Last Samurai Corps* (Rutland, VT: Tuttle, 2005).

9. Joseph Heco, *The Narrative of a Japanese: What He Has Seen and the People He Has Met in the Course of the Last Forty Years*, vol. 1 (San Francisco, CA: American-Japanese Publishing Association, 1895), https://archive.org/details/narrativeofjapan02hecoiala/mode/2up?q=stonewall.

10. Heco, *The Narrative of a Japanese.*

11. "The Development of Japanese Sea Power: 'Know Your Enemy'!" (*CinCPoc-CinCPOA Bulletin* 93-45, 1945), Naval History and Heritage Command, https://www.history.navy.mil /research/library/online-reading-room/title-list-alphabetically/d/development-of-japanese -sea-power-cincpoa-93-45.html.

12. "Title: March 4, 1868: Gun Salute for U.S. Concierge *Kotetsu* Warship," Japan Center for Asian Historical Records; National Archives of Japan, reference Code C11081520500.

13. "Yanaka, Sakuragi and Ueno Park Alley Tour Guides," Kamitani Sakuraike, http:// ya-na-ka.sakura.ne.jp/nakajimaSako.htm.

14. "Title: Item Ministry of Military and Naval Affairs Documents Extract Warship *Kotetsu* Crewing Personnel Number Investigation," Japan Center for Asian Historical Records; National Archives of Japan, reference code C09090003900; "Yanaka, Sakuragi and Ueno Park Alley Tour Guides."

15. *Crete Democrat*, August 8, 1894; *Leavenworth Times*, August 7, 1894.

16. "Asians and Pacific Islanders and the Civil War," in *U.S. National Park Service (NPS) Handbook* (2015), cited in "Two Japanese Nationals Fought in US Civil War," JAVA Research Team (JRT), https://archive.org/details/asianspacificisl0000unse_n9z3.

17. "French Military Mission to Japan (1867–68)," Infogalactic, https://infogalactic.com /info/French_military_mission_to_Japan_(1867%E2%80%9368).

18. Marco Margaritoff and John Kuroski, "Jules Brunet: The Military Officer behind the True Story of 'The Last Samurai,'" All That's Interesting, May 2020, https://allthatsinteresting .com/last-samurai-true-story-jules-brunet.

19. Yamakawa Kenjirō, *Aizu Boshin Senshi* (Tōkyō: Tōkyō Daigaku Shuppankai, 1931).

20. National Institute of Information and Communications Technology (NICT), trans.,"Shinsengumi," Japanese Wiki, https://www.japanesewiki.com/history/Shinsengumi .html.

21. Beatrice Heuser, "Ends, Ways, Means: Clausewitz and Other Prophets," *Military Strategy Magazine* 8, no. 3 (February 2012), https://www.militarystrategymagazine.com/article/Ends-Ways-Means-Clausewitz-and-Other-Prophets/.

22. A. C. Yu, "Japanese-English Bilingual Corpus of *Wikipedia*'s Kyoto Articles," trans. National Institute of Information and Communications Technology (NICT), Japanese Wiki, https://www.japanese-wiki-corpus.org/history/The%20Boshin%20War.html.

23. Andrew Marshall, "What Was the Boshin War (1868–1869)?," Boot Camp Military Fitness Institute, January 20, 2022, https://bootcampmilitaryfitnessinstitute.com/2022/01/20/what-was-the-boshin-war-1868-1869/.

CHAPTER 26: BULLETS LIKE RAIN

1. "Tactics in Warfare during World War I," Anzac Portal, https://anzacportal.dva.gov.au/wars-and-missions/ww1/military-organisation/tactics-in-warfare#:~:text=After%20World%20War%20I%2C%20Winston,the%20war%20in%20an%20afternoon.

2. Ken Yamaguchi, *Kinsé shiriaku: A History of Japan, from the First Visit of Commodore Perry in 1853 to the Capture of Hakodate by the Mikado's Forces in 1869*, trans. Ernest Mason Satow (Yokohama: Wetmore, 1876).

3. Ueno, "Walking in the Steps of the Last Shogun," Google Arts and Culture, https://artsandculture.google.com/story/0AWhTrVJLsafrw.

4. Ryōtarō Shiba, *The Last Shogun: The Life of Tokugawa Yoshinobu* (New York : Kodansha International, 2004), https://archive.org/details/lastshogunlifeof0000shib/page/76/mode/2up?q=Iemochi.

5. Romulus Hillsborough, *Shinsengumi: The Shogun's Last Samurai Corps* (Rutland, VT: Tuttle, 2005).

6. Hansgeorg Jentschura, Dieter Jung, and Peter Mickel, *Warships of the Imperial Japanese Navy, 1869–1945* (Annapolis, MD: U.S. Naval Institute Press, 1977).

7. Japan Center for Asia Historical Records, National Archives of Japan (website), https://www.jacar.archives.go.jp/aj/meta/result?DB_ID=G0000101EXTERNAL&DEF_XSL=default&ON_LYD=on&IS_INTERNAL=false&IS_STYLE=eng&IS_KEY_S1=ironclad&IS_TAG_S1=InfoSDU&IS_MAP_S1=&IS_LGC_S1=&IS_KIND=detail&IS_START=1&IS_NUMBER=1&IS_TAG_S18=eadid&IS_KEY_S18=M2009090311022825397&IS_EXTSCH=F2006083118101851446%2BF2006083118133052046%2BF2006090107053643613%2BF2009070114211367619%2BF2009070114223067621%2BF2009090311020825163&IS_ORG_ID=M2009090311022825397.

8. "Bakumatsu & Meiji Era Ships," in *Naval Encyclopedia*, https://naval-encyclopedia.com/industrial-era/bakumatsu-meiji-era-ships.ph2; "Title: June 15, 1868: Minister of War Visits and Boards on *Kotetsu* Warship, *Kasuga* Warship, *Yoshun* Warship, *Teibo* Warship," Japan Center for Asian Historical Records; National Archives of Japan, reference Code C11081522000.

9. Thomas T. Wiatt, *The Stonewall: The True Story of a Ship without a Port* (Brisbane, Australia: Limelight, 2021).

10. "Cherry Blossoms and Red Leaves at Hakodate Goryokaku Fort," J Histories, June 14, 2023, https://jhistories.com/goryokaku-fort/; citing National Diet Library, Japan.

11. Bearbeitet Berend Wispelwey, comp., "Bankichi Matsuoka," *Japanese Biographical Index* (München: Saur, 2004), https://books.google.com.au/books?id=4UkhAAAAQBAJ&pg=PR3&source=gbs_selected_pages&cad=2#v=onepage&q&f=false.

12. "Bakumatsu & Meiji Era Ships."

13. "Boshin War," in *New World Encyclopedia*, https://www.newworldencyclopedia.org/entry/Boshin_War.

14. A. C. Yu, "Japanese-English Bilingual Corpus of Wikipedia's Kyoto Articles," trans. National Institute of Information and Communications Technology (NICT), Japanese Wiki, https://www.japanese-wiki-corpus.org/history/The%20Boshin%20War.html, cited in Kurt Meissner, "General Eduard Schnell," *Monumenta Nipponica* 4, no. 2 (1941), https://doi.org/10.2307/2382634; https://typeset.io/papers/general-eduard-schnell-s8wsqhw0cj.

15. Cited in Meissner, "General Eduard Schnell."

16. "Hijikata Toshizo Vice-commander of the Shinsengumi," Shinsengumi.net, September 20, 2020, https://shinsengumi.net/?s=Hijikata+Toshizo; "Edo Samurai," Samurai Life, June 14, 2019, https://www.everydaysamurai.life/budo/tennenrishinryu/hijikata-Toshizō/; "'The 'Demonic Second-in-Command' Who Never Let Go of His Sword until the Very End," Samurai vs Ninja, September 8, 2023, https://samuraivsninja.com/en/contents/why-did-hijikata-Toshizō-fight-through-the-battle-of-aizu-and-the-battle-of-hakodate-to-the-end-even-when-the-odds-were-so-slim/.

17. "Toshizō, as Seen by His Contemporaries," Shinsengumi Archives, January 3, 2022, accessed October 1, 2024, https://shinsengumi-archives.tumblr.com/post/672375749843501056/Toshizō-as-seen-by-his-contemporaries; "Hijikata Toshizo," Japan's Samurai Revolution, https://samurairevolution.omeka.net/exhibits/show/shinsengumi--losers-then-and-w/hijikata-toshiz--.

18. Yamaguchi, *Kinsé shiriaku.*

19. "The Meiji and Taisho Eras on Photographs: The Aizu War and Wakamatsu Castle," National Diet Library, Tokyo, https://www.ndl.go.jp/scenery/e/column/tohoku/the_aizu_war.html, citing Aizuwakamatsu-shi Hisho Kocho Ka and Aizuwakamatsu-shi Shi Kenkyukai, eds., *Aizu no Bakumatsu Ishin: Kyoto Shugoshoku kara Aizu Senso* (Fukushima Prefecture, Japan: Aizuwakamatsu-shi, 2003).

20. Kallie Szczepanski, "A Long History of Japanese Women Warriors," ThoughtCo, January 22, 2020, https://www.thoughtco.com/images-of-samurai-women-195469.

21. Ernest Satow, *A Diplomat in Japan* (1869) (Tokyo and London: Stone Bridge Press, 2007).

22. John Breen, "The Imperial Oath of April 1868: Ritual, Politics and Power in the Restoration," *Monumenta Nipponica* 51, no. 4 (Winter 1996): 407–29.

23. S. Araki, "Ruins on the Ocean Floor (Salvaging the Kaiyō Maru)," in *Diving for Science*, ed. C. T. Mitchell (La Jolla, CA: American Academy of Underwater Sciences for the Conference Diving for Science, 1985); archived from the original on April 15, 2013.

24. "Battle of Hakodate," Alchetron, updated Jun 01, 2022, https://alchetron.com/Battle-of-Hakodate; "Japanese Warship *Chōyō Maru*," Alchetron, November 29, 2022, https://alchetron.com/Japanese-warship-Ch%C5%8Dy%C5%8D-Maru.

25. "Hokkaidō," in *New World Encyclopedia*, https://www.newworldencyclopedia.org/entry/Hokkaid%C5%8D#:~:text=The%20largest%20city%20on%20Hokkaid%C5%8D%20is%20its%20capital%2C,the%20number%20of%20Japanese%20living%20on%20the%20island.

26. "Title: The Trouble Report from Captain Ito of the Warship *Azuma* to the Navy Minister Kawawmura," Japan Center for Asian Historical Records; National Archives of Japan, August 22, 1904, reference code A03030657400; reference code A03030680900.

27. Andrew Marshall, "What Was the Boshin War (1868–1869)?," Boot Camp Military Fitness Institute, January 20, 2022, https://bootcampmilitaryfitnessinstitute.com/2022/01/20/what-was-the-boshin-war-1868-1869/.

28. Joseph Heco, *The Narrative of a Japanese: What He Has Seen and the People He Has Met in the Course of the Last Forty Years*, vol. 1 (San Francisco, CA: American-Japanese Publishing Association, 1895), https://archive.org/details/narrativeofjapan02hecoiala/mode/2up?q=stonewall; "The History of Shipbuilding in Scotland," Scottish Built Ships, https://www.clydeships.co.uk/view.php?ref=18462.

29. "Ezo Republic: Japanese-English Bilingual Corpus," Hakuouki History, https://hakuouki-history.tumblr.com/post/166063584664/ezo-republic-2010-japanese-wiki-entry.

30. "Boshin War."

31. James B. Lewis, *Frontier Contact between Choson Korea and Tokugawa Japan* (New York: Routledge, 2003), 25.

32. John R. Black, *Young Japan: Yokohama and Yedo* (London: Trubner, 1881; repr., Yokohama: Kelly & Co., 2001), 2:240–41.; "Dajōkan: Imperial Japanese Council of State," in *Encyclopedia Britannica Online*, https://www.britannica.com/topic/Dajokan-imperial-Japanese-council-of-state.

33. Christian Polak, *Soie et lumière: L'âge d'or des échanges Franco-Japonais* (Tokyo: Hachette Fujingaho, 2002).

34. "Under Six Flags: The Intriguing Saga of the CSS *Stonewall*, the Confederate Ironclad That Helped Forge an Empire," From Small Causes Great Events, August 25, 2020, https://fromsmallcausesgreatevents.org//2020/08/25/under-six-flags-the-intriguing-saga-of-the-css-stonewall-the-confederate-ironclad-that-helped-forge-an-empire/.

CHAPTER 27: STEALING *KOTETSU*

1. "Ikunosuke Arai," in *Prabook Biographical Encyclopedia*, https://prabook.com/web/ikunosuke.arai/3718871.

2. "Title: Item Ministry of Military and Naval Affairs Documents Extract Warship *Kotetsu* Crewing Personnel Number Investigation," Japan Center for Asian Historical Records; National Archives of Japan, reference code C09090003900.

3. "Ezo Republic: Japanese-English Bilingual Corpus," Hakuouki History, https://hakuouki-history.tumblr.com/post/166063584664/ezo-republic-2010-japanese-wiki-entry.

4. Bayard Taylor, *Japan: In Our Day* (New York: Scribner, Armstrong, 1872).

5. Taylor, *Japan: In Our Day*.

6. Eugène Collache, "Une aventure au Japon," *Le Tour du Monde* 77 (1874), https://gallica.bnf.fr/ark:/12148/bpt6k34402b/f52.item.

7. Lee Kennett, "The Strange Career of the *Stonewall*," *U.S. Naval Institute Proceedings* 94, no. 2/780 (February 1968), https://www.usni.org/magazines/proceedings/1968/february/strange-career-stonewall.

8. "The Biography of Captain Koga Gengo," Kogagengodenkannkokai, March 10, 1933; David C. Evans and Mark R. Peattie, *Kaigun: Strategy, Tactics, and Technology in the Imperial Japanese Navy, 1887–1941* (Annapolis, MD: U.S. Naval Institute Press, 1997).

9. "The Biography of Captain Koga Gengo."

10. Evans and Peattie, *Kaigun: Strategy, Tactics, and Technology*; "Kōga Gengo," Wikipedia, last updated February 13, 2024, https://simple.wikipedia.org/wiki/K%C5%8Dga_Gengo.

11. "Kōga Gengo."

12. Ken Yamaguchi, *Kinsé shiriaku: A History of Japan, from the First Visit of Commodore Perry in 1853 to the Capture of Hakodate by the Mikado's Forces in 1869*, trans. Ernest Mason Satow (Yokohama: Wetmore, 1876); Nagayo Ogasawara, *Life of Admiral Togo* (Tokyo: Shorin, 1934), https://archive.org/details/lifeofadmiraltog0000vari/mode/2up?q=kasuga.

13. "How Many of the Top 10 Loudest Noises Have You Been Exposed To?," Industrial Safety and Hygiene News, https://www.ishn.com/articles/105610-how-many-of-the-top-10-loudest-noises-have-you-been-exposed-to#:~:text=At%20the%20155%2D160%20decibel,it%20temporarily%20difficult%20to%20swallow.

14. "The Evolution of Naval Weapons," Bureau of Naval Personnel; Naval History and Heritage Command, March 1949, https://www.history.navy.mil/research/library/online-reading-room/title-list-alphabetically/e/evolution-of-naval-weapons.html.

15. Romulus Hillsborough, *Shinsengumi: The Shogun's Last Samurai Corps* (Rutland, VT: Tuttle, 2005).

16. "Preface Map," in Taylor, *Japan: In Our Day*.

17. Hillsborough, *Shinsengumi*.

18. Ogasawara, *Life of Admiral Togo*; Hillsborough, *Shinsengumi*.

19. Ogasawara, *Life of Admiral Togo*; Hillsborough, *Shinsengumi*.

20. "Bakumatsu & Meiji Era Ships," in *Naval Encyclopedia*, https://naval-encyclopedia.com/industrial-era/bakumatsu-meiji-era-ships.ph2.

21. Bearbeitet Berend Wispelwey, comp., "Bankichi Matsuoka," in *Japanese Biographical Index* (München: Saur, 2004), https://books.google.com.au/books?id=4UkhAAAAQBAJ&pg=PR3&source=gbs_selected_pages&cad=2#v=onepage&q&f=false.

22. "History of Hokkaidō: The War of the Last Samurai in Hakodate," Hokkaidō Treasure, September 10, 2021, https://www.facebook.com/hokkaidotreasure/posts/452212416250657/.

23. Hillsborough, *Shinsengumi*.

24. Morton S. Schmorleitz, *Castles in Japan* (Rutland, VT: Tuttle, 1974); "Goryokaku Fort," Japan Atlas, https://web-japan.org/atlas/historical/his01.html#:~:text=There%20are%20five%20V-shaped%20projections%20from%20a%20central,area%20of%20251%2C400%20square%20meters%20%28about%2062%20acres%29.

CHAPTER 28: MY SPIRIT GUARDS MY LORD IN THE EAST

1. Romulus Hillsborough, *Shinsengumi: The Shogun's Last Samurai Corps* (Rutland, VT: Tuttle, 2005).

2. Lieutenant (J. G.) Hyman Kublin, "Admiral Enomoto and the Imperial Restoration," U.S. Naval Institute, April 1953, https://www.usni.org/magazines/proceedings/1953/april/admiral-enomoto-and-imperial-restoration.

3. "Bakumatsu & Meiji Era Ships," in *Naval Encyclopedia*, https://naval-encyclopedia.com/industrial-era/bakumatsu-meiji-era-ships.ph2.

4. Ken Yamaguchi, *Kinsé shiriaku: A History of Japan, from the First Visit of Commodore Perry in 1853 to the Capture of Hakodate by the Mikado's Forces in 1869*, trans. Ernest Mason Satow (Yokohama: Wetmore, 1876); Nagayo Ogasawara, *Life of Admiral Togo* (Tokyo: Shorin, 1934), https://archive.org/details/lifeofadmiraltog0000vari/mode/2up?q=kasuga.

5. "Bakumatsu & Meiji Era Ships."

6. Raphael Semmes, *Memoirs of Service Afloat during the War between the States* (1869; repr., Chicago: Revell, 1909).

7. Yamaguchi, *Kinsé shiriaku*.

8. Yamaguchi, *Kinsé shiriaku*.

9. Edwin Albert Falk, *Togo and the Rise of Japanese Sea Power* (New York: Longmans, Green, 1936), 292.

10. Yamaguchi, *Kinsé shiriaku*.

11. "Bakumatsu & Meiji Era Ships."

12. Yamaguchi, *Kinsé shiriaku.*

13. Ogasawara, *Life of Admiral Togo.*

14. Keisuke Otori, *Memoirs of the Ezo Republic: The Life of Keisuke Otori*, trans. T. K. E. Ueda (Seattle: University of Washington Press, 2002).

15. Ogasawara, *Life of Admiral Togo.*

16. Ogasawara, *Life of Admiral Togo.*

17. Ogasawara, *Life of Admiral Togo*; "The Boshin War: The Tokugawa Shogunate vs. the Imperial Court," Yabi, http://yabai.com/p/3217.

18. Ogasawara, *Life of Admiral Togo.*

19. Toshizō Hijikata, *The Shinsengumi: The Shogun's Last Samurai Corps*, ed. and trans. J. P. M. Huber (Rutland, VT: Tuttle, 2003).

20. "Hijikata Toshizo," Shinsengumi, September 28, 2020, https://shinsengumi.net/index .php/welcome-to-shinsengumi-no-makoto/hijikata-Toshizō/; "Edo Samurai," Everyday Samurai Life, June 14, 2019, https://www.everydaysamurai.life/budo/tennenrishinryu/ hijikata-Toshizō/; "The 'Demonic Second-in-Command' Who Never Let Go of His Sword until the Very End," Samurai vs Ninja, September 8, 2023, https://samuraivsninja.com /en/contents/why-did-hijikata-Toshizō-fight-through-the-battle-of-aizu-and-the-battle-of -hakodate-to-the-end-even-when-the-odds-were-so-slim/.

21. Kathe Roth, trans., "Goryōkaku," in *Japan Encyclopedia* (London and Cambridge, MA: Harvard University Press, 2002).

22. "Boshin War," in *New World Encyclopedia*, https://www.newworldencyclopedia.org /entry/Boshin_War.

23. Yamaguchi, *Kinsé shiriaku.*

24. "Cherry Blossoms and Red Leaves at Hakodate Goryokaku Fort," J Histories, June 14, 2023, https://jhistories.com/goryokaku-fort/; citing National Diet Library, Japan.

25. Jeffrey P. Mass and William B. Hauser, *The Bakufu in Japanese History* (Stanford, CA: Stanford University Press, 1985); National Institute of Information and Communications Technology (NICT), trans., "Soma Kazue," Japanese Wiki, https://www.japanesewiki.com /person/Kazue%20SOMA.html.

26. Kawai Atsushi, "The Meiji Restoration: The End of the Shogunate and the Building of a Modern Japanese State," Nippon, November 29, 2018, https://www.nippon.com/en /views/b06902/.

27. John A. Harrison, "The Capron Mission and the Colonization of Hokkaidō, 1868–1875," *Agricultural History* 25, no. 3 (1951): 135–42, https://www.jstor.org/stable/3740831; Walter A. McDougall, *Let the Sea Make a Noise* (New York: HarperCollins, 1993), 355–56.

28. "The Daybook: Civil War Navy Special Edition-Technology," Hampton Roads Naval Museum, https://www.history.navy.mil/content/dam/nhhc/browse-by-topic/War%20 and%20Conflict/civil-war/cwsetech.pdf.

CHAPTER 29: THE IMPERIAL PACIFIC

1. Kallie Szczepanski, "Overview of the Tokugawa Shogunate of Japan," ThoughtCo, updated on June 21, 2019, https://www.thoughtco.com/tokugawa-shoguns-of-japan-195578.

2. William R. Hawkins, "The Emperor's Confederate Ironclad," *Naval History* 18, no. 6 (December 2004): 57–60.

3. Donald Keene, *Emperor of Japan: Meiji and His World, 1852–1912* (New York: Columbia University Press, 2005), 165–66.

4. Jonathan Clements, *A Brief History of Japan: Samurai, Shogun and Zen: The Extraordinary Story of the Land of the Rising Sun* (Rutland, VT: Tuttle, 2017).

5. "Title: Officers of Crew of Warships *Kotetsu*, *Chōyō* and *Yoshun* Were Awarded Rice for Their Special Services in Hakodate and It Was Sent with Bond of Mitsui Bank by Ministry of the Army," Japan Center for Asian Historical Records; National Archives of Japan, reference codes C09090720400 and C11080972000.

6. Andrew Gordon, *A Modern History of Japan* (New York: Oxford University Press, 2014).

7. Harry Parkes, *The Life of Sir Harry Parkes: A Memoir*, ed. J. W. C. Smith (Edinburgh, Scotland: William Blackwood and Sons, 1898).

8. M. G. Haynes, "Samurai Invasion: Japan's 1609 Conquest of Ryukyu," HistoryNet, August 13, 2022, https://www.historynet.com/japan-invasion-of-ryukyu/.

9. A. C. Yu, "Japanese-English Bilingual Corpus of Wikipedia's Kyoto Articles," trans. National Institute of Information and Communications Technology (NICT), Japanese Wiki, https://www.japanese-wiki-corpus.org/history/The%20Boshin%20War.html.

10. "Meiji Imperial Japanese March Medley," JMS Translation, YouTube, https://www.youtube.com/watch?v=498v91CLAUw (included in a wider period medley); W. M. Swan, "A Century of Japanese Intelligence—Part 1," *Naval Historical Review*, September 1974, https://navyhistory.au/a-century-of-japanese-intelligence-part-1/2/.

11. "Meiji Period (Japan, 1868–1912)," World History Education Resources, http://world-history-education-resources.com/articles/meiji-period-japan.html.

12. "Imperial Japanese Navy Deck Officers: Captain Kuranosuke," Archive Today, https://archive.md/20121204191935/http://homepage2.nifty.com/nishidah/e/px00.htm.

13. Kawai Atsushi, "The Meiji Restoration: The End of the Shogunate and the Building of a Modern Japanese State," Nippon, November 29, 2018, https://www.nippon.com/en/views/b06902/.

14. S. Araki, "Ruins on the Ocean Floor (Salvaging the Kaiyo Maru)," in *Diving for Science*, ed. C. T. Mitchell (La Jolla, CA: American Academy of Underwater Sciences for the Conference Diving for Science, 1985), archived from the original on April 15, 2013.

15. Nihon Rekishi-gakkai, ed., *Meiji Ishin Jinmei Jiten* (Tokyo: Yoshikawa Kobunkan, 1981), n.p.

16. National Institute of Information and Communications Technology (NICT), trans., "Soma Kazue," Japanese Wiki, https://www.japanesewiki.com/person/Kazue%20SOMA.html.

17. Nihon Rekishi-gakkai, *Meiji Ishin Jinmei Jiten*.

18. Casey Baseel, "An Up-Close Look at One of Japan's Five Ryuseito Swords, Forged from Meteorites," Japan Today, September 26, 2019, https://japantoday.com/category/features/lifestyle/an-up-close-look-at-one-of-japan%E2%80%99s-five-ryuseito-swords-forged-from-meteorites?comment-order=popular.

19. "Biographies: Enomoto Takeaki," Japan Reference, March 1, 2012, updated July 22, 2017, https://jref.com/articles/enomoto-takeaki.104/.

20. Margaret Mehl, "A Long Retirement: Tokugawa Yoshinobu, the Last Shogun," June 16, 2018, https://margaretmehl.com/a-long-retirement-tokugawa-yoshinobu-the-last-shogun-2/. Mehl is citing Ernest Satow, *A Diplomat in Japan* (1869) (Tokyo and London: Stone Bridge Press, 2007), 299; and Yoshinobu quoted in Ōkuma Shigénobu and Marcus Bourne Huish, *Fifty Years of New Japan* (London: Smith, Elder, 1909), 1:67, 1:69, https://wellcomecollection.org/works/ek6pjaj4.

21. Mehl, "A Long Retirement."

22. Kawai Atsushi, "After the Shogunate: The Last Shōgun and a New Direction for the Tokugawa Clan History," Nippon, September 15, 2023, https://www.nippon.com/en/japan-topics/b06914/.

23. Donald Keene, *Emperor of Japan: Meiji and His World, 1852–1912* (New York: Columbia University Press, 2005), 165–66.

24. Satow, *A Diplomat in Japan*; Keene, *Emperor of Japan*, 143.

25. "The Development of Japanese Sea Power: 'Know Your Enemy'!" (*CinCPoc-CinCPOA Bulletin* 93-45, 1945), Naval History and Heritage Command, https://www.history.navy.mil/research/library/online-reading-room/title-list-alphabetically/d/development-of-japanese-sea-power-cincpoa-93-45.html.

26. "Title: Enquiry about Payment of Expenses to the Two Warships *Azuma* and *Ryōshō* for Sailing to China Sea," Japan Center for Asian Historical Records; National Archives of Japan, reference code A01100043100.

27. Marius B. Jansen, *The Making of Modern Japan* (Cambridge, MA: Harvard University Press, 2000), OCLC 44090600.

28. F. W. Seal, "Oda Nobunaga," Samurai Archives, https://web.archive.org/web/2017 0606234308/http://www.samurai-archives.com/nobunaga.html#2.

29. Kato, "Saigō Takamori, the 'Last Samurai,'" Samurai World, 2018, https://samurai -world.com/Saigō-takamori-the-last-samurai/.

30. Kōichi Hagiwara, *Illustrated Life of Saigō Takamori and Okubo Toshimichi* (in Japanese) (Tokyo: Kawade Shobō Shinsya, 2004), 34–35.

31. "The Meiji and Taisho Eras on Photographs; The Aizu War and Wakamatsu Castle," National Diet Library, Tokyo, https://www.ndl.go.jp/scenery/e/column/tohoku/the_aizu _war.html; citing Aizuwakamatsu-shi Shi Kenkyukai and Aizuwakamatsu-shi Hisho Kocho Ka, eds., *Aizu no Bakumatsu Ishin: Kyoto Shugoshoku kara Aizu Senso* (Fukushima Prefecture, Japan: Aizuwakamatsu-shi, 2003).

32. Andria Pressel, "Why Did the Samurai Lose? Rebellion and the Last Warrior," The Collector, September 16, 2021, https://www.thecollector.com/samurai-warriors-satsuma -rebellion/.

33. Mark Ravina, *The Last Samurai: The Life and Battles of Saigō Takamori*, 1st ed. (New York: Wiley, 2005).

34. *Shinsengumi Encyclopedia* (Tokyo: Shin Jinbutsu Oraisha, 1978); Kato, "Saigō Takamori."

35. Yukio Hiyama, "How Japan Honors Its War Dead: The Coexistence of Complementary Systems," Nippon, August 21, 2013, accessed December 26, 2013, https://www.nippon .com/en/in-depth/a02402/.

36. Kanji Sakaguchi, *The Medical Activities of Sōha Hatono VIII and His Welfare Activities*, Kenkyuu Kiyō 27 (Natori: Shokei Junior University, 1995).

37. Eugène Collache, "Une aventure au Japon," *Le Tour du Monde* 77 (1874), https://gal lica.bnf.fr/ark:/12148/bpt6k34402b/f52.item.

38. "Ezo Republic: Japanese-English Bilingual Corpus," Hakuouki History, https:// hakuouki-history.tumblr.com/post/166063584664/ezo-republic-2010-japanese-wiki-entry.

39. Académie des Sciences d'Outre-Mer, *Présences françaises outre-mer* (Paris: Éditions Karthala, 2012), 1:712.

40. "Biographies: Enomoto Takeaki."

41. "Ikunosuke Arai," in *Prabook Biographical Encyclopedia*, https://prabook.com/web/iku nosuke.arai/3718871.

42. Denis Ashton Warner and Peggy Warner, *The Tide at Sunrise: A History of the Russo-Japanese War, 1904–1905* (New York: Charterhouse, 1974).

43. Anthony J. Watts, *The Imperial Russian Navy* (London: Arms and Armour, 1990).

44. "Toshizō, as Seen by His Contemporaries," Shinsengumi Archives, January 3, 2022, https://shinsengumi-archives.tumblr.com/post/672375749843501056/Toshizō-as-seen-by-his-contemporaries; "Hijikata Toshizo," Japan's Samurai Revolution, https://samurairevolution.omeka.net/exhibits/show/shinsengumi--losers-then-and-w/hijikata-toshiz--.

45. Romulus Hillsborough, *Shinsengumi: The Shogun's Last Samurai Corps* (Rutland, VT: Tuttle, 2005).

46. "Yanaka, Sakuragi and Ueno Park Alley Tour Guides," Kamitani Sakuraike, http://ya-na-ka.sakura.ne.jp/nakajimaSako.htm.

47. "Asia for Educators: The Meiji Restoration and Modernization," Columbia University, http://afe.easia.columbia.edu/special/japan_1750_meiji.htm.

48. Franklin K. Van Zandt, "Boundaries of the United States and the Several States," U.S. Geological Survey Professional Paper 909 (Reston, VT: U.S. Geological Survey, 1976), 1–2.

49. Margaret Mehl, "Emperor Meiji (1): Monarch for a New Era," April 17, 2019, https://margaretmehl.com/emperor-meiji-1-monarch-for-a-new-era/.

50. Mark Schreiber, "Japan Focus: A Century of Japanese Assassination: Reflection and Commemoration," *Asia Pacific Journal*, September 15, 2022, https://asiatimes.com/2022/07/a-guided-historical-tour-of-tokyo-assassination-sites/.

51. Mehl, "Emperor Meiji."

52. "Emperor Meji," Google Arts & Culture, https://artsandculture.google.com/entity/emperor-meiji/m01bsgq?hl=en.

53. "Meiji Jingu: Fun Facts about the Wooded Shrine amidst the Main Venues of the 1964 Tokyo Olympics," The Olympians, https://theolympians.co/2017/11/28/meiji-jingu-fun-facts-about-the-wooded-shine-amidst-the-main-venues-of-the-1964-tokyo-olympics/.

CHAPTER 30: PASSING THE TORCH

1. "Imperial Japanese Navy," in *New World Encyclopedia*, https://www.newworldencyclopedia.org/entry/Imperial_Japanese_Navy; citing Romulus Hillsborough, *Shinsengumi: The Shogun's Last Samurai Corps* (Rutland, VT: Tuttle, 2005).

2. Arthur Judson Brown, *The Mastery of the Far East* (Cambridge, MA: Harvard University Press, 1919).

3. "Bakumatsu & Meiji Era Ships," in *Naval Encyclopedia*, https://naval-encyclopedia.com/industrial-era/bakumatsu-meiji-era-ships.ph2.

4. Karthick Nambi, "How a Japanese Navy Doctor Eradicated Beri Beri in Japan: Poor Diet in Japan Caused Widespread Cases of Beri Beri until a Japanese Army Doctor Found Its Root Cause," Lessons from History, April 7, 2023, https://medium.com/lessons-from-history/how-a-japanese-army-doctor-eradicated-beri-beri-in-japan-5ebe9b58afb1.

5. Hansgeorg Jentschura, Dieter Jung, and Peter Mickel, *Warships of the Imperial Japanese Navy, 1869–1945*, trans. Antony Preston and J. D. Brown (London: Arms and Armour, 1976).

6. David A. Norris, "Ironclad Clash at Lissa," Warfare History Network, March 2017, https://warfarehistorynetwork.com/article/ironclad-clash-at-lissa/.

7. Roger Chesneau and Eugene M. Kolesnik, eds., *Conway's All the World's Fighting Ships, 1860–1905* (New York: Mayflower Books, 1979).

8. David Evans and Mark R. Peattie, *Kaigun: Strategy, Tactics, and Technology in the Imperial Japanese Navy, 1887–1941* (Annapolis, MD: U.S. Naval Institute Press, 1997).

9. "Title: Item Ministry of Military and Naval Affairs Documents Extract Warship *Kotetsu* Crewing Personnel Number Investigation," Japan Center for Asian Historical Records; National Archives of Japan, reference code C09090003900.

10. Robert Eskildsen, "An Army as Good and Efficient as Any in the World: James Wasson and Japan's 1874 Expedition to Taiwan," *Asian Cultural Studies* 36 (2010): 52–56.

11. "Title: Enquiry about Payment of Expenses to the Two Warships *Azuma* and *Ryōshō* for Sailing to China Sea," Japan Center for Asian Historical Records; National Archives of Japan, reference code A01100043100.

12. "Title: Notification of Dispatching Warship *Azuma-kan* to Kyushu Area," Japan Center for Asian Historical Records; National Archives of Japan, reference code A07060197300.

13. William L. Neumann, *America Encounters Japan: From Perry to MacArthur* (Baltimore, MD: Johns Hopkins University Press, 1963), 78–79.

14. "Title: Inquiry about Navigating Warships *Ryōshō* and *Azuma* to the Coastal Sea of China because of Taiwan Situation," Japan Center for Asian Historical Records; National Archives of Japan, reference code A01100066100.

15. "Title: Telegraph from the Branch Office, on Shakedown of the *Azuma*, Departure of Takasago-maru, Employment of Englishman by Consul Shinagawa, Correspondence to the Ministry of Navy," Japan Center for Asian Historical Records; National Archives of Japan, reference codes A03030240600 and A03030245000.

16. "The Very Short Career of CSS *Stonewall*," in *Naval Encyclopedia*, https://naval-encyclopedia.com/industrial-era/1870-fleets/japan/kotetsu.php.

17. "Title: The Trouble Report from Captain Ito of the Warship *Azuma* to the Navy Minister Kawawmura (August 22)," Japan Center for Asian Historical Records; National Archives of Japan, reference codes A03030657400 and A03030680900.

18. A. J. Watts, "Japan," in *Conway's All the World's Fighting Ships 1860–1905*, ed. Roger Chesneau and Eugene M. Kolesnik (New York: Mayflower Books, 1979), 216–39.

19. Andrew Blackley, "The Enduring Legacy of the War of Jiawu," *Naval History Magazine* 35, no. 2 (April 2021), https://www.usni.org/magazines/naval-history-magazine/2021/april/enduring-legacy-war-jiawu.

20. Mike Coppock, "How the South's European Spymaster Built a Formidable Fleet That Challenged the Union Naval Power," HistoryNet, January 7, 2021, https://www.historynet.com/how-the-souths-European-spymaster-built-a-formidable-fleet-that-challenged-union-naval-power/.

21. Navy Department, *Dictionary of American Naval Fighting Ships* (Washington, DC: Office of the Chief of Naval Operations, 1959), 11; Electric Power Historical Museum, "4-1, Egasaki, Tsurumi-ku, Yokohama, 230-8510, Japan," archived at https://www.tepco.co.jp/shiryokan/.

22. Denis Ashton Warner and Peggy Warner, *The Tide at Sunrise: A History of the Russo-Japanese War, 1904–1905* (New York: Charterhouse, 1974); Watts, "Japan," 216–39.

23. Tom Huntington, "From Dixie to the Land of the Rising Sun," HistoryNet, October 27, 2016, https://www.historynet.com/from-dixie-to-the-land-of-the-rising-sun/.

CHAPTER 31: A WORLD OF IRON

1. William R. Hawkins, "The Emperor's Confederate Ironclad," *Naval History* 18, no. 6 (December 2004): 57–60.

2. Arthur Judson Brown, *The Mastery of the Far East* (Cambridge, MA: Harvard University Press, 1919).

3. Lydia T. Black, *Russians in Alaska 1732–1867* (Fairbanks: University of Alaska Press, 2004), https://books.google.com.au/books?id=NSRxrDm0JYYC&lpg=PA176&ots=MeRg0 z6Ezh&dq=khvostov+1806+japan&pg=PA176&redir_esc=y#v=onepage&q&f=false.

4. "Japanese Ministry of Military Affairs; 1874," National Institute for Defense Studies, February 20, 2024, https://www.nids.mod.go.jp/english/; Donald Keene, *Emperor of Japan: Meiji and His World, 1852–1912* (New York: Columbia University Press, 2005), 165–66.

5. Philip Kuhn, *Rebellion and Its Enemies in Late Imperial China: Militarization and Social Structure, 1796–1864* (Cambridge, MA: Harvard University Press, 1970), ch. 6.

6. Nagayo Ogasawara, *Life of Admiral Togo* (Tokyo: Shorin, 1934), https://archive.org /details/lifeofadmiraltog0000vari/mode/2up?q=kasuga.

CHAPTER 32: THOSE WHO SERVED

1. "Title: Item Ministry of Military and Naval Affairs Documents Extract Warship *Kotetsu* Crewing Personnel Number Investigation," Japan Center for Asian Historical Records; National Archives of Japan, reference code C09090003900. Letter dated September 25, 1965, from Susumu Nishiura, Chief, War History Office, Defense Agency of Japan to Faith Kravitz, Researcher, Eleutherian Mills, Hagley Museum (Delaware), regarding history of the Confederate Navy ship *Stonewall*, Internet Archive, https://archive.org/details/KravitzNishi-uraLtrJapanese/Kravitz-NishiuraLtr-Japanese/page/n1/mode/2up?q=azuma. William Param Brooks, *Personal Steam Logs of W. P. Brooks, 1st Assistant Engineer C.S.N.*, digitized from the collection of the Virginia Museum of History & Culture; Virginia Historical Society. U.S. Naval War Records Office, *Official Records of the Union and Confederate Navies in the War of the Rebellion*, series 1, vol. 18 (Washington, DC: Government Printing Office, 1894). U.S. Naval War Records Office, *Official Records of the Union and Confederate Navies in the War of the Rebellion*, series 1, vol. 3, *Operations of the Cruisers—Union, April 1, 1864, to December 30, 1865* (Washington, DC: Government Printing Office, 1896), 453–500. U.S. Naval War Records Office, *Official Records of the Union and Confederate Navies in the War of the Rebellion*, series 2, vol. 2, *Navy Department Correspondence, 1861–1865, with Agents Abroad* (Washington, DC: Government Printing Office, 1921), 1861 Contents. "Officers Table: Register of Officers of the Confederate States Navy 1861–1865," compiled and revised by the U.S. Office of Naval Records and Library of the United States Navy Department, from all available data (Washington, DC: Government Printing Office, 1931), https://civilwarnavy.com /wp-content/uploads/2020/04/Register-of-Officers-of-the-Confederate-Sates-Navy.pdf. J. Thomas Scharf, *History of the Confederate State's Navy: From Its Organization to the Surrender of the Last Vessel* (New York: Rogers & Sherwood, 1887), https://archive.org/stream/his toryconfeder01schagoog/historyconfeder01schagoog_djvu.txt. "The Civil War: Search for Sailors," National Parks Service, https://www.nps.gov/civilwar/search-sailors.htm#sort =score+desc&q=STONEWALL.

2. "Title: Item Ministry of Military and Naval Affairs Documents Extract Warship *Kotetsu*"; "Yanaka, Sakuragi and Ueno Park Alley Tour Guides," Kamitani Sakuraike, http://ya-na-ka .sakura.ne.jp/nakajimaSako.htm.

SELECTED BIBLIOGRAPHY

Allen, Charles Maxwell. *Dispatches from Bermuda: The Civil War Letters of Charles Maxwell Allen, United States Consul at Bermuda, 1861–1888.* Kent, OH: Kent State University Press, 2008.

Ballard, George Alexander. *The Influence of the Sea on the Political History of Japan.* Boston: Dutton, 1921.

Baxter, James Phinney. *The Introduction of the Ironclad Warship.* Cambridge, MA: Harvard University Press, 1946.

Beasley, W. G. *The Japanese Experience: A Short History of Japan.* Oakland: University of California Press, 1999.

Bigelow, John. *France and the Confederate Navy, 1862–1868.* New York: Harper, 1888.

———. *Retrospections of an Active Life.* New York, Doubleday, Page, 1909–1913.

Black, John R. *Young Japan: Yokohama and Yedo.* Vol. 2. London: Trubner, 1881. Reprint, London: Adamant, 2001.

Bramsen, Bo. *The House of Glücksburg: The Father-in-Law of Europe and His Descendants.* 2nd ed. In Danish. Copenhagen: Forlaget Forum, 1992.

Brooks, William Param. *Personal Steam Logs of W. P. Brooks, 1st Assistant Engineer C.S.N.* Digitized from the collection of the Virginia Museum of History & Culture; Virginia Historical Society.

Brown, Arthur Judson. *The Mastery of the Far East.* Cambridge, MA: Harvard University Press, 1919.

Bryant, Anthony. *Sekigahara 1600: The Final Struggle for Power.* Osprey Campaign Series 40. Oxford: Osprey, 1995.

Bulloch, James Dunwoody. *The Secret Service of the Confederate States in Europe; or, How the Confederate Cruisers Were Equipped.* New York: Putnam, 1884. https://archive.org/details/secretserviceofc02bulluoft/page/36/mode/2up?q=coal.

Campbell, R. Thomas. *Confederate Ironclads at War.* Jefferson, NC: McFarland, 2017.

Canney, Donald L. *The Old Steam Navy: The Ironclads, 1842–1885.* Vol. 2. Annapolis, MD: U.S. Naval Institute Press, 1993.

The Case of Great Britain. Vols. 1 and 2. London: Printed for T. Becket and P.A. de Hondt, George B. Butler, and Gervase Parker Bushe, 1869. Reprint, Anatiposi Verlag, 2023.

Chesneau, Roger, and Eugene M. Kolesnik, eds. *Conway's All the World's Fighting Ships, 1860–1905.* New York: Mayflower Books, 1979.

Civil War Encyclopedia. Vols. 3 and 5. New York: Appleton, 1868.

Clements, Jonathan. *A Brief History of Japan: Samurai, Shogun and Zen: The Extraordinary Story of the Land of the Rising Sun.* Rutland, VT: Tuttle, 2017.

Clodfelter, Micheal. *Warfare and Armed Conflicts: A Statistical Encyclopedia of Casualty and Other Figures, 1492–2015.* 4th ed. Jefferson, NC: McFarland, 2017.

Clowes, W. Laird. *The Royal Navy: A History from Earliest Times to the Present.* Vol. 1. London. Sampson, Low, Marston, 1897.

Collache, Eugène. "Une aventure au Japon." *Le Tour du Monde* 77 (1874).

Cooper, William J. *Jefferson Davis, American.* New York: Knopf Doubleday, 2000.

Coppock, Mike. "The Unsinkable CSS *Stonewall.*" *Sea Classics* 43, no. 6 (June 2010): 42–45.

David, William C. *Duel of the First Ironclads.* Essex, CT: Stackpole Books, 1994.

Demaree, Albert L. "Our Navy's Worst Headache: The *Merrimack.*" *U.S. Naval Institute Proceedings* 88, no. 3/709 (March 1962). https://www.usni.org/magazines/proceedings/1962/march/our-navys-worst-headache-merrimack.

Denney, John. *Respect and Consideration: Britain in Japan 1853–1868 and Beyond.* Leicester: Radiance Press, 2011.

Dodson, Aidan. *The Kaiser's Battlefleet: German Capital Ships 1871–1918.* Barnsley: Seaforth, 2016.

Edmonds, Adam C. "Confederate Wooden Gunboat Construction: Logistical Nightmare." PhD diss., East Carolina University, May 2011.

Evans, David, and Mark R. Peattie. *Kaigun: Strategy, Tactics, and Technology in the Imperial Japanese Navy, 1887–1941.* Annapolis, MD: U.S. Naval Institute Press, 1997.

Fairbank, John King, and Kwang-ching Liu, eds. *Late Ch'ing, 1800–1911.* Cambridge History of China Series 11, part 2. Cambridge, MA: Cambridge University Press, 1980.

Falk, Edwin Albert. *Togo and the Rise of Japanese Sea Power.* New York: Longmans, Green, 1936.

Ferreiro, Larrie D. "The Wrong Ship at the Right Time: The Technology of USS *Monitor* and Its Impact on Naval Warfare." *International Journal of Naval History,* May 13, 2021.

Flickema, Thomas O. "The Settlement of the Paraguayan-American Controversy of 1859: A Reappraisal." *The Americas* 25, no. 1 (July 1968): 49–69.

Foreman, Amanda. *A World on Fire: An Epic History of Two Nations Divided.* London: Penguin, 2011.

Freeman, Douglas Southall. *R. E. Lee: A Biography.* Vol. 2. New York: Scribner, 1934.

Fuller, Howard J. *Clad in Iron: The American Civil War and the Challenge of British Naval Power.* London: Bloomsbury Academic, 2008.

Gallaway, Lowell E., and Richard K. Vedder. "Emigration from the United Kingdom to the United States: 1860–1913." *Journal of Economic History* 31, no. 4 (December 1971): 885–97.

Gordon, Andrew. *A Modern History of Japan: From Tokugawa Times to the Present.* New York: Oxford University Press, 2014.

Gould, William B., IV. *Diary of a Contraband: The Civil War Passage of a Black Sailor.* Stanford, CA: Stanford University Press, 2002.

Grammaticus, Saxo. *The Nine Books of the Danish History of Saxo Grammaticus.* Translated by Oliver Elton. Reprint, n.p.: Leopold Classic Library, 2016. Originally published in 1894.

Gray, Edwyn. *Nineteenth-Century Torpedoes and Their Inventors.* Annapolis, MD: U.S. Naval Institute Press, 2004.

Greene, Jack, and Alessandro Massignani. *Ironclads at War: The Origin and Development of the Armored Battleship.* New York: Hachette Books, 1998.

Gröner, Erich. *German Warships: 1815–1945.* Vol. 1, *Major Surface Vessels.* Annapolis, MD: U.S. Naval Institute Press, 1990.

Hagiwara, Kōichi. *Illustrated Life of Saigō Takamori and Okubo Toshimichi*. In Japanese. Tokyo: Kawade Shobō Shinsya, 2004.

Hale, John Richard. *Famous Sea Fights from Salamis to Tsu-Shima*. Boston: Little, Brown, 1911.

Haraguchi, Izumi. "The Influence of the Civil War in the US on the Meiji Restoration in Japan." *South Pacific Study* 16, no. 1 (1995).

Heco, Joseph. *The Narrative of a Japanese: What He Has Seen and the People He Has Met in the Course of the Last Forty Years*. Vol. 1. San Francisco, CA: American-Japanese Publishing Association, 1895. https://archive.org/details/narrativeofjapan02hecoiala/mode/2up?q=stonewall.

Hillsborough, Romulus. *Shinsengumi: The Shogun's Last Samurai Corps*. Rutland, VT: Tuttle, 2005.

Howard, Frank. "Early Ship Guns. Part I, Built-up Breech-Loaders." *Mariner's Mirror* 72 (1986): 439–53.

Howath, David. *A Brief History of British Sea Power: How Britain Became Sovereign of the Seas*. London: Robinson, 1974.

Hozier, H. M. *The Seven Weeks' War: The Austro-Prussian Conflict of 1866*. London: Macmillan, 1867.

Hsu, Hsuan L. "Personality, Race, and Geopolitics in Joseph Heco's *Narrative of a Japanese*." *Biography* 29, no. 2 (Spring 2006).

Jansen, Marius B. *The Making of Modern Japan*. Cambridge, MA: Harvard University Press, 2000.

Jentschura, Hansgeorg, Dieter Jung, and Peter Mickel. *Warships of the Imperial Japanese Navy, 1869–1945*. Translated by Antony Preston and J. D. Brown. London: Arms and Armour Press, 1970.

Jones, John William, Robert Alonzo Brock, and James Power Smith, eds. *Southern Historical Society Papers*. 52 vols. Richmond, VA: Southern Historical Society; Virginia Historical Society, 1876–1959.

Kanazawa, Hiroyuki. *The Rise and Fall of the Shogunate Navy: Japan Naval Construction at the End of the Tokugawa Shogunate*. Tokyo: Keio University Press, 2017.

Keene, Donald. *Emperor of Japan: Meiji and His World, 1852–1912*. New York: Columbia University Press, 2005.

Kenjirō, Yamakawa. *Aizu Boshin Senshi*. Tōkyō: Tōkyō Daigaku Shuppankai, 1931.

Kuhn, Philip. *Rebellion and Its Enemies in Late Imperial China: Militarization and Social Structure, 1796–1864*. Cambridge, MA: Harvard University Press, 1970.

Lambert, Andrew. *The Alabama Affair: The British Shipyards and the American Civil War*. London: Constable, 1989.

Lewis, James B. *Frontier Contact between Choson Korea and Tokugawa Japan*. New York: Routledge, 2003.

Lossing, Benson. *The Pictorial Field-Book of the War of 1812*. New York: Harper, 1868.

Luraghi, Raimondo. *A History of the Confederate Navy*. Annapolis, MD: U.S. Naval Institute Press, 1996.

Marolda, Edward J. *The Washington Navy Yard: An Illustrated History*. Washington, DC: Naval Historic Center, August 22, 2019.

Mass, Jeffrey P., and William B. Hauser. *The Bakufu in Japanese History*. Stanford, CA: Stanford University Press, 1985.

Maynard, Douglas H. "The Confederacy's Super 'Alabama.'" *Civil War History* 5 (March 1959): 80–95.

McDougall, Walter A. *Let the Sea Make a Noise*. New York: HarperCollins, 1993.

McOmie, William. *The Opening of Japan, 1853–1855*. Folkestone, UK: Global Oriental, 2006.

McPherson, James M. *War on the Waters: The Union and Confederate Navies*. Chapel Hill: University of North Carolina Press, 2012.

Merli, Frank. *Great Britain and the Confederate Navy, 1861–1865*. Bloomington: Indiana University Press, 2004.

———. "A Missing Chapter in American Civil War Diplomacy: The Confederacy's Chinese Fleet, 1861–1867." In *Global Crossroads and the American Seas*, edited by Clark G. Reynolds. Missoula, MT: Pictorial Histories, 1988.

Miller, Edward Stokes. *Civil War Sea Battles*. New York: Combined Books, 1995.

Mitchell, Joseph R., and David Stebenne. *New City upon a Hill: A History of Columbia, Maryland*. Cheltenham, UK: History Press, 2007.

Morton, Robert. *The Japan Society: A. B. Mitford and the Birth of Japan as a Modern State: Letters Home*. Tokyo: Renaissance Books, 2017.

Murphy, Jim. *The Boys' War: Confederate and Union Soldiers Talk about the Civil War*. New York: Clarion, 1990.

Murray, David. *Japan*. New York: Putnam, 1896.

Museum of Fine Arts Boston. *Japan at the Dawn of the Modern Age: Woodblock Prints from the Meiji Era, 1868–1912*. Boston: MFA Publications, 2001.

Navy Department. *Dictionary of American Naval Fighting Ships*. Washington, DC: Office of the Chief of Naval Operations, 1963.

Neumann, William L. *America Encounters Japan: From Perry to MacArthur*. Baltimore, MD: Johns Hopkins University Press, 1963.

Ogasawara, Nagayo. *Life of Admiral Togo*. Tokyo: Shorin, 1934. https://archive.org/details /lifeofadmiraltog0000vari/mode/2up?q=kasuga.

Owen, John Fletcher. *Treatise on the Construction and Manufacture of Ordnance in the British Service*. London: Her Majesty's Stationery Office, 1877.

Owsley, Frank Lawrence, Jr. *The C.S.S. Florida: Her Building and Operations*. Tuscaloosa: University of Alabama Press, 1987.

———. *King Cotton Diplomacy*. Vancouver: University of British Columbia Press, 2008.

Page, Thomas Jefferson. *La Plata, the Argentine Confederation and Paraguay: Narrative of the Exploration of the Tributaries of the River La Plata during the years 1853, '54, '55, and '56 under the Orders of the United States Government*. New York: Harper, 1859.

Perry, Horatio J. *Memorial of Horatio J. Perry*. Boston: Little, Brown, 1886.

Peterson, Clarence Stewart. *Admiral John A. Dahlgren: Father of United States Naval Ordnance*. New York: Hobson Book Press, 1945.

Polak, Christian. *Soie et lumière: L'âge d'or des échanges Franco-Japonais*. Tokyo: Hachette Fujingaho, 2002.

Price, Roger. *The French Second Empire: An Anatomy of Political Power*. Cambridge: Cambridge University Press, 2004. https://books.google.com.au/books?id=l0LMNRvWaLIC&pg=PA 407&redir_esc=y#v=onepage&q&f=false.

Quarstein, John V. *The Monitor Boys: The Crew of the Union's First Ironclad*. Charleston, SC: History Press, 2011.

———. "Proving the Power of Iron over Wood." *Naval History Magazine* 26, no. 2 (April 2012). https://www.usni.org/magazines/naval-history-magazine/2012/april/proving -power-iron-over-wood.

Rable, George C. *The Confederate Republic: A Revolution against Politics*. Chapel Hill: University of North Carolina Press, 1994.

Ravina, Mark. *The Last Samurai: The Life and Battles of Saigō Takamori*. 1st ed. New York: Wiley, 2005.

Reed, Edward J. *Our Ironclad Ships, Their Qualities, Performance and Cost*. London: John Murray, 1869.

Rekishi-gakkai, Nihon, ed. *Meiji Ishin Jinmei Jiten*. Tokyo: Yoshikawa Kobunkan, 1981.

Roberts, William P. "James Dunwoody and the Confederate Navy." *North Carolina Historical Review* 24, no. 3 (July 1947): 315–66.

Rodger, Nicholas. *The Command of the Ocean: A Naval History of Britain 1649–1815*. New York: Penguin, 2004.

Rogers, Hiromi. *Anjin—the Life and Times of Samurai William Adams, 1564–1620*. Amsterdam: Amsterdam University Press, 2016.

Rolle, Andrew F. *The Lost Cause: The Confederate Exodus to Mexico*. Norman: University of Oklahoma Press, 1965.

Sadler, A. L. *The Maker of Modern Japan: The Life of Tokugawa Ieyasu*. London: Allen and Unwin, 1937. Reprint, Rutland, VT: Tuttle, 1978.

Saint Hubert, C. de. "Builders, Engine Builders, and Designers of Armored Vessels Built in France 1855–1940." *F.P.D.S. Newsletter* 14, no. 3 (1986): 2–8.

Sajima, Naoko, and Kyochi Tachikawa. *Japanese Sea Power: A Maritime Nation's Struggle for Identity*. Foundations of Thinking on Sea Power 2. Canberra: Sea Power Centre, Royal Australian Navy, 2009.

Sakaguchi, Kanji. *The Medical Activities of Sōha Hatono VIII and His Welfare Activities*. Kenkyuu Kiyō 27. Natori: Shokei Junior University, 1995.

Sato, Hiroaki. *Tokugawa Yoshinobu: From Shogun to Retired Shogun*. Oakland: University of California Press, 2003.

Satow, Ernest. *A Diplomat in Japan*. 1869. Tokyo and London: Stone Bridge Press, 2007.

Scharf, J. Thomas. *History of the Confederate States Navy: From Its Organization to the Surrender of the Last Vessel*. New York: Rogers & Sherwood, 1887.

Schencking, J. Charles. *Making Waves: Politics, Propaganda, and the Emergence of the Imperial Japanese Navy, 1868–1922*. Stanford, CA: Stanford University Press, 2005.

Schlürmann, Jan. *The Schleswig-Holstein Rebellion*. Kiel, Germany: University of Kiel, 2012.

Schmorleitz, Morton S. *Castles in Japan*. Rutland, VT: Tuttle, 1974.

Schneller, Robert J. "A State of War Is a Most Unfavorable Period for Experiments: John Dahlgren and U.S. Naval Ordnance Innovation during the American Civil War." *International Journal of Naval History* 2, no. 3 (December 2003).

"Sharecropping." In *Gale Encyclopedia of U.S. Economic History*, edited by Thomas Carson and Mary Bonk. Vol. 2. Farmington Hills, MI: Gale, 2000.

Shaw, David W. *Sea Wolf of the Confederacy: The Daring Civil War Raids of Naval Lt. Charles W. Read*. Dobbs Ferry, NY: Sheridan House, 2005.

Shewmaker, Kenneth E. "Forging the 'Great Chain': Daniel Webster and the Origins of American Foreign Policy toward East Asia and the Pacific, 1841–1852." *Proceedings of the American Philosophical Society* 129, no. 3 (September 1985). https://www.jstor.org/stable/987008.

Shiba, Ryōtarō. *The Last Shogun: The Life of Tokugawa Yoshinobu*. New York: Kodansha International, 2004.

Shigénobu, Ôkuma, and Marcus Bourne Huish, *Fifty Years of New Japan*. Vol. 1. London: Smith, Elder, 1909.

Smith, Gene Allen, and Larry Bartlett. "'A Most Unprovoked, Unwarranted and Dastardly Attack': James Buchanan, Paraguay, and the *Water Witch* Incident of 1855." *Northern Mariner / Le Marin du Nord* 19, no. 3 (2009).

Sondhaus, Lawrence. *Naval Warfare 1815–1914*. New York: Routledge, 2001.

———. *Preparing for Weltpolitik: German Sea Power before the Tirpitz Era*. Annapolis, MD: U.S. Naval Institute Press, 1997.

Spencer, Warren F. *The Confederate Navy in Europe*. Tuscaloosa: University of Alabama Press, 1983.

Stern, Philip Van Doren. *The Confederate Navy: A Pictorial History*. New York: Da Capo, 1992.

———. *The Confederate Navy: The Ships, Men and Organization, 1861–65*. New York: Doubleday, 1962.

Taniguchi, Mako. *Kiri-sute Gomen*. Tokyo: Yamakawa Shuppansha, 2005.

Taylor, Bayard. *Japan: In Our Day*. New York: Scribner, Armstrong, 1872.

Thompson, Stephen C. "The Design and Construction of USS *Monitor*." *Warship International* 27, no. 3 (1990).

Thulesius, Olav. *The Man Who Made the Monitor: A Biography of John Ericsson, Naval Engineer*. Jefferson, NC: McFarland, 2007.

Totman, Conrad. *The Collapse of the Tokugawa Bakufu, 1862–1868*. Honolulu: University of Hawai'i Press, 1980.

Tregel, Joseph Jr. "The Political Apprenticeship of John Slidell." *Journal of Southern History* 26, no. 1 (February 1960): 57–70.

Tucker, Spencer C. "Confederate Naval Ordnance." In "Special Commemorative Naval Issue: CSS Alabama, 1864–1989," edited by Frank J. Merli, special issue, *Journal of Confederate History* 4 (1989).

Turnbull, Stephen R. *The Samurai: A Military History*. New York: Routledge, 1996.

———. *Samurai Invasion: Japan's Korean War, 1592–98*. New York: Cassell, 2002.

Turner, George E. *Victory Rode the Rails: The Strategic Place of the Railroads in the Civil War*. Indianapolis and New York: Bobbs-Merrill, 1953.

Van Deusen, Glyndon G. *William Henry Seward: Lincoln's Secretary of State, The Negotiator of the Alaska Purchase*. Oxford: Oxford University Press, 1967.

Warner, Denis Ashton, and Peggy Warner. *The Tide at Sunrise: A History of the Russo-Japanese War, 1904–1905*. New York: Charterhouse, 1974.

Watson, William. *The Adventures of a Blockade Runner*. London: Unwin, 1892.

Watts, Anthony J. *The Imperial Russian Navy*. London: Arms and Armour, 1990.

Wells, Tom H. *The Confederate Navy: A Study in Organization*. Tuscaloosa: University of Alabama Press, 1971.

Wiatt, Thomas T. *The* Stonewall: *The True Story of a Ship without a Port*. Brisbane, Australia: Limelight, 2021.

Widerman, John C. *Naval Warfare: Courage and Combat on the Water*. New York: Metro Books, 1997.

Wilson, Beckles. *John Slidell and the Confederates in Paris: 1862–65*. Minton: Balch, 1932.

Wilson, J. G., and J. Fiske, eds. *Appleton's Cyclopædia of American Biography*. New York: Appleton, 1900.

Wilson, Walter E., and Gary L. McKay. *James D. Bulloch: Secret Agent and Mastermind of the Confederate Navy*. Jefferson, NC: McFarland, 2012.

Winters, John D. *The Civil War in Louisiana*. Baton Rouge: Louisiana State University Press, 1963.

Wise, Stephen R. *Lifeline of the Confederacy: Blockade Running during the Civil War*. Columbia: University of South Carolina Press, 1988.

Wood, John Taylor. "First Fight of Iron-Clads." In *Battles and Leaders of the Civil War*, edited by Robert U. Johnson and Clarence C. Buel. 4 vols. New York: Thomas Yoseloff, 1956.

Yamaguchi, Ken. *Kinsé shiriaku: A History of Japan, from the First Visit of Commodore Perry in 1853 to the Capture of Hakodate by the Mikado's Forces in 1869.* Translated by Ernest Mason Satow. Yokohama: Wetmore, 1876.

CORRESPONDENCE AND RECORDS

Abraham Lincoln Online. "Letter to Horace Greeley, Washington, August 22, 1862." https://www.abrahamlincolnonline.org/lincoln/speeches/greeley.htm.

Balch, Thomas Willing. "Charles F. Adams to Earl Russell, October 23, 1863." In *The Alabama Arbitration*. N.p.: Allen, Lane & Scott, 1900.

General Records of the Department of State. *Despatches from U.S. Consuls in Belfast, 1796–1906.* National Archives Microfilm Publication T368. RG 59. College Park, MD: National Archives.

———. *Despatches from U.S. Consuls in Liverpool, England, 1790–1906.* National Archives Microfilm Publication M141. RG 59. College Park, MD: National Archives.

———. *Despatches from U.S. Consuls in London, England, 1790–1906.* National Archives Microfilm Publication T168. Roll 32. RG 59. College Park, MD: National Archives.

Glasgow University Archives. CBF Private Letter Book, No. 3. UCS 1/11/1.

"Letter to Robert Bontine Cunninghame Graham." In *Joseph Conrad: A Biography*, by Jeffrey Meyers. New York: Scribner, 1991.

Library of Congress. "Letter from Akamatsu Noriyoshi to Yoshizawa Genjiro." https://www.loc.gov/item/2021667500/.

National Archives and Records Administration. Letters Received by Confederate Treasury Secretary. Record Group 365. Roll 35.

———. Record Group 45. Entry 502 AD. Box 51. Folder 10.

Naval Records Collection of the Office of Naval Records and Library. Record Group 45. National Archives.

U.S. Naval War Records Office. *Official Records of the Union and Confederate Navies in the War of the Rebellion.* Series 1. Vol. 3, *Operations of the Cruisers—Union, April 1, 1864, to December 30, 1865.* Washington, DC: Government Printing Office, 1896.

———. *Official Records of the Union and Confederate Navies in the War of the Rebellion.* Series 1. Vol. 5. Washington, DC: Government Printing Office, 1884–1927.

———. *Official Records of the Union and Confederate Navies in the War of the Rebellion.* Series 1. Vol. 7, *North Atlantic Blockading Squadron—March 8, 1862 to September 4, 1862.* Washington, DC: Government Printing Office, 1898.

———. *Official Records of the Union and Confederate Navies in the War of the Rebellion.* Series 2. Vol. 1. Washington, DC: Government Printing Office, 1894.

———. *Official Records of the Union and Confederate Navies in the War of the Rebellion.* Series 2. Vol. 2, *Navy Department Correspondence, 1861–1865, with Agents Abroad.* Washington, DC: Government Printing Office, 1921.

U.S. Steamer *Sacramento* Watch. Quarter & Station Bills, 1866–1917 (bulk 1866–1867). MS 72. Special Collections & Archives, Nimitz Library at the United States Naval Academy.

Van Zandt, Franklin K. "Boundaries of the United States and the Several States." U.S. Geological Survey Professional Paper 909. Reston, VT: U.S. Geological Survey, 1976.

Whittle Papers. Folder 2, nos. 36 and 38. Southern Historical Collection. University of North Carolina Library. Chapel Hill: University of North Carolina.

WEBSITES

Abbeville Institute. https://www.abbevilleinstitute.org.

American Battlefield Trust. https://www.battlefields.org.

Britannica. https://www.britannica.com.

Dawlish Chronicles. https://dawlishchronicles.com.

HistoryNet. https://www.historynet.com/.

Japan Center for Asia Historical Records, National Archives of Japan. https://www.jacar .archives.go.jp.

Lowcountry Digital History Initiative. https://ldhi.library.cofc.edu.

Mariners Museum and Park. https://blog.marinersmuseum.org/.

National Institute of Information and Communications Technology (NICT). https://www .japanesewiki.com.

National Library of Medicine. https://www.ncbi.nlm.nih.gov/.

National Museum of Civil War Medicine. https://www.civilwarmed.org.

National Parks Service. https://www.nps.gov/index.htm.

Naval Encyclopedia. https://naval-encyclopedia.com/.

Naval History and Heritage Command. https://www.history.navy.mil/research/library /online-reading-room/title-list-alphabetically.

ThoughtCo. https://www.thoughtco.com.

290 Foundation. https://sites.google.com/site/290foundation/history/c-s-s-stonewall.

U.S. Naval Institute. https://www.usni.org.

Warfare History Network. https://warfarehistorynetwork.com.

White House Historical Association. https://www.whitehousehistory.org/.